Fire & Ice

Whangaehu Hut is perched on the edge of a rocky knoll, watched over by Ringatoto Peak (formerly known as Mitre Peak, 2591m). Peter Laurenson/ The Occasional Climber

Fire & Ice

Secrets, histories, treasures and mysteries of Tongariro National Park

Hazel Phillips

MASSEY UNIVERSITY PRESS

THE WILD
AND
CHAOTIC GRANDEUR
OF
TONGARIRO
NATIONAL PARK
N
W
E
S
Lake Otamangakau
Lake Te Whaiau
47
Lake Rotopounamu
The Gurgler (water vortex)
Otukou
Ketetahi
Papakai
Lake Rotoaira
46
Taurewa
WHANGANUI RIVER
Ketetahi Hot Springs
Blue Lake (Te Wai Whakaata o Te Rangihiroa)
TONGARIRO 1967m
Sly grogging tracks
Soda Springs
TE TATAU POUNAMU WILDERNESS AREA
Mangatepopo Hut
Pukeonake
NGĀURUHOE 2287m
Oturere Hut
Haunted Whare
Holl's Rock
Tama 1623m
47
48
Upper Tama
National Park (Waimarino)
Mangahuia Campsite
Mangahuia Track
Whakapapa Village
Waihohonu Hut
Lower Tama
Waikune
Iwikau Village
TONGARIRO NATIONAL PARK
Hauhungatahi 1521m
Erua
Summit rock with mystery inscription
Whakapapaiti Hut
4
Stanton Memorial
Whakapapa ski field
Aero Commander wreckage
Airspeed Consul wreckage
MAKATOTE RIVER
Paretetaitonga 2751m
Dome 2672m
Ringatoto Peak 2591m
Tukino ski field
Round The Mountain Track
Kaka wreckage
Whangaehu Hut
Tahurangi 2797m
Girdlestone Peak (Peretini) 2658m
MANGANUIOTEAO RIVER
Pokaka
RUAPEHU
Holl's Cairn
Tūroa ski field
WHANGAEHU RIVER
Mangaturuturu Hut
Rangipo Hut
MANGATURUTURU RIVER
TE ONETAPU
Ohakune Hut (old Blyth Hut)
Park employees memorial
Ghost Bush (Ngā Motu a Taka)
Te Roro o Taitearíki
Blyth Hut
Lupton Hut
WAHIANOA RIVER
Horopito
Mangaiti Hut
Mangaehuehu Hut
Round Bush (Ngā Rimutāmaka)
Bergersen's Hut
1
Lake Moawhango
KARIOI FOREST
RANGATAUA CONSERVATION AREA
Disused dam
Rangataua
OHAKUNE
Karioi

Ruapehu's Summit Plateau and Te Wai ā-moe Crater Lake in winter conditions. Mandy Rothe Photography

Contents

Two members of the Auckland Tramping Club peering into crevasses on the Mangaehuehu Glacier at Easter, 1933. Auckland Libraries Heritage Collections, 282-0426

A note on the text

This book focuses mostly on the European footprint on the mountains of Tongariro National Park. I'm a Pākehā writer, and I take the view that the stories of tangata whenua are not mine to tell. In places, the book occasionally brushes up alongside narratives and histories from te ao Māori. In other places, there are concepts and language that are recognised as offensive in today's context — for example, where a European explorer refers to Māori guides as 'my natives'. I've let these stand; this book focuses on the site that lies at the intersection between these magical mountains and the notion of 'this is what we used to do'. Members of the relevant iwi were consulted on sections of the text, and I am grateful for their kōrero.

The text is centred on Ruapehu, which I occasionally choose to refer to as male, but incorporates Tongariro and Ngāuruhoe, and generally takes Tongariro National Park as its boundaries of scope. Roderick Gray, a mountain enthusiast and a shepherd who lived at the head of the Mangatepopo Valley for some years, wrote that the names had once been inverted: 'The volcano "Ngauruhae" [was known] as "Ruapehu", the great crater to the east as "Ngaruhae" . . . the whole range took the name "Tongariro" — "Gone south, the place of the departed".' He referred principally to Tongariro, whereas I look more towards Ruapehu as the object of my interest — a mountain Gray called 'an object of wild, chaotic grandeur'.[1]

This book is a story about mountains, but it's a story about other things, too. You'll read about ghosts, fires, avalanches, crevasses and plane wrecks. There's also love, mysteries, a secret inscription on a summit stone, conscientious objectors being arrested at gunpoint in the bush, sly grogging and carrot waving. It was great fun to research and write, and I hope it's equally fun to read. Most of all, I hope you, too, feel the urge to embrace the wild and chaotic grandeur of Tongariro National Park.

Bathers at Te Wai ā-moe, Ruapehu's Crater Lake, 1962. Photo by Ronald Fox. Alexander Turnbull Library, PAColl-5342

Introduction

I became obsessed with Ruapehu about a decade ago, when I saw a photo of people bathing in Te Wai ā-moe, Ruapehu's Crater Lake, in the 1960s. In the shot, a woman in a fashionable bikini is waving at someone. A pair of skis is stuck upright in the snow, and another swimsuit-clad woman reclines nearby. It's summer, and three men and a woman are bathing happily in the lake's tepid waters. The photo was commissioned by the New Zealand Tourist and Publicity Department to promote travel to Tongariro National Park. Things have changed — Crater Lake is known to be acidic, access is challenging, and it is now recognised that swimming there is culturally offensive — but for a time this was considered the ultimate in shiny tourist glamour: to take a snowcat ride up the Whakapapa Glacier, strip down to your swimwear, have a dip, and ski down.

The photo of the bathers appeared in a book called *Skiing on the Volcano: Historical images of skiing on Mount Ruapehu* by Karen Williams and Dave Bamford. After I came across a copy in my ski club's lodge I pored over the pages, scrutinising each image to get a picture of what mountain life used to be like. I became the proud owner of a life pass to the ski fields on Whakapapa and Tūroa, climbed the peaks, ski-toured the glaciers, tramped all the tracks and visited all the huts several times over. I thought I knew the mountains, but every time I turned a corner, something new surprised me.

I wanted to know Ruapehu, the mountain I loved so much, more thoroughly — not just the ski fields, the huts, tracks and summits, and not just what was declared openly on the map. I also wanted to know what existed once you stepped off the path. What lay in places people seldom trod? What were the stories? Were there treasures still out there that people didn't really know about? What would Ruapehu allow me to find if I went gently and asked respectfully?

Skiing on the Volcano represented a slice of time in the history of Ruapehu, and so does this book. Ruapehu and Tongariro have been affected by the very European-coloniser perspective of using mountains as tools for tourism or as tools for capitalism. They've also been touched by the equally European notion of 'conquering', especially summits. I wanted to create for myself a nuanced shift in mountaineering, to go beyond the question of 'should I stand on a summit' and to overhaul the whole way we think about our relationships to mountains and our wild spaces. A mountain is more than just a summit, and a peak is such a small part of a mountain's whole being.

I came across the term 'orophile' — someone who loves mountains — but the emphasis here is on love, really, more than on mountains. I think you can be a mountaineer who loves climbing and thrives on physical challenge but doesn't truly, properly love the mountains. And in the same way, you can be an orophile, someone who loves mountains, without ever 'conquering' a summit.

This book is structured according to the elements, a classical concept of defining matter as simpler substances. Earth, air, fire and water were common elements across ancient cultures, and many also had a fifth element such as 'void'. Aristotle included the fifth element, aether, to describe something that defied encapsulation by tangible material. His reasoning was that the stars were not made from any of the four elements but from a completely different, heavenly substance.

It's hard to define why Ruapehu holds such magic, but its allure is felt by the many people who are drawn to its slopes every year when the snow falls. Ruapehu on a good day, we agree, is the best place in the world to ski. A good day, when the snow is stardust beneath our feet. Elements, even aether, will never properly capture the seductive attraction of Tongariro National Park, but Ruapehu's ice and fire is a captivating portal that will let us in.

In the 1870s George Beetham, today acknowledged as the first known European to have properly summitted Ruapehu, saw himself very much as an outsider. He was disappointed when his prospective companion, William Birch, couldn't climb or travel with him to the mountains. Beetham wrote that not only had he looked forward to the pleasure of Birch's company, but he also felt 'rather like a poacher attempting Ruapehu, I being a manuhiri (visitor), without the countenance of one of the old settlers of the district'.[1]

I also still felt like an outsider, a pretender, even though I lived a mountain life. Yet in other ways, being on or around Ruapehu always felt like being home. I realised I'd become addicted to Ruapehu, but my obsession wasn't about peaks; I'd begun to view Ruapehu as a greater whole, a feeling, or perhaps, a person. I knew the mountain contained some kind of magic, for all of us, and I wanted to capture that and put it on the page.

Our historic ascensionist George Beetham, too, was deeply touched with the Ruapehu infatuation. 'During the month of March, 1878, I found myself for the first time for many years with a few weeks' spare time at my disposal,' he wrote. 'Therefore, I determined to gratify a wish that had taken possession of my mind for many years, to visit the volcanic district of Ruapehu and Tongariro.'[2]

The volcanic mountains of the central plateau have gripped me and held me tight. I've spent two years writing and researching, looking for locations and coordinates, rifling through archival material, and walking and climbing to find memorials, plane wrecks, old hut sites and more, in the wild world of Tongariro National Park.

This is the story of how Ruapehu and Tongariro took possession of my mind.

Two climbers on the edge of Te Wai ā-moe, Ruapehu's Crater Lake. Tahurangi (the highest peak) is in the background. Auckland Libraries Heritage Collections, 1865-54

The mighty volcanoes of the central plateau lined up. From left: Ruapehu, Ngāuruhoe and Tongariro. Mike Heydon/ChopperWorx

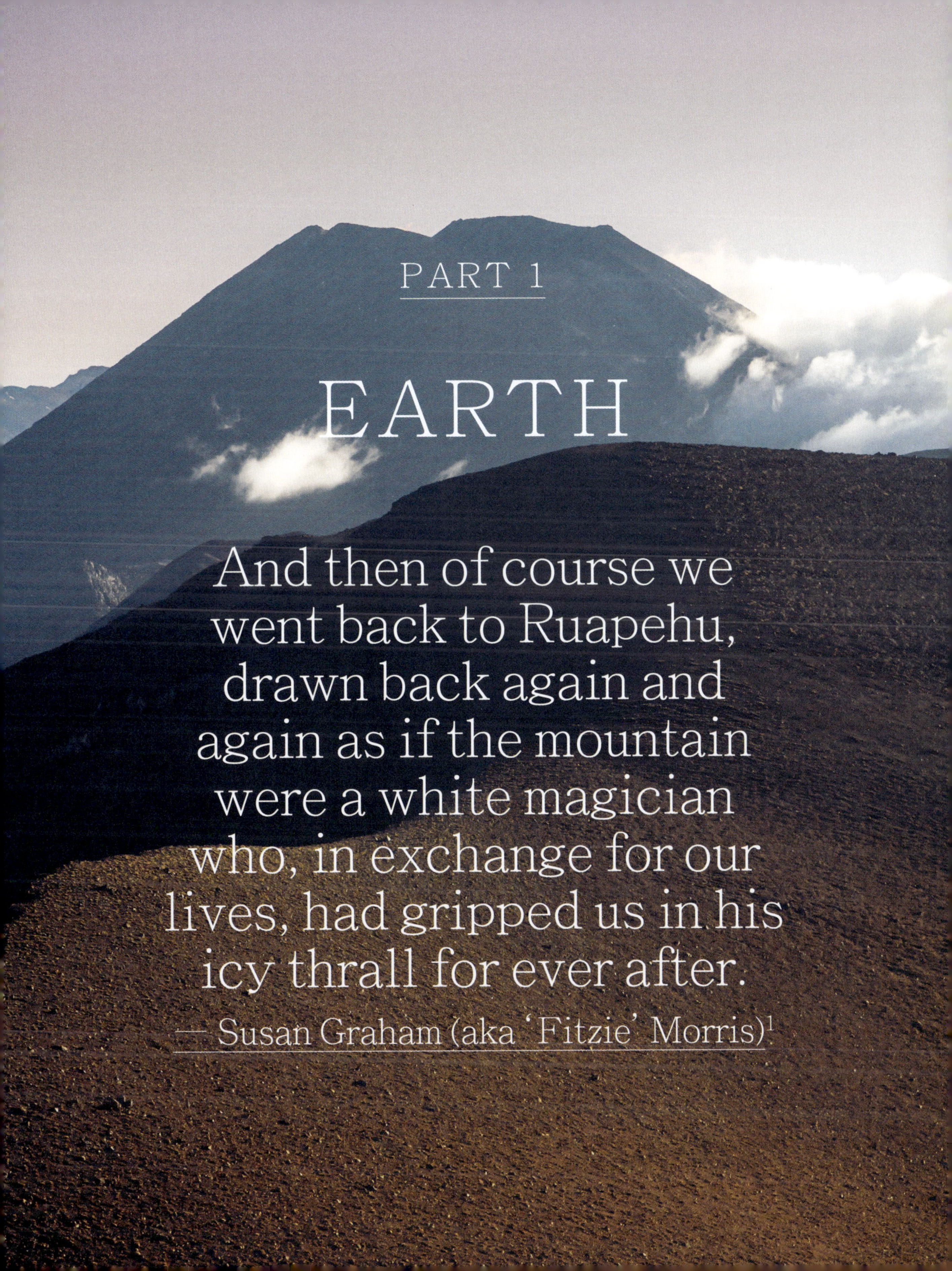

PART 1

EARTH

And then of course we went back to Ruapehu, drawn back again and again as if the mountain were a white magician who, in exchange for our lives, had gripped us in his icy thrall for ever after.

— Susan Graham (aka 'Fitzie' Morris)[1]

Makahikatoa Stream
Lava Streams and Des
NGAU
7515
SNOW
PROPOSED TRACK
24000
180°0'
HAUNTED WHARE
2160 sc.
87°20' pro.
A Ta
5276
Nga Puna a T
Nga Puna a Tama
Mountain Beech
137,900
Manganuia Stm.
Shrubby Steppe with patches of Bog
Mountain Beech
Desert
62,280
Good Camp
Pinnacle Ridge
Leading Spur
Waterfall
Subalpine Scrub, Grass and Shrub Steppe
Te Kahatu
5535
Te Heu Heu Peak
SOURCE OF WAIKATO Rr.
Waikato Gla.
Waterfall
Pare-te-tai-tonga
9025'
Mangaturuturu Gla.
Wangaehu Gla.
LAKE
RUAPEHU
9175
High rocky shoulder
Waterfall
Strong
Medicinal
Little Matterhorn Peak
Mangaehuehu Gla.
Wahianoa Stream
18100 sc.
40°16'52"
D
Good leading spur
12800 sc.
55°0'
Ruapehu No. 2
Waterfall
Ruapehu No. 1
Subalpine
Roto Kaua
B
4420
Tufa

Map of Mount Ruapehu showing Little Matterhorn Peak (Peretini/Girdlestone Peak). Lands and Survey Department, 1909, National Library of New Zealand, MapColl-2729

CHAPTER 1

The smashed summit stone

In 1922 a team of climbers installed a plaque on Ruapehu's 'Little Matterhorn' Peak in memory of Hugh Girdlestone, an early surveyor and explorer, and the peak was officially renamed in his honour. Nearly 100 years later, an angry local went up and smashed the plaque, planning to go back and chuck the remnants off the peak. Was the memorial history, or was it rubbish? I climbed Girdlestone with Henry, the plaque smasher, in an attempt to make sure it didn't become the latter.

When we ascended Girdlestone Peak in 2023, the skies above Ruapehu's massif stretched clear and starkly blue above us. At the tail end of a spell of fine but windy weather, the atmosphere had abruptly settled before the wind swung round and the rain came. The day dawned crisp but the sun soon reflected off the volcanic rocks around us as we sweltered up the black hill.

When a group of mountaineers had ascended Girdlestone just over 100 years earlier, they had needed three attempts to carry out their mission. Clouds surrounded them, their clothes froze stiff, and the misty wind picked up rocks and fired them at the party. You'd almost think the mountain didn't want them there.

We were climbing up a short section of the Skyline Ridge above Tūroa, rolling over east to the Mangaehuehu Glacier, navigating blocky sections of rock and looking for a way to get onto the ice of the glacier itself, which was separating from the smooth rock, creating a chasm between the two. I stopped to breathe.

'What pseudonym do you want in my book?' I yelled out.

'Henry,' he called back immediately. Then turned and laughed. 'I dunno, call me whatever you want.'

'Henry' stuck. I didn't know any Henrys in real life, so that helped.

The day I had first crossed paths with Henry up on Ruapehu we'd got talking, and he had quietly told me what he'd done. 'That plaque on Girdlestone, I went up and smashed it.'

I only had a vague knowledge of the plaque, and the fact that it had been smashed, but Henry pointed me to a post about it on Facebook. Outdoors enthusiast and writer Dave Bamford, one of the authors of *Skiing on the Volcano*, the book I loved so much, had gone up Girdlestone for the third time at Easter 2021. The climb was in memory of his grandfather Owen Campbell, a keen climber on Ruapehu who had been a member of the party that placed the plaque in 1922. Topping out on the summit of Girdlestone, Bamford found the plaque broken.

'It was initially a shock to discover the granite plaque to Girdlestone had been shattered fairly recently by the ravages of time and nature — frost and thaw,' he wrote in his Facebook post. 'Yes, man passes but the land endures.'[1]

Bamford and his party spent an hour or so in good conditions putting together a few of the pieces of the plaque. 'It was a reflective time,' he wrote. 'Memories, families, colonial times and their actions.'

Henry had climbed Girdlestone with a mate the summer before Bamford discovered the plaque was broken. Henry had had no idea a plaque existed on the summit, and he was shocked when he found it. After thinking about it a bit, he went back up the next week with the specific intention of destroying the memorial. Grabbing a big rock, he pounded it repeatedly into the face of the plaque. It took many blows to smash the granite tablet, pinned as it was to the large, smooth face of the rock by its four thick copper pins. Finally freeing the tablet, he picked up the shattered pieces and cast them off the peak.

Later, after seeing from Dave Bamford's post that the plaque had been partly jigsawed back together, Henry went back in my company to finish the job.

ABOVE: The broken plaque and valves on Girdlestone Peak.

BELOW: The rock that formerly bore the plaque, with the remnants of the valve stems.

Our climb up was uneventful, to a point. I knew the ascent to the top chairlift would be easy — I'd gone up via the handrails of the lift line to Tahurangi col solo a few weeks earlier — and the trek across the low-angled glacier would be just a plod. But I recalled that the final stretches to the peak itself, perhaps two or three 20-metre contour lines, were steeper and had required climbing down facing in towards the punchy snow for extra security.

The top section was a mess of craggy, splintered rock waiting to free itself from the peak. Imagine a growing crystal with healthy fingers sticking straight up, but with thick cracks threatening to shatter. Henry, an experienced rock climber, pointed out which rocks to rely on and which ones to avoid putting weight on. (A friend later told me: 'With New Zealand rock, you test them by pushing on them, not pulling.') We scrambled up a short rocky gully that thankfully had enough handholds for my short limbs, but my heart rate shot up anyway.

'I'll turn you into a rock climber yet,' Henry laughed. I'd tried rock climbing many times and it just wasn't for me, despite friends trying to persuade me to the contrary.

'Henry, I'm out of my comfort zone now,' I called out. 'I can get up this, but I don't know how I'm going to get down again.'

'That's great you're out of your comfort zone, good news,' he yelled. 'We'll hatch a plan. Or I'll just throw you off the summit.'

I sat on a nearby rock, staying well clear of Henry as he attempted to remove the copper pins — valves from an old car engine. They were a pale shade of verdigris and protruded about 5 centimetres from the rock. Ugly. A scar on the landscape, on the mountain Ngāti Rangi call Koro — their grandfather, ancestor and the source of their identity.

Henry used a hammer to bash at the valves sideways, pushing them around to weaken them on the neck. The sound of the blows echoed off the summit of Tahurangi nearby, creating tinny ding-ding-ding noises.

'You write in there that the fulla who did this is as white as they come,' he said. 'Who the fuck are you to come up here and put this up here? Go and plant a fucking tree, a tōtara or a rātā or something that's going to be around for ages. Plant it in your backyard and go sit under it, for fuck's sake.'

He picked up his ice axe and used the sharp adze, knocking the hammer on the shaft to create an indent in the neck of the valves. Then, once the indent was sizeable enough, he went back to knocking the head of the valve around with the hammer. Soon enough the first one popped off. I picked it up to examine it, surprised at its heft. The oxidised green had been sheared off by the hammer, revealing bright copper in the spots where it had been hit, and on the inside stem, after it had been protected from the elements for more than 100 years.

'From back in the day when they made things to last,' Henry observed as he handed me another one.

I snapped some photos, careful not to include Henry in any of them; he was reluctant to be identified. Shots of nearby peaks. A summit selfie, with clouds in the background behind me.

Huge bugs were crawling over the summit, overly friendly in their approach, and whenever the breeze dropped, clouds of sandflies plagued us. A bug got in Henry's way. We were, after all, disturbing their home, crusading invaders in their peaceful environment.

'Look out, bug, you'll wear it,' Henry warned as he brandished the hammer.

'There are people on top of Tahurangi,' I said. My eyesight wasn't great, but I could see something in the distance. Clouds were beginning to form around us, lower down in the rugged and craggy Wahianoa catchment on the northeastern side, hiding the faraway terrain from view.

'Fucking white people and their sense of entitlement,' Henry said, referring possibly to the climbers on Tahurangi, the mountaineers who had placed the plaque a century ago, or humans in general. I didn't ask him to expand.

The last valve popped off. Henry straightened up, released the hammer and picked up his water bottle. He gazed around, then bowed his head to the scarred rock face. 'Sorry, mate, couldn't get it all out this trip.'

The valves had stuck fast and refused to come out cleanly, so the stems were still embedded inside the rock. Four round scars told the tale, each with a broken piece of copper stem shining brightly. Hopefully they'd fade over time.

Henry had wanted to chuck the broken tablet off the peak again, but we decided to take it down, to remove it from the terrain and environment entirely; I felt that throwing it off the peak would change it from history into rubbish. We split up the pieces, Henry stronger and fitter, and carrying a lot more of the load than I did, while I stashed the weighty valves and springs in the top pocket of my pack. I'd found an old newspaper report that indicated the tablet weighed nearly 16 kilograms, and the valves would have been extra.

We took a final look at the last of the scenery below that was still visible from the summit.

'Koro's let us up today,' Henry observed.

A thin wisp of mist flicked through from the south, between me and Henry. Koro had let us up, but now it was time to go.

Much of the time I had spent watching Henry abuse the valves until they succumbed had been filled with anxiety about the descent. These things are always worse inside your head, though, and the way back down was achievable, a lot easier than I'd imagined. However, I did have to lower my pack down to Henry through the most difficult section of the gully.

It helped that the terrain below us was hidden from view behind cloud, which had touched us on the way down from the peak. Reaching a tongue of snow, we donned crampons in the mist and descended a short, steep section to the gentler slopes of the Mangaehuehu Glacier.

'We'll need to boogie across this bit,' Henry said. Rocks were falling, creating brown streaks in the snow underneath a small bluff. Henry went first. Neither of us had

Hugh Girdlestone in uniform.
Bagnall Collection, Massey University Library

brought helmets, but our heads stayed intact. I felt Koro's protection in the enveloping cloud — like a hug, but also a gentle push back to the bottom of the mountain.

Despite the fog that now surrounded us, we managed to find our way back to our exact entry point onto the glacier. I dropped my pack and refilled my water bottle from a nearby stream, snow-fed and refreshing. We had a snack break and cycled through conversation topics, constantly returning to Girdlestone and the plaque.

'I'd be so embarrassed if someone put a plaque up for me because I fell off a mountain or something,' Henry said. 'I'd fucking haunt them.'

As we descended, Henry told me he had once been caught up on Ruapehu's Summit Plateau in a thunderstorm. 'It was one of the freakiest things I've ever experienced,' he said, shaking his head. 'Just surrounded by this booming thunder and being so close to the lightning.' I'd heard of people getting caught on the Summit Plateau after the weather closed in. They'd accessed it via the Notch, a small gap in the crater rim that allows a passage through, and not been able to find their way back out again.

Hugh Girdlestone, bastion of climbing, mountain enthusiast and surveyor of Tongariro National Park, a man who spent his days ascending peaks and his nights camped beneath stars on the rocky volcanic slopes of the maunga, a man stout of stature and blessed at times with a bushy handlebar moustache, did not die on the mountains of the central plateau he loved so much; he did not come to grief crossing a swift river of glacier melt, nor did he perish from speeding ballistics ejected violently from Ruapehu's crater; no — Hugh Girdlestone died from shrapnel flying across a battlefield, piercing his tent and then his flesh. Girdie, they called him affectionately. Girdie died not on the mountains he adored, but at the hands of the nation's enemy, in wartime, in his sleep.

On 17 January 1921, an advertisement appeared in the *New Zealand Times*: a meeting was to be held to consider a proposal to erect a memorial on Mount Ruapehu in memory of Hugh Girdlestone, climber and officer of the Department of Lands and Survey. Those interested in discussing the proposal were directed to present themselves at the Wellington offices of solicitors Buddle, Anderson and Kirkcaldie at 5 p.m. on the 19th.[2]

The men at the meeting decided to erect a tablet on 'some high peak in Tongariro Park' with Girdlestone's name engraved to permanently record his 'supreme sacrifice for the Empire' as well as acknowledge all he had done for the region in bringing before the public the beauties of the national park. The chaps thought a granite tablet would be the most suitable to withstand the 'severe climatic conditions' on the peak. They appointed a committee, invited subscriptions to fund the project, and organised a party to ascend the mountain and fix the tablet in place, which would be done — so they thought — no later than Easter that year.[3] In fact, they were so confident about erecting the tablet that they had it engraved with the intended date: 23 March 1921. But the mountain had other ideas; Ruapehu wouldn't let them up there until March the next year, after two foiled attempts.

At Easter 1921 they made their first foray, setting out from Ohakune. Late in the day they endured two hours of tough step-cutting a 'devious trail amongst the crevasses' of the Mangaehuehu Glacier, crevasses that were much deeper cracks than the small and shallow slots the glacier has now. Girdlestone's friend T. Arthur Johnston described the ascent attempt to newspaper reporters:

> The calm of the glacier and warm sunlight gave way to clouds of flying scud and whirling mists. Keeping under the shelter of the ridge however the party worked along to a rocky pile to adjust swags for the final ascent. The wind rapidly increased to a gale. The rocks were found to be covered with ice, and the party travelling slowly were soon halted by a formidable drop. Ominous clouds were sweeping lower and lower, hands and feet were becoming numb with cold, and after consultation it was reluctantly decided to leave the stone in a safe place until another opportunity.[4]

They were forced to abandon the tablet and tools beneath the upper ramparts of the peak, caching their stash just 100 metres from the summit. Heinrich Ferdinand von Haast gave a brief speech about Hugh Girdlestone and the Reverend Peter Keller prayed. The fierce weather showed no signs of abating, and so the party bailed.

They tried again a few weeks later on Sunday, 9 April, this time leaving from Round Bush at Karioi, a track considered much cleaner and easier than the muddy trail from Ohakune. A storm burst over their heads and the heavy rain and whipping winds warned them not to ascend, but the wind abated slightly and they became determined to carry on. They made it to around 2500 metres altitude, just 160 metres or so off the summit proper, on the southern side, when the weather again became ferocious.

'All our wet clothes froze on us like boards,' Peter Keller later wrote in a letter to Wellington MP W. H. Field. 'We had been cutting steps for over an hour up a very steep ice-bound shingle slope, and made the foot of the big cliffs just under the summit, when we got caught.'[5]

They had a fresh stock of drills to create holes for the Ford car engine valves they would use as copper bolts to pin the tablet to the rock and they left these there, to be picked up on the next trip. Using a rope, they descended to levels they deemed safer. It was after 5 p.m. and a thick fog enveloped them, requiring them to feel their way down the mountain, navigating by exposed rocks in the dark, moonless night. They reached their camp low on the mountain at 1.30 a.m. on Monday. They had been out on their mission for 15 hours.

Since they had to return to work, another immediate attempt wasn't possible. Keller wrote: 'We talked the matter over pretty thoroughly and decided it was getting rather late in the season to attempt any more weekend efforts until after the winter is over. The ice on this occasion was much worse than on the glacier at Easter time.'[6] He reckoned they would each need a full week of leave to get a weather window that would allow them up there.

ABOVE: Hugh Girdlestone at work surveying Tongariro National Park. He wrote 'your old friend in fighting costume' on the back of the photo. Bagnall Collection, Massey University Library

BELOW: The plaque installation team at camp. Bagnall Collection, Massey University Library

'[We] are extremely keen to get our work finished, and do not care to postpone longer than can be avoided, but Girdlestone Peak was not named "Matterhorn" by "Girdie" without just cause. It is not a peak to be trifled with in winter time,' he wrote.[7]

Although the tablet hadn't yet been placed, the government officially altered the peak's name from Little Matterhorn Peak — the name Girdlestone had ascribed to it in the course of his surveying work — to Girdlestone Peak. On some maps it appears as Matterhorn Peak, and on others as Little Matterhorn or Lesser Matterhorn. Ngāti Rangi call it Peretini, a name lost to the official maps for now.

Finally, they managed to fix the stone to the summit on the third attempt, on 12 March 1922. Again the party took the Karioi and Round Bush route, using horses to trek the tools and cement to their camp. They gained the summit just after midday, picking up the tablet from where it had rested for the past year under the upper rampart. Here they encountered difficulties, as the tools they had stashed with the stone were found frozen stiff in the sack they had been buried in.

During an earlier recce they had selected a large rock, chosen for its smooth face and its position right on the very summit. They bored four holes using a hammer and drill to fit the valves, with springs behind to allow for the expansion and contraction that would happen with the extreme temperature shifts. They prepared mortar by melting snow in a spirit stove and cemented the tablet into position.

The text read: 'Girdlestone Peak. Erected in loving memory of the late Sergeant Hubert Earle Girdlestone F.R.G.S., killed in France on 28 August 1918. Erected 23 March 1921'. It had taken them another year and three attempts to achieve their goal.

One party member described the eerie atmosphere: 'The restfulness of the oncoming evening settled down on us amid the weird silence of the heights and solitudes around, and with our last look at the memorial the knowledge came home to us that our dear friend also rested, and that his memory, like his name, would have an abiding place among the mountains that he loved so well.'[8]

After a dedication speech and a few words about their 'gallant comrade', they turned around to descend, reaching camp at 9.30 p.m., then Ohakune the next day, Monday, and finally returning to Wellington on the Thursday.[9]

A photo exists of the 'Girdlestone plaque team' with their tablet on the summit before it was fixed in place. Seven men stare down the barrel of the camera, some with exhaustion marking their faces. Tweed jackets and collared shirts are standard dress. Two men sport giant bushy moustaches in the style of Girdie himself. One chap grasps the end of an ice axe, two of which are crossed behind the plaque, and a rope is coiled in front. The plaque is only just readable and its smooth newness sings out from the centre of the posed group. The four car engine valves shine with a bright copper hue, popping light to the camera for the image. The men look strong, capable and perhaps a little wistful as they remember their friend Girdie.

CLOCKWISE FROM BELOW:
The plaque team on the summit of Girdlestone after installing the memorial. Bagnall Collection, Massey University Library; Girdlestone in one of his many camps around the mountains. Bagnall Collection, Massey University Library; climbers on the Mangaehuehu Glacier showing crevasses and the 'Lesser Matterhorn' in the background, date unknown. Bamford collection

In May that year, one of the party, named only as 'Gentian', wrote an account of the plaque's installation for the *Otago Witness* newspaper that included several pages of photographs. There's one of Hugh Girdlestone resplendent in his army uniform, badges affixed, shiny buttons and neatly trimmed moustache. His eyes are filled with a cheeky humour, perhaps tinged with a little sadness. Gentian wrote:

> He did more than any one man to popularise the park, and most of his holidays for a number of years preceding the war were spent in taking up large parties for rambling, climbing, and general exploration purposes. His interests were wide and his circle of friends great and real. As a sportsman and a comrade he was sought and valued everywhere, whilst even those who came within but casual contact of his personality were impressed by his sunny manliness. Popularity never spoiled 'Girdie'. His true heart and loyal nature preserved him as a real Sir Galahad of modern life.[10]

Gentian claimed that the peak had never had a name before Girdlestone named it Little Matterhorn Peak (it was, of course, Peretini to Ngāti Rangi), but a tradition existed that it was originally known by tangata whenua as Paretetaitonga ('parapet on the southern side') and the name had since wrongly been attributed to the second highest point of the summit ridges. Then, in 1908, Girdlestone had named it Little Matterhorn Peak, a title that became established on the maps of Tongariro National Park.

Gentian's account, in particular the mention of the name Paretetaitonga, raised the hackles of University of Otago Professor James Park, a geologist and the director of the School of Mines. While he applauded the plaque's placement and the initiative required to achieve this 'notable feat of daring and hardihood', Park wrote at some length about his own adventures on 'that grand old mountain' in 1886. '[I] ascended first what I called the South-East Peak, since called Little Matterhorn, and then Parataetaitonga [sic], the highest peak of Ruapehu . . . Mine was the first ascent of the Little Matterhorn and of the summit of Ruapehu.'[11] (Despite his claims, Park wasn't the first European to climb Ruapehu; George Beetham and Joseph Maxwell have that honour.)

Park said he had inquired with Māori at Karioi and found that the native name of the highest peak was 'Parataetaitonga'. However, Gentian's narrative indicated that the name Paretetaitonga had now been attributed to the second-highest peak. 'This is surely a matter for regret,' Park thundered. 'Place names lose their historical value when changed for new ones. Mr Girdlestone called the South-East peak the Little Matterhorn, and it certainly bears a close resemblance to the classical Matterhorn in Switzerland as viewed from Zermatt. I have a notion that Mr Girdlestone would have preferred his old name to stand.' (Park's abrasive character is summed up neatly in the *Dictionary of New Zealand Biography*: 'Park's rigorous teaching methods, coupled with an inability to suffer fools gladly, inspired more respect than affection.'[12] He was known for a bitter and long-lasting scientific dispute with another professor, who probably resigned over it, and Park's wife abandoned him.)

Hugh Girdlestone's mates of course applauded the name change they had driven through. As his friend T. Arthur Johnston commented: 'It is fitting that among the old Maori names one peak should perpetuate a European name honoured alike by the pakehas and Maoris [sic], for amongst the Native race Girdlestone had many true friends.'[13]

Girdlestone was a peak with a spirit and a personality, I thought, and a history to match.

In autumn 1894, the New Zealand colony's assistant survey-general, Walter Dunnage, had warned of the dangers of the peak, at that point 'unnamed' by Europeans. 'The extreme southern peak is a comparatively low one, but very precipitous,' Dunnage wrote. 'Tourists, or people wishing to climb the mountain, have plenty of choice, as there are four or five different peaks. But . . . the sharp, extreme southern peak must be given a wide berth, as it is beset with precipices and dangerous snowfields. I have climbed the extreme southern peak once, and must warn any one from trying to reach the main peak that way.'[14]

In the height of summer 1927 a group climbing Girdlestone were plagued by electrical disturbances and 'uncanny experiences' on the southeast ridge leading up to the final arête, bordering the Wahianoa Glacier. According to an account in the *Gisborne Times*, 'Only a strong spirit of intrepidity could have inspired the climbers to complete the ascent. The lightning appeared to be striking the peak and, when within 150 feet of the top, shocks were experienced by every member of the party.'[15] Their ice axes began to buzz and hiss, and when they got to the top, they found the summit rocks charged with electricity and 'hissing like gas jets'. One of the party was Horace Arthur Holl, an experienced climber who was well known for guiding people in the Ruapehu area.

In July 1975 climber Roger Mann described in a piece for the *New Zealand Alpine Journal* how he and two others were swept 400 metres down the Mangaehuehu Glacier in an avalanche while descending from Girdlestone. If the avalanche had taken them another 100 metres, they'd have been swept over a bluff.

'Something made me stop our three-man rope and turn around,' Mann wrote. 'Was it a sound I heard or some inner instinct? I don't really know but I have had that feeling in the mountains (and elsewhere) before, a feeling of being in or near a dangerous situation.'[16]

A metre-deep crack appeared just above them, and they found themselves caught in a 40-metre-wide slab avalanche. Mann dug his ice axe into the firm snow beneath him but the rope got caught around his leg and he swam in the snow, struggling for air.

'We were travelling at a tremendous speed and I began to think the end was near: images of my wife and two children flashed through my mind. Then suddenly I was popped out like a cork into the sunshine.' He stood up, impaling his companion with his crampon — the only injury the party received. 'The only thing hurt was my pride,' Mann wrote. They'd seen a small slide earlier but it was on steeper terrain and none of them had thought the comparatively flat Mangaehuehu Glacier would avalanche.

The author carrying a foam pad out of the Mangawhero Stream. These pads detach from ski lift towers and end up in waterways.

In May 1982 two climbers died on the slopes beneath Girdlestone, either in a fall or in an avalanche. Police found their bodies at around 2300 metres altitude and believed they'd fallen down a cliff. The men, aged 26 and 28, were well equipped and found in full climbing gear.

'Girdlestone has teeth,' climber Ian Young wrote in a love letter of sorts to the peak in the *New Zealand Alpine Journal* in 1991. 'Since I first walked on Ruapehu, Girdlestone has had a fascination for me. For Young, the peak had seemed to be 'a bastion of inaccessibility' until he finally climbed it one New Year's Day. But once gripped by the lofty spire he returned again and again: 'I have stood on its top but my interest has not flagged,' he wrote.[17] Young took friends with him on what was perhaps his fifteenth summit of Girdlestone — he'd lost count — introducing them to the peak's delights, including the plaque, without commentary on its existence.

Whenever I ascend the upper slopes of Ruapehu, I think about it a lot the night before, filled with a mixture of trepidation and excitement, fear and respect. Afterwards I feel grateful, maybe honoured, that the mountain allowed me access. To see Te Wai ā-moe Crater Lake hidden until the final moments of a climb when you tip over the edge of a ridge or a peak. To walk up ridges encrusted with shimmering diamonds of rime ice. To dance on the rooftop of the North Island.

The day after ascending with Henry I woke up to winds starting at 50 kilometres per hour and snow in the forecast for the upper peaks of the mountain. Cloud gathered around the mountain but rested only on Girdlestone. It was as if the peak was hiding from us, healing while out of sight.

My body had weathered the 1000-metre ascent and seven-hour day well, but a rest day of sorts was in order. A chill settled over Ohakune, and in spite of it being nearly summer, I put on some socks and a beanie.

I'd recently been spending time wandering around the South East Basin below the ski field lifts on Tūroa, between the Mangawhero Stream and the Mangaehuehu Stream, the latter of which drains from the glacier of the same name. Both catchments have picturesque and pure, impossibly aqua swimming holes, and the Mangawhero in particular had become dear to my heart. In these catchments I began picking up rubbish from the ski field — gloves, ski passes, drink bottles — and stashing it in my pack.

Then I stumbled across rubbish that was more 'macro' in nature — long, thick black rubber lines that were used for snow fencing; the foam pads that are wrapped around ski lift towers to protect skiers who crash into them; and the tarpaulin skins from the foam pads. The foam is particularly toxic once it begins breaking down in the waterways, so grabbing it while it was still whole was a triumph. None of it would fit in my pack, so I'd borrowed a couple of old-school frame packs from my ski club to haul it out.

I needed muscle, so I asked a male friend who had more strength than me to come along and help haul the big stuff out of the stream beds. I'd tried to pull the tarpaulins out but they were embedded between rocks, and as they tended to fill up with water

and sand they were difficult to move without serious muscle. Between us, we managed to remove a Subaru Impreza hatchback's worth of foam, skins and rubbish, then we dropped it off at the rear of a building on Tūroa and let the ski field staff know. They said they'd take care of its disposal; untrusting of how well the operations were running given Ruapehu Alpine Lifts (RAL) was in financial difficulty, I regularly kept an eye on it, and relaxed when it finally disappeared.

Seeing the rubbish in catchments that fed the best swimming spots I'd seen in my lifetime changed my perspective on the ski field infrastructure swiftly and radically.

'Some of the iwi reckon Koro's been scarred by the ski field,' Henry had said to me. 'And they reckon that's why RAL's in the shit.'

A thought took hold in my brain, an opinion sure to be unpopular with many: I'd like to see the top lift, the High Noon Express, which protrudes too high on the mountain for my comfort, off the mountain and the landscape restored and healed, within my lifetime.

Henry had told me he has some Māori heritage somewhere in his family, but he's never really been engaged in te ao Māori. 'I don't say Pākehā or European or even New Zealand European when I have to tick the box on the forms,' he said. 'I just say I'm a New Zealander. I don't think you need to be Māori to want to see the backcountry kept clear of this shit. Why do we feel the need to mark wherever we've been? You know, the Māori have stories behind all their place names. But white people, we just name the peaks after ourselves.'

I read back through the comments on Dave Bamford's Facebook post about his summit trip and the plaque. On the whole, people were enthusiastic about the trip and the notion of a memorial stone, commenting that it was an amazing journey in family history, a great effort, lovely story. And it was.

One person said he had been to check on the plaque in 1961, back when there was a fund for its maintenance, and another had seen it in the late 1980s and it was then intact. Dave, who said the plaque appeared to have shattered recently, noted he personally had 'little enthusiasm for any replacement'.

It's here that all my thinking on memorials in a national park started to unravel and go round and round in the great washing machine of environmental values. One of the key management philosophies in the Tongariro National Park Management Plan is 'to protect the ancestral, historical, archaeological and cultural landscape of Tongariro National Park'.[18] Under the management plan, historic features include memorials, and the protection of these sites is provided for in legislation; the Historic Places Act 1993 promotes the protection and preservation of the historical and cultural heritage of New Zealand.

Moreover, the Tongariro National Park Act 1922 dictates that a £50 fine awaits anyone who 'wilfully breaks or injures any fence, building or erection' or 'wilfully breaks, cuts, injures or removes any, or any part of any, wood, tree, shrub, fern, plant, stone, mineral, furniture, utensil, tool, or thing of any kind'.[19] (Incidentally, the Act also applies the same fine to anyone who takes the nest or egg of any bird. Girdlestone was a known nest-robber, having been attacked by sparrow hawks on a trip in November 1899 after he stole three eggs from their nest. The eggs were, according to a report in the *Press*, 'handsome trophies'.)[20]

Were Henry and I undoing history by removing the plaque from the summit? Were we carrying out a radical act of decolonisation? Were we committing an offence? Or were we restoring the environment to its natural state? Perhaps we were doing all of those things, somehow, in a big contradictory mix.

The management plan offers a list of 'actively managed historic resources', which includes Waihohonu Hut (the historic red shed built in 1903–1904), the Chateau Tongariro, Glacier Hut on Whakapapa's Hut Flat, and the Ohakune Old Coach Road. It also identifies 'passively managed resources' such as the site of the Haunted Whare, the Stanton Memorial in the Whakapapaiti Valley, the Whakapapa ski club lodges, and 'Hollis or Holls cairn' in the Mangaturuturu Valley on the southern side of Ruapehu. The highest 'resource' on either list is Glacier Hut, which sits at just under 1800 metres. The Girdlestone plaque isn't mentioned at all. In fact, the words 'Girdlestone' (or 'Peretini') don't appear at all in the management plan.

Would I crusade to knock down Waihohonu Hut or to destroy my ski club lodge? Not at all, no more than I would attempt to burn down the Chateau.

The plan has a section on memorials, plaques and cairns, which acknowledges that the park is associated with 'many historic public events and intense personal memories', which often leads to 'a desire to commemorate an occasion or event through a physical tribute'. In an admirable piece of linguistic fence-sitting, it also states: 'It is not in the best interest of this predominantly natural area to provide for every request.' According to the plan, existing memorials, plaques and cairns should be maintained as they are, where they are, unless they are destroyed by natural events. (There is no prescription for memorials destroyed by human hand, by force and with intent.)

In 1990, six soldiers died on Ruapehu after being caught in a blizzard. They'd tried to get to Dome Shelter but couldn't; it later turned out they were only 150 metres away. A plaque in their memory was installed in the shelter, but when the structure was removed from the mountain in 2018 a replacement plaque was placed outside the DOC office at Whakapapa Village, under a tiny tōtara.

Unfortunately, Private Jason Menhennet's name had been spelled incorrectly on the plaque, and his family had tried in vain to have it redone and his name corrected.[21] In 2020 they went to the lengths of designing a new plaque (with correct spelling) as a replacement. They raised money for it and assumed it was full steam ahead. Iwi said no, and DOC supported the decision. The family was given a range of reasons: a plaque already exists; the families aren't benefactors of the park; it's not consistent with park values; there are health and safety reasons. These all related to paragraphs in the management plan, but sound heartless and needlessly bureaucratic when taken out of that context and cited in a media story.

Iwi representative Bubs Smith from Ngāti Hikairo ki Tongariro told me he supported a 'like for like' replacement, but suggested the army museum at Waiouru was

The memorial to the soldiers who died on Ruapehu in 1990.

perhaps a better place for a memorial. 'It didn't sit well with us,' he said. 'We don't want the mountain to become a graveyard.'

I told Henry about the plaque, as well as another one that's very visible within Tongariro National Park, and I think he put them in his crosshairs. His view tallied with Bubs' perspective. 'That sort of thing should be at the army museum at Waiouru, not on the mountain,' he said. I held my breath a bit, at that.

The Girdlestone plaque and copper valves sat in my living room for a while until a visitor saw them and, bug-eyed, demanded to know whose grave I'd been desecrating. They also spotted a giant disc from an angle grinder that Henry had picked up near the chairlift as part of our rubbish collection, and concluded that somehow we'd used battery-powered tools in our destruction. Assumptions can be damaging.

The plaque wasn't all there; we had removed about half of it, and the remnants were lost forever around and underneath the peak. The pieces felt heavy in my hand, as did the valves — weighted not just by their innate heft but also by the heaviness of what we'd just done. A couple of pieces were distinctly pointy and resembled the shape of Girdlestone itself. They were dirty, but once dusted off they looked as shiny as if the tablet had been made last week. I turned them over and over, examining each one in turn.

Eventually I packed it all away in a box and slid it to the back of a dark, lockable cupboard, to be addressed and dealt with at some later stage. I didn't want to just chuck it out — it was a piece of history, after all — but I'd been an accessory to removing it from the backcountry. There had been a reason, even if I hadn't yet identified that reason precisely to myself.

I looked up Dave Bamford and went to have a coffee with him at his place in Wellington. 'I've got a confession, Dave,' I said, shaking internally. 'That plaque was actually smashed, on purpose.' I told him the whole story of the trip with Henry, Henry's motives, and my desire to ensure the plaque wasn't consigned to rubbish on Ruapehu.

Dave wasn't angry, just interested, and he reiterated that he had no desire to see a plaque reinstalled on the peak.

'The plaque was a reflection of the time,' he said. 'I mean, do we really want to keep ramming colonialism down the throats of iwi?' Dave was an enthusiast for the original te reo Māori name, Peretini, being reinstated, and he noted it was already becoming more widely used, such as by what was then Ruapehu Alpine Lifts. 'Hopefully the future management of the national park will reflect a greater say by iwi.'

I also had a chat with a cultural rep from Ngāti Rangi and told them the plaque had been intentionally smashed. Their thoughts were that it was best to 'leave nature to do what it needs to do'.

The day we went up Girdlestone I came away covered in finely milled rock dust and ochre-coloured dirt, so I walked to my favourite mountain swimming hole, a jewel-coloured spot surrounded by smooth rocks made hot by the summer sun. There's a view up to the maunga, including Girdlestone. I dunked myself completely and repeatedly in the water, full-body immersion in snow melt, some of which had probably trickled down from the glacier I'd been on earlier that day. It felt pure and cleansing, appropriate after spending the day up on the rooftop of the maunga.

Words I'd read by Ngāti Rangi leader Che Wilson in an article in *Backcountry*, the Federated Mountain Clubs magazine, echoed back to me from the mountain: that there are different interpretations of the notion of 'tapu' and associated practices. 'You went at a certain time of year, and did karakia to invoke your ability to see the unseen,' Wilson wrote. 'There are key guardians in the mountains that we talk to to ask permission to go up, and also to give respect to them as they look after those places.'

As a New Zealander of European descent, these were cultural practices I didn't have access to, but we had some things in common. Wilson pointed out the key to a relationship with Koro Ruapehu was to enjoy him, but respect him, and I felt that. 'Know that for some people you're walking on their cathedral, on their Vatican, on their Westminster Abbey, on their Blue Mosque.' Don't just treat recreation on the maunga as a walk in the park.

'Irrespective of culture, the lofty peaks are a recognition of that which is special and unseen,' he wrote. 'Going to those lofty places is all about being inspired and given a spiritual recharge.'[22]

In March 1924, two years after the plaque was installed, a small party climbed Girdlestone to check on the state of the memorial tablet. The *Evening Post* reported: 'Despite the powerful disintegrating forces which are continually acting against this precipitous pinnacle, the monument displays no sign of deterioration and the party are now of the opinion that its permanency is now assured.'[23]

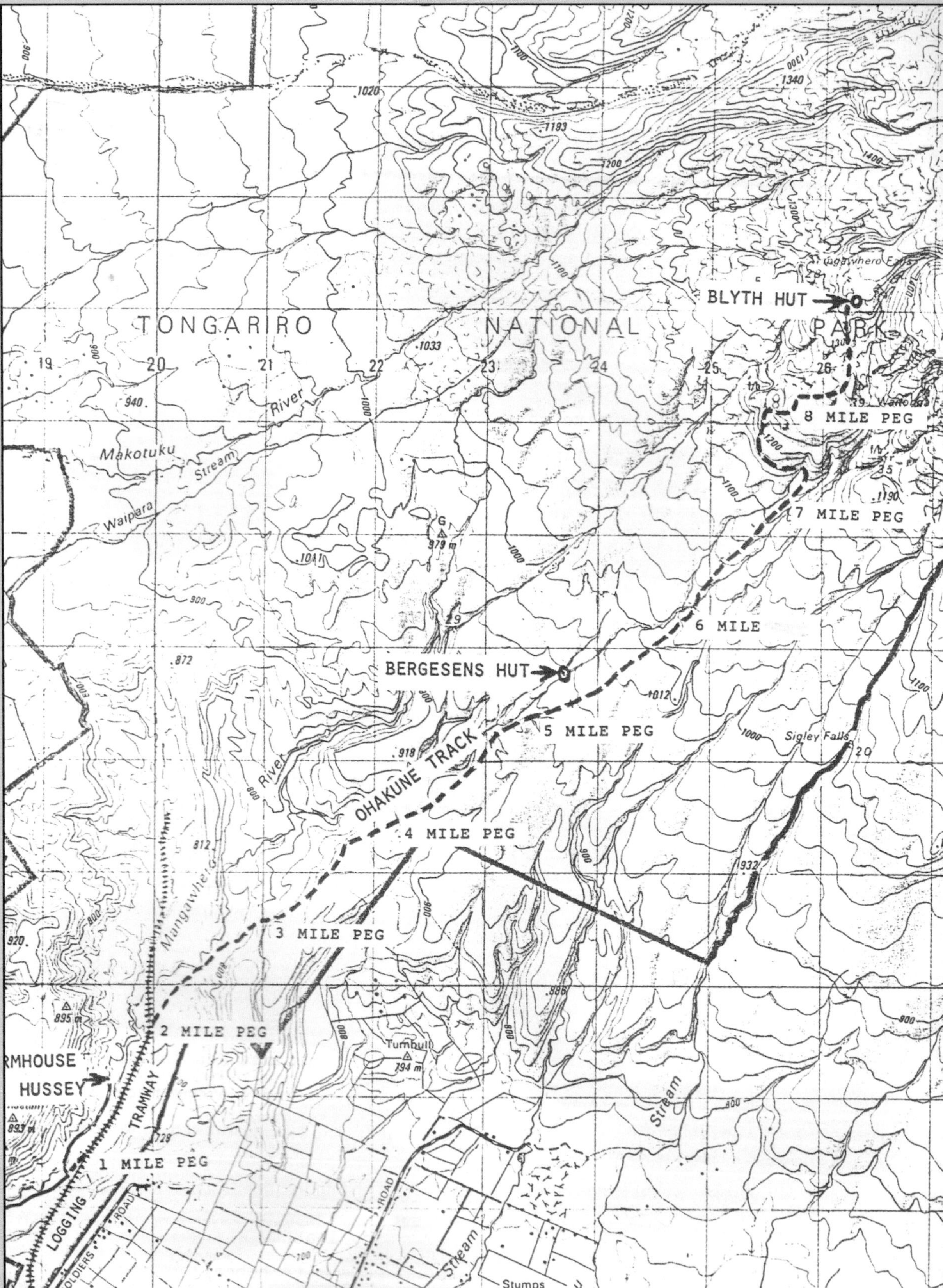
TONGARIRO NATIONAL PARK
BLYTH HUT
8 MILE PEG
7 MILE PEG
6 MILE
BERGESENS HUT
5 MILE PEG
OHAKUNE TRACK
4 MILE PEG
3 MILE PEG
2 MILE PEG
1 MILE PEG
RMHOUSE
HUSSEY
LOGGING TRAMWAY
SOLDIERS ROAD
ROAD
Makotuku River
Waipara Stream
Mangawhero
River
Sigley Falls
Turnbull
Stumps
Stream

Map showing the rough location of the upper Bergersen hut. Ashley Cunningham collection, Ohakune Library

CHAPTER 2

Secret huts on the southern slopes

During the Second World War, two men called Bergersen built a couple of huts on the southern side of Ruapehu to avoid conscription. Both men were labelled conscientious objectors and one was arrested at gunpoint. Could we find their huts, nearly 80 years later, in the tangled and frigid Mangawhero Stream?

Ohakune, 1942. Auckland, gripped by an ongoing dry spell, was relying almost entirely on the small mountain town for its supplies of green vegetables; pigeon racing was hotly contested between the regions, and birds were liberated from Ohakune to race more than 177 kilometres; a track was cut from the Junction to Mangaiti Hut; and a long-haired defaulter was captured on the southern slopes of Ruapehu.

Ohakune gardener Merv Bergersen had failed to report for military service when he was first called up on 27 April the previous year. Instead, he took to the bush, where he built a hut, fitting it out with bunks, tools and goods.

Six weeks before Merv's arrest, members of the Ohakune Home Guard had been exploring the bush on the mountain and were about five miles from Ohakune when they came across a sign placed incorrectly on a track. They quickly figured out that it was a ruse, designed to divert trampers from a new track that led to Merv's hut. They spotted two men in the vicinity, and one was their man. A warrant for his arrest was issued and police organised a search party, pushing their way through the dense bush for five hours to reach the hut. It was empty. A note that read 'Gone down Horopito track' did not put them off the scent: Merv was found hiding in a paddock behind the shack. He'd been hiding for a year by that stage, and hadn't seen a haircut in several months. He also sported a thick, bushy beard.

Merv pleaded guilty in the Ohakune Magistrate's Court and was sentenced to one month in jail followed by detention in a camp for military defaulters. It's unclear how long he was detained for, but archives suggest he spent at least the next three years in the camp; the authorities denied his application for release in August 1945, just a month before the war ended.[1]

In 1943, a year after Merv was caught, his uncle Les, a carpenter who also lived in Ohakune, was called up for military training along with scores of other men from the Whanganui military district. Four were from Ohakune and 'L. J. Bergerson' was among them. The surname, a Norwegian one, is often misspelt, but it was Lesley John Bergersen, Merv's uncle. Les was having none of it. He'd appealed the ballot in July 1942 on personal grounds and had only got a short stay of relief until 30 September. Les was married with a family, and his desire to avoid war had been influenced by his brother's experiences in the First World War. Les also took to the bush, where he built his own hut. Although avoiding conscription was controversial and generally frowned upon, a few local supporters assisted Les by stashing supplies in the thick forest around the lower southern slopes of Ruapehu.

It's thought that the Bergersens built more than just the two huts. One was reported to be close to the bottom of what is now the Ohakune Mountain Road, and the other not far from the Old Blyth Track, which was then reached by a foot and horse track. The upper hut demonstrated Les's carpentry skills; it was hewn from kaikawaka, felled using his broadaxe, which he stashed under a loose floorboard. The hut had a corrugated-iron roof and a shingle on the door that read: Bergersen's Hut.

Some reckon Les was captured at that hut in 1944, but there's a thread of a story that he avoided getting snapped until much later, when he was out of the area altogether.

ABOVE: From left: Les Bergersen, Merv Bergersen and Tom Reynolds. Susan Pulman collection

BELOW: Merv Bergersen at a mountain hut (but not the hut where he hid out). Susan Pulman collection

I stumbled across the story of Les Bergersen first, while researching another historical thread entirely. An online search provided a link to an ebook compiled by a master's student in archaeology that had site records of historical interest listed at the end. It described the Bergersens' huts as two sites in the Ohakune area occupied by Les and Merv Bergersen while they were evading conscription at different points during the Second World War. The upper hut site had last been visited in 2012 and was considered to be in 'fair' condition, the report stated — the site, I assumed, not the hut itself. It was highly unlikely that the structure was still standing, no matter how good a builder Les had been.

As I began to search, initially for information about Les, the spellings threw me off track: Bergerson, Bergesen, Bergeson, Leslie, Lesley. I put in a request to the National Library in case an archivist there could offer me a lead. Neither Les's nor Merv's births were registered in New Zealand, I was told, and although there was a death registered for Leslie Alfred Andes Bergersen, he had been born in 1938 and had died in 1979, so he couldn't be the Les I was looking for.

Eventually I found some more concrete information, settled on what I deemed to be their correct names: Lesley John Bergersen and Mervyn Stanley Bergersen. Their middle names helped — searching for newspaper stories about 'Mervyn Stanley' meant that although a few other unrelated Mervyn Stanleys were thrown into the mix, it didn't matter how the surname was spelled, and it yielded results.

I got coordinates for the upper hut site from the ebook, and then found more while rifling through old papers in the DOC archives in Wellington. After placing them all on my topo map app, I had a total of four potential sites to check out. Three were consistent with reports that the upper hut was 'west of the five-mile peg' on the Old Blyth Track, while the fourth lined up with the intel that a hut was situated 'not far' from the Ohakune ranger station.

But man, they were hard to find.

I started with the Old Blyth Track. It is named for Joe Blyth, the only person who was probably more obsessed with Ruapehu than I am. A keen tramper and climber, he reportedly ascended the maunga 147 times — and that would've been from Ohakune Hut just below 1200 metres, making it a 1400-metre day out. This was a far more arduous and extensive undertaking than my habit of 'popping up' from the top of the Far West T-bar on Whakapapa, a 'summit trip' of perhaps 400 metres' ascent to visit one of the peaks (I was totally cheating).

Blyth wore a few different hats. He was appointed headmaster of Ohakune School in 1909 and was instrumental in constructing the Blyth Track (now the Old Blyth Track), which runs parallel to the Ohakune Mountain Road and joins with the Waitonga Falls Track. If you really wanted to climb Ruapehu while maintaining historical integrity, you'd start from the bottom of the Old Blyth Track at around the

8-kilometre mark on the road, then grovel up through mud and bush before joining the track to the new Blyth Hut. Blyth and co cut rounds of logs and tree branches and laid them across the track to try to mitigate the mud, but even then horse traffic cut it up very badly and Blyth himself labelled the track in its earliest days 'an elongated bog'.[2]

The cut wood was designed as an anti-bog tool, a corridor, but in its modern incarnation this is a failure; the smooth wood, once wet, becomes hilariously slippery. Imagine railway sleepers, only closer together, but then interspersed with sections where they are absent altogether and where it behoves the cautious tramper to poke around at muddy areas with a pole before committing. Some of these areas have wood hidden just below the wet surface while others allow the unsuspecting tramping boot to plunge in above its top, filling it with mud and making that concerning sucking sound when retrieved by force.

The Old Blyth Track is at such a gentle gradient at that point on the mountain that the water simply doesn't run off. I don't mind a gentle gradient, so on my first foray to find the Bergersens' huts I wombled right past the point where I was meant to turn off and begin bush bashing.

I reckoned the men would've wanted a good reliable water source, so they'd have placed their huts close to a stream but not so close as to get flooded if the stream ran high. The site would need to be far enough off the main Old Blyth Track that passers-by wouldn't inadvertently stumble across it and ask inconvenient questions, but again, not so far that it required a large effort of bush-crashing to reach.

I backtracked, watching my GPS for just the right spot, then left the track and made for the stream nearby, looking around as I went for a potential clearing, signs of an old track, or anything that might tip me off to a prior human presence, albeit a long time ago.

Sometimes you get a sense that Ruapehu is allowing you in, and this was one of those days. Gaps at just the right places in the bush called my name and subsequent gaps allowed me to pass through without having to battle too many obstructions. I don't really like the idea of 'bashing' Ruapehu or his slopes and forest; I prefer the idea of moving quietly and stealthily through, just touching him gently.

I navigated sections of bush lawyer, wet and mossy limbs, overgrown grasses and an inordinate amount of bush litter on the forest floor. It occurred to me that any hut remnants could be covered by decades and decades of leaf matter, twigs and windfall, and unless there was something incredibly obvious that had stood the test of time — a chunk of corrugated-iron roof, for example — realistically I was unlikely to actually find anything.

Eventually I stumbled upon a clearing, a small but distinct clearing, with a view directly above to bright blue sky, unobstructed by treetops. I checked the topo map. I was right on top of the pin I'd set. This could well be it.

I fancied, though, that this site was marginally too far away from the stream. It also had a steep drop down to the water source, which wouldn't be ideal for daily living. The ground was covered with layer upon layer of years of windfall, too hard to lift or poke through except on its surface layers, as well as leaves, broken branches and mud. This could well be it, but I'd never know.

I became properly obsessed with the Bergersens and their lives. A research approach of wearing out the soles of my tramping boots was one thing, but I knew I'd need to do some more desk research if I really, properly wanted to know about Les and Merv and their huts. I fired up my laptop and shot off information requests, starting with the National Library and Archives New Zealand. A researcher at Archives New Zealand replied swiftly: they held nothing on either man, and had tried all the various spellings of their names. They pointed me to the Police or perhaps the New Zealand Defence Force.

I put in an Official Information Act request to Defence and promptly forgot about it, until one day when I was up on the mountain cleaning up rubbish in the waterways I got a call from a withheld number.

'Hello Hazel,' a rushed female voice said. 'I'm from NZDF Personnel Archives and Medals.' She said it so quickly that my brain scrambled to make sense of the name. 'Look I've got these files on the Bergersens. What's your address and I'll courier them to you? We're on a deadline.'

I knew nothing about a deadline but I rattled off my address, and the next day a slim volume arrived at my door. Two branded folders contained all that the New Zealand Defence Force held on the Bergersens. Les's file was inexplicably thicker than Merv's; I knew Merv had been caught but I had thought Les might have evaded the authorities entirely. I'd found a media report about Merv's capture and nothing about Les.

Reading the files, Les was an enigma. Incongruently for a man who'd gone to some lengths to avoid conscription, it seemed — if I was reading the files correctly — that he had either been awarded, or been recommended for, two medals — the War Medal and the New Zealand War Service Medal. The file also confirmed that he'd appealed his call-up in May 1942 on grounds of public interest and undue hardship and had been given a stay until September. I asked an army mate to check the paperwork and he confirmed I was interpreting it correctly: Les had been awarded both medals.

After his stay ended in September 1942 Les had disappeared for the next couple of years. He'd left his home town of Ohakune to go bush, or to join a shearing gang in the Wairarapa, or to go to the South Island where he was later caught, or possibly all of those options. He'd failed to notify his change of address, an act that could result in a charge of desertion. By late 1942 the hunt for Les was in full swing. Police memos noted he was 31, stood five foot nine (he was definitely taller, though, well over six foot), of good physique and fresh complexion, with brown hair and grey eyes, and letters went back and forth between police and the army.

Reading the correspondence in the file felt like the written version of an episode of *Fawlty Towers*. Les might be with a shearing gang over in the Wairarapa, his wife told police; she hadn't heard from him in ages. 'That is all I know,' she finished, and sent Les's conscription letter back to the military. The military wrote back: 'Please treat this matter as urgent as Mr Bergersen is regarded as a defaulter and the usual defaulter action is being instituted forthwith.'

LEFT: Les Bergersen.
Susan Pulman collection

RIGHT: Merv Bergersen.
Susan Pulman collection

A police memo sent to the military area officer in February 1943 summed up the situation as the Whanganui Inspector of Police knew it:

> You may recall that his cousin [sic], Mervyn Stanley, was arrested by police when he was or had been living in a hut on the side of Mt Ruapehu. Leslie John Bergersen [sic] was suspected of carrying supplies to the cousin. Masterton police cannot trace [him]. Ohakune police say that information received indicates that Bergersen had been seen prior to Xmas last or during Xmas holidays in the vicinity of Aramoho [near Whanganui]. Mrs Bergersen claims she has not heard from her husband since the receipt of the Masterton dated letter. It is unlikely that she will assist in any way. Enquiry is being made at Aramoho.[3]

Les was finally arrested two years later, in January 1945, not in Ohakune or Aramoho or anywhere near Ruapehu, but instead in Blenheim. He was caught using a false name, Les Jensen, and given two months' imprisonment for the false name and another two months for failing to report. In one of the notes from the time of his arrest it says he was 'fit for detention with hard labour'. He was in prison only until mid-March 1945, when he was released, but evidently he was compelled to serve in the military, six months before the war would be over. He was almost 35 when he was discharged, in October 1945, just a month after the war ended, with medals pinned to his chest.

Merv's file is stamped with a large scarlet brand: 'Conscientious Objector. Refuses to take oath', the oath being, 'I, Mervyn Stanley Bergersen, do sincerely promise and swear that I will be faithful and bear true allegiance to our Sovereign Lord the King, and that I will faithfully serve in the New Zealand Military Forces against His Majesty's enemies, and that I will loyally observe and obey all orders of the Generals and Officers set over me, until I shall be lawfully discharged. So help me God.'[4]

Merv had shown up for a medical examination and to be 'graded' in June 1941 but disappeared shortly after. He was caught 11 months later and sentenced to one month's imprisonment, followed by detention in a defaulters' camp on a charge of failing to report. Merv's file showed he 'failed to report' four times.

'Prior to his arrest he had been living in a newly built hut on the side of Mt Ruapehu,' a note from the Whanganui Inspector of Police informed the area officer. 'This information had been supplied to you by members of the Home Guard stationed at Ohakune but no action could be taken by police until your request for prosecution was received.'

Turns out Merv was targeted by an angry local. His file shows it was an Ohakune resident, T. Gover, who was irate that Merv hadn't reported for duty; Gover had penned several letters to police complaining about it. The first one read:

> I am taking this opportunity of writing to you. This concerns a young chap by the name of Mr Mervyn Bergerson [sic], who has been called up five times to enter camp, it's a year in May since he was called in an overseas ballot. He has no intentions of going into camp and there has been nothing done or said

> about it. It's not that he's a conchie objector as it's nothing to him to go shooting animals etc. Don't you think it's about time someone looked into the matter. Do you think it's fair that other mothers and fathers have to part with their sons, as I did, with three of mine, to fight for the likes of this Mr. Bergerson [sic] who's had his freedom for a year and still having it. Another chap would have been collected before this time. The police can't do anything until they have a warrant for his arrest, as they can't make it out themselves why he's not in camp and all the other chaps have gone. This chap lives in Rangataua Road, Ohakune. If it's good enough for other boys and wives' husbands it's good enough for him. Hoping you'll see into the matter.[5]

A lack of action prompted Gover to write again. He continued to complain about Merv's continued freedom, 'which makes it the fourth time and yet there has been nothing done about it and he is still walking about having his freedom while the rest of the boys are fighting for him'.

During the First World War, the National Registration Act 1915 required every man aged between 17 and 60 to register for service. They were required to state their willingness to fight in the war, specifically to serve beyond New Zealand. During wartime, it became a common sight in small towns for men to parade to service accompanied by the sound of martial music, men dressed in Army khaki or the blue Air Force uniform and the still bluer hue of the Navy dress. From the earliest, 'defaulters' who failed to register faced consequences, including social persecution. Shortly after the Act was passed, Prime Minister Bill Massey stated that there would be 'consequences' for those who didn't comply: 'We cannot allow any individual to shirk the responsibility.'[6]

Conscription was introduced the following year, requiring all non-Māori men aged 20–46 to register, sorted into married/recently married and bachelors. Men could object and appeal to the Military Service Board on grounds such as family hardship or conscientious objection. If their appeal was declined and they still refused to serve, they were imprisoned.

Archibald Baxter, father of poet James K. Baxter, was arguably the country's most famous conscientious objector. He was imprisoned and wrote of his experiences in his book *We Will Not Cease*. In 1918, Baxter was sent to the front line in France, to a place called Mud Camp, where he and three others were sentenced to 'field punishment number one' in a bid by the military to make an example of them. The punishment consisted of being tied to a tilted post in a field, their hands, knees and feet tightly bound. Blood would drain to their feet and it was known to be excruciatingly painful. The punishment was usually applied for eight hours, but on two occasions Baxter was left there for 12 hours or more. He collapsed and was taken to a French hospital, where he was diagnosed with 'confusional insanity'.

There was intense public feeling over conscientious objectors, which continued in the Second World War, as can be seen by the lengths the police and military (and locals like the angry T. Gover) went to with Merv and Les Bergersen. Employers were forbidden to employ men who weren't enrolled, newspapers reinforced the need to show up, with headlines admonishing 'Remember! You MUST do your duty!', and men who didn't go were publicly shamed by being handed a white feather, to label them a coward.

In the First World War around 600 men objected, and about half were imprisoned. All seven of the Baxter brothers refused to fight and were classed as 'defiant objectors'. Newspaper cartoons of the time illustrated the depth of emotion against so-called 'conchies'. There's one by Frank Holland that shows a man reclining in a chair smoking a cigarette surrounded by cards showing others who are serving — father, brother, mother, sister, uncle, cousin — the subtext is clear: they are all doing their part. The nail in the coffin is the caption, which reads: 'This little pig stayed at home.'

There's a famous photo of conscientious objectors during the Second World War, snapped at Hautu Detention Camp near Tūrangi. Nine men smile at the camera, which is separated from its subjects by close rows of barbed wire. Some are shirtless in the heat. One has a long and hairy beard. Behind them are 'public works' huts, road-worker style, just small huts, presumably no insulation, shared facilities. It would've been freezing there in winter. The men look like a rag-tag bunch.

Jeff Bergersen, son of Merv, told me he showed his father the photo once. Merv looked at it for a while, then pointed to each man in turn and named them, every one.

'How do you know all that?' Jeff asked.

'Because I was there,' Merv said.

I tracked Jeff down thanks to social media. I posted on a Facebook group for enthusiasts of local Ohakune and Ruapehu history, and a few people got in touch, some who knew more than others. Jeff was one of them. He's 69, lives in the Coromandel now, and I eventually found him via that age-old method of contactability, the White Pages, and called him for a chat.

In 2006, Merv was suffering ill health, so Jeff had resigned from his job to spend more time with his dad. Merv and Jeff would sit in the sun and chat. In 2007, Jeff got a computer and introduced Merv to the internet. 'I pulled up the subject of the conscientious objectors' movement in New Zealand,' Jeff told me. 'My father didn't openly profess to be a conscientious objector — it was just circumstance — and because of his manner, he didn't make any protest or any attempt to front up to conscription. He didn't explain things in a lot of words, he just expected you to understand things. It took a bit of chiselling info out of him. Some of those camps were pretty tough places.'

Hautu was one; Whitaunui and Paiaka near Shannon were the others. In 2012, Mary Bielski, a woman who lived near Shannon, got curious about the historical items she uncovered on her own land, and after a bit of research found out she was sitting on the old Whitaunui Detention Camp. It covered around 8 hectares of land and comprised a hospital, kitchens, ablutions, gardens and the sleeping huts. Bielski began to investigate. The camps operated from 1941 to 1946 and housed men from around the

ABOVE: Merv Bergersen during his time as a bushman. Susan Pulman collection

BELOW: Conscientious objectors at Hautu Detention Camp, 1943. Alexander Turnbull Library, 1/2-037724-F

country. They seem to have been fed adequately, if photos are anything to go by, but the huts would've been miserably cold.

Bielski pointed out that the camps were a huge waste of time for those men. 'Young people are now puzzled about why people were so angry about the conscientious objectors — people have moved on, and can't understand how intense the feelings were,' she told a reporter.[7]

I was much the same, and I said as much to Jeff. I also couldn't comprehend how something like compulsory service would fly in a modern environment. 'It took me a lot of time to get information out of my father,' Jeff told me. 'There are others who won't talk about it, because of the stigma about conscientious objectors. Now that I'm older, I see the different generational perspectives on these things, if that's a way of putting it. It's hard to even begin to understand — I was only born in 1955. Trying to understand what happened with those generations, what they went through and how it affected families, it's hard for newer generations now to appreciate how things went down.'

Jeff remembered Les from his childhood, although he doesn't recall a lot about him or his activities on the mountain. 'I just learned everything when Dad was ill and I'd sit there and talk to him, just chip info out of him.' He reckons Les had no time for warfare and was extremely anti-authoritarian, particularly about the structure of governments, the military and the English. Jeff recalled that Les wasn't arrested on Ruapehu like Merv was, and knew he was caught in the South Island somewhere. 'He got arrested in the end because he dropped his ration book and it had his name on it.'

Jeff stumbled across one of Les and Merv's huts when he was out deerstalking on Ruapehu one day, totally by accident. 'I thought, I'll be beggared. There was a noticeable clearing and I thought it wasn't natural. I could see iron sticking out of the ground and hewn timber around. I made a note of it in my mind. I could find it again — I'd walk straight to it.'

Living in the cold huts in a detention camp at Hautu was one thing, but Merv must've been a tough cookie already. Jeff described him as a proper Kiwi bushman, used to hunting and living off the land — he'd been all over the Moawhango, now within the Waiouru military zone. Merv would've been used to snow and ice, living rough and making do with whatever he had. He'd also lived through one of the worst disasters to hit Ohakune, and it happened while he was at large in the forest. In fact, it's hard to imagine that the hut he was in wouldn't have been affected.

In January 1942 a torrential flood, one of the biggest in history, hit Ohakune. The Mangateitei and Mangawhero rivers burst their banks and a railway bridge was washed away. Debris piled up against a bridge at Ohakune, diverting floodwaters into the street, pushing into people's homes. It happened suddenly when a slip let go. Cars were overturned and the streets were littered with dead animals — trout, eels, birds. It was the era of outhouses, and any longdrop near the riverbank was swept away. Ohakune became a wasteland of silt, slush and slash.

Ole Olsen was 79, had an artificial limb and walked with a stick. The owner of

Ohakune's billiard saloon, Olsen was last seen alive at his premises in Clyde Street as the waters began to rise. The back door was about 20 metres from the raging Mangateitei Stream, and it's thought he went to attend to some cattle. Search parties went down the Mangawhero River and up from Raetihi. His house had received the full force of the floodwaters — a later inspection found the bath was full of silt and water, indicating how badly flooded the dwelling had been. After a couple of weeks, Olsen's body was found in Memorial Park, 120 metres from his house, covered in driftwood and silt. Debris was banked up against trees up to a metre and a half high and included large logs and wrecked longdrops.

The damage had occurred over just two hours during the afternoon. Farmers arrived with tractors to pull logs out of the main street, and a fund was opened for cleaning up and rebuilding. Ohakune stank; the stench from decaying mud, dead animals and debris was obnoxious, and locals were wary of an outbreak of disease, particularly from the filthy outhouses gone rogue.

Merv lived through the storm and flood, presumably huddled up by himself in one of the huts, a single man against the elements. He was a survivor.

Les's granddaughter Susan Pulman also got in touch after seeing my Facebook post. I was finding people were slightly wary of a random researcher/writer asking probing questions about their ancestors, but Susan was amenable enough. She wondered if Les ever got caught at all, because he had a close group of friends who helped him and supported him during the war.

'Les would visit my grandmother semi-regularly, and he'd ride his bicycle up to the bushline, hide it in the scrub and then hike, usually one or two days, to one of his huts,' Susan said. 'There were two or three huts, all a good couple of days' hike from each other.' This all tallied with the multiple sets of coordinates I'd found.

'He was a very adept bushman and was quite self-sufficient living off hunting and fishing. I don't think Merv was with him, but I believe there were a couple of other men, they would meet from time to time but generally were quite solitary.'

Susan said Les spent time down south and in Australia shearing and working as a labourer or builder in the 1940s, and ironically he was employed by the Ministry of Works as a carpentry foreman during the building of the Waiouru army camp.

Les and Merv have a bit more in common. Both were habitual diary keepers — documents the families still hold — and both actually attempted to join other war efforts than the army. Les tried to join the Air Force as a single young man when he was 18 but because he couldn't produce a birth certificate, as apparently his records had been lost in a fire, they wouldn't let him in. And I found proof in Merv's file that he had volunteered for the navy.

'I've read some of Les's diaries from that time,' Susan said. 'You can understand, as a married man with a young family — three kids under five years old — he was not keen. His father-in-law at the time was a World War I veteran who had suffered terribly with lung problems and also PTSD after being gassed in the trenches on the front line.'

I found a description of the Bergersens' huts while rifling through material at the Ohakune Library one day. Tramper Ashley Cunningham had collated a book of historical information, including photographs, and donated it to the library in the 1980s. He had been to one of the huts just a few months after Les Bergersen was captured, led to the spot by a friend. His information tallied with the other material I'd found about the brothers and their huts. He wrote:

> I believe he built, and used, two huts, one of which was not very far from the present Ohakune Ranger Station. The other was beside the stream west of the five-mile peg on Blyth Track. A friend showed me Bergersen's hut a few months after his capture. We delighted in the workmanship of it. It was built of kaikawaka, broadaxed so perfectly that the timbers and woodwork seemed almost to be sawn. It had a single room with a large open fireplace, bed, bookcase, table, chair and food cupboards. Under a loose floorboard was his broadaxe, but that had disappeared by 1949 when I last used the hut.[8]

The last time Cunningham had been to the site was in May 1987, when he found it challenging to locate because of the many changes in the forest and the stream. It took him hours to find. 'By then,' he wrote, 'the hut had been reduced to scraps of decaying wood, and some old corrugated iron.'

Buoyed up by Ashley Cunningham's booklet, I struck out up the Mangawhero Stream one day, dropping into the water itself via a well-worn deer track. It was only autumn, but the cold hurt my bones. The water was thigh deep in places, and the sides of the stream formed a sort of gorge. I soon turned back; although I'd left my intentions — details of where I planned to go and when I'd be back — it occurred to me that if I slipped on a mossy rock and knocked myself out, I'd drown long before anyone knew.

I resolved to head back when daylight hours were longer, and I hassled my old mate Pete, aka Papa Smurf, for many months to come with me. I lured him in with occasional tales of the Bergersens until he finally relented and drove over from Hawke's Bay for a mission. The Smurf had long been involved in Land Search and Rescue, and now that he was retired he was regularly chasing kiwi in the Kaweka as part of a tracking programme. Not only was he admirably fit for an old bugger, he was also adept at moving swiftly and stealthily through the bush.

We'd bashed up the stream, Papa Smurf finding animal tracks on the sides and moving far faster than I had on my last trip, and we got onto a sort of terrace between two catchments. I noticed he made almost no noise as he slipped through the trees, like fingers of fog swirling across the landscape. I turned back and looked at my other mate Pete, who'd also come with us. 'It's like he can smell it, eh?' I said. 'Years of experience.'

Pete nodded. 'I can see why you wanted him to come.' This Pete, in contrast to Papa Smurf, is a larger-format human and often had to do combat with fallen branches rather than duck under them, but he didn't complain. I recalled a scene in Barry Crump's

ABOVE: Les Bergersen's hut near the Mangawhero Stream. Ashley Cunningham collection, Ohakune Library

BELOW: Pete and Papa Smurf surveying what would have been Les Bergersen's bath in the Mangawhero Stream.

book *Wild Pork and Watercress* in which young Ricky Baker realises he's learning how to weave his way through ferns, vines and branches. His Uncle Hec had chastised him: 'If you try to break off every twig and fern that gets in your way, you'll be worn away long before you've made any impression on the Urewera.' I reckoned Papa Smurf was Uncle Hec in human form, and without the Child Welfare issues and police involvement.

We cleared the first set of coordinates easily — they were sitting straight on the stream bed and seemed to be wrong from the outset, because what flavour of idiot would build a hut in a stream? Then we headed to the second set, up on another terrace. We split up and conducted grid searches, staying within calling distance of each other and without result, but when we dropped down to the stream again we were all struck by the sight of a distinctive small waterfall and rock pool, fringed with moss and greenery.

'Holy smokes,' I said. 'This would've been their swimming pool — Bergersens' Bath.'

Pete agreed. 'You'd make sure your hut was near to a good water source if things dried up, and having a bathtub like this would be handy long term.'

Back up on the terrace again, Papa Smurf asked a question he should have asked some time ago. 'What exactly are we looking for, Shorty?' (Although the Smurf is not so much taller than me.) 'Is the hut still standing?' And I realised I'd failed to include some critical information: that the 'hut' was mere scraps on the ground, if that, and that when Ashley Cunningham visited it in the 1980s there already hadn't been much left.

Papa Smurf didn't care, though, that I'd conned him into a wild goose chase; any mission was a good mission. It turned out he was familiar with Cunningham, who had been a proper bushman and known the Kaweka well. We concluded that his map markings were likely quite correct, but everything had been covered up during the four decades since anyone was last known to have been in there.

We had two needles, good strong needles, but a very large and unwieldy haystack.

In 2023 I tracked down Kaye Rabarts and David Wilton, two researchers and volunteers who had actually been to two Bergersen hut sites in 2008. Their photos showed that the upper site, in the Mangawhero and off the Old Blyth Track — in fact, the very set of coordinates we'd dismissed because they seemed to be right in the stream — sported corrugated iron remnants, a pile of stones that was a possible fireplace, and some broadaxed planks. They also supplied a photo of the distinctive metre-high waterfall in the stream that would work as a positive landmark for finding the hut, just up on the true right terrace. Wilton said they'd used Cunningham's information the first time they looked for the hut, unsuccessfully, but the second time they went straight up the stream. 'Bear in mind it's just a scatter of overgrown rubble lying on the ground,' he added.

Rubble was enough for me. Pete and I went back for another go in spring, while Papa Smurf was waylaid chasing kiwi or slashing through the Urewera with a machete, or some other such bushman pastime. It took us 40 minutes to wind our way up the stream in warm, flowy conditions. The small waterfall worked as a stopping point, and from there we pushed up to the terrace, 10 metres above the stream, and there it was. There it was! Corrugated iron rose out of the ground, interspersed with plainly broadaxed planks, so cleanly hewn that they could have been sawn yesterday. An old beer flagon stuck up out of the dirt. I spotted a door hinge and a pile of stones almost entirely covered in moss. We snapped photos and circled around the site, and hunted further for any other residual signs of life.

We were about to leave when I looked down at my feet. Unthinkably, on the ground, unobstructed by any other material, was the head of an axe. I picked it up, its heft weighing on my hands. Les's axe, or one of them, anyway. Probably used to split wood rather than craft the hut. But still: a clear sign, a remnant of the mighty Bergersen who had built the structure.

I read through sections of both Merv's and Les's diaries, which gave me an idea of what daily life was like for them. Both Bergersens were occasionally poetic in their scribblings. Merv wrote in March 1942 of going for a swim in the twilight in a pool in the Mangaturuturu Stream:

> I noticed a waterfall and knowing there would be a fine swimming pool under it down I went. And there was a beauty, although a bit late I couldn't resist . . . the water looked very tempting and stripping off, in I went, but there was already ahead of me two lady birds and a locust which had got out of their depth and were struggling like hell to get back. Rescuing these, I settled down to a quiet bit of splashing around.

Merv routinely made trips back to Ohakune to see his family and get vegetables, and in fact Jeff reckoned the newspaper reports were wrong: he wasn't arrested at the bush hut, but in the paddock behind the family's home while helping them harvest potatoes.

He constructed a window in his hut, and wrote: 'I am beginning to be a champ (not chump) carpenter with a hatchet, hammer and saw. The sun will be able to shine in on the table now, when it shines . . . now as I see the moths crawling on the window, trying to get in to the candle light, it looks more like home . . . goodnight.'

He also wrote about going deerstalking with a friend he calls simply 'X'. Their stag weighed about 45 kilograms, and they carried it from high up on Ruapehu down to the hut, stopping at Ohakune Hut on the way. Some trampers had just left and the fire was still burning. Merv and X had no food with them, but the trampers seemed to have had plenty; in the fire was about a pound of luncheon sausage, which was ruined but they ate it regardless. Outside in the tussock was a discarded small loaf of bread, a bit damp but a welcome find, and inside they found butter, tea and milk. 'After scraping the mouse droppings off, this seemed alright, so with what we found outside and inside, it made quite a good supper.'

ABOVE: An axe head found in 2023 that probably belonged to Les Bergersen.

BELOW: The remnants of Bergersen's hut in 2023.

They sandwiched themselves between the mattresses in front of the fire, which Merv deemed much better than sleeping out in the bush. 'When the trampers threw away that loaf of bread they would have had no idea that some hungry deerstalkers would find it and be very thankful.' On their way home the next day, Merv and X came across half a cake of Cadbury's chocolate in the creek, which they consumed with delight. 'We are living on what they have chucked away,' Merv commented to X. 'First the bread, now the chocolate.' X responded: 'Yes, if we knew where they lived, we wouldn't have to work any more.' On returning to his hut, Merv cut some maggots off a piece of old roast pork and ate it with roast potatoes, rice and a cup of coffee.

At one point in 1942, Merv described a trip with a friend to Waihohonu Hut, where they arrived late and exhausted, to discover the hut was full of soldiers. The chaps gave up their bunks and offered them chocolate, and peaches covered with condensed milk. Merv reflected: 'Little did these soldiers know that I was a conscientious objector that had ignored four notices to proceed to camp — if they had known their hospitality might not have been so great.'

Les's diaries make for a gripping read; he records several close calls where he nearly got caught, and at times had to hide in long grass until darkness fell. He was supported by a couple of close friends, whom he trusted and relied on for help when needed. 'What a beautiful world this would be if the masses were to see, believe and act as my friends do,' he wrote. 'Help one another. All men equal, no race or class distinction and no war.'

Les often made trips back to the family home in Ohakune, driven by the desire to see his kids. He had close calls there, too, and wrote of one incident where his son got excited and revealed to visitors that his daddy was home. 'It's a fine flag we live under when one has to punish his children for telling the truth all because his father refuses to murder for the stinking capitalist . . . I love my family and want to be where I can see them now and then.'

In a February 1943 entry, Les wrote of telling his son he had to leave again — either he had to head off to go shearing, or go to war and kill some other little boy's daddy, he told him — and his son cried.

'If he only listens like he did tonight and takes heed of what I tell him in regard [to] war he will never don the khaki and cause sorrow and grief to millions.'

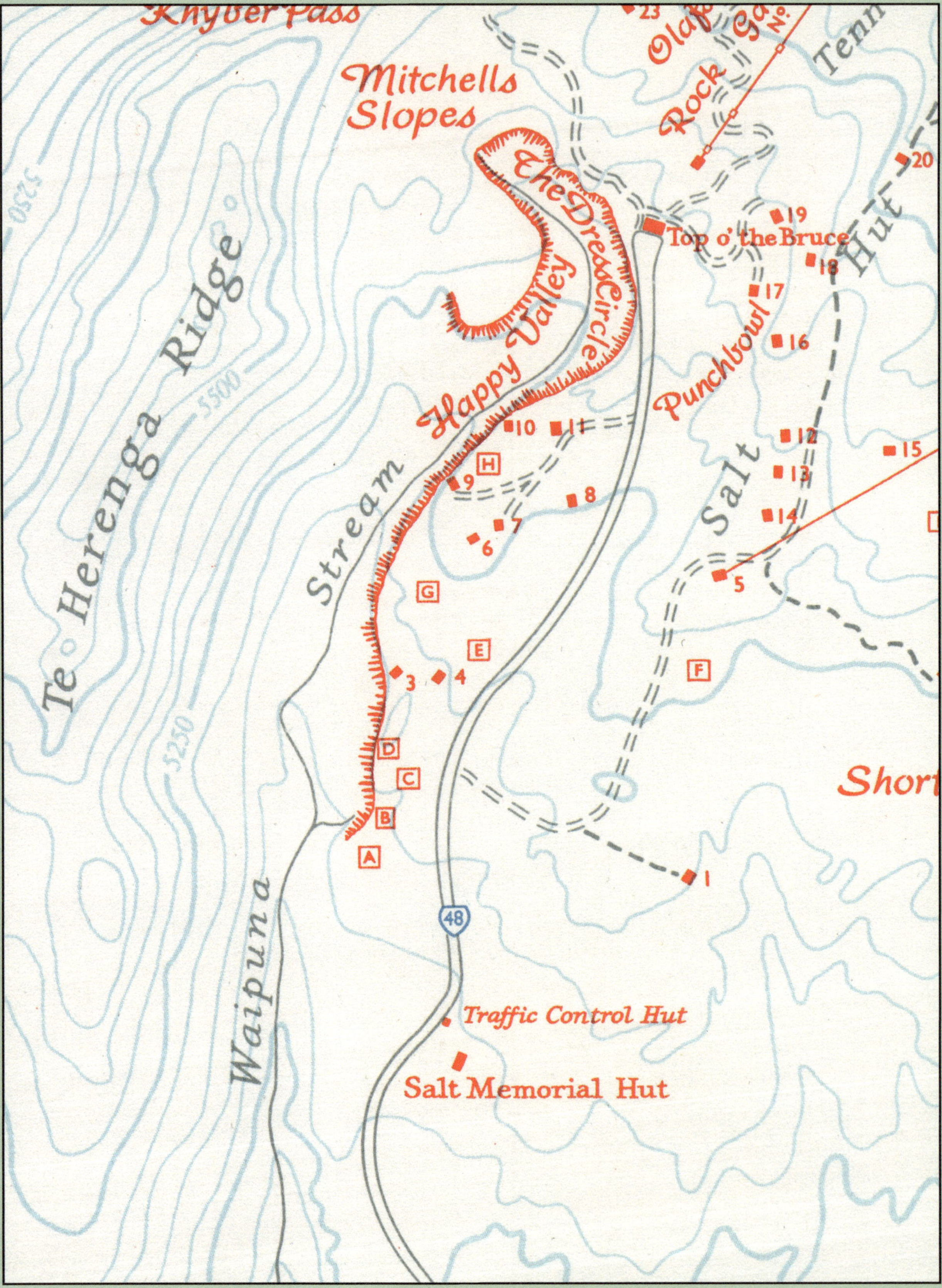
Khyber Pass
Mitchells Slopes
The Dress Circle
Happy Valley
Te Herenga Ridge
5250
5500
5250
Waipuna
Stream
Top o' the Bruce
Punchbowl
Salt
Hut
Rock
Traffic Control Hut
Salt Memorial Hut
48
1
3
4
5
6
7
8
9
10
11
12
13
14
15
16
17
18
19
20
23
A
B
C
D
E
F
G
H

Map showing Salt Hut on Whakapapa, 1963. National Library of New Zealand, 38239544_1963

CHAPTER 3

Lost on Ruapehu — the Stanton search

In 1931 a party of university students left the Chateau Tongariro to climb Ruapehu. A blizzard struck and they were forced to spend the night at a huge boulder on a plateau bounded on all sides by precipitous gorges. It ended fatally for one of the party, but for others, enduring love developed. The 'Stanton episode' — as it came to be known — was one of the biggest searches in Ruapehu's history.

The week of 24 August 1931 was a big one on Ruapehu. Alpinists from all around New Zealand were clustering at the Chateau for the New Zealand skiing championships, organised by Ruapehu Ski Club (RSC). The Chateau was heaving, with around 350 guests, 80 of whom hailed from the ski club itself. The championships were to open on the Wednesday and conclude on Friday, with skiers staying on for the weekend. The snow the weekend before had been plentiful and powdery, and there had been excellent skiing earlier that week.[1]

The weekend would be big, too; a new hut, Salt Hut, was due to open at Upper Scoria Flat on the Saturday, overlooking the main ski ground and runway for the races. The hut was a memorial to former RSC president William Salt, who had died two years earlier. Built of straight-grained rimu specially selected for the purpose, and secured by rocks stacked around the foundations, the hut could shelter a hundred people at a push, with storage space for 150 pairs of skis. The structure had been blanketed by snowfall earlier that month when Ruapehu received a record dump, with around half a metre of white gold blessing the new hut.[2] The skiers didn't know it, of course, but the new hut would come in unexpectedly handy in the days to come.

Meanwhile, influenza and winter germs were sweeping across the region. Chateau manager Richard Cobbe had been confined to bed with the flu, in spite of the full house. Well-known mountaineer Rod Syme was struck down, and a member of RSC also took ill and had to turn around and go home to Whanganui. Championship skier and RSC member Mary Mitchell had arrived earlier in the week from Auckland with a slight chill and gone straight to bed on arriving at the Chateau. Tonsillitis developed into double pneumonia, and Mitchell died on the morning of Thursday, 27 August. Privileged and popular, Mitchell had been educated at the exclusive girls' boarding school Woodford House in Hawke's Bay, then at Auckland University College. She was mourned by a wide circle of family and friends, and as a mark of respect the events scheduled for that day were postponed.[3]

Conditions remained challenging. On the Friday, 15 members of the Tararua Tramping Club climbed Ruapehu successfully. The party enjoyed clear weather, but the cold wind kept the surface of the Whakapapa Glacier slick and icy and they had to stamp firmly on their skis to get purchase. They only paused briefly at the Crater Lake to enjoy the view in the strong, bitterly cold winds. They arrived back at the Chateau late in the day after a long and careful descent to avoid an 'unexpected glissade'.[4]

That night, as the Tararua group reported on the tough conditions, a party of 19 enthusiastic trampers from the Auckland University Field Club assembled. They planned to climb Ruapehu the next day, taking lunches made by the chefs at the Chateau. Among the trampers was 18-year-old Warwick Stanton, a talented young law student at Auckland University College. Stanton was known to be quiet and a little shy, but he opened up with people he knew. Dark-haired and tanned, he was a promising athlete with a clean runner's build. He had set new running records at university and was known for always holding back some energy for the finish. He kept himself trained to a hair in season and out, friends said, and was thought to be the very incarnation of physical fitness. He was renowned for always zipping on ahead of any party he was

ABOVE: Salt Hut on Whakapapa. Alexander Turnbull Library, 1/2-030084-F

BELOW: Chateau Tongariro, the base for the Stanton search. Archives New Zealand, AAQT 6539 W3537 A2117 R21010634

tramping with, perhaps too impatient to stick with others who were slower. But he was always happy, friends said, because he put more into life than most people, and hence got more back.[5]

Stanton had some mountain experience — he'd been educated at Waitaki Boys' High School in the South Island, where he'd made a few excursions to Aoraki Mount Cook. This was his first visit to Ruapehu, where his habit of running off ahead of others would ultimately lead to his demise.

Saturday the 29th dawned clear and cold. Graham Bell, a 32-year-old man with good knowledge of mountaineering, was the leader of the party, backed up by Harold Addis, a master from Nelson College. They all left the Chateau at 5 a.m., aiming for the Crater Lake. Bell told friends that if the ice was hard, he'd leave the women in the party at Salt Hut and pick them up on his way back.

Each climber was clad in good heavy boots, a raincoat, two woollen jumpers, a cap and scarf. The group collectively carried one day's rations for 19 people, two 40-foot ropes, four ice axes, a compass and an aneroid barometer, a supply of maps, a spyglass and a torch. Four of the original group of 19 failed to show for the alpine start, but they took all the food with them anyway. One, Edome King-Mason, walked for a few kilometres and turned around after deciding that doing a full 28-kilometre day was too much.

Among the group was Jock Graham, a lean, tall, dark-haired 19-year-old. Graham had grown up in the Auckland suburb of Mount Eden and been an elite scholar at Auckland Grammar, winning a national scholarship that took him to Auckland University College to do his Bachelor of Arts. His writing had appeared in the *New Zealand Herald* and he was already enjoying an outstanding career as a scholar.

Another was Susan Morris, known as 'Fitzie', an 18-year-old who was no stranger to danger. She had twice been on board Pacific interisland ships that had caught fire. The first time the crew managed to put the fire out, in a situation where rescue would have been impossible had the ship gone down; the second time, the fire couldn't be put out but the ship made it back to Auckland safely. On top of that, Fitzie had also been knocked down by a car on an Auckland street and invalided for six months, passing her exams only by special grant. She had been educated at various schools in Niue, Rarotonga, Sydney and New Zealand and had come to Auckland as a 14-year-old, attending Epsom Girls' Grammar School, then Auckland University College, where she'd met Jock at a second-hand book sale when they both reached for the same book at the same time. They shared classes, they discovered — English, history, French — and began spending a lot of time together.

Fitzie's parents had only been persuaded to let her go on the trip to Ruapehu after meeting Jock and being reassured by him. 'Parties from the Ruapehu Ski Club and the two Boys' Grammar Schools, two other large parties and all the ordinary tourists will be there with us, and so, we won't be likely to get lost,' she convinced them. After she arrived at the Chateau she wrote a letter home enthusing about the climbing, tramping, dancing, skiing and eating they had been indulging in: 'At this furious pace every minute of the night and day, I shall return an Amazon or dead.'[6]

The whittled-down group of 14 achieved the crater area around 12.30 p.m. and had lunch. Clouds had blown up but there was nothing to indicate heavy weather coming. A few climbers wanted to ascend one of the summit peaks, so some of the party began to cut steps, but they abandoned the effort about 10 metres from the top when it got too dangerous. The wind changed direction, and around 3.15 p.m. the group began to descend. In true Ruapehu style, the weather then deteriorated rapidly. They'd hardly left the summit ridge when it began to snow, thick and cold. Soon a blizzard was shrieking all around them, so strong that they couldn't see each other, and Bell got all 14 to rope up. Bell's goggles froze over, and he discarded them.[7]

Down at the new Salt Hut, conditions had become so bad that the winter sports activities were abandoned. More than a thousand people had gathered at Upper Scoria Flat but nobody reported seeing the party of climbers return. Guide Olaf Pedersen and Auckland University College professor Frederick Worley became concerned, and they remained glued to the spot while others left to seek shelter. The pair watched anxiously through the raging blizzard for the students' return, then, when darkness fell, they returned to the Chateau and raised the alarm.

Up top, Bell had set his compass for the correct line down the Whakapapa Glacier, but the instrument froze over. He cut steps down the glacier in the blizzard, keeping everyone together on the rope. On one particularly dangerous part of the descent he divided the party into three groups, each with a leader who wielded an ice axe. Two of the groups anchored while the third moved. Fitzie later described the ordeal in her book *Susan in Springtime*:

'Now, One and Two, anchor!' Bell yelled.

'Right!' called One, and 'Right!' called Two.

'Three, move!'

With this drill they inched downwards. Once, Fitzie was tugged off her feet.

'Jock!' she screamed.

'Got you!' he yelled, ramming his ice axe into the ice to anchor her. Bell's drill had worked perfectly.

Fitzie could hear Jock behind her singing that year's popular song, 'Honey' by Rudy Vallée, not quite in tune, but reassuring nevertheless. Whenever they stopped for a quick break, Jock embraced Fitzie in a bear hug of love and comfort.

'You do look pretty,' he said. 'You have a halo of tiny little icicles all around your forehead where your hair has frozen.'

They smiled at each other in the darkness.[8]

Strong winds blew the group off course, and in the whiteout they veered too far left on their descent. Instead of returning to Whakapapa and the Chateau, they descended further west, towards the Whakapapaiti Valley. They got bluffed after descending a gully, where they encountered a steep, icy slope, too dangerous in the dark and difficult

ABOVE: The climbing party below Paretetaitonga, next to the Crater Lake, just before everything went wrong. Alan Graham collection

BELOW: Searchers depart the Chateau in rain and wind. Alan Graham collection

conditions. Retracing their steps, they reached higher ground around 8 p.m., in the pitch dark and howling snow. Then they found a plateau and rejoiced, thinking it was Scoria Flat. However, the plateau was bound on three sides by impossible bluffs and deadly gorges. They were stuck.

A boulder sitting alone on the plateau offered some shelter, and the party dug in on the lee side of the rock using their ice axes. Jock led the men in building a snow wall for shelter, and they all kept warm by exercising, stamping their feet in the snow and clapping their hands. The men made the women get up and exercise any time they showed signs of falling asleep. Jock in particular refused to let Fitzie go to sleep, no matter how much she pleaded, and all night long he bullied her into survival.[9]

They all tucked in to their rations: two tins of sardines, half a loaf of bread, butter, a pound of cheese, some oranges, and whisky and brandy mixed together. There was nothing further to be done but to bivvy out and wait for daylight, and hopefully for the weather to clear.

Over at the Chateau, the hundreds of guests put their revelry on hold and organised a search party. Manager Richard Cobbe strongly opposed the notion of searchers leaving before 3 a.m., but Rod Syme dragged himself out of his sickbed to insist on immediate action, backed by members of RSC. Syme led the first party, which left the Chateau at 11 p.m. and searched all night with torches and lanterns at Scoria Flat and up to the base of the Whakapapa Glacier. It was fruitless: any footprints had already been snowed over. Syme, suffering badly from the flu, fell asleep in the snow and had to be woken by his companions.

Other parties searched near Silica Rapids, but everyone returned on Sunday morning empty-handed.[10] Winter parties and social gatherings were postponed, and doctors and nurses called in. Worried relatives flooded to the Chateau, desperate for news. Local mountaineers such as Joe Blyth joined the search party, which now numbered in the hundreds. Salt Hut became an important base for searchers on the mountain.

Over at the giant bivvy rock, the group continued on at first light. Once again they found the chute they'd looked at the previous night and had deemed too icy. Now it had several inches of soft snow, and they decided to glissade down it in groups of two or three. They found a stream but didn't know for certain which waterway they were on; they thought it was the Whakapapanui, closer to the Chateau, but in fact they'd descended into the Whakapapaiti, one catchment further away.

The parties began to spread out. Warwick Stanton and several others got further ahead. Bell didn't yell out and attempt to stop them as he wasn't concerned — thinking, of course, that they were in the Whakapapanui and would soon be able to sidle over to Scoria Flat and reach the Chateau. At that point, in fact, he still didn't think they were lost. But when they reached the bush, they realised their mistake. The leading party — Warwick Stanton, Bruce Spooner, Harold Addis, Gordon Harris, Jula Rennie, Esme Brockett, and Fitzie and Jock — became separated from Bell and the others, and they didn't see each other again.

The rear party — Graham Bell, Eva Ellett, Moya Watkins, Gweneth Watkins, Stuart MacDiarmid and Alan Flynn — was rescued on the Sunday afternoon and taken back to the Chateau. Flynn was so exhausted that he dropped unnoticed from the rescue party, which had to go back and retrieve him. When they found him, he was wandering about in a daze in the bush with no idea how he'd become separated from everyone. Once back at the Chateau, Bell reported to rescuers where he thought the others were, collapsed into a brief sleep, then went out again to help in the search effort.

Meanwhile, the other party ended up in the Whakapapaiti, then later in the Mahuia catchment at the base of Hauhungatahi, where the bush is so thick that searchers needed machetes to make any progress, and even then they could only inch along.

The sleep-deprived trampers hallucinated regularly. Fitzie talked to a man milking a cow, while one of the men insisted he could call for help from the telephone box around the corner. Someone else saw the lights of a farmhouse and waved to the farmer's wife.[11]

They were almost constantly on the move, in the midst of the seemingly endless blizzard. The group had only a couple of hours' sleep each night, and otherwise kept moving to try to stay warm. Their thick alpine clothing helped — without it, they would have died. They'd eaten their rations, but were later cheered by the discovery of a forgotten half-block of chocolate, which was shared out. They couldn't light a fire, and they had to drink water from deep clefts in the ground. Without a cup to hold water, Jock would hold Fitzie by the feet and dangle her down to drink water directly from the source. She protested out of exhaustion: 'I'm not thirsty! Enough snow blows in when I open my mouth.' But Jock was determined to keep Fitzie alive. 'You must drink to keep you going. Down you go.' As she would later relate, Jock saved her life, over and over, in different ways.[12]

Warwick Stanton became the de facto leader of the smaller party and wore himself out running up any hill that might give them a clue as to their location and how to get back. He was the fittest, by far, and the women regularly begged him to slow down so they could keep up. Eventually the group split again. Bruce Spooner took off on his own, and was later found wandering around the snow slopes above the Whakapapaiti Gorge in a confused state. Then Harold Addis and Warwick Stanton decided to push on to get help when the others became too exhausted — one of the women was frostbitten, and Harris had hurt his leg.

Jock, Fitzie and the others were bivvied in a clump of trees about 10 kilometres west of the Chateau. During the night Fitzie went out to stretch her legs and talk to Jock, who was continually working to improve the bivouac, ripping up tussock and braiding it in and out of the bushes to keep the frost off. They stood together in the darkness. Jock put his arms around Fitzie.

'I think we must face it now, that this may be the end for us,' he said.

'I would rather die with you than go on living without you,' she said.

'Everything will be all right so long as we are together.'[13]

Reassured, they returned to the bivvy with the others, huddling together and rubbing each other to keep the blood moving. Jock sat upright to avoid falling asleep, so he could ensure the others were awake in the morning.

The next day, Monday, 31 August, their spirits were raised when a plane flew overhead — planes were rare enough that they had no doubt the pilot was searching for them. Jock and Fitzie decided to strike out together to get help. The weather had cleared and they could now see Ruapehu and Ngāuruhoe, and they knew that the road went between the two.

Harris, Brockett and Rennie were too weak even to move out into the sun, so Jock tied a white handkerchief to a high, bare tree near them as a marker, and the pair struck out hand in hand with renewed strength and hope.

After about an hour of walking they saw smoke. Initially they assumed it was mist or a hallucination, then they realised its warmth and pinky-blue hue were surely from a fire. They called out, but nobody responded. They went towards the smoke anyway, hoping to warm themselves by the residual fire. Then a man emerged from the bush, with white hair, rosy cheeks and bright blue eyes, looking like Santa. Was it another hallucination? Fitzie ran up and embraced him. The man cried, and reached out a hand to grab Jock.

'Were you looking for us?' Fitzie asked him.

He shook his head slowly. 'We were looking for your bodies.'[14]

More men then materialised from the clump of trees: bushmen, lumberjacks, mill-hands, all huge, rugged men who soon took care of the pair. They discovered that Fitzie and Jock were both in a decent state, although Fitzie's hands were bandaged. They gave them hot drinks and food, then stripped them both and rubbed them down with whisky to warm them up.[15] (I am reliably informed that stripping someone and rubbing their naked body with whisky is no longer accepted search and rescue practice.)

The men made stretchers by hacking down trees and nailing sacks and overcoats to them, although Jock refused to be carried until they were out of the bush — a five-hour scramble. The rescuers were rather touched to discover that Jock and Fitzie were hopelessly in love, and carried their stretchers side by side when they could.[16]

When Fitzie and Jock were finally delivered back to the Chateau they found it infested with newspaper reporters who had raced to the mountain to cover the story. 'The girls were wonderfully plucky, especially Miss Morris,' Jock told them. 'On the first night she got a bad kick on the head. She fell down a hole with two others on top of her and was dazed for a time, but she tramped gamely on. She was one of the fittest in the end.' They had been relieved to wake up to fine weather that morning, he said. 'Every other morning it had been too misty for us to see where we were making for, and it turned out that we had gone hopelessly astray.'[17]

For Fitzie, the worst thing had been the constant false alarms of rescue, of thinking they'd discovered a way out or that they'd been found.[18] At one point they'd heard noises and called back, but later realised it was just a morepork. Then they'd seen what they thought was smoke from a fire, but it turned out to be mist. Later, they saw footprints in the snow with the mark of a ski pole beside them and they followed the trail for some way, thinking it would take them to safety. The trail ended abruptly,

This map showing where the members of the party were eventually found was published as part of the extensive coverage of the search. *New Zealand Herald*

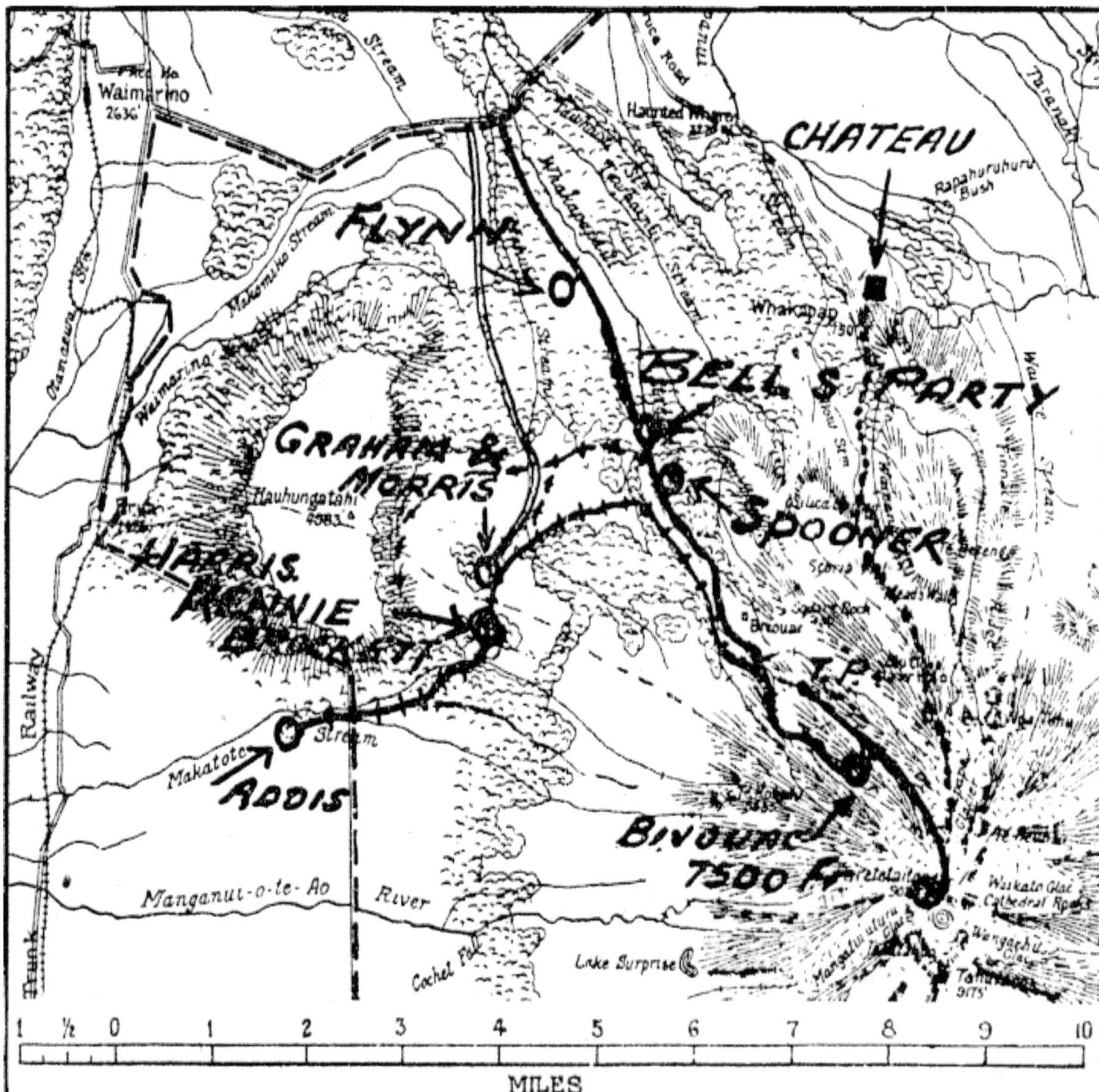

SEARCH FOR LOST CLIMBERS ON RUAPEHU.

The map, which is fully explained in an accompanying article, illustrates the route (dotted line) taken by the party from the Chateau to the summit on August 29; the line of descent (heavy line), which is extended to show the track followed by Mr. Graham Bell and five others; and the track (crossed line) of the other eight members of the party. Points at which the successive rescues were effected are marked by circles.

though, with just a lump of frozen snow on the ground, and they realised that was how the track had been made in the first place — a piece of frozen snow rolling down the mountain side. But they kept their spirits up and maintained absolute confidence that everything would come right in the end.

Fitzie said they hadn't felt all that hungry, but they tried to find food anyway. They'd heard of Māori eating fern roots and tried to do the same, but found them to be 'horribly fibrous', with a distasteful smell. Still, plenty of fresh, clean water from mountain streams helped. They later found out there was nothing they could have eaten on the mountain.

The other three of the group of five were soon picked up by rescuers. Jula Rennie told reporters that for her it was the first night, when they'd bivvied out at the big rock in the snow, that was the worst. 'On Sunday morning when we failed to find the Chateau I thought I would die, but I bucked up and followed the boys down to the bush. We sheltered on Sunday night in some bush with the snow falling all round us, and it got so cold we had to move to a more sheltered place. Our last camping place was infinitely better.'

Jula was full of admiration for the dashing Jock Graham and his survival skills. 'Jock Graham was marvellous,' she said. 'When Mr Harris was too weak to do anything, Jock kept us warm by cutting grass and sticks and making a roof for us.'[19]

Esme Brockett had been a Girl Guide and was well versed in bushcraft. Her parents had once been lost for seven days in the Tararua Ranges. 'It all seems like a nightmare now,' she said. 'We did not discuss our chances of getting out. We purposely kept off the subject. I don't think we stopped shivering all the time we were up there. The cold was harder to bear than the hunger. We spent part of the time that we were in the bush planning menus. Our clothes were soaking wet all the time we were out. We had no matches, so we could not light a fire.'[20]

Fitzie remained optimistic about her relationship with Ruapehu. 'Some people think that because we are young we did not fully realise the seriousness of our position, but I can assure you that we did, although we were confident throughout that we would eventually be found,' she said. 'Next year I hope to visit the mountain again.'[21]

While these five were warming up and describing their experiences to the reporters, Harold Addis and Warwick Stanton remained missing.

Addis and Stanton had mistaken the peak of Hauhungatahi, west of Ruapehu, for Ngāuruhoe and had attempted to travel on its western side. Had they been correct, they would have come out all right. Unfortunately, as their fundamental navigation assumptions were wrong, things went from bad to worse. They ended up in the ferocious Makatote River, a scoured gorge with impossibly steep sides.

The Makatote River starts high on the western slopes of Ruapehu, several hundred metres below the peak of Paretetaitonga (2751 metres), and tumbles down the southern side of a rock known as Te Kohatu (1725 metres) in a series of cascades that explorer and surveyor Hugh Girdlestone described as 'magnificent'. A 55-metre

Fitzie Morris and Jock Graham at the Chateau after recovering from their ordeal. Alan Graham collection

waterfall leads to another 28-metre fall, and further down in the bush several smaller cascades dot the waterway. Several fingers of water lead through the bush, joining up with another source on the northern side of Te Kohatu, cutting around the base of Hauhungatahi. For several kilometres between the road and the river's upper reaches near Hauhungatahi, it cuts violently through the landscape, scouring out a deep ravine.

Addis and Stanton had had to bash their way through the thick bush, Stanton doing most of the leading, which consisted of throwing himself into the undergrowth to break a track, then getting up to do it again. They moved at a crawl. Several times they found themselves deep in the ravine and had to swim while clinging to ferns on the banks. The river got so deep they decided to go up and around it. When Addis pushed his hand underneath Stanton's boot to give him a foothold, Stanton's remarkable strength suddenly began to fail, and he gave in. He got a strange look in his eyes and became incoherent.

Stanton repeatedly collapsed; several times he lay down and became motionless until Addis managed to revive him, pulling him to his feet and forcing him to continue. Finally, Addis decided that he would have to push on alone to get help. He found a snug place beneath a tree with a lot of growth around it, hollowed out a hole and dragged Stanton into it. Stanton was now safely tucked away, but this also hid him from the searchers' view. Addis turned back several times, doubting his decision, but he knew the only chance for both of them was to battle on alone.

Addis hallucinated too. The running water spoke to him and the trees called out: 'Take my hand and I will bring you to the Chateau,' he heard them say. He went up to the trees, thinking they were people until he touched them. At first light he saw a survey marker, which gave him hope.[22]

Meanwhile the searchers persevered. The sheer cliffs of the Makatote are sometimes up to 80 metres high, and the terrain around it, although flat once out of the ravine, is obstructed by *Griselinia lucida* (puka) and *Coprosma foetidissima* bound together with bush lawyer, a plant that grips you and rips you. *Coprosma foetidissima* is also known as stinkwood, or hūpiro, and the disgusting smell emanating from the bush made the searchers feel physically sick. The rescue parties split up, covering both sides of the ravine, calling out to keep in touch with each other. They were almost 6 kilometres up the river from the road when a shout from one of the men was met with a response from below. They scrambled down the cliff to investigate. Addis was clinging to a tree next to the river.

'Are you fellows looking for me?' he asked.

'We are indeed,' said one of the searchers.

'Thank God,' he said. 'Tell Mother I'm safe.'

Then he, too, collapsed.

After Addis came to, he remained incoherent and unable to give any account of where he'd been and how he'd ended up in a ravine in the Makatote. When he was asked where the others were, he responded: 'They've gone to the Chateau.' He was utterly exhausted, and suffering from frostbite; several times his feet had frozen to the soles of his boots. His rescuers stripped him, rubbed him with whisky and got a fire going, while Addis kept saying, over and over, 'The snow, the snow.' Finally the rescue party, which included a pharmacist from Taumarunui and a St John Ambulance worker, carried him out on a stretcher. He'd been out in the open — the wind, rain, hail and snow — for 72 hours.

Tuesday, 1 September was initially clear with unlimited visibility, but the weather soon turned again. There were now more than 500 men searching for Warwick Stanton, the last unaccounted-for member of the party. Women helped by cooking food at the Chateau and ferrying it in heavy backpacks out to the men as the search continued through the next few days. Women from tramping clubs got into the kitchen and helped with the dishes until well after midnight each night. Those staying at the Chateau gave everything they had to the searchers, if it would help in some way. The men in the field had bloodshot eyes through lack of sleep, were drenched through, and many were so hoarse from calling out that they could no longer speak. Fighting through dense bush on foot had exhausted them, and many had put their own lives in danger. Most had been wading through freezing, waist-deep water in the various streams and rivers around the park.

The Chateau was now bursting with searchers, guests and worried friends and family. At one point there was not a spare blanket, mattress or pillow to be had, and people were sleeping wherever they could. Rod Syme and Richard Cobbe got out of their sickbeds to help. Cobbe's wife worked for 60 hours straight until she fainted on her feet, and the head waitress, Miss Tonkin, presided over meals for 700 people, then she too passed out after 60 hours without sleep. There was a continual stream of enquiries from anxious people, and as a result two young telephonists collapsed at the Chateau's switchboard and were put under the care of a doctor.[23]

Experienced Ruapehu mountaineer Joe Blyth encouraged people not to give up hope. 'At Passchendaele during the war, I saw a German brought in alive after being out in the mud of No Man's Land in midwinter with a broken thigh for six days,' he said.[24] People clung to Blyth's words — after all, nobody knew the mountain like he did.

But by Friday, 4 September, no hope remained for finding Stanton alive. So many searchers had covered such a wide area that if he'd been alive, surely he would have responded to their calls. Snow and heavy fog continued.

Eventually Addis regained his senses and was able to give searchers information on where in the Makatote catchment he'd left Stanton. He said he had helped Stanton out of the river and onto the bank, and had left him next to a log covered with bush lawyer and other vegetation. He was in a hollow next to the log, but on the side away from the river — searchers wouldn't be able to see him from the river and instead would need to check all the logs. They scoured the Makatote again, to no avail. If Stanton was there, he wasn't responding.

Stanton was known for his limitless grit, so the searchers thought he would have continued to fight for his life. A theory developed that he had revived after Addis left him and had attempted to find his way out but got into the river, and in his weak and fatigued condition was swept off his feet and drowned. Others theorised that after he recovered he tried to get to higher ground to get his bearings.

On Monday, 7 September another blizzard swept Ruapehu, even worse than the storm the weekend before. Icicles a metre long were hanging from trees, and if Stanton had left any tracks they would certainly have been obliterated by the rain and snow.

The parents of the students, including Stanton's parents, gave a statement to the press thanking everyone for their efforts: 'It has proved once more the essential unity which lies beneath the surface of human nature. To everyone who helped in any way, we tender heartfelt thanks.'[25]

Although all hope of finding Stanton alive was now lost, searchers continued their work in an effort to find his body. The terrain was their main enemy. As the *Evening Post* described it:

> Unless one has visited this country one can have little idea of the difficulties of getting through it at all, let alone searching every hollow and sheltering rock outcrop for a man who must by now be in too weak a condition to help himself far towards searchers. The stream runs in a broken, rocky bed between sheer rock cliffs, and elsewhere, where the gully sides slope less abruptly, the bush is a tangled mass right down to the rocky bed. The searchers have had to cut their way for the greater part of their struggle up the stream with slashers and hand axes, exceedingly hard and exhausting work. Many of them, bush workers of long experience, know the bush of that locality well, but all come back with the same story: that the going is the very devil.[26]

More than three weeks after the ill-fated climb, Warwick Stanton's body was found on the banks of the upper Makatote River, lying under the limb of a tree in dense undergrowth about 150 metres from the river. He was discovered by Department of Lands and Survey staff who had come up from Wellington to help. His body was found where Addis had left him, as described, in a hollow next to a log covered in tangled vegetation. The body was face down and almost concealed from view by the thick tangle of undergrowth, now covered with recent snow. There were no marks on his body, no indication that he had moved, and no injuries, although his hands and nose were slightly frostbitten. It was clear that Stanton hadn't revived after Addis saw him that final time.

In the inquest that followed, Harold Addis and Graham Bell were exonerated of blame. Coroner A. Laird said Bell displayed great judgement in leading the party down the mountain, and the trouble that followed was not due to his leadership but rather by a section of the party deciding to break away. Addis, the coroner said, was sensible to leave Stanton and push on for assistance. The verdict: Warwick Stanton died due to syncope (loss of consciousness) caused by exposure and exhaustion.[27]

Two years later, Stanton's friends had a brass memorial tablet made in his honour.

Groups of his friends journeyed from the Chateau up to the Whakapapaiti Gorge and mounted the plaque on the rock where the whole party of 14 had spent their first night sheltering from the storm. It was set in a concrete bed and bolted to the rock. They found an empty pineapple tin at the base of the rock, its contents having been consumed by the climbers while they were bivvying and waiting for dawn.

'The rock is almost a landmark in the vicinity and can readily be picked out by climbers visiting the upper Whakapapaiti,' newspapers reported. 'The place where the memorial has been erected is an extremely desolate one, rough scoria boulders covering the ridges as far as eye can see and, in winter, a dreary expanse of ice and snow.'[28]

The plaque, which includes a quote from Tennyson's famous poem 'Ulysses', reads:

In Proud and Affectionate Memory of
WARWICK STANTON
Who Passed this way in August 1931 Aged 18 Yrs.
One equal temper of heroic hearts
Made weak by time and fate, but strong in will
To strive, to seek, to find, and not to yield.

The going was indeed the very devil in the Makatote and I had little inclination to experience it for myself; the Stanton Memorial, though, was unobstructed by jungle, and I had a reliable set of coordinates from my mate Ken. He'd declined to come on this trip as he'd been several times before, and he warned me that there were several false leads.

'I once did a recce prior to taking a tramping group out there,' Ken told me. 'I got down to the "plateau", headed to the large rock, and there wasn't a plaque. Two weeks later I discovered my mistake — there's a second flat lower down with the real rock.'

There are, in fact, several plateaus and many gorges and waterfalls waiting to snare the unwary. Ken's intel helped, though. I roped in a couple of interested mates — Pete and Papa Smurf, whom I'd taken on one of the forays to find the Bergersens' huts.

We set out on the Ruapehu Round the Mountain Track off Scoria Flat on the Bruce Road and hung a sharp left, heading up a leading ridge to Pehi's Bluff (named after Pehi Tūroa, a Whanganui chief who had a whare in the Hauhungatahi area). The bluff is a splintered mass of vertical columns, created from a lava flow that cooled from the top and bottom, rather than the sides. Rounding the top of the bluff, we angled across several gullies, some with sparkling swimming holes that I pinned on the topo map so I could revisit them later in the summer heat. We stood at the top of a large plateau and stared down.

'That's it,' Papa Smurf said, pointing to a huge rock on the far left. Several other boulders competed for attention, but this one was far more distinctive. 'Sticks out like the proverbial.'

Papa Smurf took off in a straight line to the boulder, and sure enough, a weathered

ABOVE: The photo of Warwick Stanton published alongside a tribute to him in the Auckland University College student magazine *Craccum*. Bagnall Collection, Massey University Library

BELOW: The Stanton plaque above the Whakapapaiti Gorge. It has weathered time well.

plaque still clung to the downhill side, bolted into the smooth rock. Lichen had taken over the rock but not the plaque, which was still perfectly readable. One of the bottom corners had snapped off and a careful visitor had rammed the piece behind one of the upper corners for safekeeping.

'Presumably they all sheltered on this side,' Pete said. 'Not actually a lot of room given there were fourteen of them.'

'You know, I reckon it's amazing they were able to get back here and find the spot again,' Papa Smurf said. 'Especially as they were here in the dark initially and then took off the next morning.'

We stared up the hill at a line of bluffs the boulder must have initially come from. A long way, and a big traveller. Nothing else around, just a huge expansive plateau and a tiny bit of hope for survival.

From the memorial we bounded down a nearby gorge, presumably the same one the party glissaded down. I could see how in winter and filled with snow it would be easy to gather speed and take off. In places it got tricky and required some wriggly moves to get around small rocky bluffs and waterfalls, but it eventually spat us out onto the smoother slopes of the upper Whakapapaiti Stream, where the going was deceptively easy. If only they'd stopped there and sat tight.

'Never would have happened if they'd all stuck together and just stayed in one place,' Papa Smurf said.

In the months and years following the Stanton search, people and organisations called for increased safety measures and more control on activities in the national park. The New Zealand Alpine Club and the Federation of Mountain Clubs[29] lobbied Prime Minister George Forbes for legislation governing alpine climbing. Alpine Club president A. P. Harper asked for controls around ensuring alpine guides were fully qualified and licensed, and pointed out that he'd been advocating for this since 1922 without result.[30]

'The whole thing wants systematising,' Harper said. 'Speaking with all seriousness, as a climber of forty-six years' experience, I say advisedly that unless this scheme is put into operation before next session we shall run the risk of grave accidents.'[31]

Prime Minister Forbes said he would do his best to bring a bill before Parliament.

'We must have more control over people wandering up mountain sides and getting lost, causing danger to the lives of other people and expense in finding them,' Forbes said. 'It seems to be a very haphazard business. The occurrence on Mount Ruapehu had the makings of a first-class tragedy.'[32]

Meanwhile, Chateau manager Richard Cobbe thundered along on his own soapbox, still steamingly angry that Rod Syme and other searchers had disobeyed him. 'It is necessary that the rule laid down that searchers must not go out until the early morning be strictly enforced,' he said. 'My orders, that no man must leave until three o'clock on Sunday morning to search for the students, were disobeyed by members of the [Ruapehu] Ski Club. They left at 11 o'clock on Saturday night and were unable to do any good because of the darkness and weather, and were so exhausted the next day when every experienced man was needed their services were not available.'[33]

The Federation of Mountain Clubs held its annual meeting in Wellington the month after the search, where they endorsed Syme's decision to dispatch searchers as soon as the students were announced missing, noting in the annual report: 'A commendable feature [of the search] was the speed with which help was organised and got away [as soon as] it was reasonable to suppose the missing party had met with difficulties. Under the circumstances it is indeed fortunate that further lives were not lost and that the consequences not much more serious than they were to the survivors.'[34]

The organisation also called for a policy of safety measures, and recommended that a bridle track be constructed between the Whakapapa huts, near the Chateau, and Ohakune Hut, near what is now the Ohakune Mountain Road.[35]

Graham Bell, the leader of the climbing party, wrote to the coroner after the inquest, in October 1931, urging him to recommend that the Unemployed Relief Board make a grant to the National Park Board for funds to cut tracks that summer. There should be tracks around the mountain, he said, but as an additional measure of safety, tracks should also be cut down the valleys of the Whakapapaiti, Mahuia and Makatote to the various roads. 'The existence of such outlets would considerably minimise the danger of the repetition of such a tragedy as the death of Mr Stanton,' Bell wrote. Coroner Laird made the recommendation 'in view of the loss of a valuable life, the great expense incurred and the loss of time involved by the search parties'.[36]

In his book *Ruapehu: Tribute to a mountain*, published in 1963, Jock Graham observed that the loss of life was not in vain. 'Ruapehu became safety-minded . . . tracks were cut to permit exit from the Whakapapaiti Valley, and eventually the Alex Bivvy (Whakapapaiti Bivvy) provided shelter in the area.'[37]

The Tongariro National Park Board created a special committee, including warden John Cullen and Joe Blyth, tasked with considering suggestions on improving safety measures. The mayor of Auckland set up a 'Ruapehu Mountain Calamity' fund to compensate people who had helped in the search, and £50 was allocated for the construction of a poled track between the Chateau and Ohakune Hut. It would be around 18 kilometres in total, 3 kilometres of which had already been marked with poles in 1930 by the forward-thinking Joe Blyth.

Work began in early 1932 and was quickly complete, using packhorses but mostly manual labour. The new route consisted of 440 marker poles traversing the scoria and tussock slopes of western Ruapehu, and so the Ruapehu Round the Mountain Track came to be.

Joe Blyth was applauded for his work at a parliamentary level. The 1932 Department of Lands and Survey annual report included a direct quote from a letter Blyth had written to the Park Board chairman: 'The new route will provide a popular tramp when the weather is too stormy to permit of a trip across the top, and, what is of greater importance, it will provide a most valuable safeguard against lost parties wandering into the bush. The knowledge that such a line exists should prevent a repetition of the disaster of last year.'[38]

Newspaper coverage of the rescue appeared beneath an unrelated heading, 'BRIDAL GROUP', which the couples were teased about. Gordon Harris is at lower left and Esme Brockett is at lower right. They eventually married. Bagnall Collection, Massey University Library

The press was still following the matter and reported approvingly on the work. The *New Zealand Herald* echoed Blyth's words:

> The new line that has been poled above the bush-line will become a popular traverse of the slopes . . . more important still it will be a most valuable safeguard against lost parties wandering into the bush as occurred last winter when Mr Warwick Stanton lost his life. Even in foggy weather when poles may not readily show up, the knowledge of their existence will keep lost climbers to the open land above the bush, where they will be bound to pick up the guiding line and follow it to safety.[39]

Blyth eventually persuaded the Park Board against the notion of cutting tracks down the river valleys as Bell and the coroner had recommended. As a safety measure, the value of these tracks would be very small indeed, he said: 'The well-meaning people who urge its improvement cannot have a first-hand knowledge of the locality.' Lost trampers would have a better chance by travelling across or intersecting the new track between the Chateau and Ohakune Hut rather than trying to happen upon the Mahuia track running downhill.

Today, the old track that was slashed by bushmen during the 1931 search up the Mahuia still stands. It runs past the old Alex Bivvy site and Whakapapaiti Hut to join up with the upper part of the original Chateau to Ohakune Hut track. No tracks of note run down the imposing river valleys on the western side of the Makatote, Mangaturuturu and Manganuioteao. Trampers who enter this country are on their own.

Around a year after the construction of the new track, it was already paying safety dividends. In 1933 Blyth wrote to the chairman of the Tongariro National Park Board:

> I must say that this poled route is becoming more popular with mountaineering parties. The last three parties to occupy the Ohakune Hut have used it to proceed to the Chateau and this, in a small way, here fits the latter hostelry. The value of the poles was proved at Easter when two climbers, who had wandered a long way from their route gladly espied the poles just at dusk and followed them along till they reached the hut.[40]

After the events of 1931, old biddies at the Chateau whispered about the inappropriateness of males and females spending the night out together without a chaperone. Two love stories fell out of the 'Stanton episode', as it came to be known. Fitzie and Jock, of course, but also Gordon Harris and Esme Brockett, who later married. The *New Zealand Herald* featured a montage of photos of the climbers, with Fitzie and Jock

RESCUED CLIMBERS AT THE CHATEAU. BRIDAL GROUP. TEST CRICKET.

FAMOUS TENNIS PLAYER.
Mr. Norman E. Brookes, the former Australian international tennis player, who is a passenger on the Sierra, which arrived at Auckland yesterday.

SHIPPING COMMODORE.
Captain J. H. Trask, captain of the Sierra, who is also commodore of the Matson Shipping Line.

FURTHER MEMBERS OF THE LOST TRAMPING PARTY PHOTOGRAPHED AT THE CHATEAU WHILE RECOVERING FROM THEIR ORDEAL ON RUAPEHU.
From left, top: Miss Gweneth Watkins, of Devonport, one of the first party to be located; Miss Fitzie Morris, of Whangarei, and J. C. Graham, of Mount Eden, who were found together on Tuesday; and Miss Moya Watkins, who was rescued at the same time as her sister. Lower: Mr. G. Harris, of St. Heliers Bay, found on Tuesday; Miss Eva Ellett, of Helensville, saved with the first party; Mr. H. Addis, of Ponsonby, and Miss Esme Brockett, of Masterton. Both the latter were found on Tuesday.

at the top, arms linked, looking 'dewy-eyed' as she later described it. At the bottom left, Gordon Harris leaned in, newspaper tucked under one arm, seemingly looking directly at Esme Brockett on the far right, her hair pinned up demurely and clad in jumper, blazer and necklace. Above the photo montage, the heading: 'BRIDAL GROUP', which referred to a different item on the page, prompted telegrams to Jock and Fitzie and 'ribald comments'.[41]

Rumours of their wilderness romance abounded around the university. 'Those two were having quite the little romance,' one person said.

'Oh yes, quite palpable,' said another. And they were known from then on as 'the Palpables'.

For Fitzie and Jock, it was enduring love. 'But fate sets devious traps for lovers,' Fitzie later wrote in her memoir, *Susan in Springtime*.[42] Fitzie graduated with an MA (Hons) in history and both she and Jock completed a diploma in journalism. Jock went on to work as a journalist for the *New Zealand Herald*, and from the 1950s to the 1980s he was the New Zealand correspondent for the *New York Times*. Fitzie wrote for the *Weekly News* and the *Herald*, and published eight books under her married name, Susan Graham.

Fitzie and Jock married in Whangārei in 1935. They had a son, Alan Graham, whose book *Mount Ruapehu: 100 years of skiing*, written for the Ruapehu Ski Club's centenary, matched his father's *Ruapehu: Tribute to a mountain*, published for the club's fiftieth anniversary. Fitzie and Jock co-founded the Ruapehu Ski Club magazine *The Bulletin* and edited it for 41 years before handing it over to Alan. They were together for 68 years, until Jock died in 1999, aged 87. Fitzie moved to Wellington to be closer to Alan, and died in 2007, aged 95.[43] Their infatuation with Ruapehu persisted, and Fitzie and Jock remained undeterred by their experience and the wrath of Ruapehu. Fitzie wrote of her attraction to the mountain: 'And then of course we went back to Ruapehu, drawn back again and again as if the mountain were a white magician who, in exchange for our lives, had gripped us in his icy thrall for ever after.'[44]

A few months after finding the Stanton Memorial I had the opportunity to get lost and rescued myself. I got a message from Conrad Smith, the local policeman in National Park. Conrad is a member of the Ruapehu Alpine Rescue Organisation (RARO), something you wouldn't guess from his habit of wearing jandals in alpine environments. Perhaps more like a sandal, on reflection — a Jesus sandal. In summary, you can think of Conrad as a sort of Alpine Jesus, saving the unsaved from mountain danger.

Conrad and an acquaintance of mine, Elly, were organising a SAREX (search and rescue exercise) in a few weekends' time.

'We're looking for a few people to get lost for the weekend so the search and rescue teams can find them,' Conrad messaged me.

Then another message. 'Hey Hazel, what are you up to on the eleventh and twelfth of May?'

I replied: 'That is right up my river valley.'

'Yeah,' Conrad responded. 'We thought you'd be good at getting lost.'

I wasn't sure whether to take that as a compliment or an insult, but I decided on the former.

It was all super top secret, Conrad said, but the SAREX would be kicked off with a theoretical eruption at 8 a.m. on the Saturday. There'd be people in the Whakapapaiti Valley who'd been knocked over by a lahar and injured, and while they were being rescued my job would be to go and get lost. I'd also need to lay a trail of clues for the field teams to decipher and follow. Trickily, I'd also have to avoid crossing paths with the field teams. This required backcountry ninja skills of the highest order and was, I concluded, clearly why my specialist skills had been called in.

'We don't want them to find you on the Saturday — ideally they should find you Sunday morning around 9 to 10 a.m.,' Conrad said. 'So you can commando crawl around past the searchers. In the tussock. Like the movies.'

I roped in Pete again, and crafted a scenario. Pete and I would pretend to have camped out at Stanton Memorial on Friday night. Then, terrified by the 'eruption', we'd leg it down the Whakapapaiti Valley to get away from residual ash and flying rocks. I'd fall over in the Whakapapaiti River and get cold, leading to mild hypothermia and the need for an emergency bivvy. I'd possibly also add on a token head injury and some garden variety confusion.

'Perfect,' Conrad said. 'You do realise you're setting a precedent now and you'll be my full-time SAREX scenario writer from now on.'

'It helps that I've obsessively read and researched every Ruapehu rescue scenario from all time,' I acknowledged.

Two days before the SAREX weekend I went into the petrol station at National Park, bought something, and made sure I was in full view of the security cameras while I took off my multicoloured buff, shook it out, and put it back on. I tucked the receipt away to leave at Whakapapaiti Hut. This was all Conrad's idea — to leave a clue rather than signing the hut book, and see if the field teams could figure it out.

It had been a busy week already, with five rescues for Land Search and Rescue (LandSAR) and RARO to sort out. One of them was a guy who had attempted the Tongariro Alpine Crossing in spite of being told not to because of horrific weather. He got as far as the top of the staircase and made 22 calls to 111, but his phone kept cutting out. (Emergency services registered him as a 'distressed female'.) He cried when he saw the RARO team, and again when Conrad spoke to him back at the National Park base, because he knew he could have died up there.

'I wasn't even being mean,' Conrad reflected.

'See, this is why you're Alpine Jesus,' I said. 'Saving people but inspiring them to atone for their sins at the same time.'

On the Friday I made a public Instagram post — also Conrad's idea — showing a selection of photos for the intel teams to glean information from. There was a photo of me wearing the multicoloured buff, a selfie showing Pete in the reflection of my sunglasses, and a company logo on a shirt; I even included a shot of my boots, showing the footprint. The post read: 'Very successful day chasing mountain history . . . one of the most dramatic Ruapehu events ever, from a cold snap in 1931. Found an excellent camp spot up high, set up for the night, star watching and fending off the frost. Doesn't get better than that! A few kilometres put onto the old boots today, might be heading for a replacement soon.' If anyone in the teams knew about the Stanton episode, the mention of a 1931 Ruapehu event would lead them to conclude I'd been at Stanton Memorial on Friday night.

It was minus 2 degrees on the way in on Saturday morning, but entirely windless with bright sunshine. I destroyed hoar frost with my boots and poked the ice crust of puddles with my poles as we tramped over the ridge below Pehi's Bluff. We had a quick stop at Whakapapaiti Hut, where I left the receipt on the fireplace along with a couple of wrappers, and briefed a tramper who was staying there not to touch it and to tell anyone who asked that he hadn't seen us, but that he'd been in and out all day so really anything could have happened.

I hit the radio. 'Alpine Jesus, Alpine Jesus, this is Rubber Ducky.'

The radio crackled to life. 'This is Alpine Jesus, go ahead Rubber Ducky.'

'The first clue is in position and we are departing Whakapapaiti Hut.'

We had heaps of time, Conrad said, and he told us to make lots of footprints in the mud as we walked. Further down, past the Whakapapaiti River crossing where I would theoretically fall over and get soaked, I left my buff hanging on a bush. In places the mud was frozen and it was impossible to create footprints leading off the track, but Pete lit on the idea of leaving mandarin peel as a sign.

We set up camp behind several stands of beech forest, in a little hollow that had just enough room for the tent and fly. Conrad on the radio had gone silent. I radioed in our coordinates and somebody else took them. More silence.

'Something's gone wrong, I reckon,' I said, and Pete agreed. It wasn't unheard of for a SAREX to turn SAROP (search and rescue operation) if someone got hurt for real.

Several hours later Conrad re-emerged. Someone had broken a leg on the Tongariro Crossing and the RARO team had been redeployed to retrieve him. There'd been other delays, too — we'd expected the field teams to have gone past us by now.

'How are they going so far?' I asked.

Conrad paused slightly. 'We have a few things to work on,' he said.

The teams hadn't made it out into the field for a few hours, and they were unlikely to go past us that day. One team was camped out not far from us, and the others were all at Whakapapaiti Hut. Conrad formed a plan: we'd get up early next morning and move from our camp, head down and find somewhere just off the track to park up and see if they could hunt us out. We signed off for the night, compared the comfort ratings of our respective sleeping bags, and did some reasonable damage to a hip flask of toffee-flavoured vodka.

At stupid o'clock the next morning Pete fired up the billy. We shook ice and frost off the tent and fly, then packed in a hurry and hared off down the track towards the Chateau. We came to Slippery Gully, where we walked around a bit to create footprints in the hoar frost, then nipped up a ridge. There, we found a campsite we wished we'd seen the day before. It had a flat, mossy area, was perfectly sheltered and out of the way, with a pure and delicious water source just nearby, and a view.

Elly was in the team that found us. I'd met her years before, tramping in Nelson Lakes National Park, and although we were friends on Facebook, we seldom saw each other in real life.

It was time to fake a head injury. I looked at Elly and squinted.

'What's your name?' I asked. Her facial expression altered just slightly. I could see her wondering: Is this part of the scenario or does Hazel really not remember me?

I moved on so she didn't have to answer. 'I fell over in the river but I've had a lot of hot drinks now,' I said. I looked at the other two. 'What's your name?' The other guys introduced themselves.

About 10 minutes later I looked up at one of the guys. He was wearing rugby shorts in Otago colours.

'What's your name?' I asked.

'Corey,' he said, and laughed slightly.

'Oh,' I said. 'You have very nice Dunedin shorts.'

They clicked that something was 'wrong' with me and soon diagnosed my head injury. I asked them if they were going to strip me and rub me with whisky, like they did during the Stanton rescue, but Elly said that wasn't in the search and rescue field manual, and anyway, we didn't have any toffee-flavoured vodka left. Then we called the scenario complete.

Conrad later gave me a tour of the new search and rescue centre in National Park, built in 2023 and funded entirely via grants and donations. Having a purpose-built facility so close to the mountains gives rescue organisations a central hub for operations rather than being fragmented in various places, and the potential time saved could mean the difference between life and death for someone.

'You know the Stanton family was involved in this, eh?' he said. I didn't, actually. But yes — incredibly, the Stanton estate had made a rather hefty bequest in the memory of Warwick Stanton, the young and enthusiastic runner who lost his life on icy Ruapehu in 1931, so that future rescues in the national park could be well supported.

In 1951, one of Warwick Stanton's friends, known only as 'J. M. B.', penned an obituary in the Auckland University College student newspaper *Craccum* after it was clear Stanton wasn't coming back, but before his body was found. 'Warwick Stanton *accepted* life more completely and unquestioningly than anyone else I have known,' J. M. B. wrote. 'And by this . . . he was nearer the great secret of the Art of Life, that redeems the Pain of it with the Beauty.'

Before Stanton left for his ill-fated Ruapehu trip, they had been shopping for watches together. 'That watch is ticking on my wrist as I write,' J. M. B. wrote. 'The mate of it, somewhere on Ruapehu, does not tick. But if a watch has stopped, and a life stopped with it, it is for us to keep a memory alive. It may be we can learn from a death; it is very certain we can learn from a life.'[45]

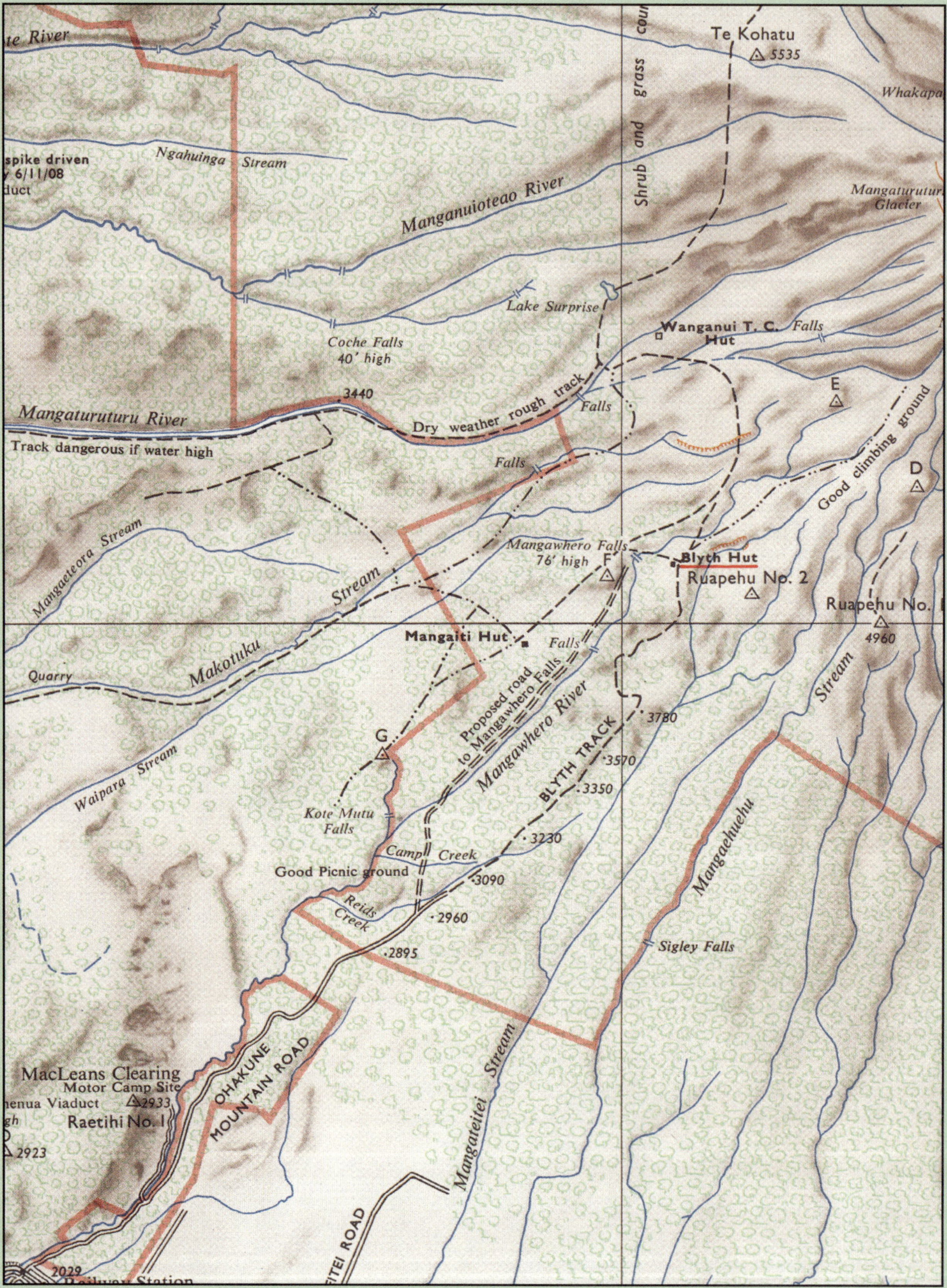

te River
Te Kohatu
5535
Whakapa
spike driven
y 6/11/08
duct
Ngahuinga Stream
Manganuioteao River
Shrub and grass cou
Mangaturuturu Glacier
Lake Surprise
Wanganui T. C. Hut
Falls
Coche Falls
40′ high
3440
Mangaturuturu River
Dry weather rough track
Falls
E
Track dangerous if water high
Falls
Good climbing ground
D
Mangaeteora Stream
Mangawhero Falls
76′ high
F
Blyth Hut
Ruapehu No. 2
Stream
Makotuku
Ruapehu No.
4960
Mangaiti Hut
Falls
Quarry
Proposed road to Mangawhero Falls
Mangawhero River
Stream
3780
G
BLYTH TRACK
3570
Waipara Stream
3350
Kote Mutu Falls
3230
Camp Creek
Good Picnic ground
3090
Reids Creek
2960
2895
Mangaehuehu
Sigley Falls
OHAKUNE MOUNTAIN ROAD
MacLeans Clearing
Motor Camp Site
henua Viaduct
2933
Raetihi No. 1
gh
2923
Mangateitei Stream
TEI ROAD
2029
Railway Station

Map showing Mangaiti Hut and the surrounding tracks, 1958. National Library of New Zealand, 37103234_1958

CHAPTER 4

Mangaiti, the hidden hut

Mangaiti Hut, one of the earliest examples of a hut in the national park, was built in 1940. It is still standing, still cared for today by the loving members of the Tongariro Tramping Club. After catching wind of a secret hut that wasn't on the map, I struck out through a portal in the bush to find this tramping treasure.

One day at the Four Square in National Park (a very un-wildernessy place to be, I admit), I was quietly congratulating myself on having bagged my last hut in Tongariro National Park. Ice cream was in order and I bent over the freezer, peering at the choices on offer, which largely consisted of either a two-litre tub of Pams vanilla flavour or splashing out on a Viennetta, which is cemented in my mind as the absolute pinnacle of 1980s New Zealand dessert sophistication. I laughed to myself, and a chap loading 1-kilogram blocks of cheese into the chiller asked me, 'What are you laughing at?' in a friendly way.

'Viennetta desserts. I grew up in Ōrewa in the 1980s and it seemed like the fanciest thing back then. I'm getting ice cream to celebrate — I've just ticked off all the huts in the national park.'

'No you haven't,' he said, not unkindly. 'You haven't been to the secret hut.'

I nearly dropped my Viennetta. There was a secret hut?! Roll me in layers of fancy cream and chocolate and throw me in the freezer.

'Mangaiti Hut,' he said. 'It's not on the map, or not really — there's a little dot on the topo map but it's not named.' He gave me instructions about where to park. Then: 'Look for a gap in the bushes and you'll find a track. It's a bit hidden but once you're on it, you'll know. It's about twenty minutes' easy walking.'

I thanked him and departed with my Viennetta, feeling, however, that the celebration had now been rendered premature. The next day I drove around to the Ohakune Mountain Road to try to find Mangaiti Hut, the 'secret hut', fairly sure that he was pranking me. But he was right: there was a dot on the map, but no name. On older maps, the dot disappeared altogether, although I've since found one map from probably the early 1970s that names Mangaiti Hut quite clearly.

I parked my car at the instructed spot, a place where an easy, well-groomed track leads off in another direction entirely, and busied myself putting on my thick canvas gaiters. A man approached, his brows knitted together in worry.

'Ah, excuse me? Ah, are we going to need gaiters for this track? I see you're putting gaiters on. We don't have any. Ahhhh . . .'

'Oh, don't take any notice of me. I'm going into the bush that way and off track,' I told him, gesturing over my shoulder. He disappeared, relieved, and I stood for a while, surveying the wall of scrub opposite. Only one spot seemed to suggest a gap of any sort, so I parted the scrub as best I could, let it spring back into place behind me, and suddenly I was Alice, down the rabbit hole. I was on a track, no mistake. I followed the escape path lighting that promised to lead me to the nearest exit, and in spite of my thought that this was an elaborate joke Four Square workers enjoyed playing on visitors to the region, I became a card-carrying believer in the secret hut.

Tiny markers encouraged me every so often — a rusty tin-can lid nailed to a tree, a pink strip tied around a branch, a piece of permolat from an old venetian blind on a square stick — although they weren't strictly necessary as the ground trail was obvious enough . . . until it ceased abruptly in the middle of nowhere. There was a wall of forest to my left and a wall of forest in front of me. I poked around a little further, found nothing, and was about to give up and retrace my steps to the car — hmmmmph, secret

Mangaiti Hut, painted a cheerful red, sits hidden among the trees.

hut indeed — when a flash of colour caught my eye. There it was! Inside the trees, calling out to me.

I found a short path through the forest and stood in front of Mangaiti Hut, built between 1939 and 1940 and preserved as an example of early hut-building history, a plaque informed me. In fact, because old Blyth Hut (originally known as Ohakune Hut) had been demolished in the 1970s after standing for 50 years, Mangaiti Hut was almost the oldest hut in the national park, except for Glacier Hut on Whakapapa (which the Park Board attempted to remove because, hilariously, they deemed it an eyesore).

Mangaiti was built of corrugated iron and painted a bright, fresh red, with clean white trim on the windows. The door was locked, and when I peered inside I couldn't see much, although I could make out an upstairs loft area. I contented myself with dancing around a little, overjoyed that I'd found the hut and that I wasn't currently the butt of a joke at the Four Square in National Park.

Mangaiti Hut owes a lot to Joe Blyth, the Ohakune man with a Ruapehu obsession. Back in the 1930s Blyth was a member of the Tongariro National Park Board, and in 1937 he had agreed to procure a permit to build a hut for the Tongariro Tramping Club. Whether he did actually get a permit or not is a matter of some debate — Blyth died in 1940, shortly after the hut was finished but before anyone thought to question the permit's existence or validity.

In his 1979 book *Memories of a Mountain and a River*, early ski enthusiast Bill Mead reckoned Blyth did get a permit from the Park Board. Mead wrote that Blyth thought the site would be too far down the mountain for summit trips, so the permit was for a small hut that could be moved further up if members later desired. Blyth was mostly interested in summiting the mountain, so he conceptualised the hut as a base for mountaineering activities. However, the club didn't go with Blyth's suggestion and instead decided to try out the current site of what became Mangaiti Hut.

In 1942, when the township of Ohakune flooded, the club was proven right, says Mead.

> As things dried out a number of us in the [Tongariro] Tramping Club went to look at the effects of the flood. Some members went up the Mangateitei, which had been a narrow stream overhung by trees. These had all been washed out leaving bare ground sometimes chains wide. A slip into the Mangawhero above the falls had gone right across the stream and covered a flat where we would have put our hut if we had put it higher up as Blyth had proposed.[1]

The hut was meant to have four rooms plus an outside porch, and at first the club wanted to erect two rooms and do the rest later. The board conceded that it had permitted a 'temporary camp' for one year, but the club constructed a one-room hut instead. The club appears to have been issued a permit retrospectively in 1956, but it came with an expiry date.

In the early eighties, ranger Bryan Norton wrote an extensive memo for the Park Board detailing the hut's history in a tone suffused with scepticism. 'From file correspondence it is fairly obvious that the hut had been built without permission of the Board and that the club maintained that Mr T. A. Blyth had given permission for its erection.' But the board allowed the hut to stay. 'I have some doubts as to whether or not the club was a viable organisation from say the early 1950s and even today I am not certain that the active members of the club consist of more than a few families.'[2]

The Park Board was then in the habit of conducting yearly club hut inspections, and Mangaiti Hut was not exempt. The inspections looked at the appearance of the building and the cleanliness of the surrounds. In 1969 Mangaiti Hut was awarded a 'B' grade — generally satisfactory but requiring a tidy-up and rubbish removal. Members were put on notice that as it was an offence under the National Parks Act to cut tussock and place it on muddy sections of the track they should desist from doing so. In February 1970 the status of the hut was upgraded to 'A', and club members were encouraged to 'keep up the good work'.

Chief Ranger John Mazey wrote to the Park Board in July 1970, questioning whether the club consisted of more than a few members, and asking the board to push for compliance and an up-to-date list of club members. A board secretary wrote to the club: 'Recent lodge inspections have revealed that your hut has not been used for some time. Would you please advise whether in fact your club is still operating.' The club's admin officer sent back a cursory note: 'Further to your letter of 17 July, yes.'

The club then went on the offensive, writing to the board to emphasise that hut usage had increased dramatically with the improvement of ski facilities on the southern side of Ruapehu. Minor repairs had been carried out. The hut had a new toilet! And in the annual Park Board inspection the hut had been awarded an 'A' grade. Thanks to increased revenue from skiers, there was $500 in a building fund and the club now sought permission to extend the hut in a style similar to the Lockwood huts in the park.

The application was declined, and Mangaiti Hut dropped to a B grade when inspected the following summer. The board directed the club to carry out essential maintenance to keep the hut up to scratch. The club replaced the roof, but changed it to a high gabled roof, in doing so essentially adding a second storey to the building. Mazey was either furious or phlegmatic when he wrote to inform the board of the changes: 'Without wishing to press this matter too far because obviously the hut has been there for many years and probably does little harm, there is a matter of principle. The club has deliberately extended the hut to double its usable size in such a manner that they have complied with the approval given by the Board, but have obviously set out to beat the Board.'

The club hit back. The secretary argued that they couldn't replace the roof like-for-like, but had been forced to opt for the new A-frame format because of the heavy snow and rain the area received. They had not increased the hut's sleeping capacity — there had previously been six bunks on the floor and two in the loft, and that had been reversed. 'Additional room has been made available however, for living space on

Mangaiti Hut circa 1940s, before its gabled roof was added. Brian Mosen collection

the ground floor and we feel this is now more in line with the park board's building requirements.' And the kicker: 'We were under the impression that we were carrying out maintenance work . . . we regret and apologise for any misunderstanding of instructions.'

The Park Board remained unimpressed. At a 1973 meeting, its members moved 'to censure the club for carrying out alterations so as to increase the accommodation without proper approval and that the club be advised that the board will watch the situation and act accordingly in the light of future use given the hut by the club'. The Tongariro Tramping Club was directed to hand over plans of the hut as it currently stood.

The board considered various options: maintaining the status quo (which they found intolerable, given their view that the club had 'duped' them); removing the hut and putting it somewhere else in the national park; prohibiting further maintenance and then removing it when it became decrepit to the point of being unwieldy; and (the most exciting option) upgrading it for use as a public building, preferably at the club's expense.

The Park Board eventually decided that 'because of the deliberate violations of principle in past years and because of the precedents this hut sets, option one seems inappropriate'. And the cost, both in resources and in 'public relations', meant it wasn't worth relocating the hut. Despite the opinion of a hut inspector that 'as the club currently pays no lease for the site, there appears to be some merit in allowing the public to have unrestricted access to the hut as a public shelter', no change was made to the hut's status. By 1982 more than a hundred people had used the hut book and signed their names, and all appeared to have enjoyed their time there.

Mangaiti Hut still stands as a supreme example of early hut life. Since my 'discovery' of the secret hut I've taken other people there, introducing them to the joy of pushing through the narrow entrance in the scrub and entering a whole other world, and seeing the excitement on their faces when they glimpse the happy red colour through the bush at the end of the secret track to nowhere. Mangaiti Hut is one of Ruapehu's greatest delights.

Mangaiti Hut enthusiast Bill Mead set out from the hut one day to locate a 'wonderful acre' of *Ranunculus insignis* (insignia buttercup) he'd seen during his outings in previous years, but to his disappointment he found just a bare desert — all the flowers were gone. 'Perhaps the plants had all been exterminated by the deer which had spread all round the mountains,' he considered. 'Or it may have been that the climatic change in recent years had left the area too dry in the summer.'[3]

Ranunculus insignis also goes by the name of korikori, or, my favourite: 'hairy alpine buttercup'. The name comes from the Latin word 'rana', meaning 'little frog', which probably refers to the propensity of frogs to live around the plant in marshy areas, and 'insignis', meaning outstanding or remarkable. The plant sports bright yellow flowers and waxy green leaves, and it is often dotted around the lower slopes

Bill Mead, standing at right with skis, was one of the founders of the Ruapehu Ski Club. Alan Graham collection

of Tūroa ski field in summer, accompanied by its mates *Celmisia spectabilis* (common mountain daisy) and *Celmisia incana* (white mountain daisy, which has furry green-grey leaves; 'incana' meaning 'hoary').

I always look out for Bill Mead's wonderful acre of hairy alpine buttercup when I visit Mangaiti Hut and its surrounds, but as yet I haven't spotted it, although the buttercup abounds in other spots.

In 2023 I tramped into Blyth Hut for a short overnight midweek mission with Lois, who works for the Department of Conservation (DOC). At university Lois had been on a geography field trip where she had to choose to study plants, birds or animals. She couldn't decide, and took so long choosing that only plants were left. She returned from the field trip totally obsessed with plants. 'Mum said when I was little, I put tags on the feijoa tree to figure out if the flowers or fruits were producing, so I must have always had an obsession for plants there somewhere,' she told me.

I told her about an experiment I'd done as a child. I had several sets of plants that I kept separate, giving good feedback to one group in a loving tone of voice but yelling insults at the others. The scientific integrity of the experiment fell apart when my brother intentionally ruined it by yelling at all the plants indiscriminately while I wasn't looking. I complained to my mother and got punished for being cruel to plants. My brother suffered no consequences, and I ended up in the 'dumb' class for School Certificate science.

Lois immediately understood my plant-yelling experiment and I wondered if she might be of a mind to repeat it herself, but with more scientific rigour. (There are probably groups of plants out the back of a DOC office somewhere now, waiting for her daily address.)

As we were exhaling our way up a small hill towards the boardwalk at Rotokawa on the way to Blyth Hut, she told me that the national park had an 'illegal carnivorous plant enthusiast'. It took me a bit to get that phrase sorted in my head. 'They're doing something criminal, but that sounds harsh, so we call them an enthusiast,' she added, affirming my view that DOC is probably the only government department to be of a mind to soften the wording of an illegal activity.

Someone had been planting *Pinguicula grandiflora*, aka butterwort (carnivorous, as it eats insects by trapping them with its tiny sticky hairs, and illegal, as it's not native and shouldn't be in the wild in New Zealand) in places around Tongariro National Park. Lois showed me spots on the topo map where it had been found — one on the Taranaki Falls Track from the Chateau, and another at the beginning of the Silica Rapids Track just above that. Butterwort loves clay pans, apparently, and really thrives, outcompeting the native wetland species.

'One of the spots I'd noticed was just off the boardwalk here,' Lois said. 'We can go have a look. I like to check on the sites if I go past. Got to be careful though because your boots can spread the seeds if you walk around the area.'

We were looking for the stunning purple flowers of the illegal butterwort but, like Mead's *Ranunculus insignis*, none could be found. (I shudder to think of a 'wonderful acre' of butterwort and what it would take to remove it.) I stuck topo pins on my app

LEFT: Lois Cooper carrying rubbish out of the bush near Blyth Hut.

BELOW: *Ranunculus insignis*, the alpine buttercup Bill Mead enthused over. iNaturalist NZ

and made a mental reminder in my head to check on the various sites any time I was there, in case of new activity.

'What's the point of planting this stuff, though?' I asked Lois as we stood on the boardwalk looking across the Rotokawa tarn. I came across here frequently but only occasionally got to see Ruapehu's reflection in the waters, which were usually rippled, or just reflected cloud if Koro was hiding.

'Sometimes they just think the species is cool, or looks nice, so they want it to take hold here, or they think New Zealand's biodiversity needs to be more, well, diverse,' Lois said. 'Or maybe they think it's threatened elsewhere so it will help it globally to take hold here. Or possibly there's a black market — if they establish a population in the wild, then they can trade it.'

New Zealand is a signatory to the Convention on International Trade in Endangered Species of Wild Fauna and Flora, an agreement that aims to ensure global trade in plant specimens or wild animals doesn't threaten their survival. Right now, butterwort is covered by the convention.

'Butterwort is hard to get rid of, too — we were spraying the sites and thought it was gone but then the plants popped up again.'

'I'm fascinated by the intersection of criminal acts and the conservation estate,' I said. 'Actually I'm surprised there aren't more unauthorised secret huts in the national park.' I was thinking of a mate who had been talking loosely of building a secret bivvy on the southern side of Ruapehu. I'd not come across any illegal huts in the national park, but the nearby Kaweka Forest Park was dotted with huts and bivouacs that weren't on the map and theoretically didn't exist.

'Not in the *national* park,' Lois said. 'But the Tong Forest has a problem.'

The Tongariro Forest Conservation Area sits to the north of the national park. It was milled extensively in the past for kahikatea to make butter boxes, and mataī and rimu for construction. The New Zealand Forest Service wanted to convert the area to farmland and pine plantations in the 1980s, but locals campaigned to have it preserved, and it was transferred to DOC in 1987. Now it's home to whio (blue duck) and kiwi, among other threatened species, and it's been labelled the 'forest of the future'.

'There are at least forty secret huts in the Tong Forest that shouldn't be there,' Lois said. 'Some of them are really flash, too — Colorsteel cladding and brand new fireplaces.'

Tongariro Forest has one official hut, called Ten Man Hut. A hunters' hut, it was initially built illegally, but DOC made a compromise and allowed it to stay on the condition it go on the map and be available for public access. I hadn't been there, having been informed by others that it was infested and filthy. I knew you could get there not just by foot but also by dirt bike and possibly by four-wheel drive. As a general rule, any hut that can be accessed by four-wheel drive is usually a den of filth of the highest order — a rule that runs counter to logic, because if you drive in, surely you could at least take your rubbish out.

But these new huts had taken 'oops' to the extreme. DOC had uncovered problems with rubbish, illegally stored ammunition and firearms, and dumping of human waste. Some huts had LPG gas bottles installed without safety compliance certification, putting the hut at risk of fire and explosions. Many of the hut builders were chopping down trees to create driveways for their huts so they could get right up to them without having to walk. There were fights when people used huts they hadn't built, and in some places, hut builders were also damming streams so they had a water source nearby.

Well, a Colorsteel hut in the wilderness is one thing — tolerable, perhaps — but once you touch our trees, that is a red rag to DOC's sleeping bull. The hut numbers had been increasing exponentially over the past 10 years, and that meant no room for kiwi.

'DOC decided to demolish them,' Lois said. 'We posted notices on all the huts and gave them a time period, like 30 days or something, to remove them. With "Call this number if you need more information".'

DOC principal investigation officer Matt Davis expanded on this: 'While the people who constructed these structures consider them as their private property, it is public conservation land. These are buildings, built without permission, on land they don't own. The area has very high conservation values, including a kiwi sanctuary and many other protected native species — these activities are a major threat to conservation.'[4] Davis described this as a nationwide issue for DOC; the expanse of land managed by the department is so vast that it has no idea how many illegal structures exist.

The Tongariro Forest seemed a curious mix of bad factors (four-wheel drives chewing up the ground, unauthorised huts, dumped rubbish, and I thought of munter-hunters oozing testosterone, carting in large amounts of alcohol and waving their guns around rather than actually going hunting) with good (the 'forest of the future', happy native birds being left in peace, trees).

On one hand, I loved the idea of a secret hut in the bush, a treasure only known to a few. On the other hand, if we *all* did it . . .

Top of the Bruce
IWIKAU VILLAGE
Ski Patrol H.Q.
PINNACLE RIDGE
1750
N.Z. Alpine Club Hut
Te Heuheu
Bluffs
Whakapapa Glacier
Glacier Shelter
Mangatoetoenu
2250
Area usually covered by snowfield
Paretetaitonga
Whangaehu Glacier
Crater Lake
Mangaturuturu Shelter
N.Z.A.C.
1800
Mt. Ruapehu
2797
Wahianoa Glacier
Mangaehuehu Glacier
2500
Girdlestone Peak
1750
TUROA SKIFIELD
2000
2150

Map from 1975 showing some of the shelters searched during the Dudley rescue. National Library of New Zealand, 37100114_1975

CHAPTER 5

The Dudley rescue

In bad weather in 1972, experienced alpinists Bryan and Anne Dudley only ever intended to camp out on Ruapehu for one night, but their overnight trip sparked a long and extensive search.

In 2010, I went tramping in the Richmond Ranges, south of Nelson, with my friend Jane Dudley. Loaded up with heavy packs we inched along, two snails on the track. I was unfit, Jane wasn't, so I puffed while she talked, I think in an attempt to distract me from the task at hand. She also told me stories. One, about her parents, lingered in my imagination beyond that trip.

Long before Jane and her brothers came along, her parents went to Ruapehu for an overnight trip, intending to camp high on the mountain. It was a long weekend in 1972, and it turned out even longer for Bryan and Anne Dudley; the weather turned bad and instead of their planned overnight trip, they were up there for more than a week. They built an igloo and enlarged it for rescuers as they arrived. Then, just as the weather finally broke, three rescuers in another snow cave were buried and nearly died.

Jane was tough and resilient — much more so than I was — and had the sort of robustness that only comes from being used to an outdoor existence from a young age. One of our earliest trips together was to the Kauritatahi Hut, a three-bunk corrugated-iron shack nestled on the eastern side of the flat-top Te Hanga Ridge in the Kaimai Ranges. We followed her mother's self-published tramping guide to the ranges, which gave some unlikely sounding directions such as 'turn left at the plastic bag tied to a tree branch' — but sure enough, there was the plastic bag.[1]

Two minutes after we had arrived at the hut, the heavens opened. I'd found the tramp gruelling, so I got changed immediately then more or less sat on a bunk rocking back and forth in a state of quiet desperation. Meanwhile, Jane merrily set about lighting the fire and cooking dinner as if she'd just been for a short walk around the block and could keep going for another couple of hours. The third member of our party, Krystle, perched on the top bunk reading out celebrity gossip from her iPhone (this was in the era when the iPhone was new and unusual). In between rocking back and forth I made resolutions to improve my fitness.

Years later I got to witness Jane's proficiency at building igloos during a ski-touring weekend on Tukino. Other people cut blocks while Jane efficiently built the shelter from the inside, and the swiftness with which she strategised the construction impressed me. I appreciated, too, how sheltered it was from the inside — I'd snowcaved several times before, and had built snow shelters, protective ramparts and even an iceblock toilet of sorts, but there is something truly silencing and cosy about igloo life in particular.

Jane's story of her parents' adventure stuck with me, but it was difficult to find more information about it. The 1970s were a bit of a black hole for research — newspaper archives went up to the 1960s, while internet search history and Newztext, a New Zealand media search engine, went back to the 1990s if you were lucky. I put in a request to the National Library to see what they could find on my behalf, and found the 'Dudley search', as it was known, in a history book of Land Search and Rescue (LandSAR). Turns out, it was one of the major incidents that prompted the formation of both LandSAR and the Ruapehu Alpine Rescue Organisation, because when the Dudleys went missing in 1972, it was up to their tramping and alpine friends to stage a rescue.[2]

Building an igloo near the Tukino ski field.

Bryan and Anne had only ever intended a three-day trip. Both were schoolteachers and at the end of their mid-term break. They nailed down a plan: they'd take the train from Auckland to Ohakune, walk up the Ohakune Mountain Road to the high faces, traverse over to the Wahianoa Glacier on the eastern side, climb around the crater and drop down to the park headquarters at the Chateau.

They left Auckland on Friday, 7 July and by late on the Saturday they had achieved their objective of reaching the Wahianoa Glacier, where they camped in their tent. But when they woke up on Sunday, the weather had deteriorated. They left to climb around the crater but it was so misty they couldn't see, and both feared the lack of visibility would cause an accident. Getting down to the Chateau was off the agenda, but the pair knew of another escape route: down a snow bowl to the Whangaehu Glacier. What they didn't know was that eruptions the year before had changed the terrain, and what used to be an easy snow slope was now a large cliff, a ring of impassable rocks. The way was blocked.

The Dudleys retreated. Conditions were getting worse and they knew it would be safer to dig in. They were both adept at building snow shelters, so they constructed an igloo. Together they had pioneered a new method of building igloos, based on New Zealand conditions: one cut blocks with an ice axe, while the other sat in the middle of the igloo doing the construction work. They then settled in for the night, hoping that better weather in the morning would let them get down the mountain.

Better weather didn't come. Weakened by cold and lack of food, they knew they could only make a break for it if the weather cleared substantially. Every night they spent in the igloo reduced their chances of self-rescue, leaving them reliant on others — not only to come to their aid, but first to also realise they were missing. The Dudleys had only made one error: they hadn't left their intentions with friends or family.

On Sunday, 9 July, as the Dudleys dug into the snow, across the North Island in Te Urewera two Venturer Scouts had gone missing. Colin Arthur and Bruce Galloway, both 18, had been on a hunting and bush-familiarisation exercise with 15 other Scouts from Te Aroha. The two were following a track that stopped abruptly, and from there they found themselves walking around in circles.

They kept walking, for days. Then one of them dropped his pack and the pair heard a distinctive crunch. Their compass was broken, the needle wouldn't turn, and they couldn't see more than a few metres in front of them as the storm that had pinned down the Dudleys swept across the North Island. Their matches were too wet to start a fire. Weakened with fatigue, they slept under logs.

'We thought we knew direction, but we didn't,' Colin Arthur said later. 'We couldn't even see the sun.' They ran out of food, and after three days of walking they decided to sit tight and stay in one place. They knew people were usually found after three days, but nobody came and they began to lose hope.[3]

But a search for them had been launched.

On Monday, 10 July, the school term resumed. When Anne Dudley didn't turn up to teach her class, people began to worry. Police and the Tongariro National Park Board headquarters were notified on the Wednesday and searchers began to assemble. Teams checked the New Zealand Alpine Club's Whangaehu Hut, down on a knoll beside the Whangaehu Glacier, as a likely location where the pair might have sought shelter, but without success. They attempted to check the Tūroa emergency shelter — Mangaturuturu Shelter, at 2300 metres on the western side of Ruapehu — but bad visibility and violent weather prevented any progress. The Wellington Face Rescue Team was called in.

As the public held its collective breath for news of both the Dudleys and the Scouts, the media latched onto the stories: 'MOUNTING FEAR FOR COUPLE', a headline in the *Auckland Star* read. An Auckland couple had 'disappeared' on a climbing trip, the newspaper announced: 'Conditions on Mt Ruapehu today were exceptionally bleak, and snow, gusty winds and very poor visibility is reported.'[4]

Anne Dudley's father, Jim, took his wife to the RSA to take her mind off things. One of the regulars approached them. 'Sorry about your daughter, Jim. I guess you're starting to organise the funeral.'

'Actually,' Jim said, 'we're hoping for a better outcome.'

'Not a chance,' the man scoffed. 'They'll be dead as mutton by now.'[5]

Glacier Shelter stood at the edge of the Whakapapa Glacier, near a spot known as the Notch, at just under 2600 metres. Like Mangaturuturu Shelter, it's also since been removed, but it used to offer shelter to those in need. Word filtered through that the Dudleys had been seen there. But by Friday, 14 July, teams had cleared Glacier Shelter and reported no sign of the Dudleys and no logbook entries that might provide a clue. The searchers who managed to reach the shelter reported 75-kilometre-per-hour winds, extreme cold, visibility down to zero metres at some points, and bullet-proof ice. Fresh snow loading up in places increased the risk of avalanche.

People flocked to help, largely from the New Zealand Alpine Club, the Auckland University Tramping Club and the Auckland Catholic Tramping Club. Everyone knew the Dudleys; they were popular and well known in climbing circles, and they had a reputation for being sensible about mountain safety.

By the end of that Friday, a total of 60 people were searching for them, in teams of four.

As the search continued, journalists grasped for a new angle. 'LOST CLIMBERS WERE TRYING WARMTH TEST', declared the *Auckland Star*.[6] The Dudleys had been planning to test the insulating properties of newsprint as an experiment in keeping themselves warm, the *Star* reported. It sounded irresponsible, but several paragraphs down the newspaper admitted that the Dudleys were in fact carrying full climbing gear as well as the experimental newspaper, and were thoroughly equipped for rugged conditions.

Visibility was still nil, but rescuers and police were confident that, because the Dudleys were experienced climbers, they would have holed up somewhere until the weather cleared — either in their tent or by digging a snow cave. They were now thought to be high up on the Wahianoa Glacier, which hadn't had any visibility above 1700 metres since they first went up.

Bryan's mother was unbothered. She told reporters that both Bryan and Anne knew what they were doing — Bryan had climbed extensively in Peru, and Anne had climbed in the Himalaya — and while she was concerned, she was more worried about the two missing Venturer Scouts, and perhaps searchers' efforts would be better focused there. 'My kids are very experienced climbers. They're just weather-bound on Ruapehu. That's nothing compared with some of the climbs Bryan has pulled off.'[7]

Teams checked other huts on the southern side of Ruapehu, finding no sign of the couple. The ferocious weather did not abate, and teams had to turn back from the top of the mountain. Rescuers hoped to get a helicopter up high on the weekend, to no avail. A chopper tried to get two searchers up top but 'due to a hair-raising flight in the wind and minimal visibility it was aborted'.[8] Down at Whakapapa ski field, mountaineer Graeme Dingle and well-known skier Roy Turner had just arrived at the Top of the Bruce in Turner's Land Rover. Dingle was living near the mountain at the time, setting up the Outdoor Pursuits Centre (now known as Hillary Outdoors). He was dressed in street clothes but had his boots in the wagon. Someone recognised him.

'We need you, Dingle,' they yelled out. 'We've got a panic on. Get in the chopper.'

Dingle donned his boots and jumped into the helicopter alongside the pilot, Otto Gram, a highly experienced flyer who would later be awarded an MBE in the Queen's Birthday Honours.

Gram had had 30 or so jobs in between school and his early twenties, then discovered his love of flying, first with topdressing planes, and later with helicopters. He was an expert at manoeuvring machines, from aerial spraying and lifting jobs to stringing power lines, conducting deer recovery and, of course, rescue missions.[9]

Gram was known for being able to set his machine down with absolute precision. The year before, he'd been smacked publicly for taking 'wild risks' when helping scientists from the Department of Scientific and Industrial Research (DSIR) to carry out essential research at the Crater Lake. One newspaper had described him as displaying 'great daring in venturing close to, and actually over, the turbulent and unpredictable crater of the volcano' — words that reflect a media beat-up, or as Gram described it, exaggeration and over-dramatisation.[10]

But the article was spotted by the owner of the helicopter, and Gram was ordered to stop flying over the Crater Lake. Scientists protested that they'd be unable to carry out their research; they pointed out that samples were taken in two seconds by lowering instruments into a corner of the lake, and that flying up the side of the mountain was a greater risk than actually taking the samples. The owner of the helicopter relented, and Gram, from then on, refused to talk to media apart from one trusted local newspaper.[11]

Now, with Dingle on board, Gram took off for the top. The chopper had an operating ceiling just under the height of Ruapehu (which is 2797 metres at its highest point) but when Gram took it up to nearly 3000 metres, beyond its operating capabilities, it suddenly dropped out of the sky, falling about 1200 metres. Dingle thought he was going to die, but Gram managed to get the machine back under control near the expansive saddle between Ruapehu and Ngāuruhoe. Radio traffic went wild, and the search controllers called Gram to stand down.

By Sunday, 16 July, the Dudleys had spent more than a week in their igloo, and had been without food for three days. They were cold, hungry and occasionally despondent but otherwise fit and well. They'd also witnessed two 'incredibly violent thunderstorms' from the igloo, which seemed to light the sky up blue through the snow and ice, flashing their eyeballs.

Finally, a four-man rescue team reached the Summit Plateau, on the Whakapapa Col underneath Paretetaitonga. They were using whistles to call to the Dudleys, and heard a reply of metal banging on metal — it was Bryan banging tin plates together, a noise that rang out clearly through the mist and wind. Inching forward, it took the team another hour to circumvent the Crater Lake and reach the Dudleys' igloo on the southern side, underneath Tahurangi. The team joined the couple in their snow cave, finding that Anne was feeling the exposure slightly but that Bryan was largely fine. Together the group enlarged the igloo to fit the now-expanded party.

Meanwhile, other teams still trying to get up to Glacier Shelter were forced to retreat. The storm continued.

Finally, news filtered through that the Dudleys had been found alive, and so had the Scouts, in a rugged area down the side of a ridge about 10 kilometres from Pukahunui Hut. The Scouts were flown in an RNZAF Iroquois helicopter from nearby Te Hoe Hut to Napier Hospital, where they were put into intensive care but soon released. Their parents, who'd been waiting at Murupara since the Monday, had all but given up hope. Jubilant, they shouted a round of drinks at the local pub.

'We couldn't stop crying, but at least they were tears of the right kind,' said Val Arthur, mother of Colin. 'And we are so happy, too, for the people found safe on Ruapehu. We couldn't have felt so happy if we'd known they were still missing.'[12]

It was touch and go for the Scouts; the boys had been found mere hours before the search organisers were to decide whether or not to continue.

On the Monday another rescue party, including a doctor, had struck out to reach the Dudleys, battling in a whiteout and roping themselves together as protection against the 90-kilometre-per-hour winds. Around midday they made voice contact with the igloo party, and reached them shortly after with food and dry clothes. The doctor checked the Dudleys over and pronounced them in adequate health. The igloo was maxed out with its party of six, so the team proceeded to dig another snow cave.[13]

Meanwhile, other teams who had lugged up sleds in case they were needed to rescue the Dudleys had dug in on the slopes below Paretetaitonga. One of the teams included three climbers from Auckland: Fraser Clark and Mark Prebble, both 21, and Graham Langton, 25.[14] They were young, capable and comparatively fit. Another

ABOVE: Searchers departing to find the Dudleys. Bagnall Collection, Massey University Library

BELOW: Newspaper coverage of the eventual rescue. Auckland Libraries Heritage Collections

rescuer, Robert Bruce, had a pee in the snow before turning in to bed in his team's cave nearby. That pee, unremarkable at the time, was to become a game changer — a life saver — the next morning.

On Tuesday, 18 July, the weather finally relented. The RNZAF had its Iroquois helicopter on standby, waiting for the break they all needed. It pounced, doing two trips to retrieve the Dudleys and the eight rescuers at the cluster of igloos with just 20 minutes to spare before the weather closed in again. The Dudleys, still in good condition, got on board the helicopter without assistance, although they later described themselves as 'weak-legged and grubby'.

Rescue organisers initially thought that an abundance of fresh powder snow and the topography of the bowl-like area below Tahurangi where the igloos sat would cause problems for the helicopter, and that the teams would have to move to a level area. But the RNZAF dismissed all such problems with a wave of its metaphorical hand and simply swooped in, taking the Dudleys directly to Waiouru military hospital for a medical check-over, scones and hot tea.[15]

Bryan and Anne had kept their spirits high during their igloo stay. They'd sung to each other, prayed, and — down to just one slice of bread a day, then none — talked about what they'd eat when they got out. Every morning they'd peer out of the igloo's small entrance to check the weather, only to see fresh snow and no visibility. Every night, they went to bed shivering in their sleeping bags, hopeful that the next day would be fine enough to leave. And every morning they were disappointed.

'Our moods varied from good to very depressed,' Bryan said. 'We wanted to get out from our igloo but knew we had to wait.'

Their faith helped. 'We enjoy life and didn't want it to be taken away,' Bryan said. Anne agreed: 'We are both Catholics and times like this praying helped a lot.'[16]

Nearby on the Summit Plateau, danger was about to grip three young men. Up high, Fraser Clark, Mark Prebble and Graham Langton had woken up in their snow cave to discover the entrance had become blocked by snowdrifts overnight. The 10-day blizzard had blown a huge volume of loose snow around. They had noticed the snow accumulating in the entrance around 10 p.m. the night before, but knew that was fairly normal. What they didn't expect, after the wind had changed direction, was that a 5-metre snowfall would build up on the side they'd predicted would be sheltered.

At 7 a.m. they began to dig, knowing that they only had limited time before the oxygen inside the small space ran out. They dug a tunnel, which eventually extended to around 2 metres long — when Prebble took his turn in the tunnel, it was long enough that his feet had disappeared from the cave and his arms could be fully extended. The length reduced the amount of digging needed to rescue them.

'We weren't able to rescue ourselves,' Prebble recalled, 'but our efforts increased our chances of survival. Without our tunnel, it's uncertain whether the rescuers would have gotten to us in time. Fraser deserves most of the credit for digging the tunnel — he worked on while Graham and I could no longer contribute.'

RESCUERS REPORTED "IN BAD SHAPE" AFTER BURIAL IN SNOW

The rescue team left on Mt Ruapehu after a helicopter picked up Auckland climbers Mr and Mrs Bryan Dudley today fought for two hours to rescue three of its members buried under a snowfall.

"They are in pretty bad shape and we now have the problem of getting them off the mountain," said Senior Sergeant D. R. Mowat.

The three men, Mark Prebble of Auckland, Geoffrey Ian Clark of Howick, and Graham Gordon Langton of Onehunga, were members of a support team on its way to assist the sledging of the Dudleys down Mt Ruapehu.

They were buried when 10 to 15ft of wind-driven snow covered their overnight snow cave at 8500 ft.

Mr Mowat said 11 rescuers reached the scene at 10 a.m. and began trying to reach the trapped men.

The Press Association reports the men were freed shortly before noon.

Earlier, an RNZAF Iroquois helicopter, in two quick trips to Mt Ruapehu, brought Mr and Mrs Dudley and eight rescuers to safety with just 20 minutes to spare before the weather closed in again.

The rescue swoops were made during a brief break between advancing fronts, starting about 7.30 a.m.

The 10 were flown 14 miles to Waiouru while the other rescuers still left on Ruapehu were to make their way down in whiteout conditions along a pole-marked route.

SLEDGE IDEA

Police Sergeant I. J. McDonald said Mr and Mrs Dudley walked to the helicopter and climbed aboard without assistance.

At rescue headquarters in the Tongariro National Park office, it was thought powder snow and the topography would cause lift-out problems.

It was thought the Dudleys would have to be moved some distance to a level area on rescue sledges which this morning still had not arrived at the trapped party's position.

However, the RNZAF dis-

Voices in snow: Of song, prayer and saviours

From NIGEL HORROCKS

RUAPEHU, Today. — Auckland couple Bryan and Anne Dudley spent five days singing to each other, praying and talking about what menus they would have when they got out while they were snowed in near a summit of Mt Ruapehu.

"Down to one slice of bread a day, cold and hungry, we sat and waited and waited and waited but nothing happened," Mrs Dudley told me shortly after the couple were snatched to safety by helicopter today.

Complaining only of appearing grubby and being weak-legged, they talked of going home as they ate scones and tea at Waiouru Military Hospital.

"We enjoy life and didn't want it taken away," said Bryan.

"Our moods varied from good to very depressed. We wanted to get out from our igloo but knew we had to wait."

Every morning the couple, battling to keep warm in their sleeping bags, would peer out of a hole in their igloo (of about 4ft diameter) and find nil visibility and fresh snow.

"Every night we thought the next day would be fine and all would be well but when we woke up the weather was just as bad," said Anne.

"At night we shivered in our sleeping bags.

"There were two incredibly violent thunderstorms," said Bryan,

It's time to smile for

No recipe to stop 'cook book'

WELLINGTON, Today (PA). — An application by Miss Patricia Maureen Bartlett for an interim injunction to restrain publication of a book was dismissed in the Supreme Court here today.

Mr Justice Roper said it was an impossible task to decide that a book about to be published was "unquestionably libellous" unless the book was before the Court.

Miss Bartlett, primary school teacher, of Lower Hutt, had sought the injunction to restrain publication of "The Patricia Bartlett Cookbook."

The defendant was Mr Alister Taylor, publisher of Wellington. His Honour awarded the defendant $40 costs and disbursements.

On behalf of Miss Bartlett, Mr G. W. Alderdice said his client alleged the proposed book contained references to her that were libellous and which would bring her into public redicule and contempt.

It appeared that publication of the book was imminent but the plaintiff was in some difficulty as the defendant had failed to make available the manuscript, pictures or other material in the book, Mr Alderice said.

A subpoena had been served on Mr Taylor requiring him to produce the material to the Court. Counsel was in some difficulty as the exact contents of the book were not known.

The plaintiff had acted in good faith and relied on the established right of every citizen not to be drawn into disrepute by libellous publication.

Mr H. C. MacNeill, counsel for Mr Taylor, submitted that on the plaintiff's affidavit there was not a shred of admissible

LIZARDS DIE

They got through about 2.5 metres of snow, but the cave was only about 2 metres by 1.5 metres, and they were soon out of air. By 10.30 a.m. the three men were overcome by carbon dioxide poisoning and were unable to do much. They were all close to unconsciousness.[17]

The 11 other searchers who were nearby began to dig. It wasn't clear where the entrance to the snow cave was, so they initially dug at a face 6 metres wide. Then Robert Bruce recognised his yellow pee stain in the snow, which offered a crucial clue to the three men's position. The rescuers began digging with more focused attention. Between 10 and 11.45 a.m. they shifted more than 60 cubic metres of snow.

The three men were prostrate and in shock. Shivering violently, they had constricted pupils, a pink-purple skin colour and low pulse rates. Two of them needed oxygen. Chief Ranger John Mazey's subsequent report on the incident observed that they would not have survived another hour. The three were sledged back down to Whakapapa, and with everybody safe the whole Dudley episode was finally closed off at 3.28 p.m. that day.[18]

It was not, Mark Prebble told me when I corresponded with him in 2023, the most helpful contribution they could have made to the Dudley rescue. 'We ended up with photos on the front page of the *New Zealand Herald*, while more deserving people weren't mentioned.' Prebble reckons the Dudleys deserve huge credit. 'They didn't just keep themselves alive, they also figured out how to attract the attention of searchers in zero visibility and howling gales.'[19]

Likewise, in his history of LandSAR, Roger Bates concluded that the Dudleys were well equipped, competent at building an igloo for shelter, and wise to sit out the weather and ration their food.[20] Mazey's incident report also acknowledged their skills: 'In no way is it considered that Bryan and Anne Dudley were irresponsible. Their actions proved their competence and fitness to survive.'[21]

The first and second teams that reached the Dudleys were also outstanding, Prebble told me, both for their endurance and their navigation. 'Tom Clarkson [one of the searchers] commented that the day they battled across the crater area was among the hardest days of his search and rescue experience. I find that comforting, because I thought it was off the scale.'

John Mazey also deserved huge respect for his part in the search, Prebble said. 'He maintained an oversight of the search that was informed by his intimate knowledge of the mountain. His report mentions a point where he suggested the bearing that the second team should follow in zero visibility — and he was right. I recall other occasions when he was offering detailed advice over the radio to searchers and rescuers as they called in for directions about what they should do next. Somehow he seemed to know where parties were on the mountain when they were unsure themselves. He held the whole thing together for a week.'[22]

One thing that was true in 1972 still holds true today: shelter saves lives. In August 1990, six young men on an army training exercise died from exposure just 200 metres from Dome Shelter. At the same time, a 27-year-old Japanese climber, George Iwama, survived on the mountain by remaining in his snow cave, where he listened on the radio to details of his own attempted rescue. After six days the weather cleared, and he left his snow cave, walked down the mountain, approached a snow groomer and said, 'Hi, I'm George, the missing climber.'

Dome Shelter sat just under Dome, 2672 metres, on the peak's southeastern side, for 57 years from its completion in 1961 until its removal in 2018. The shelter survived multiple eruptions, extreme rime ice each winter and constant winds.[23]

In his book *Ruapehu: Tribute to a mountain*, Jock Graham recorded an era of intense building activity on Ruapehu in the 1960s, when club lodges were being constructed and the mountain was as busy in summer as it was in winter:

> It was an exciting time with an irresistible surge of enthusiasm which overcame all obstacles. Every weekend the scoria ridges rang with the sounds of pick and shovel, blasting, bulldozers, tractors, concrete mixers . . . almost anywhere, any weekend, human beasts of burden strained slowly upward under heavy loads. Some clubs employed paid tradesmen for key parts of the construction, but the donkey work, the unpaid, unskilled labour, was almost always done by members, both men and women.[24]

Graham records that Dome Shelter was built by ski clubs in partnership with the Park Board, and partly funded by Ruapehu Ski Club as a memorial to Joe Blyth's efforts at promoting safety on the mountain. The project was easy to get agreement on but difficult to execute in reality, and was only completed thanks to the 'refusal of such moving spirits' as several Ruapehu Ski Club members. The Air Force dropped materials on Dome but many pieces were lost into crevasses and when the Air Force later refused to drop larger items, they had to be lugged up the Whakapapa Glacier by hand and foot. It was, says Graham, 'all very heavy labour cheerfully performed by men who loved the mountain'.

Just four years after the shelter's completion, a 23-year-old foreign student's life was saved after he went missing for four days during the worst summer on Ruapehu for years. Anek Chelling was found on the Summit Plateau by three Park Board rangers who took him to the shelter, where they holed up for three nights while the weather raged. Temperatures dropped so low that their radio equipment iced up and communication back to park headquarters was impossible.

Chelling had set out the Sunday before to climb to the Crater Lake with three friends, who all turned back because one of the party felt sick. However, the weather was clear and he decided to continue. Within minutes he had zero visibility and was being pushed around by the wind and bashed by hailstones. He crawled up Dome and saw the shelter: 'the most beautiful sight in the world'. Inside, a box labelled 'open only in emergency' contained essential supplies — food and blankets — that would save his life.

During the same storm, four mountaineers from Wellington had to dig a snow cave to survive after their tent was blown away. They descended slightly down the Whangaehu Glacier, just 100 metres from the plateau, and constructed a snow shelter.

Former ranger Alex Salmon enthused publicly about the success of Dome Shelter: 'If it saves no other lives than these, it has shown the wisdom of the park board in putting it there,' he said in 1965.[25]

In 2007, mountaineer William Pike and his climbing buddy James Christie were caught in an eruption while staying overnight in Dome Shelter. Pike lost his leg, but the shelter saved their lives. The pair had dug a shelter initially but the snow proved too soft, and although they had a tent they opted to stay in the shelter. Pike reckoned the decision saved them — if they'd pitched the tent they would have been blown off the mountain, and if they'd been in the snow cave, they would have drowned. 'It was a good call.'[26]

Dome Shelter was finally removed in 2018. Its top hatch was usually iced shut, it hadn't served as an effective actual shelter for a long time, and essential volcanic monitoring equipment was by then located at the Matarangi shed on Glacier Knob. A DOC representative described the removal of the structure as a way of acknowledging the cultural significance of the sacred Summit Plateau area.[27]

With the removal of Dome Shelter complete, the top area of Ruapehu, sacred to iwi, was free of huts and shelters. Mangaturuturu Shelter (aka Tūroa Shelter), at 2300 metres on the western side, was gone. So was Glacier Shelter, at just under 2600 metres at the northern end of Dome Ridge. Today, the highest huts on Ruapehu are the New Zealand Alpine Club huts, Ruapehu Hut on Whakapapa at 2020 metres, and Whangaehu Hut at 2060 metres on the eastern side. Otherwise, it's up to backcountry users to know how to construct their own snow shelter, just as the Dudleys did in 1972.

The winter before the Dudley search, three men had been stranded for four days at Whangaehu Hut by extreme weather. Tom Clarke, Craig Rowley and Paul Hazelwood had climbed up from Tukino on Saturday, 28 August, intending to climb further on the eastern side, but were hampered by sleet, snow and gales. The trio bunked down at Whangaehu Hut. They had enough food for two days, but by Monday morning their supplies had run out and they decided to bail. For two hours they walked down the eastern slopes in what residents later described as the worst blizzard since 1968.

Eventually, although Tukino was extremely close, they encountered sharp bluffs they couldn't get past. They spent four hours toiling back to the hut, battling thigh-deep snow. At one stage, they thought they might need to bivvy out because they were simply too exhausted to continue; had they done so, they would have had to be carried out by rescuers later. After they finally reached the hut at 4 p.m., they sat tight for another three nights, listening to the wind howling outside, with very little food and no source of heat. Eventually the weather broke and a rescue party reached them as they strolled out in the first sunshine Ruapehu had seen for more than a week.

'We were on a starvation diet at the end,' Hazelwood said. 'One of our dishes consisted of custard powder and water.'[28]

After any alpine search, fingers are often pointed at those who are lost, and the search and rescue processes are scrutinised. Inevitably someone proposes new restrictions on access to the mountains, which is frankly never a workable solution. For their part the Dudleys (and the searchers) come out of this episode clearly competent, skilled and sensible, and the rescuers as at least mildly heroic. As John Mazey wrote after the event:

> Numerous well-intentioned people will undoubtedly make comment about climbers and other users of our mountains placing other people in danger. I cannot believe that any true climber, tramper, skier or member of the National Park Service would not willingly go through the same type of search and rescue operation again, knowing full well that a similar situation could involve them as the missing party rather than the search or rescue team. Inevitably on some similar search or rescue operation, people will die, however, I for one accept this as an acceptable risk and would resist most strongly any attempt to restrict the use of our mountains by responsible people.[29]

Mark Prebble considers that the Dudleys' survival ranks up there with the most remarkable survival stories in New Zealand. 'They did brilliantly. Building an igloo in a storm is not easy. They could do it, though, because it was a skill they had practised — how many of us have done that? They kept each other going when everything looked desperate. They did everything right, and that is why they survived.'[30]

Now, Bryan and Anne Dudley's daughter Jane Dudley teaches igloo building, using the method her parents pioneered. Passionate about safety in the outdoors, she believes in pushing personal boundaries in a managed way rather than trying to eliminate all possible risk in life.

'More people should learn to build igloos,' Jane told me. 'They save lives.'

NATIONAL PARK
48
4
Whakapapaiti
Mahuia Campsite
Stream
Waikare
Stream
Tawhai Fa
Moturoa Bush
Makokomiko Stream
Waimarino Stream
Mangahuia Stream
Whakapapaiti
WHAKA
WHAKAPAPAITI VALLEY
Waikune Prison
Grass Country
Silica Spring
Whakapapaiti Biv.
Hauhungatahi
1519
Whakapapaiti Hut
Stream
ERUA
EST
Shrub and grass country
River
HAUHUNGATAHI WILDERNESS AREA
Mangatur
River
850
900
950
1000
1050
1100
1200
1250
1300
1350
1500
800

Map from 1975 showing the old track over Hauhungatahi, now part of a wilderness area. National Library of New Zealand, 37100114_1975

CHAPTER 6

Hauhungatahi's secret stone

Hauhungatahi is almost unnoticeable next to the imposing lines of Ruapehu but it's a volcanic cone in its own right, and part of a scrubby, boggy wilderness area. After my first trip up Hauhungatahi, I swore I'd never do it again, but after I was told that there was an inscription chiselled onto one of the summit rocks, I had to find it and see it with my own eyes.

Ken pushed through the thick bush a couple of metres to my right, branches cracking and flicking back. Using my pole, I carefully hooked some bush lawyer around a twig so I wouldn't get ripped to shreds by its grippy barbs. I was also conscious of Mandy, who was sensibly sticking behind me but keeping her distance.

'So,' Mandy said, in her clipped German tones, 'this is what you people do for fun.'

She knew what she'd signed up for, having come on 'exploratory' trips with me before, but she'd be broken by the time the day was over.

'We'll sign cut it,' Howie decided. Which meant we'd space out and bush bash until one of us found the track. Shouldn't take long, he reckoned.

By the time we found the secret track, we were a bit too far away from each other for sensible communication. Ken stumbled across the trail lower down, marked by a piece of black plastic tied to a branch, while Howie found remnants of a camping bedroll higher up — a sign someone had crashed through the bush at some point. Howie messaged me and Ken, but down where we were, nestled in the trees and shielded from civilisation by the slopes of Hauhungatahi, we had no phone reception. Eventually we all ended up together on the same track, a bit higher up.

Had I looked more closely at the info I'd gathered from my last trip up Hauhungatahi, taking the secret track to the open spaces above the bushline, we could have found it much earlier. We might have even saved ourselves five to six minutes of bush bashing, and a couple of expletives. I'd gone up five years before with my old mate Papa Smurf, and although I'd sworn never to go back, I'd taken the precaution of setting a pin on the topo map and snapping photos of a distinctive tree in the middle of the track where the secret trail began. You know, just in case.

Apparently tramping trauma takes five years to resolve because here I was again for another go. The four of us — me, Ken, Howie and Mandy (although Papa Smurf professed to be keen, he'd wisely elected to be 'busy') — were heading for the summit of Hauhungatahi, and we knew it would be a long day. The peak is only 1521 metres high — Ruapehu's highest point, Tahurangi, is 2797 metres — but it takes longer to ascend the 620 metres of the former than it does to climb the 1200 metres of the latter. Why do I do this to myself, I wondered. What's more, why do I do it to other people?

I'd been happy to wallow comfortably in the secure knowledge that I'd never again set foot on Hauhungatahi, until my mate Ron Thomas from Whanganui mentioned a stone on the summit with a mystery inscription. 'Of course, you'll have seen the secret tablet with the carving on it on the summit,' he said to me during one of those conversations where we'd both rave and hand-wave violently about Ruapehu's history and the mysteries of the maunga.

'Nope,' I said. 'Got a pic?'

Ron pulled out a shot of the rock. It was a light ochre colour, with dark lichen in spots all over, so dark the growths were almost black. I could make out some letters but they didn't seem to spell anything obvious, and I could see some sort of date, but it was hard to tell: the numbers could have been either '3' or '8' in places. Some of the shapes could have been letters chiselled in, or they could have been lichen growing in letter-shaped formations. It was irritatingly unclear, and I could feel my curiosity inconveniently piqued by the alluring and mysterious idea of a secret stone on the summit.

'Bloody hell, Ron, now I'm going to have to go back up there.'

He laughed. Sort of cackled with delight.

'Do you have any idea what it means?' I asked.

'Not the foggiest, and like you, I can't make out what the letters are.'

And so, because of bloody Ron and his bloody mystery inscription, I had to go back.

There's not a huge amount to be gleaned about Hauhungatahi Wilderness Area other than that it's 8498 hectares and was gazetted in 1966. It seems to fly under the radar compared to Tongariro National Park. Hauhungatahi itself is the fourth highest volcanic cone after Ruapehu, Taranaki and the Tongariro massif, including Ngāuruhoe, and it is thought to be about 900,000 years old, making it the oldest in the Tongariro Volcanic Centre. It's mostly covered in spongy tussock, with a line of bush around its base, and its northern slopes contain charred tree fragments from the AD232 Taupō eruption, meaning that Hauhungatahi was at the eruption's southern limits. A small and seemingly insignificant peak tacked onto the lower slopes of the giant Ruapehu, unnoticed by visitors who stare in awe and longing at the spires of snow-clad summits higher up, it's a bump compared to Ruapehu and feels a rather unlikely addition to its much more statuesque volcanic companions. But boy, does it have a sting in its tail.

On the Mangahuia Track, just above the 1140-metre mark, there's a sharp 90-degree bend, the sort of bend that's often a clue that a track junction once existed there, and for whatever reason one section of track has been simply sliced off. Indeed, older maps show the track continuing on in a westerly direction, across boggy ground and up a ridge to the bushline. The track appears on maps as late as 1979, well after the wilderness area had been gazetted, but is scrubbed clean on the 1989 version. At this sharp junction there's a wooden sign that hasn't been painted in many years. Its metal fixings are rusted in places, and just visible through a coating of light-green moss are carved letters that read:

> You are now entering the Hauhungatahi wilderness of
> Tongariro National Park. Because of the wilderness status
> there are no marked tracks to follow in this region.

It reminds me of the sign at Checkpoint Charlie in Berlin: 'Sie verlassen den Amerikanischen Sektor. You are leaving the American sector.' Proceed at your own risk. If you don't know of the dangers that await you, you're about to find out.

It's part of the idea, the allure, of wilderness areas that there's not much information about them. As tramper and climber Carl Walrond said, in a *New Zealand Geographic* magazine article in 2016, 'By definition, wilderness areas do not have a high profile — you have to dig into national park management plans to find them on maps.

Mandy Rothe (left) and the author on Tongariro, with the summit peak of Hauhungatahi in the background. Mike Heydon

If there is no shelter from the storm, no bridge across swollen waters, no route marked, then it is no country for the inexperienced. And publicity could lead to overuse, which would defeat their very purpose.'[1]

Hauhungatahi's boundary snuggles up to the Whakapapaiti Valley Track and the Mangahuia Track (sometimes called the Mahuia Track), on their western side. It's swampy, spongy country, deceptively difficult to walk across, with holes, rocks and unstable soil waiting to snare the unsuspecting tramper. Some call Hauhungatahi Baldy or Old Baldy, probably referring to its seemingly bald top, although once close up it's not as devoid of scrubbery as you'd think from afar. A mate has tried to convince me that the locals call it 'Brown Top', but I suspect this is simply a localism and has been verbal only.

I've not been able to find Baldy (Old or otherwise) on any maps, and the area was referred to as Hauhungatahi as far back as the 1886 Surveys of New Zealand report. Uenuku chairman Aiden Gilbert told me that the iwi knows the mountain as Puketiti: 'puke' meaning hill, and 'titi' referring to the muttonbirds that were gathered in the area. Although Hauhungatahi is in Uenuku's rohe, their name for the peak hasn't been acknowledged on maps.

Like its sister wilderness area Te Tatau Pounamu, on the northeastern slopes of Tongariro National Park, Hauhungatahi is too small and not remote enough to be considered a big-boy wilderness area under a policy that was established after both were gazetted. But because they snuck in before the policy they've been retained as wilderness areas, sometimes referred to as 'remote experience zones', in a quiet sweeping under the carpet of a conservation problem nobody really cares about sufficiently to try to air out and/or resolve. That's fine. The Tongariro National Park Management Plan 2006–2016 makes an acknowledgement of support for the semi-wild spaces of both areas: 'In a park such as Tongariro, where the pressure for development, commercialisation and inappropriate use — both from within and outside the park — is high, it is imperative that some very significant areas receive protection from development.'[2]

Wilderness areas are different to conservation spaces in that they are devoid of infrastructure and human interference. That means no huts, tracks or bridges, and no concessions for commercial operators — ideologically, anyway, if not in practice, because these things don't always work so strictly. You won't find a coffee cart at the summit of Hauhungatahi, but you will find a major tramping track cutting through its higher reaches (the Ruapehu Round the Mountain Track), and Whakapapaiti Hut is just within the area's boundaries, depending on how closely you scrutinise the map.

The Round the Mountain Track, developed as a result of the Stanton search, was already firmly in place between the Chateau and the Ohakune Mountain Road by the time the wilderness area was gazetted. It's a popular, well-used track, and so it remains. When trail runners do the 'Goat' mountain run each year they likely have little clue they're actually running across a wilderness area. The Stanton Memorial and a plane wreck from 1948 also lurk inside the boundaries of the wilderness area.

In an essay in *Wild Heart: The possibility of wilderness in Aotearoa New Zealand,*

ABOVE: The author, Mandy Rothe and Howie Nicholson on the scrubby tops of Hauhungatahi, having just left the bushline.

BELOW: Ken Mercer by the summit rock with its mystery inscription. Mandy Rothe Photography

wilderness writer Shaun Barnett acknowledged that Hauhungatahi and Te Tatau Pounamu really aren't big enough to serve their purpose. He rightly pointed out the existence of the Round the Mountain Track, and the fact that any competent tramper could completely traverse the wilderness area in a day. 'To protect its core, a good wilderness actually needs a buffer zone around it, what managers call a "remote experience zone",' he wrote. 'Having said that, Tongariro National Park does not have any better options. And by simply stepping off the track, you can go from a crowded environment into solitude.'[3]

Unable to find out much about Hauhungatahi online, I looked at the Tramping in New Zealand group on Facebook; surely someone had been up there?

Indeed, someone had tramped it in 2019 and had concluded it was 'something different to do if you are looking for a day's tramping with nobody else around'. They had found the old poled route to the summit, and noted that it was a lifetime since any track up to the peak had been shown on a national park map, but they hadn't responded to users' requests for intel about the route.

Then in 2021, another user had begged for information: 'Summiting Hauhungatahi. Tell me what you know.' I scrolled through the posts and came across a reply that read: 'I WILL NEVER DO THIS AGAIN.' The comment had my name on it. I further expounded: 'This is a "worst tracks of NZ" episode looking for a victim.' I couldn't remember writing the post, but there it was.

And yet here I was, again, with victims in tow. We'd better find this mystery rock, I thought; I didn't want to have to go up a third time.

The secret track through the bush was easy enough to follow once we were on it. Sporadic markers of all kinds — plastic ties, tin-can lids — lit the way. Then it spat us out into the open, on the tops of Hauhungatahi, onto the part that looks super easy-going from a distance. Although Howie didn't voice the thought at the time, later that day he mentioned he had eyed up the spongy scrub underfoot, looked at the distance to the summit, and concluded quietly that we were in for a very long day.

I suggested a break at this point so we could stuff ourselves with snacks and lather on sunscreen. We perched on lumps of tussock and attended to our individual needs. A cloud lurked up high, looking like a UFO waiting to pick us off the summit later on. I pointed it out.

'Do you believe in aliens?' I asked.

Generally, the others agreed — aliens were likely to exist in some form. This was excellent news for the cloud UFO waiting to pick us up. I took it one step further: 'Do you reckon you'd like to be abducted by aliens?' I asked.

'Well, that defeats the point of abduction, doesn't it?' Howie pointed out. 'If you're going willingly, it's not a proper abduction.'

'Imagine it'll be a nice, fun abduction. Maybe their spaceship goes really fast and it's like being on a rollercoaster, and their alien food is tasty, and when they probe you it feels pretty good,' I replied.

OSPREY

Ken thought for a minute. 'Well,' he said, 'I wouldn't want to have to eat something weird, like chocolate ants.'

In a sense, you could say I had abducted these guys for this trip, but in another sense, they had come willingly. None of them had been up Hauhungatahi before, something I found surprising given Ken and Howie had been Ruapehu regulars for decades.

The terrain of the supposedly 'bald' top was hard going. Not technically difficult, just exhausting and sweaty. Although it looked bare and rocky from afar, the exposed top was covered in soft scrub, so that for each step we had to lift our feet quite high to get on top of the growth, which would then compress back down again. It was like trying to walk up an escalator that was going down.

It was only 3 kilometres from the bushline to the summit, and a mere 300 metres' gain in altitude, but it took us just over two hours — probably double what I'd usually allow for those variables. We were about halfway and alternating between sweating in the sun and from the exertion and freezing in the chilly breeze, when we paused for another restorative snack stop.

'Mary tried going up Hauhungatahi once,' Ken said. Mary is Ken's wife, also a fit and enthusiastic tramper. 'They went up from Erua on the other side. And they walked and walked and it felt like they'd been going forever, and the summit never got any closer, so eventually they gave up and went back down.'

It is possible to ascend from Erua, a tiny settlement on the western side of the park, just south of the creepy abandoned prison at Waikune. It requires marginally more ascent than going via the Mangahuia Track, and in recent years there have been reports that it comes with the risk of angering some of the landowners there. The known workaround is to park further south, walk up the train tracks, not get run over, and look out for a track marker. Somewhere. Maybe. I couldn't possibly give you directions, because that would be cheating.

My face was crusted in salt and sweat by the time we finally made it to the top, exhausted, after five hours' slog. First to a rusty old trig at the summit proper, and then a short bash over to a second summit, which looks higher — especially from a distance — but is actually just a smidgen lower. Visual trickery at its finest. We took in the unique view towards Ruapehu, Ngāuruhoe and Tongariro, as well as the bushy lower slopes of Hauhungatahi and its tiny tarns. We could see the vestiges of the track from Erua trickling down towards the bushline.

Mandy was starting to feel the pain by this point, but she didn't say anything until we were descending, and for the moment she seemed deceptively robust in that German hiker sort of way. The soles of my feet were burning. In two days' time I would have the biggest migraine of my life. I put it down to the bright sunshine and the sheer effort I'd expended.

The mystery rock, our secret tablet, was easy to find — almost disappointingly so. It was quite readable up close — LTEIKA, 3-5-53 — on a rusty-coloured rock, matching the trig, with spots of black lichen taking over. I'd brought a scrubbing brush in case we needed to clear away the growth in order to read it, but once we got there it just didn't seem right to interfere with nature's work. The letters had been chiselled in neatly;

Howie pointed out they were in a distinctive serif font, so some sort of lettering stamps had probably been carried up, and a hammer used to make the indentations. Ruapehu glowed steadily with his white top in the background, and the tussock surrounding the mystery rock wavered in the consistently stiff breeze.

What had happened on 3 May 1953, just over 70 years ago? My search began.

In 1953 Ed Hillary reached the summit of Mount Everest, but that didn't happen until later that month, on the 29th. The Tangiwai disaster was also local — just on the southern side of Ruapehu, where the Whangaehu River becomes a lahar path in an eruption — but that didn't happen until December.

In 1953, the Social Credit Party was formed. Auckland introduced parking meters — the first in the country — and the first Family Planning Association clinic opened. Godfrey Bowen broke the world record for sheep shearing, shaving 456 sheep in nine hours, which turned him into a celebrity (well, in New Zealand, anyway). And — wait — six climbers died on Taranaki, and another two climbers died a week later. But no, that also happened later in the year.

It did occur to me that the inscription could have been made at any time, and wasn't necessarily chiselled in on that exact date. Howie sensibly pointed out it was probably three people with their first and last initials, LT, EI and KA, and the date they summited — sort of wilderness graffiti or tagging, the tramping equivalent of writing your name on a bathroom wall. I don't necessarily blame them; it had taken us hours of grovelling, and that was with the secret track to make the going quicker. Bush bashing back in 1953 would have been far worse.

But did they even bush bash? Old maps consistently show a track from Erua in the west, taking an almost direct line up to the summit, then angling east-northeast to descend a sloping ridge, dropping down through the bush to the swamps and connecting with the Mangahuia Track.

In fact, a track was cut very early, leading up from Erua and over the summit peak. It must have been a good track, too, allowing for swift travel. In 1909 Hugh Girdlestone, who was then working as an assistant government surveyor, wrote that the journey up Hauhungatahi took about an hour and a half, and another hour to come back down. (A far cry from our nine hours.) He mentioned that a previous party travelling over Hauhungatahi had camped on the flat, boggy slopes in between Hauhungatahi and Ruapehu, and ascended some 1500–1700 metres to summit Paretetaitonga in just four hours. I guess without the desk life and with fewer visits to KFC, folks were a lot fitter back then — or Baldy really was bald, which would have made the going a bit swifter.

You can almost hear Girdlestone modestly shrugging off the effort: 'Ruapehu can be ascended almost anywhere, as the spurs all rise in steady slopes, there being no difficult rock-climbing on any of them.'[4]

In the 1908 Lands and Survey report on Tongariro National Park, pioneering botanist Leonard Cockayne and his sidekick Edward Phillips Turner, a botanist, surveyor and Inspector of Scenic Reserves, wrote of their concern that Hauhungatahi

ABOVE: Heading towards the false summit of Hauhungatahi in the distance. Mandy Rothe Photography

BELOW: Tongariro and Ngāuruhoe from Hauhungatahi. Mandy Rothe Photography

and its steep sidewalls with 'extremely beautiful' forest might be lost forever if logging took hold.[5] Cockayne and Turner diplomatically dropped in a mention that the timber was of little use for milling purposes anyway. So, they argued, the Hauhungatahi area should really be added to Tongariro National Park (this being a suggestion already made by the Scenery Preservation Board — imagine that there once was such a department!). This was all happening in an era when the gents in power assumed that the land along the Main Trunk Line around Ruapehu was 'destined to play a great part in the farming industry of the future',[6] but it was around this very time that a farm was failing over on the Desert Road.

As we trudged back down again, I overheard Howie muttering something about heather; he may have used the term 'bastard'. Indeed, *Calluna vulgaris* was intentionally introduced to the slopes of the central plateau by park warden and former police commissioner John Cullen, starting around 1912. Cullen was on a bender to create an environment similar to the Scottish moors to attract grouse for recreational game shooting. He used local prison labour to plant heather extensively — ling heather and several other kinds — and although the plant took off, the grouse didn't. Cullen was backed by Prime Minister William Massey and the Department of Tourist and Health Resorts, which then administered the park.

In 1914 Cullen had inspected the heather to find 95 per cent of the plants doing well, although it was early days, and he trumpeted his success in a letter to the Minister of Justice: 'Now that the heather planting experiment has proved a success, I beg to apply for authority to spend, say, any sum up to £50 this season in purchasing all the heather plants I can obtain and in planting them out during next month.' During a recent visit to Otago and Southland he'd found heather going to seed, so he arranged for seed to be saved for him, 'with the result that I have now over a bushel of New Zealand grown heather seed ready to sow out on the plains when the plants are being planted out next month'. He had also sourced two dozen plants from Campbell Island.[7]

'The primary objects in establishing heather on the National Park,' Cullen continued, 'are to beautify the place and to provide food for grouse, blackcock and ptarmigan when they are introduced later on'. He was full of ideas of things to plant — rowan trees, hawthorn plants, wild cherry, wild strawberry, bilberry. 'As the quantities of heather plants and seeds which can be obtained in New Zealand are very limited, it would take a lifetime to establish a good supply of heather on the National Park. This being so, I beg to suggest that the High Commissioner be requested to try and enter into arrangements with persons in England, Ireland and Scotland for a good supply of heather seed to be saved this coming autumn.'[8]

Cullen wanted to get in touch with the Board of Irish Agriculture and have sacks of seed sent from various counties, and then move on to any similar boards of agriculture in Scotland and England. He concluded: 'I may say that neither the heather nor bilberry plants can become noxious weeds.'

The plan went a bit wrong, as these things often do, and by 1990 heather was

proliferating wildly in the national park. Today, heather is widespread in the park, although for a long time it was thought to be rarely fertile above 1200 metres.

Throughout the year, as the seasons change, the whole Tongariro landscape switches from golden tussock to purple, depending on when the heather is flowering. It's possible this will change as the planet warms up; in 2019, DOC rangers found about 20 small adult heather plants at around 1700 metres altitude in Central Crater on Tongariro, well beyond their usual happy place.

If you think this is absolute horse shit, it almost literally is; it's thought that other common invasive weeds seen in the national park, such as gorse, broom and lupin, probably first arrived via horse droppings, as they were the main means of transport in the early years.

From 1993, scientist Dr Harry Keys led a project to introduce the heather beetle *Lochmaea suturalis* to combat the spread of heather. The beetles didn't enjoy their big OE and only one population survived, but a hardy bunch of renegades set to work and eventually, with help from scientists from Manaaki Whenua Landcare Research, they spread many kilometres from their original transplant sites. The beetles have been a success (and in some places they have thoroughly decimated the heather) and now there are only 20,000 hectares remaining for them to spread into. This means the New Zealand Defence Force no longer needs to spray herbicide over its army training area on the eastern side of Ruapehu, in the zone adjacent to the national park. Researchers at Manaaki Whenua are now checking to see how the beetles respond to higher-altitude placement. The future is bright, though: it seems that the hardy heather-destroying Ruapehu beetle can 'rediscover recovering heather and repeat its demolition job'.[9]

The bastard heather made the going tough for us, too. It's a springy enough plant, growing up to a metre high, with tiny green leaves and small purple flowers. It's meant to flower in the summer, and we were there in October, but the lack of snow and unseasonably warm temperatures meant that the little mauve flowers were already poking through in places.

In 1975, Greta Stevenson wrote in *Forest and Bird* magazine:

> A narrow bush track, clearly marked where it begins, leads up the main ridge south of the railway station with some easy grades and many steep stretches. Where it emerges from the upper bush zone there is a narrow belt of alpine shrubbery before the trail leads into the open sub-alpine tussock grass with its own association of native alpine plants. *Calluna vulgaris*, the introduced heather with its pretty purplish flowers, is vigorously invasive of much of the upper slopes leading to the summit of Hauhungatahi. The track leads on over the summit and back to the Chateau, a long day's tramp for those who want something strenuous and very well remembered by some of our party who completed this marathon on a previous visit.[10]

(Readers who are excited by Latin names of flora — I am, sadly, not one of you — may read specifics of the growths on and around Hauhungatahi by looking up the article, and there are plenty of others on the topic in academic journals.)

Vulgaris indeed; the plant's rate of reproduction is faster than two bunnies on a Netflix date in a romantic warren — each year one plant can produce 161,000 seeds, which remain viable for at least a decade and possibly up to 45 years. But *calluna*? It comes from the Greek 'kalluno', which means 'to brush' or 'to clean' — referring to the use of the plant as a broom. And it's hardy (just not as hardy as the beetles) — heather isn't bothered by frost or bog, and it can resprout after physical damage such as animal grazing, and even after being razed by fire.

As I was getting beaten up by the springy undergrowth of Hauhungatahi's unassuming-looking slopes, I contemplated the extent to which I would enjoy being as resilient as a heather beetle. Were I one of these beetles, I should take to the slopes of Hauhungatahi with abandon, munching a path up to the summit and over the other side, so that the humans of today could enjoy a mere hour and a half wander, in the fashion of that fit bastard Hugh Girdlestone, up and over the top.

LTEIKA, 3-5-53. A mystery I'm acutely aware I will likely never solve. I've come to terms with that — I'm just glad we found the rock with the inscription in the first place, given it could have been a proper needle-in-a-haystack mission, and I would've felt the need to keep banging my head against that particular mystery until I solved it.

As we descended in silence, each of us lost in thought, I realised that I had properly broken Mandy the German. Lagging behind somewhat, she had gone extra quiet, and was snapping fewer and fewer photos. I was sure she'd eventually look back and decide the outing had indeed been fun, but I realised it might take a year or two for the trauma to subside. After all, it had taken me five years to recover sufficiently to get to the point of deciding to go back for another taste of Hauhungatahi's stiff medicine.

Maybe in another five years I'll have recovered enough to go back again, to retrace the line of the old track across the boggy lower slopes, up over the summit peak and down to Erua. It's marked on so many of the old maps, and vestiges of it can be picked out on satellite images, so it's still there. Somewhere. Hidden away, with the mystery of LT, EI and KA, standing on the summit on a chilly autumn day in 1953.

Te Heuheu peak (2732m), the 'killer peak' the Airspeed Consul crashed into on 11 December, 1951. Mike Heydon/ChopperWorx

PART 2

AIR

If Tongariri is the right way of spelling the name of the volcano, instead of Tongariro, it is a very appropriate name, as it means 'angry south wind'.

— Ernst Dieffenbach[1]

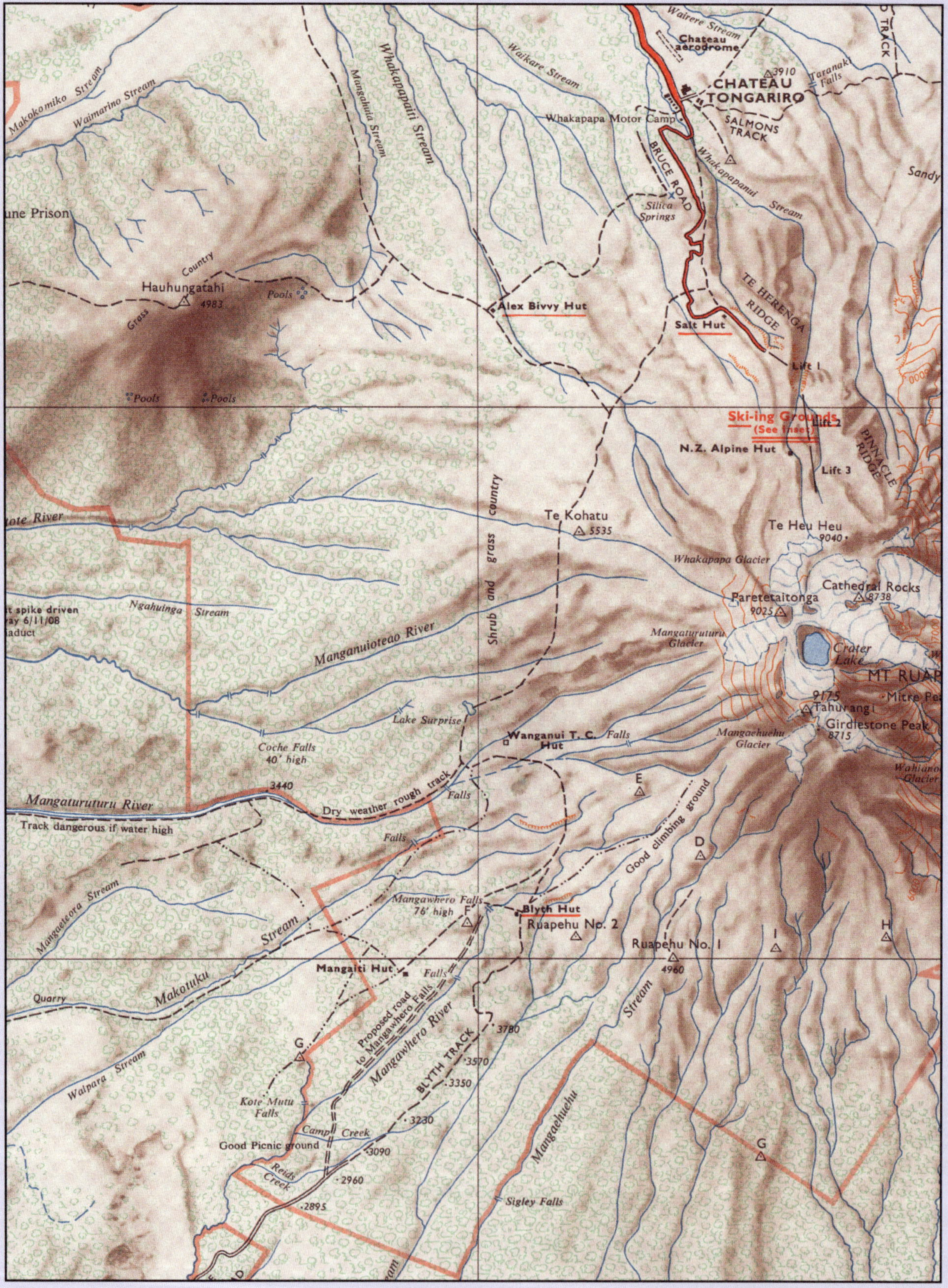

Wairere Stream
Chateau aerodrome
CHATEAU TONGARIRO
Taranaki Falls
3910
Waikare Stream
Whakapapa Motor Camp
SALMONS TRACK
BRUCE ROAD
Whakapapanui Stream
Silica Springs
Sandy
Makokomiko Stream
Waimarino Stream
Mangahuia Stream
Whakapapaiti Stream
Prison
Country
Grass
Hauhungatahi
4983
Pools
Alex Bivvy Hut
Salt Hut
TE HERENGA RIDGE
Lift 1
Ski-ing Grounds
(See Inset)
Lift 2
N.Z. Alpine Hut
Lift 3
PINNACLE RIDGE
Te Kohatu
5535
Shrub and grass country
Te Heu Heu
9040
Whakapapa Glacier
Cathedral Rocks
8738
Paretetaitonga
9025
Ngahuinga Stream
Manganuioteao River
Mangaturuturu Glacier
Crater Lake
MT RUAP
9175
Tahurangi
Mitre Pea
Girdlestone Peak
8715
Lake Surprise
Wanganui T. C. Hut
Falls
Mangaehuehu Glacier
Coche Falls
40' high
3440
Mangaturuturu River
Dry weather rough track
Track dangerous if water high
Good climbing ground
Mangaeteora Stream
Mangawhero Falls
76' high
Blyth Hut
Ruapehu No. 2
Ruapehu No. 1
4960
Makotuku Stream
Mangaiti Hut
Quarry
Proposed road to Mangawhero Falls
Mangawhero River
BLYTH TRACK
3780
3570
3350
3230
3090
2960
2895
Waipara Stream
Kote Mutu Falls
Camp Creek
Good Picnic ground
Reids Creek
Mangaehuehu
Stream
Sigley Falls

Map showing the Mangaturuturu Glacier and Lake Surprise. The *Kaka* was found about halfway between the two. National Library of New Zealand, 37103234_1958

CHAPTER 7

The wreck of the *Kaka*

In 1948, a plane smashed into a ridge on the western side of Ruapehu in almost zero visibility, instantly killing its 13 occupants and sparking one of the toughest recoveries in the mountain's history. The wreckage was gone — or so I was told.

It was 23 October 1948. Wet and windy conditions buffeted most of the North Island, but it was Ruapehu that bore the brunt of the fierce weather, sticking up out of the centre of the motu. Beth Gilberd's laundry was flapping about on the line in the squalls that blew through Rangataua, just out of Ohakune. She had mixed up a sponge cake and placed it in the oven, carefully noting the time so she would know when to take it out — it was precisely 2.06 p.m. — and went out to get more wood to stoke the stove.

Gilberd stepped out the back door, heard a plane overhead, and looked up. She was 19 years old and obsessed with planes, so she always watched when aircraft went over. Gilberd wanted to be a transport pilot in the war but it all wrapped up a month before she turned 18 and she missed her chance. Her interest in aircraft remained, though.

The clouds, which had been relentless all day, parted momentarily, and for about three seconds she saw the plane. She noted its direction of travel, and that it was a National Airways Corporation (NAC) Lockheed — she could tell by the twin tail and tapered wings. It wasn't a good day to be flying, and Gilberd thought they were mad. What she didn't know was that the plane shouldn't have been there in the first place — if it had been on course, it would've been further west and flown between Raetihi and Pipiriki, not over Rangataua. The clouds closed over again, and her attention turned back to gathering firewood to ensure the sponge cooked properly. Not many people were given credibility for what they saw and heard that day, but Gilberd was.[1]

Robert Schofield, the stationmaster at Rangataua, was at home for a late lunch. Around 2 p.m. he had occasion to go outside, and he was just about to go inside again when he heard the engines of a plane. It passed through his mind that it was a bad day for aircraft to be flying. He stopped at his back door and waited. After a spell, he saw a plane pass through a break in the clouds, just for a few seconds. It was a twin-engined silver monoplane with tapered wings, he later told police.[2]

Deep in a valley on Ruapehu, three deerstalkers had broken camp early that morning and ascended to a plateau on the eastern side of the Mangaturuturu Stream. Visibility was very bad, about 10 metres, and a strong wind was carrying heavy rain sideways. Edward Ross, a bushman with the local Pokaka Timber Company Mill, wondered how sleet and fog could exist in such a wind. Around 2 p.m. they were walking in single file when they heard a plane overhead. The man in front stopped. The aircraft sounded quite close but higher than they were, and it seemed to be coming from Ohakune and travelling towards the mountain.

Ross turned to the others. 'That plane is going to hit the mountain,' he said.

'Perhaps it's above the clouds and flying in bright sunshine,' one of the others suggested.

Then the engines seemed to cut out. They didn't hear the plane again, and didn't hear the sound of a crash, so they assumed it had passed over the ridge and out of earshot. The men thought no more of it until they returned to Pokaka the next day to discover a large-scale hunt for a missing plane, and they fronted up to tell what they knew.[3]

ABOVE: The *Kaka* in service at Rongotai, Wellington, May 1945. Whites Aviation, Richard Waugh collection

BELOW: Freight being loaded into the nose of the *Kaka*. It carried passengers and mail around the country. Transport Accident Investigation Commission

The *Kaka*, a shiny silver and vermillion Lockheed 10A Electra ZK-AGK, was flying from Palmerston North to Hamilton that afternoon. It was a long weekend, and all the seats were full. The captain relayed the last radio message at 1.38 p.m., near Whanganui, as the plane turned and climbed in heavy rain and dense cloud. Back then, aircraft flew beneath the altitude of the highest peaks of the North Island mountains Ruapehu and Taranaki. Pilots flew from Palmerston North directly towards Whanganui, where a homing beacon was installed — they knew they were above the beacon when a sort of compass needle would swing around violently — then they took a 'dog leg' route, turning to fly north to Hamilton. This approach ensured they passed safely between the two mountainous areas.

The wind that day was ferocious — wind speeds were recorded as 44 miles per hour at Waiouru and 30 miles per hour at Ohakune. The weather report noted 'squalls' at Ohakune. Electras were known for being large, robust but heavy machines that got battered around by the elements at their relatively low altitude. Inside the *Kaka*, the seatbelt sign was illuminated and co-pilot Brian Russell moved through the cabin, reassuring apprehensive passengers. They were all seated and holding on tightly, except for one: William Mumford, an engineer and a Member of the Order of the British Empire, had left his seat to use the lavatory.

The *Kaka* was due in Hamilton at 2.50 p.m. It never arrived. Flying in zero visibility, the aircraft skidded on a flat section of the western slopes of Ruapehu, shot across a gully around 40 metres wide, and smashed directly into a steep slope opposite. One wing stuck in the steep, snow-covered face, then broke off, while the rest of the plane slid back into the gully below, never to move again. All 13 on board — two pilots and 11 passengers, including a toddler, four-year-old Keith Collinge — died.

If the *Kaka* had been flying just 100 metres higher, it would likely have passed over the Mangaturuturu ridge and those aboard would have arrived safely in Hamilton, in blissful ignorance of the fate they had narrowly escaped.

The first searchers to find the wreck, a week after the crash, confirmed the aircraft's occupants had died immediately on impact, as there were no signs of any movement after the crash. 'They never knew what hit them,' several of the searchers were reported as saying.[4] At most, pilot Max Hare would have seen a split second of rock face speeding towards him after the plane skidded across the flat spot.

The scene was gruesome. Pieces of metal were scattered for a hundred metres around the crash site, indicating the force of the impact. The fuselage had been bent into a reverse S shape, and the nose was completely stoved in.

'I flew with the Air Force in the war and witnessed bad crashes, but never anything to equal this,' one man said. 'It was a terrible sight. I wish I had not seen it.'[5]

I loosely knew about several aircraft wrecks on Ruapehu, but they were brought to the forefront of my thinking after I saw a post on social media. A New Zealand Alpine Club member had posted on the club's Facebook group, asking for information on where the wrecks were, as he was hoping to go for summer walks to find all three sites.

ABOVE: The *Kaka* came to rest in a sharp gully. Richard Waugh collection

BELOW: Wreckage of the *Kaka* lodged in the snow. Richard Waugh collection

We corresponded, and I began digging out information from newspaper archives and asking questions of local folk about the *Kaka*.

Although a wealth of information existed about the crash and ensuing search and recovery operation, the wreck itself as it existed (or didn't exist) in contemporary times seemed to be shrouded in myth and mystery. Several friends had been out looking for it more than once without success. Someone told me the engine blocks were at the base of a waterfall in the upper part of the Mangaturuturu River, somehow having travelled downstream and over the waterfall's edge. Many people said nothing was left. Yet others said the wreck was still there, just in a remote spot and not where most people thought it was.

I questioned the narratives that nothing was left. The *Kaka* was a sizeable aircraft — it weighed 4.5 tonnes and could carry 13 people — and something of that magnitude doesn't just disintegrate or disappear off a mountain side. The engine blocks were massive and had two large propellers. The common theory seemed to be that the wreckage had first been scattered over a wide area by the force of the impact, and then had been ground into pieces over the years by rockfall, ice, snow and avalanches. Certainly the steep slope bordering the gully would have been avalanche-prone, and if the wreckage sat in a gully, it would've been hammered by avalanche debris and the weight of snow drifts. But still. A wreck does not just disappear.

Mystery aside, a veil of environmental gatekeeping seems to shroud things such as plane wrecks in the backcountry. Posts on social media get quickly shut down by dissenting locals, or by the backcountry elite who want the hills to remain free of pesky tourists. On one Facebook group where we discussed the various wrecks on Ruapehu, a local chap wrote: 'Until I read this post I was mildly aware of this wreckage and in many ways I wish it had stayed off social media. You may disagree with me on that but I sincerely hope it does not encourage souvenir hunters.' Another responded: 'I'm fairly confident the climbing/mountaineering fraternity is a good bunch who respect environmental and historical values.' And the response: 'But the Facebook stalkers are not. There's a hell of lot of ones influenced by what they see posted.'

There seemed to be an idea that it was acceptable to talk about these things and pass on information in a word-of-mouth sort of way, but that widespread searchable knowledge should be tempered — that it would lead to hordes of people running off to strip the wrecks. I also regularly got smacked on the hand by another mountaineering chap for posting photos of swimming holes on the mountain, only to discover later that the old Round the Mountain Track used to cross the Mangawhero Stream at exactly the point where the best swimming hole exists, and hence had historically hosted a steady stream of foot traffic.

The problem of wreck-stripping isn't a new one. Just months after the crash of the *Kaka*, in February 1949, when the snow melted — thereby removing the need for mountaineering experience to access the site — newspapers reported that parts of the plane were being taken by souvenir hunters, who were gradually removing the aircraft 'piecemeal', although the fuselage was still in recognisable condition.[6]

The passengers' belongings had been left to rot, and a fur coat lay tattered among the wreckage. 'Unscrupulous people' had removed any personal effects that they considered could be of value — even the *Kaka*'s nameplate had been tacked onto the door of Salt Hut on the mountain's northern side.[7] It's said that a portion of the *Kaka*'s cockpit still exists somewhere in Horopito.

Five months after the *Kaka* accident, another NAC plane, the *Kereru*, a Lockheed Lodestar, crashed into the Tararua foothills and burst into flames, killing all 15 on board. Soon, souvenir hunters were looting whatever they could find at that site, too. Newspaper editorials condemned the act, one calling it ghoulish and callous.[8] Another said: 'It is unfortunately true that too many members of the public cannot be brought to exercise not only common restraint but even common decency in the face of such a happening as the present disaster. The souvenir hunter has not the slightest trace of a conscience.'[9]

The contemporary narrative seemed to be that if these things appeared on social media, hordes of tourists would go up to strip the wreck, but that had already happened — back in 1949, just months after the crash of the *Kaka*, and without the existence of Facebook to help circulate information. Souvenir-hunting didn't, in fact, seem to be a problem that stemmed from increased availability of information via social media, but of human desire and conscience. Moreover, the wreck's location was so hard to pinpoint, and the terrain anything but simple; going on an expedition to find the *Kaka* was a far cry from walking up Roy's Peak to get a sunrise yoga photo for Instagram.

Back in 1948, fingers pointed furiously and assertions flew that the public shouldn't have been allowed near the wreck. Some responsibility perhaps lies with NAC. In December 1948, R. G. Phyn, whose son Roderick had died in the accident, wrote to the Minister of Civil Aviation trying to get his belongings returned to the family. 'I wish to ask you what is being done about the personal effects of the victims who lost their lives in the crash,' Phyn wrote. 'When I was at Ohakune to identify my son I was told that all the luggage would be salvaged and I would receive notice at a later date.' Police had told him it was the responsibility of NAC to salvage and return belongings. 'I will be glad if you will let me know if anything will be done to recover any of the luggage from the wreckage of the lost plane,' Phyn told the minister.[10] It's unclear if he was successful.

In late December, a 17-year-old schoolboy tramped from the Chateau to the wreck site and together with friends spent three hours combing the wreckage. He found a diary, with recently penned words: 'Huge cloud bank over Ruapehu and over mountains. A pity, as I went by the Desert Road to see them.'[11] The diary belonged to 38-year-old William Mumford, the man who'd been up to go to the lavatory at the time of the crash. The diary was forwarded to NAC to return to Mumford's relatives.

I knew that going tramping on the mountain to find the wreck without some indication of its location would be a pointless proposition. I thoroughly enjoy a good wild goose chase, but the terrain in and around the Mangaturuturu catchment is not only extensive but also precipitous and tricky. It looks smooth and doable on the topo map, but in reality, obstacles abound. Ridges are ringed with bluffs and are steeper than they

ABOVE: Some of the wreckage ended up high on the ridge. Richard Waugh collection

BELOW: Rescuers needed mountaineering experience to traverse into the gully to reach the scene. Richard Waugh collection

seem on the map, sheer waterfalls appear suddenly without warning, and the going is craggy, unstable and often difficult.

I began investigating where the *Kaka* could have crashed, examining the topo map and attempting to line it up with the information I found in newspaper reports of the day. But even that material seemed conflicting. I read that the site was 300 feet from the 'summit', then 500 feet, then 700 feet. I read that it was at the 'toe' of the Mangaturuturu Glacier. The mountain's ice fields are shrinking over time, so I searched for old maps that would indicate where the glacier had terminated back in the 1940s, but on maps back to 1969 the indication of the ice field hadn't changed — impossibly, it seemed always to reach to the 2200-metre mark. And what constituted the 'summit'? Did they mean the Mangaturuturu/Paretetaitonga Col, at 2600 metres, or one of the summit peaks itself, such as Paretetaitonga (2751 metres) or Te Ataahua (2757 metres)? An altitude of 150 metres makes quite a bit of difference when searching on the ground. And did they mean 300 feet in vertical distance or horizontal?

I also kept finding mentions of the location as being around 1.5 kilometres northeast of Lake Surprise. That made me suspect it wasn't in the bed of the Mangaturuturu proper but rather up on the ridge, which was contoured and featured many small gullies and dips up on its flanks. I'd found some old coordinates in the DOC archives, and they seemed to tally up with the description of the wreck in relation to Lake Surprise.

I roped in a trusting friend, Emma, to go on an overnight expedition to hunt for the wreck. We tramped in from the Ohakune Mountain Road to Mangaturuturu Hut then on and up towards Lake Surprise. There, we chose a campsite near the lake, dumped our overnight gear, and continued up on the Round the Mountain Track.

'Some of the information I found in the DOC archives said the crash site was between the Mangaturuturu and Manganuioteao streams,' I told Emma. She was incredibly patient about my propensity for backcountry haystacks, and also confident that I knew the material. Emma stared at the topo map on her phone, scrolling up and down, examining the ridges.

'The whole ridge does really stick up out of nowhere,' she said. 'It's just hard to imagine how a plane could get into here without hitting something else, though.'

We left the Round the Mountain Track and headed up the hill, making for the location I'd pinned on my map, going by the DOC coordinates. It sat on the rounded part of a ridge, and I felt that it was unlikely to be the site simply because of the shape of the terrain, but I wanted to 'clear' the area and rule it out. The reports said the plane had skidded on a flat part of the mountain, shot across the gully and smashed into a steep face; the terrain we were on didn't offer any sort of gully, and the rounded nature of the hill was angled away from the southern side where the plane would have travelled from.

'I don't think this is it,' I said.

'I don't either,' Emma agreed. 'But this bit over here, further to the east — maybe it's in there. It's a sort of gully, and a steep face.'

We climbed up the ridge, peering down into the gully, then dropped down off

ABOVE: Ray Christensen, one of the first to reach the wreck. Richard Waugh collection

BELOW: The plane hit a rock face, tearing off a wing and an engine. Richard Waugh collection

the ridge and into it, examining the ground for any sign of wreckage. I'd saved some old photos showing various rocks, bluffs and terrain features, and we lined those up with the ground we were on. The features sort of matched, but it wasn't a complete, dead-cert verdict. We gave up and returned to our campsite. That night, looking out at the lake from under the fly, we went back and forth on what we'd seen. Eventually we decided we'd probably found the site but not the wreck. We'd need to come back and check higher up the ridge, where the reports had indicated it was at the toe of the Mangaturuturu Glacier. Just in case.

Six young men from Taihape were the first to reach the site of the wreck, on 30 October 1948.[12] Rod Winchcombe was 19, and he and his mates had heard radio reports of a plane crash near Lake Surprise the weekend before. They took the Wellington–Auckland Express train from Taihape at 9 p.m., reached Ohakune at 11 p.m., and immediately set off walking up the mountain. There was no road, then — they followed the Old Blyth Track to Ohakune Hut at its former location on a ridge above the Mangawhero Falls. By the time they got there, dawn was filtering across the slopes of Ruapehu. The boys had a cup of tea at the hut and kept going.

Winchcombe and his friends had climbed the mountain before, but they only had basic equipment with them. They had no ice axes, and after a night Rod described as 'pretty frosty', the slopes were firm. One of the party slipped and was pulled up by another who was wearing better boots. It was a steep and arduous climb, and the mood among the group became increasingly sombre as they drew near to the crash site.

They reached the wreck around 9 a.m., just ahead of the main search party, which was coming in from Horopito. Winchcombe's friend Ray Christensen recorded in his diary that it was the saddest scene of his life. The aircraft was a twisted wreck and a pungent smell of fuel plagued the gully. A gap had been torn in the side of the fuselage and they could see right into it. There were no survivors. A week had passed since the crash and the bodies sat there, waiting, chilled in the spring snow.

Winchcombe snapped some photos of the wreck area, which he later sold to a newspaper. There's one with Ray Christensen in the foreground, kneeling in the snow in front of the downed plane. At first glance he looks like a wartime Air Force hero in a leather jacket. The letters 'AGK', part of the *Kaka*'s call sign, are just visible. A few heads can be seen just above the silver fuselage, glinting in the strong sun — not bodies, but rescuers planning the body retrieval. The gully is steep and fringed with bluffs. Christensen's hands are on his knees, his dark hair swept to one side. He's maybe smiling, perhaps a hint of a smile, but on second look his face is tinged with sadness. It wasn't the boys' last visit to the wreck — Winchcombe and Christensen went back several times later on and souvenired some pieces of the twisted plane.

The Otaihape Ski Club still has an old hut book where other trampers recorded their outing that night as they followed the Winchcombe party and arrived on the scene shortly after:

KAKA
NZ
NAC

> The plane a complete wreck and all passengers and crew look as though killed instantly. Large party arrive later and removes all victims who were a sight we will never forget. The plane apparently struck a rock face tore a wing and an engine off, spun around, leaving an engine halfway down, while the remainder of fuselage, wing, tail slid off. The victims were very mutilated and looked as though they didn't know what struck them.'[13]

The reality for the recovery team was far more gruesome. The only intact body was that of four-year-old Keith Collinge. Police cut the fuselage open, assembled the bodies and removed them by stretcher. Initially dragged over snow like sleds, the stretchers were then lashed to tree poles so they could be carried through the forest, and later put onto logging carts to go down the tramway to Horopito. Given the rugged nature of the terrain, the fact that the bodies were ever recovered at all is an incredible feat.

The recovery operation brought together people from the Police, Air Force, Army and Navy, as well as local bushmen, experienced mountaineers, Ruapehu mountain guides and forestry officers. A tramway existed from Cowern's Mill near Horopito, and a rough track extended into the lower Mangaturuturu Valley. They set up base camp on a plateau in the Mangaturuturu, and bushmen set about slashing a track up to Lake Surprise, hacking through dense scrub and uncooperative forest to reach the snow line.

Ruapehu was heavily coated with an unseasonable volume of snow and stood out in stark relief against a bare blue sky. Over Ruapehu's shoulder, Ngāuruhoe watched on, emitting a small but steady stream of cloud and steam, which the rescuers used as a reference for the strength of the spring wind that buffeted the mountain's slopes. The Air Force dropped stretchers, food and supplies to the base camp.

Back at Horopito, the wreckage could be seen with the naked eye as a dark spot against the whiteness of the snow. Mountain guides who had come across from the Chateau reported they'd also seen it, and it could just be made out from Ohakune.

A group of policemen were the next on the scene after Winchcombe's group. Constable Ward, Constable Adsett and a band of about 40 men arrived at around 9.15 a.m. after leaving base camp just three hours earlier. They found the victims were for the most part strapped to their seats, although some of the seats — with people attached — had been ejected from the fuselage on impact. Constable Ward wrote: 'A further painstaking search around and near the wreck digging and groping in the snow with anything we could get to shift the snow, the body of the co-pilot was eventually located almost under the tip of the starboard wing of the plane under approximately 2'6" of snow.'[14]

All the bodies were accounted for except William Mumford's. The rescuers were extremely tired, hadn't eaten for many hours, and had no tools to try to dig for him. Constable Ward gave instructions to leave, with the intention of returning to base camp before dark, with the bodies in tow.

Three days later, Constable Ward returned to the site, this time with a couple of guides: 'Snow' Mace and Franz Skadarasky. They finally found Mumford under the port wing, which had torn off and was embedded in the snow higher up the steep

Otaihape Ski Club logbook with the short narrative written by members who went to the scene. Judith Hamblyn/Otaihape Ski Club

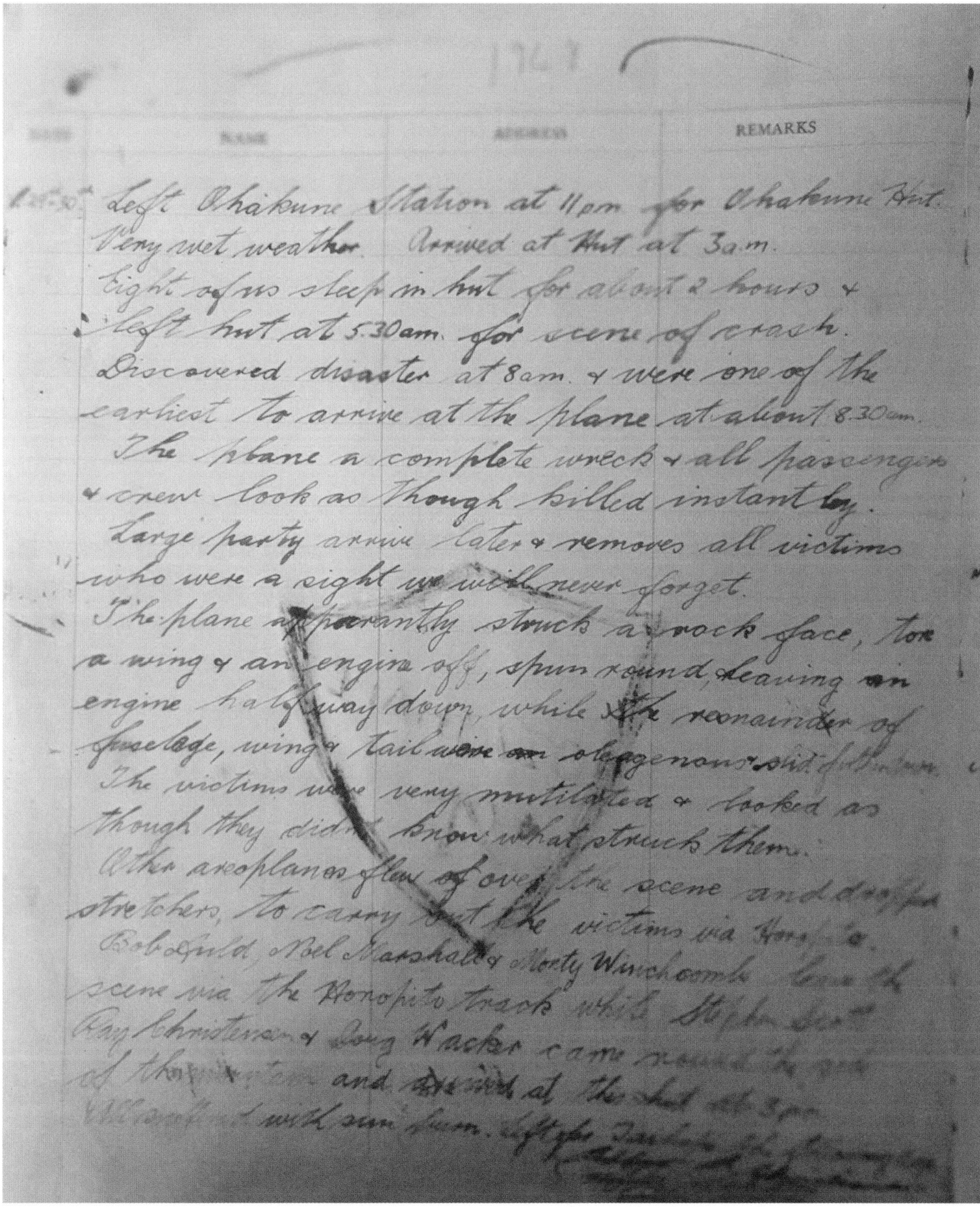

DATE	NAME	ADDRESS	REMARKS

[illegible] Left Ohakune Station at 11pm for Ohakune Hut.
Very wet weather. Arrived at Hut at 3a.m.
Eight of us sleep in hut for about 2 hours &
left hut at 5.30am. for scene of crash.
Discovered disaster at 8am. & were one of the
earliest to arrive at the plane at about 8.30am.
The plane a complete wreck & all passengers
& crew look as though killed instantly.
Large party arrive later & removes all victims
who were a sight we will never forget.
The plane apparantly struck a rock face, tore
a wing & an engine off, spun round, leaving an
engine half way down, while the remainder of
fuselage, wing & tail were on [illegible]
The victims were very mutilated & looked as
though they didn't know what struck them.
Other aeroplanes flew over the scene and dropped
stretchers, to carry out the victims via Horopito.
Bob Guild, Noel Marshall & Morty Winchcombe left the
scene via the Horopito track while Stephen Scott
Ray Christensen & Doug Wacker came round the [illegible]
of the [illegible] and arrived at the hut at 3pm
[illegible]

slope of the Mangaturuturu ridge. Constable Ward later reported that Mumford's body was covered by more than two feet of snow — much like the body of co-pilot Brian Russell. 'A great excavation had to be made before the feet could be released.' Unlike others, Mumford didn't have a seatbelt on. 'I would say that from the position of the body, relative to the lavatory fittings, water container, and also the fact of Mumford's braces being undone in front, and the buttons of his coat and vest being undone, would suggest that he had either just been or was just going to the lavatory.'[15]

The aviation industry was in its infancy in the 1930s and 1940s, and flying was a fashionable way to travel, tinged with glamour and luxury. The Electra was developed by the Lockheed Aircraft Corporation in the mid-1930s to compete with the Boeing 247 and Douglas DC-2. New Zealand's government-owned airline, NAC, purchased a fleet of Electras and named them after native birds. The *Kaka* flew alongside the *Kuaka* (godwit), the *Kahu* (hawk) and the *Kereru* (wood pigeon). The Lockheed Electra became known for another reason: it was Amelia Earhart's aircraft of choice on her ill-fated round-the-world expedition in 1937.

The *Kaka* arrived in New Zealand in 1938, was unloaded at the wharf in Wellington and taken to the local Rongotai Aerodrome for assembly. It was christened at Milson Aerodrome in Palmerston North, in what was considered 'an event of considerable importance in the world of civil aviation', attended by civic leaders 'and their wives'.[16] The *Kaka* was formally christened by aerodrome president D. F. Smillie. 'It is my great privilege to name this machine *Kaka* and may it have long, safe, and successful service,' Smillie said, as he broke the ensign from the plane.[17]

Just a month later, in November 1938, the *Kaka* was not only in service across the country, it had also established a record for speedy air travel. Aided by a 60-mile-per-hour tailwind, it managed 224 miles per hour at 8000 feet, making Wigram (Christchurch) from Dunedin in 54 minutes and beating the previous record — held by the Air Force — of 58 minutes.[18] The *Kaka* then arrived at Rongotai 23 minutes ahead of schedule. The *Kaka* performed well, alongside other Electra aircraft, throughout the Second World War.

Two and a half years before the *Kaka* crashed, the aircraft had a landing mishap in Wellington, skidding on waterlogged ground and bouncing off its proper course and over a low fence.[19] Nobody was injured, and seemingly nor were they alarmed — one woman who was carrying a basket of eggs on her lap managed to keep them all intact. The incident was attributed to the wheels skidding during braking, and although the plane was only going 10 miles per hour when it happened, the *Kaka*'s undercarriage and both propellers were damaged. The aircraft had to be pushed back to the tarmac using a crane and a bulldozer, and was prescribed four to six weeks off work.

After the crash of the *Kaka* on Ruapehu, there were two inquiries: one, to establish how and why it crashed; and the other, a parliamentary press inquiry, to appease journalists who complained that their access to the wreck site and information about the incident had been impeded.

I went to track down the inquiry reports. They were surely on record somewhere, perhaps in a cardboard box with the corners tearing, slightly dusty, new labels stuck over old ones, possibly a spider who's built a bach inside.

I located the press inquiry easily, on the Papers Past website: 'Report of Commission to Inquire into and Report on Treatment of Press Representatives: Kaka Aircraft Disaster, Laid on the Tables of Both Houses of the General Assembly by Command of His Excellency'.[20] Journalists these days are lucky if they get a free muffin at a PR launch morning tea, and here was a whole 36-page inquiry laid out for their edification.

These journalists were pretty cheesed off at the access restrictions. Police had been stationed at Cowern's Mill to head off anticipated sightseers. Women in particular weren't allowed up, and men only if they were going to help with retrieval efforts, such as scrub cutting. (You sort of sympathise with the police trying to prevent the scene from turning into a circus.) One reporter managed to get up to the base camp plateau, somehow evading the blockade, only to be told he couldn't go any further. The report is sprinkled with quotes such as 'I'm sorry, chaps, but you seem to have annoyed somebody at the Air Department' and 'I will throw you out or put you under arrest'.

In places the prose reads like a Monty Python dialogue, and in others, you can practically hear the journalists slapping each other on their robust, waistcoat-clad backs. Commissioner Harold F. Johnston eventually concluded the reporters hadn't been obstructed and were simply whingeing (my words, not his; but in my defence, I read the report so that you don't have to), and presumably needed a long lie-down after he was done. I was almost cheering by the time I got to this bit: 'Counsel for the reporters, Mr Leicester, attempted to raise the level of what are somewhat petty complaints to the ground of a fight for the constitutional and traditional rights of the press.' Too right, old chap.

I took a walk one day up Pukeonake with Conrad, aka Alpine Jesus, the policeman at National Park. Pukeonake sits alongside the road to the beginning of the Tongariro Alpine Crossing at Mangatepopo. At 1225 metres it's the lowest of all the volcanic cones on the central plateau and is hence a small hump unnoticed by most of humanity, most of the time.

We sat on the edges of the hill and got talking about a fatal mishap the previous season. A chap had gone ski touring in icy conditions, fallen and died. There were whispers locally that he was well known in the skiing and mountaineering community, but nobody knew the man's name. I hadn't thought much of it until a story appeared on the Newsroom website criticising police and conservation officials for not publicly disclosing the death. I asked Conrad for the story behind the story.

'Well, the reality was,' he said, 'we found him at 10 p.m., it was a late night and I still had to complete the paperwork for the coroner and organise mortuary procedures, so I didn't finish work until the wee hours. I was tired, I didn't see a media release as being a priority given all the other things I had to get done, and the next day I got busy with other stuff.'

Things can be made out to be much more nefarious with the help of a media headline: 'Officials quietly handle Ruapehu skiing death'.[21] Just some carefully selected words and a bit of nuance. There's actually no requirement for police to report a death to the media — people die all the time and the media have no idea.

During the *Kaka* press inquiry reporters claimed they had been subjected to 'a system of almost wartime secrecy'. I was beginning to feel that way about my quest to find concrete information about the actual location of the crash.

Both inquiries did yield more intel, however, with consistent reports that the site was at 6000 feet altitude. The press inquiry included coordinates, though the incident inquiry didn't. These were wrong, anyway, or I was misreading them — they were truncated, incomplete and showed a location over on Whakapapa that definitely wasn't correct.

Rescuers had set up their base camp at the 'plateau' near Cascade Falls, at 4500 feet (1370 metres). The first searchers left the camp at 5.30 a.m. on 30 October and reached the wreck by 9.15 a.m., then radioed back to camp and that timing was about consistent with it being in the upper Mangaturuturu. Newspaper reports couldn't always be relied on, but the incident inquiry was clear: 'The Lockheed, apparently flying on a northerly track, hit a ledge about a mile to the north of Lake Surprise and a little below the level of a main mountain spur running to the west . . . Many considered that the aircraft first struck and slid across a small flat area and then shot across a two-chain [40-metre] wide gap to hit squarely a sheer face.' The port wing remained on a ledge, while the fuselage was dashed into a deep gully 50 feet below. The debris was scattered over hundreds of metres. And the engines were still there, initially, with one buried in the snow.

Reaching the wreck in 1948 required experience moving on ice and snow. It had crashed in a gully, sure, but the searchers weren't sure which one, so they climbed the steep Mangaturuturu Ridge until they could see the deep, V-shaped gully it sat in. The press claimed that the aircraft had crashed between the Manganuioteao and Mangaturuturu streams; the former was the next catchment to the west, so I had an idea the wreck would be higher up on the ridge itself rather than in the bed of the Mangaturuturu proper.

I gleaned further details: there was no sign of life; the aircraft was completely wrecked, but wasn't burnt out; the only recognisable portion of the aircraft was the compound tail unit. And rescuers had dropped permanganate of potash to mark the scene of the crash. (That's a chemical with many uses: it can be employed as an emergency snow signal, because of its bright violet hue, but also works as an anti-fungal treatment — Canadian soldiers used it during the First World War to prevent STIs, but its lack of effectiveness merely resulted in purple-stained genitalia.)

Beyond the inquiries, there must have been more on record. I contemplated the Civil Aviation Authority but instead put in a research request to Airways New Zealand, which bumped it to an organisation I had never heard of but was enthused to discover: the Transport Accident Investigation Commission. I got access to their archives and combed through the material, which largely consisted of correspondence, newspaper clippings and some astounding photographs from the site. I read of how the victims' watches were removed by investigators to determine the time of the crash, and how that information was withheld from angry journalists. Somewhat crucially, Captain Max Hare had picked up the papers with the weather forecast before the flight but didn't wait for a briefing or look at the weather map. That morning, he'd flown southbound over the route, and remarked to the duty forecaster that he'd skirted one of the biggest thunderstorms he'd ever seen in the area.[22]

It also seemed that the mail on board the *Kaka* finally arrived some weeks after the aircraft had taken off for its final ill-fated flight. A member of the search party who was a former Post Office employee had gathered up the mail at the wreck site and handed it to the postmaster at Raetihi. There were 44 letters, and the addresses could still be read on the fronts of the envelopes.[23]

Archives New Zealand yielded a small amount of information, but one box of papers had been sealed for 100 years to 'protect the privacy of natural persons', so I applied to the police for access. (I'd done this once before for research purposes, jumped through several hoops, and found the information to be both boring and unhelpful.) I also contacted aviation historian the Reverend Dr Richard Waugh, who had written a book on the Electra aircraft. He had also organised a commemorative service to mark the fiftieth anniversary of the accident, which included placing a memorial plaque at the Round the Mountain Track entrance on the Ohakune Mountain Road. Among the wide-ranging material he sent me were many photos, including one of the wreck taken in 1970, and I had to admit there wasn't a lot left.

In 1998 Waugh was interviewed on the current affairs show *20/20* for the crash's fiftieth anniversary. He advocated for the pilots by pointing out that more recent investigations revealed some critical factors that had likely contributed to the accident. The officially sanctioned route went unnecessarily close to the mountains and beneath the summit of Ruapehu. Some experienced pilots were dissatisfied with the route and had developed their own 'dog leg' change to ensure a greater safety margin, he said. Captain Hare was new to the route, and may not have been conversant with this practice. The weather was more extreme and variable than forecast. It was consequently suggested that navigation drift calculations may have been affected, and the influence of electrical storms was raised. Waugh also explained that in 1948 the Lockheed was already obsolete, had relatively low power, a poor rate-of-climb, and had no de-icing equipment, meaning the aircraft and those on board were vulnerable on such a demanding air route in poor weather.

Seventeen years later another TV documentary about the *Kaka* was produced, one of a series called *Descent from Disaster*. It wasn't available online so I requested a viewing at the audiovisual archive Ngā Taonga Sound & Vision in Wellington. Fittingly, the programme is narrated by Jim Hickey, a former weatherman and a pilot. Jim is shown climbing up to the site of the crash on the mountain, telling the camera, 'It's a tragic yet intriguing story. It's hard not to be affected yourself.' There's a craggy ridge on the skyline. They hit the rock face suddenly, Jim says, and points to the ridge.

'The wreck of the *Kaka*, of course, was never removed from the mountain. And over

ABOVE: Access to the site is difficult, so few photos exist of the wreck over the years. This one is from March 1970. Jim Sullivan, Richard Waugh collection

BELOW: By 1970, little remained of the wreck. Jim Sullivan, Richard Waugh collection

the decades, the combined weight of snow, and of course, avalanches of rock, and snow melt, pushed and crushed the aircraft debris into the valleys, into the ravines, and it's slowly working its way down into the waterways. A silent testimony, if you like, to what happened, back in 1948.' Jim looks meaningfully at the camera, the snow-flecked mountain behind him, a green beanie on, jacket and pack. He smiles — sympathetic, empathetic, friendly Jim who is informing you the weather tomorrow will be bad but he's got your back. He's the perfect person to front this episode.

So why did a plane just smash into the side of a mountain? The official report lists 'causes which can be eliminated': radio failure, constructional defects, engine failure, instrument defects, meteorological hazards, loss of control, and meteorological forecasting errors. Then, 'causes which cannot be eliminated', and there is just one: navigational errors. The aircraft flew 'an erroneous course', causing it to hit the mountain. The inquiry concluded that the captain had made an error in calculating the aircraft's course, and no other factors had contributed to the accident.

After the *Descent from Disaster* documentary screened, Jim Hickey publicly disagreed with the official line that the pilot alone was to blame. He told the *Ruapehu Bulletin* that it was a classic case of an accident waiting to happen. 'They were flying a plane that was ill-equipped for the conditions. They shouldn't have been flying in those conditions. They were getting far more sideways drift than they thought.' And that put them on a path to smash into the mountain. The thunderstorms would have interfered with the plane's compass, and the aircraft was underpowered for the job. 'The poor old captain was on a hiding to nothing.'[24]

I tracked down the director/producer of *Descent from Disaster*, Ross Peebles, to ask if they had indeed found the wreck during filming. Peebles said his understanding was that there's no 'wreck' as such left. 'Over the years snow and ice have broken it up into probably hundreds of pieces and it's gradually spreading itself over the area,' he told me. 'We spoke to people who said there are pieces that can occasionally turn up in the river or at waterfalls beneath the crash site, but they're rarely seen. We filmed on the mountain side and looked pretty hard to find any evidence of the aircraft, but didn't find anything.'

Enough information. Actually, too much information. It was time to go hunting again.

Once again Emma and I donned pack and boots to search for the wreck, managing to align our calendars with a weather window. This time we were armed with much more information. I'd pinpointed where I thought the wreck was, based on the photos I'd found in the archives at the Transport Accident Investigation Commission, and on the episode of *Descent from Disaster*. We set off from Tūroa early in the morning, traversing out towards the upper Mangaturuturu catchment, tackling gullies and navigating around bluffs. Sunshine was forecast until midday, then we'd be battling showers and cloud, reducing visibility. Cyclone Gabrielle had left its mark on the country not long before, and the mountain was still exuding its precipitation — the Mangaturuturu is dotted with waterfalls, and they were all popping and cascading.

We peered up and down each gully in turn, wondering 'could this be it?'. But we always moved on, knowing that the gully in question had to be hard up against the major Mangaturuturu ridge. The photos showed an intimidatingly steep snow slope on one side, and none of the smaller gullies suggested that. Matching up terrain features with the historic photos had the potential to be misleading — the gullies were all filled with a winter's worth of snow when the pics were taken. We were searching in March after a bad snow year, with tiny snow patches up high and Ruapehu's 'glaciers' small enough to require quote marks around them.

I stopped just before we reached the final ring of bluffs into our target gully. I was standing in a wide expanse of smooth rock rather than scoria, a line of bluffs running down the mountain on one side, and another line on the other.

'This would fill up with snow pretty well in winter, I reckon,' I said to Emma.

She looked around and nodded in agreement. 'It could be the "flat spot" the plane skidded on. Doesn't look flat now, but it would be once the snow piled up and filled it in a bit.'

The bluffs along the gully made it impossible to enter at the bottom end, and looking at the historic pics had made me wonder if we'd be able to get into it at all. The guys who were first on the scene had come in the same way, but the snow would have helped lay a path for them in and out, while we just had bare rock and an environment that had surely changed over time. We scrambled up the ridge along the bluffs, peering over the edges to see if we could spot a way down that didn't present too much risk. Emma found one, a big blocky step, but I knew I'd be too short to get down it.

'We'll manage it,' Emma said, and made for the step. I froze, clung to the scoria and looked up towards the summit of Paretetaitonga hundreds of metres above us. A shivery chill ran over me, a sudden, inexplicable 'no' feeling about the rock step. I've learned the hard way to honour those feelings when they come to me, especially in the wilderness.

'I can't go that way,' I called out. 'I just can't do it. Let's look further up the bluffs and see what we can find.' I could see a point where the bluffs pinched in towards the terrain in the gully and was hopeful there'd be an easier way there. I became fixated on that spot. Emma must've heard the resolve in my voice, and agreed to continue our search.

Further up the ridge I was arrested by the sight of an unmistakably man-made structure in the wilderness. Someone had piled rocks up neatly on top of a small boulder sitting on the ridge. I looked around — all the other rocks in the vicinity seemed to be placed sporadically, not carefully piled up. I looked back. Emma's attention was buried in a topo map on her phone.

'Hey Emma!' I called. 'Look at this!'

She legged it up. 'That's definitely not a natural structure,' she said. 'Okay, the wreck must've been here then. Look — this is all a flat area just here where the plane maybe skidded, and those bluffs across there would match up with the ones in the photos.'

We looked at each other, excited. We were surely right on it. Now we just had to get down into the gully.

Emma seemed prepared to give up on finding a bluff entrance where we were and return to the previous blocky step, but I wanted to search a little further. I went to the spot I'd fixated on, up onto a rock that looked deeply unlikely to allow us access, just making a final check of the boxes. Peering over, I saw a few small ledges, just enough to get a foothold, and not so far away that my short legs wouldn't reach.

'Yeah, it'll go,' I called out.

Emma went first, descending step after step down through the bluffs. More confident on steep terrain, she was well ahead of me when I stopped to breathe a bit and look around. Something blue and white caught my eye to my left, inside a hole in the rocks. I turned my head fully towards it, registered that it was another human sign in an off-track area of a national park that people seldom visited, and the same cold chill as before ran all over my body.

'Emma, come back up here! I've found something. I don't know what, but it's something.'

She scrambled back up, looked at the thing. 'Wow, that'd be hard to spot.'

I went to pull it out, and as soon as my fingers made contact with it, my fingertips filled with electricity. My hand buzzed, and I pulled it away. Whatever it was, it was hard to the touch, and whoever had put it there had done so with the assumption it would never be disturbed.

'I can't do it,' I said. 'I can't touch it. You do it.'

Emma grasped the thing and pulled it out, grating pieces of flaking, decaying plastic bag on the scoria. Whatever it was, it was wrapped in several bread bags, Molenberg brand, an older design. Each bag had been put into another bag so that whatever it was had multiple protective layers.

I thought it was a skull, but thankfully it wasn't.

Emma pulled off a layer of disintegrating bread bag, unrolled the top of the innermost one and looked in. She reached in and pulled out a chunk of something hard, a small chink of the greater whole.

'It's someone's ashes,' she said.

'I wonder how long that's been there. Can you turn it over, I'll see if there's an expiry date on the bag.'

She rotated the bag carefully and I examined it. The inner bag was in perfect condition, as if it had come off the shelf yesterday. Then I realised, 'Oh, it won't have an expiry date, actually. They stamp the date on the tag, not on the bag. Oh well.'

As Emma rotated the bag back, I noticed something was printed on one side. 'Wait, what's that?' There were the words 'Fun Climb', and the outline of a rock climber. Underneath was a date: 2001. The ashes could have been there for 22 years. Ashes, stashed in a place many hours' walk from anywhere, at a spot where 13 people had perished. It couldn't be a coincidence — this had to be related to the crash of the *Kaka*.

ABOVE: The first pieces of the wreck we found during our 2023 trip to the site.

BELOW: Barbara Morris on an earlier trip to the site, with some of the same pieces we found in 2023. Barbara Morris collection

After putting the ashes back and apologising silently to the deceased person for having disturbed their slumber, we climbed down to the stream bed and began hunting for signs of the wreck. There were none. We were both certain we were on the spot where it had crashed, going by certain rock features towering above us and a slight bend in the gully.

'I suppose that where it crashed and where the wreckage ended up could be two different sites,' I said. 'It would've sat on top of a whole season's snowpack, and as that melted, it probably shifted down the stream bed. So it could be maybe 200 metres, maybe a kilometre down. But it's unlikely that it crashed here and stayed right here while the snow melted.'

Emma wanted to stop for lunch. We were in the wind, I thought. 'Let's just go down there a wee bit, it'll be more sheltered,' I said.

'Sure,' she agreed, 'but I also want to be high enough that we can look down the exit of the gully and compare photos.' She had a good point. The historic photos showed several features of the terrain in the horizon looking down the gully, with some distinctive rock outcrops. We'd tried to match these up at the other site without success, but maybe we'd get a match here in the gully.

I chose a spot with a couple of obliging rocks for seats. We'd both settled in and pulled out our lunch when Emma cried out and pointed at something a few metres directly below us. There, sitting on a rock, as if someone had placed it right there for us to find, was a collection of metal pieces. We were both gripped with excitement that we'd finally found signs of the *Kaka*, but rendered sombre by the background knowledge that 13 people had lost their lives here. We snapped some pics of the metal with the waterfalls of the upper Mangaturuturu in the background, marked the find on the topo map, then returned to our lunch.

'I could send photos to Richard Waugh and see if he thinks it's the *Kaka*,' I said. But there was no need. Leaving the site, we found sprinklings of metal down the gully, some of it no bigger than a coin and the biggest perhaps the size of an A3 sheet of paper. We stumbled upon obvious remnants where a human had gone before us. Someone had collected up metal sheets from the fuselage like a teacher taking in work for marking. In one place they were pinned down by a large rock, and in another they were wedged in between a rock and a boulder.

I'd been an unbeliever when told there wouldn't be much left of the *Kaka*. How could a giant aircraft just disintegrate into nothingness? Surely we'd find a significant section of the fuselage, as it appeared in the 1970 photo from Richard Waugh. Surely we'd find the engine blocks, sitting in the stream bed, wedged up against a boulder. Once I was in the gully and down in the stream bed, comprehension dawned. Sections of sand had washed down the catchment and come to rest in the stream, and from one side constant rockfall and splintered lava would easily cover the wreck. From the other side, huge chunks had fallen off the bluffs and smashed into the ground below. We could see recent activity, probably from an earthquake I'd felt at home in Ohakune just a couple of weeks earlier.

In reality, the wreck had been ground to pieces by nature. Ashes to ashes, dust to dust.

We reached the bottom of the gully, marking the end of our search. We'd found enough to know it was the remnants of the *Kaka*'s body, and it felt inappropriate to continue disturbing terrain where souls had departed the earth. Spirits fly up and down that gully, sending chills over the bodies of humans who go in there. Some places are better left as sacred earth in memory of those unlucky people.

Emma found a way up through the bluffs, a little gap requiring some level-five climbing moves and a shimmy and a wiggle. I handed my tramping poles up to her to free up my hands. At the top, my heartbeat pounded in my ears. Emma pointed out another cairn, this one just three rectangular rocks piled directly on top of each other, more of a marker of the route into the gully than a memorial cairn like the other one. We'd found a lot more human sign than anticipated on this trip. Human sign that had persisted.

On top of the bluffs, we took a snack break. 'The ashes,' Emma said. 'Maybe that's one of the people who died in the wreck. And they were cremated, and the family has held on to Grandma or Grandpa for years, and finally the grandkids have decided to return them to the spot where they died.'

'Could be,' I said. 'The ashes would've initially been in something else, right? Even a paper bag. It's weird that they're in a Molenberg bag. The ashes must've been transferred into that from something else. Are we sure they're human? Not a pet? I reckon it weighed about two kilograms.'

Emma agreed, and searched online: 'What do human ashes look like?' The photos looked exactly like what we'd found in the bread bag. 'Human ashes weigh around three to four kilograms for an adult male and two to three kilograms for an adult female.'

She looked up, as rain sprayed us momentarily from above, although we were in bright sunshine. 'That would match the weight of that bag — probably around two kilograms.'

'On scenarios,' I said, thinking out loud, 'it could be, say, the wife of a man who died in the crash, and she wanted to be left at the same place where he'd died.'

I wondered, also, if whoever had left the ashes there wasn't very emotionally attached to the person and was simply carrying out their wishes for where they'd like to rest for eternity. I'm not sure I could leave a loved one's ashes inside a bread bag. Or it could've been so windy on the day that they elected to stash them rather than spreading them.

'They could've been put in the bread bag back in 2001 but not placed there until more recently, too,' Emma said. 'We know they were put there after 2001, and probably not within the past few years, given how the outer bag had broken down. But if they were placed around 2001, that lines up with it being someone who was an adult at the time of the crash. Maybe in their twenties or thirties, and they died in 2001 aged 80 or so.'

When I got home I chased DOC for any guidance on scattering ashes in a national park. There didn't seem to be anything in the management plan (which expired in 2016). A spokesperson told me it wasn't prohibited by law but it did require consultation with the relevant iwi, depending on which part of the park you were talking about. In the past, they said, iwi had been strongly opposed to the idea, as the maunga are considered sacred from the peak to the borders of the park.

Our thinking has come a long way. Ohakune local Allan Whale scattered his mother's ashes in the Crater Lake back in 1995. His mother had climbed Ruapehu 13 times and had specifically requested that her ashes be scattered there. It was 23 September, her birthday (she would've been 80). Allan remarked to the pilot on how the crater lake had been warming up recently — the temperature, usually between 10 and 40 degrees, had risen to 48 degrees just three days before. 'She's going to have words with somebody,' Allan said (referring presumably to the mountain, not to his deceased mother). 'Either everything's going to go dead quiet, or it's really going to blow.'[25] Just two hours after Allan tipped the ashes out of the aircraft and into the crater lake, the mountain erupted, the ash reaching up to 10 kilometres in radius.[26]

After our successful — finally successful! — trip to find the wreck, I was fizzing, so stoked, in fact, I wanted to tell everyone. It was hard to keep my mouth shut and I was motivated only by the lure of saving my stories and corralling them into a book. Neatly lining them up, placing them on the page and making sense of it all. Finally closing the chapter on the wreck of the *Kaka*, high on Ruapehu, a sudden end, a long weekend cut short on a stormy day in October 1948.

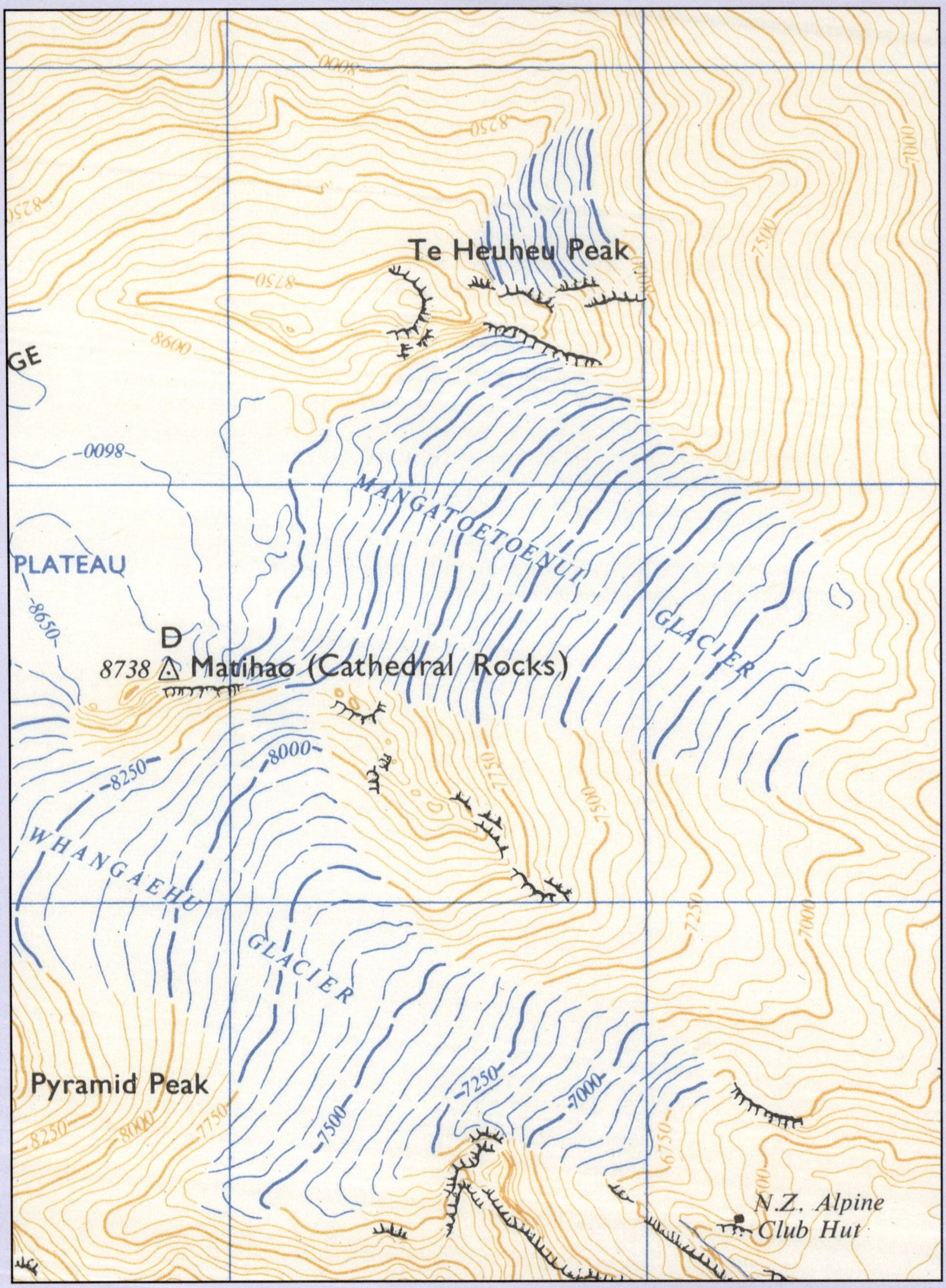

Te Heuheu Peak
GE
PLATEAU
MANGATOETOENUI GLACIER
8738 Matihao (Cathedral Rocks)
WHANGAEHU GLACIER
Pyramid Peak
N.Z. Alpine Club Hut

Map showing the Mangatoetoenui Glacier, which swallowed the wreck of the aircraft for many years. National Library of New Zealand, 23363041_1964

CHAPTER 8

A plane wreck hidden for decades

In 1951 an Air Force aircraft smashed into Te Heuheu peak, killing the three people on board. Snow covered the wreck almost immediately and it became part of the Mangatoetoenui Glacier. Thirty-two years later, the glacier finally spat out the wreck, and today it's well off the white ice, embedded in rocks.

The Airspeed Consul NZ1902 in service. Air Force Museum of New Zealand

The 1950s was an era of postwar relief and occasional glamour, a time when visitors flooded to Tongariro National Park in search of authentic backcountry skiing and tramping experiences. Ruapehu was centre stage in the North Island's era of the mountain guide, rugged, strong men with superior outdoors knowledge, called upon by tourists for their services. Such guides usually took up residence at the Chateau as part of their employment — somewhere to live, and somewhere to stash their long wooden-handled ice axes and coils of rope.

Noel Kerr was one such guide, and in 1951 he was living at the Chateau while working with Swiss ski instructor Walter Haensli to map out ski runs on the central plateau volcanoes. Haensli was a gun skier and Kerr was no less of a weapon on the snow; in 1949 Kerr had won the North Island championship at Mount Egmont, and he went on to win the Dominion Championships on Ruapehu against skiers from all around New Zealand and Australia.

Kerr, like Joe Blyth in his time, knew the volcanoes of the national park intimately, their ridges and valleys, their rivers and streams, the secrets and the treasures. On 11 December 1951, he was guiding clients on Ruapehu and had reached about 2100 metres when he paused to listen to an aircraft flying on the mountain's eastern side. It seemed to be travelling in a south–north direction. The sound died away, and Kerr continued, but tucked the observation away in the back of his mind.

Later, when a plane was reported missing, Kerr conveyed the information and along with other guides scaled Ruapehu with ice axe in hand and coils of rope to search for the aircraft — and, they hoped, the survivors.

On the morning of 11 December, Royal New Zealand Air Force flight NZ1902 had been flying from Wigram to Rukuhia, just south of Hamilton, on a mission to pick up urgently needed spare parts. The aircraft was an Airspeed Consul, a twin-engine light transport aircraft and a conversion of the Airspeed Oxford, a military trainer used during the Second World War. The pilot was 28-year-old Flight Lieutenant Pat Goddard, who was flanked in the cockpit by Sergeant Francis Stark, 37, and Sergeant Reginald Shelton, 31. They stopped to refuel at RNZAF Station Ohakea, near Palmerston North, where Goddard made a slip-up: he neglected to ask for an updated forecast.

Cloud was banking up in the central North Island, but Goddard simply refuelled and continued.

The plane was reported missing after it left Ohakea, sparking a five-day search over a wide area, up as far as Lake Taupō and across the Kaimanawa Range. It was assumed something had gone wrong in the vicinity of Ruapehu. Searchers were hopeful of finding the three men alive — they were, after all, Air Force chaps, knowledgeable and fit. The missing aircraft carried a rubber dinghy with emergency supplies, a first-aid kit, compass and food. If the airmen weren't seriously injured, and if the supply kit hadn't been burned, they could make their way out to safety. They were trained for such an eventuality. But still, they didn't show.

Kerr and other guides continued to search the mountain on foot, battling bad weather. If the aircraft he'd heard on 11 December hadn't struck a peak, it would have been on the northern side of the mountain, Kerr reasoned. The search was the biggest air search in New Zealand's history, with close cooperation between police, pilots searching from the air, mountain guides and volunteers. But it was hampered by typical bad Ruapehu weather — deep snow, drifting mist and freezing winds.

Early on 15 December the weather finally cleared enough to see properly from the air. Flight Lieutenant J. W. B. Cook, piloting an Auster aircraft, spotted something high up on the Mangatoetoenui Glacier, covered in recent snow. He recorded its position and dropped them by parachute to Kerr, who was searching just a few miles away. The item was at the head of the glacier, approximately 250 metres of horizontal distance below the summit of Te Heuheu, one of Ruapehu's distinctive summit peaks at 2732 metres. The wreckage of the aircraft sat on a flatter piece of terrain at around 2600 metres altitude.

Kerr reached the wreckage swiftly, finding it almost completely blanketed by fresh snow. He established there were no survivors and left for the Chateau to communicate the find. From there, six guides — all volunteers in the recovery — joined Kerr on foot, using ice axes, ropes, skis and crampons, and struggling through deep snow and slippery, ice-clad rocks. Flight Lieutenant Cook dropped shovels to the team of guides on the glacier and they dug through the heavy snow to unearth the wreckage. It had broken into pieces when it hit the mountain, and they soon realised that the wreckage was scattered over a wide area — wings, fuselage, tail unit and instruments were discovered down the slope. Only one engine was found, and it was assumed the other had rolled down the mountain.

Kerr found two bodies near the middle of the wreck, and the team found the third further down the slope. It was clear that their deaths had been instantaneous. The guides brought the bodies back down to the Chateau, Kerr doing multiple trips on the same day. They examined the sloping glacier and concluded the aircraft had grazed the mountain before coming to a stop. It had failed to clear the crest of Te Heuheu peak by only 15 metres. Had it been a few metres higher, or to the left or the right, they would have survived.

Conditions were so challenging that one of the rescuers later said: 'Up there you could not even hold a cigarette, let alone light one.'[1]

Investigations naturally followed, and a Court of Inquiry concluded in January 1952, but no single predominant cause could be identified. The final conclusion, as reported in the press, was that the accident was caused, ultimately, by 'poor airmanship': 'The pilot must be held blameworthy.'[2]

I jumped through a few of the usual hoops to get the report from the Court of Inquiry, and an Official Information Act request eventually yielded the conclusions. Some were obvious. The aircraft had hit 50 feet below Te Heuheu peak on Ruapehu while flying in cloud. Goddard hadn't checked for a fresh forecast when he refuelled at Ohakea. Locals around Ohakune and National Park had reported a low-flying aircraft on different courses that morning. 'It appears that the pilot flew round the Ohakune-National Park area for approximately 45 minutes to find a way through to Rukuhia under the lowering cloud base. Unfortunately, he selected a course that led the aircraft into Mount Ruapehu,' the report observed.[3]

The Court of Inquiry put on record its appreciation of those who had helped in the search and recovery including 'the Chateau guides, who carried out arduous searches on difficult terrain and in bad weather conditions'. Noel Kerr emerged as something of a hero. 'Particular mention is made of Mr N.I. Kerr who spent three long consecutive days on the mountain and made two return trips to the wreckage the day it was discovered. Mr Kerr also guided the Court of Inquiry to the scene of the crash, and conducted the party safely home under extremely adverse and dangerous weather conditions.'[4]

Nothing more was to be done with the wreckage. 'Aircraft is a total write-off,' the report concluded. The crash site made it difficult, if not impossible, to recover the remnants of the wreck, and the snow that fell almost immediately after the accident compounded the problem. In winter the glacier was snowed under, while in summer it was a deserted, desolate landscape.

I first discovered that the wreck existed when I was attempting to find out how fast the glaciers move on Ruapehu. I came across a 1988 paper that mentioned the wreck of NZ1902, citing a researcher who in 1984 had used the reported positions of the remnants to calculate a flow rate for the Mangatoetoenui Glacier of 10–20 metres per

CLOCKWISE FROM RIGHT: Rob McCallum inspecting pieces of the wreck given up by the glacier in the 1980s. Harry Keys collection; a photo taken by Noel Kerr upon reaching the wreck, which had been covered in snow and became consumed by the glacier. Te Heuheu peak is in the background. Noel Kerr; pieces of the wreck beginning to emerge from the glacier in the 1980s. Harry Keys collection

ABOVE: One of the Airspeed Consul engines, with what's left of the retreating Mangatoetoenui Glacier, and Te Heuheu peak above.

BELOW: The other engine, firmly wedged against a rock.

year. By 1984, the wreck had moved 350 metres vertically downhill from its original position. After it had been snowed on and become embedded in the glacial ice, it shifted down the mountain as the ice flowed.[5]

The incident didn't seem to have been extensively covered back in 1951, certainly not to the extent given to the crisis of the *Kaka* in 1948. Possibly, the deaths of three air force men in an aircraft didn't shock the nation in the same way 11 civilian passengers and two pilots had. I found little in newspaper archives, and although the Transport Accident Investigation Commission was helpful, it was ultimately up to the Defence Force to decide what they would tell me.

I went a little further and asked questions of the photo archivists at the *New Zealand Herald* and the news organisation Stuff. I'd found only one photo of the wreck when it was discovered, showing a tangled mess embedded in the snow with two pairs of skis planted upright uphill of the wreck. Te Heuheu peak was clearly identifiable in the background. Did an original still exist? I hoped so, and it did. The *Herald*'s archivists told me it was snapped by Noel Kerr himself. On the back of the original print is written: 'Wreck of Consul aircraft below Te Heuheu peak, Ruapehu. Photo taken early Sat (Dec 15) morning. If used pay £1-1-0 to Mr Noel Kerr, Chateau, National Park.'

The archivists said it was likely the *Herald* had syndicated the image on behalf of Kerr, who was the first person on site after the crash. The *Herald* would have used the image until it could get its own photographer there — which, given the terrain, was unlikely to happen. They had no further images of the crash, and it seemed no other media had been interested enough to pursue the story, or perhaps the Air Force had discouraged coverage.

I tried to find Noel Kerr, in the admittedly unlikely event that he was still around today, to ask permission to use the photo. He'd been a lifetime member of one ski club and belonged to several others. A few leads proved fruitless, but then one club came back to me: Kerr died in the 1980s and had no descendants or next of kin. He'd been a confirmed bachelor, perhaps married to the mountain.

I researched the wreck further, wanting to find it for myself if there was anything left. I discovered a citation via the National Library for a story that had appeared in *New Zealand Aviation News* in 2010, but I couldn't find the original piece. *Aviation News* had become part of the *National Business Review* media family, and as an *NBR* alum — I'd worked on the publication for several years as a business journalist — I contacted the editor and asked if he could send me a copy. Journalist Brian Leach had found the wreck in the summer of 2010.[6]

'Half buried in the rubble of the mountain are two corroded radial aeroplane engines, their aluminium fixed pitch propellers bent grotesquely in mute testament to a violent impact,' Leach wrote.

The piece included several photos of the engines. In one taken looking downhill towards Tukino ski field, the engine was hard up against the uphill side of a huge rock. Another engine was embedded in the rocks of a small stream, with Te Heuheu ridge and some perennial snow visible in the background. Leach had also found further pieces of the wreck, including small pieces of wood with metal fittings attached. None

of it had rotted, incredibly; Leach thought that the fungus that causes timber to rot couldn't live in such a cold alpine environment.

Leach reckoned neither engine had struck solid rock, as they were largely undamaged aside from the extremely bent propellers. Both engines were located 200–300 metres further down the slope from the rest of the wreck. Leach theorised that the engines hadn't been moved down by the glacial ice, but rather had simply bounced further down the slope than the rest of the aircraft after it broke up. That would be consistent with Kerr's experience of being unable to find one of the engines.

'The leading edges of the propellers are undamaged,' Leach wrote. 'They may have just clipped the peak and then crashed lower down on the glacier with the props cutting into the ice while still moving forward, which may explain how the tips got rolled up.'

Leach's photos would help me to find the wreck, but I still needed better intel. I messaged a well-known mountaineer who had apparently been to find the wreck and asked if he'd be happy to supply me with coordinates or an altitude to shoot for. He supplied them willingly, but when I entered the coordinates they persisted in turning up a location on the western side of National Park, at Fisher's Track, nowhere near where the wreck would be. I assumed I was incompetent at reading coordinates — that I was doing it wrong — and was too embarrassed to go back to him and query his information.

I later got a grid reference from some material in the DOC archives, and a rough altitude pointer from another mountaineering acquaintance. It was on.

I went searching one summer weekend with a friend who found the idea of a lost wreck below a glacier as intriguing as I did. We tramped up to Whangaehu Hut for a night, walking past small patches of hardy snow on the way, patches that would be gone in another week. I'd never been up this side of Ruapehu in the summer and it looked vastly different, almost violent. Near the hut, the Whangaehu River gouges through the landscape, scouring rocks and cliffs as the water persistently descends. The colours are at once starkly contrasting but somehow also the same — everything is brown, but in vastly different shades, from beige to ochre and Martian red.

Whangaehu Hut (opened in 1964 by good Sir Ed himself) is perched on a sheer cliff high above the Whangaehu catchment. Let's just say you wouldn't want to sleepwalk. We sunbaked outside the hut, drinking hot chocolates and staring at the mesmerising landscape as the sun began to dip below the ridge. In spite of being full summer, it was cold, and we were clad in puffer jackets, long pants and beanies. A starry night gave way to a blazing fireball sunrise, and we were soon on our way to wreck-hunt. We sidled over towards the Mangatoetoenui Glacier, gaining around 100 metres of vertical ascent on the way. Cold temperatures yielded to summer sun, and the glacier-fed streams began to beckon as I sweated uncomfortably.

We tramped over to the 2200-metre level where we thought the wreck could be and used Leach's photos to try to line up rock features that would help us manoeuvre into the right position. False alarms abounded, as the rusty landscape made it almost impossible to pick out anything man-made. Then we began to spot a trail of tiny slivers of what could have been wreckage. We were almost right on top of one of the engines before we realised what it was. The lower engine was in the same position as in Leach's photos from 2010, at a hard stop on the uphill side of a big rock. Eventually we found the other engine, thoroughly stuck in a stream bed and surrounded by rocks that wouldn't move.

Both engines had probably travelled 400 metres downhill from their original position and they were well off the glacial ice, which had retreated unthinkable amounts. The topographic map indicates the glacier reaches down to 2180 metres today, but I'd estimate it's more like 2500 metres, possibly 2400 metres at a push.

We found more pieces — mechanical parts, wood, unidentifiable crumpled metal items — but nothing that specifically looked like the fuselage proper. It's possible that more of the wreckage exists up high, concealed in what's left of the Mangatoetoenui Glacier.

Although I hadn't been able to use the coordinates, I messaged the mountaineer to say thanks for helping me. 'Yep,' he wrote back. 'I was holding back on you. I didn't want to fully erode the quality of your adventure.' I was initially shocked that he'd seemingly been happy to insert a stick in the spokes of the wheel by supplying the wrong coordinates, but when our paths crossed a year or so later in a ski lodge and I mentioned it, he was appalled. 'I got the coordinates from someone else and they were in an old format,' he said. 'I didn't even think to check them.' He'd only wanted me to jump through the hoop of converting the coordinates.

In September 1988, two mountaineers visited the RNZAF Museum at Wigram and happened to mention to staff there that the remains of an aircraft were starting to emerge from the face of the Mangatoetoenui Glacier on Ruapehu. This was exciting news. The museum staff were hoping to build and display an Airspeed Consul at the museum, but as the aircraft had been largely constructed from wood, any remaining examples had decayed over time and were almost impossible to reconstruct. Metal parts were scarce, too. NZ1902 held great possibilities, and the Air Force obviously had visions of a slightly damaged but salvageable aircraft that would soon be delivered by the glacier, preserved and whole. (They would, of course, be thoroughly disappointed.)

Staff at the museum called the Chief Conservation Officer in Ohakune, then followed up with a formal letter. They were interested in removing the aircraft, which, they stuffily warned DOC, still belonged to the Air Force: 'As an aside the aircraft, or wreckage, still remains the property of the RNZAF and I have enclosed a pamphlet outlining this for your interest.'

The letter reeked of officialdom — the Air Force was clearly used to talking down to other departments and giving instructions. 'At this stage it is our intention to wait till the end of the snow thaw, and then seek approval to use a helicopter to evaluate and remove as much of the wreckage as possible. You may wish to comment on this.'[7]

I hope DOC sent the Air Force an invoice for parking it on the Mangatoetoenui Glacier for 37 years.

A pamphlet outlining the obligations of groups wanting to remove wreckages was indeed attached, and I managed to access that too. Clearly, interest in crashed aircraft belonging to the military was so strong that a guidance paper was needed. And ownership was everything: 'Crashed military aircraft and their equipment are never abandoned by the Crown although, in some instances, even when their whereabouts is known, a decision has been taken not to recover them. They always remain the property of the Crown.'[8]

The guidance was extensive: any group wanting to recover a wreck had to get the Crown's consent. Any human remains must not be touched and should be treated with due respect, their discovery reported immediately to the Ministry of Defence. No information about the discovery of human remains could be given out to the media until facts had been confirmed. Any exciting or valuable items also belonged to Defence or the police. And so on.

A DOC staff member responded dutifully, including photos of the site of the wreckage from autumn that year. 'The wreckage shifts downhill gradually at up to three metres per year,' they wrote. 'It also rises and falls within the ice but has surfaced the last two consecutive summers and again with a poor snow year this year, there is every chance it will do so again in 1989.'

In May 1988 visible wreckage included port and starboard flaps and assemblies, the centre control console and instrumentation, vast amounts of cable, wire hoses and lines in tangled disarray, and up to a hundred pieces of all shapes and sizes, but none more than a metre in length. The wreck sat at 2300 metres in the middle of the glacier. Crampons and axes were essential, DOC warned.

It seemed that DOC was entirely happy for the Air Force to attempt to extricate a plane wreck from the glacier — or at least to stand by and watch with a box of popcorn as they did so. The letter continued: 'With some chipping of ice it may be possible to excavate more than is actually visible on the surface. Wreckage was spread over about half an acre so perhaps metal detection equipment could be useful. The ice is glacial and as such is very hard, digging will be difficult, if not impossible.'

The Air Force chewed this over for a few months, and finally responded in May 1989. 'Time has passed and the findings from the aerial search have been thought over and a conclusion reached,' its letter said, diplomatically employing the passive voice and thereby evading responsibility. 'Unfortunately the ravages of time and the glacial action have rendered the aircraft into such a state that there is little justification to retrieve the remains, even for pattern purposes. Consequently it has been decided to abandon any recovery attempts. However, should an engine or a substantially large section of the aircraft break free from the ice, then an attempt to recover these may be made.'[9]

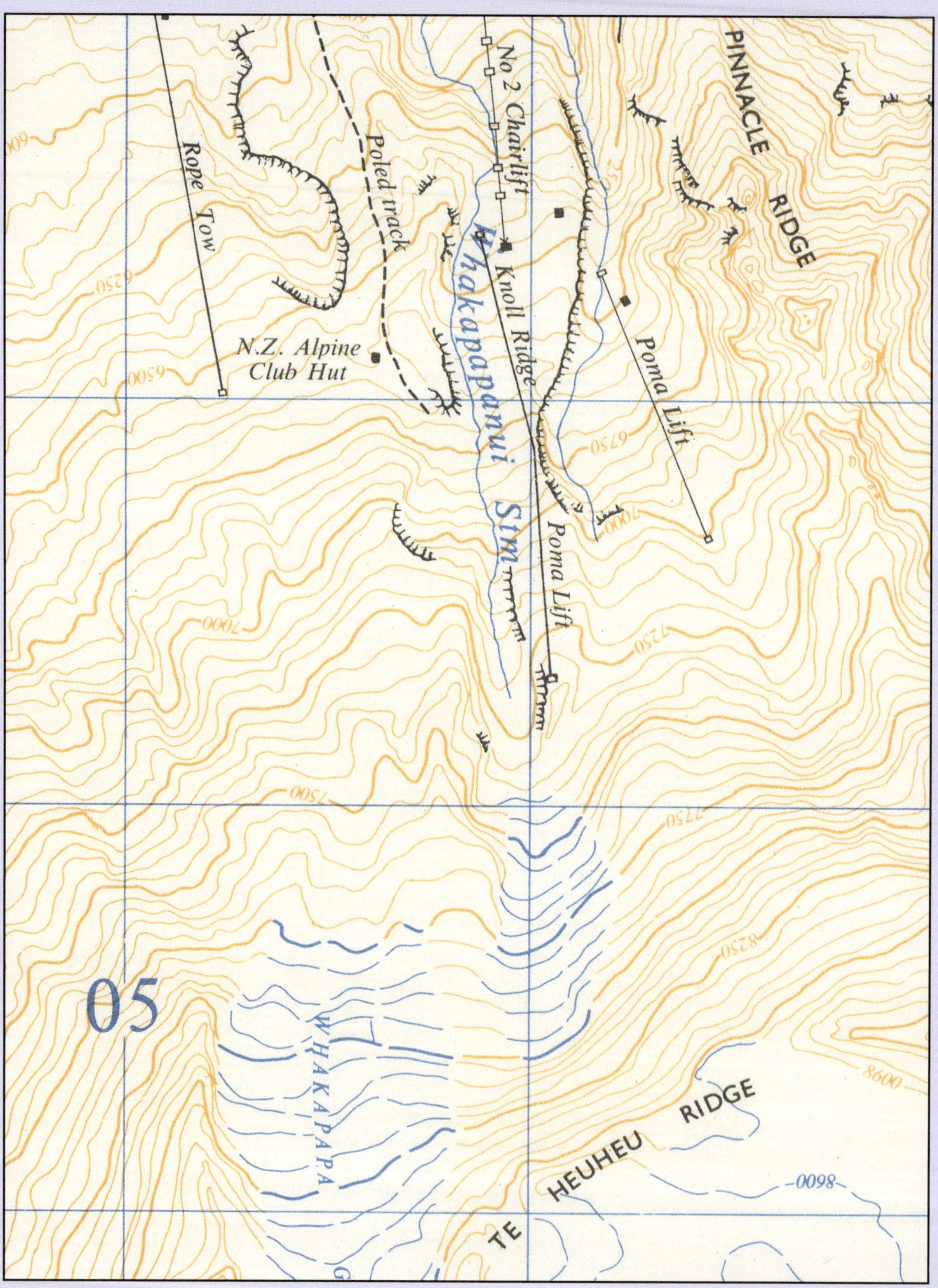

PINNACLE RIDGE
No 2 Chairlift
Rope Tow
Poled track
Whakapapanui Stm
Knoll Ridge
N.Z. Alpine Club Hut
Poma Lift
Poma Lift
6250
6500
6750
7000
7000
7250
7500
7750
8250
8600
8600
05
WHAKAPAPA
TE HEUHEU RIDGE

Map showing the old chairlifts of Whakapapa and Pinnacle Ridge. Rescuers had to climb up and over the ridge to reach the crash site. National Library of New Zealand, 23363041_1964

CHAPTER 9

A fireball above Te Heuheu peak

In 1961, onlookers watched as a wing sheared off a commercial plane above Whakapapa ski field and the aircraft erupted into flames and plummeted to the ground on the northern side of the Pinnacles. Investigators said the pilot was to blame, but was it really his fault?

The twenty-first of November 1961 was a clear-sky day. Captain Alf Bartlett greeted the five passengers on board his Aero Commander 680F Super, a modern twin-engine passenger aircraft owned by Bay of Plenty Airways. Thirty-six-year-old Bartlett had been an RNZAF pilot in the Second World War and was reputed to be very professional, not one to take risks. At 11.12 a.m. he took the plane down the Wellington runway, headed for Rotorua. Forty minutes later, he and his passengers would all be dead.

On and around Ruapehu that day, tourists, workers and trampers were out and enjoying the sunshine as the leftover snowpack from a successful ski season was melting in the hot sun. The skies above Ruapehu were mostly clear, with just a few cotton-ball puffs of cloud. High above the mountain, hot and cold air met and caused turbulence, resulting in occasional handfuls of snow being flicked off the peaks.

Against the stillness of the day, people could hear the distinctive chugging of the twin engines of Bartlett's Aero Commander. Several looked up to watch as it flew overhead, as they usually did when they heard a plane. It was 11.55 a.m.

Over on the Desert Road, a motorist saw the plane as it flew across the mountain. Down at the Chateau Tongariro, guests playing golf looked up to watch. Whakapapa ski field staff craned their necks, too, because in 1961, a plane was still uncommon enough that it warranted attention.

Those watching saw the aircraft's starboard wing shear off in mid-air. Fire flashed in the sky and an explosion followed. The plane burst into flames and plummeted to the ground on the northern side of the Pinnacle Ridge, just out of sight of the ski field workers. The many onlookers all later reported the same key fact: the wing had ripped off before the plane tanked.

Park Board Chief Ranger John Mazey heard the explosion and saw the burning plane crashing towards the ground at about 9000 feet (2750 metres). Mazey knew the terrain well and immediately began organising a search and rescue party. 'One wing came off and an engine fell,' he said later. 'There was an explosion, then the plane crashed in flames into the snow about 7500 feet up the mountain. There seemed to be a double bang when the plane hit the ground — one on the first impact and then another as it slipped over.'[1]

Tony Thrupp, a chairlift worker, was riding up on the No. 1 lift when he saw the plane fly north past the glacier. 'It seemed to be just behind the Pinnacles when I saw a cloud of white smoke appear,' Thrupp said. 'Then the right wing fell off and tumbled towards the ground with the engine attached. I heard an engine revving loudly. The plane dived, with flames and smoke pouring from it. After it had dropped out of sight, I heard a loud report.'[2]

Park Board employee Cyril Brosnan was near the Chateau when he heard the plane and looked up. 'I saw what looked like a vapour trail, but I knew it was not a jet or a top-dresser. Then more sort of vapour came out. Something fell away, and the plane started to dive as the engine revved up. It burst into flames and black smoke poured out. I counted five after that before I heard a bang.'[3]

Roy Turner, the director of Ski Enterprises who ran a rope tow on the lower region of the ski field, was working on the mountain near his hut at 1520 metres when he heard the plane approaching. (Turner and his family would later go missing on a flight themselves, in 1983, travelling from Tekapo to Fox Glacier. Their Cessna aircraft has never been found.) 'I looked up, as I usually did,' Turner said. 'Suddenly there was a scream of engine noise and the right wing separated and flew off by itself, and the remainder barrel-rolled away with both parts disappearing from sight over the ridge.'[4]

Guide Ron Manning was working above the third chairlift with Thomas Bates, the owner of the Whakapapa snowcat, and saw a wing drop from the aircraft. 'I saw the plane come down low over the peak,' Manning said. 'It appeared to drop and suddenly the right wing and the motor dropped off. Almost immediately there was a loud explosion and the whole plane suddenly burst into bright flame. It then pointed to the ground and went down at a fast pace.'[5]

Manning thought the plane might have hit Te Heuheu peak, the outcrop that towers above the ski field at 2732 metres, then crashed. He and Bates immediately set out to reach any possible survivors. Bates later tried to climb Te Heuheu to see if there was any sign of the plane having hit the peak, but turned back as it was too icy.

Ruapehu Alpine Lifts manager Lorenz Reiser was at the very top of the Valley poma lift with chairlift operator Walter Imboden. Reiser noticed the plane had come down very low. 'I thought he was trying to dive-bomb us for a while,' he said.[6] Then they, too, saw the plane burst into flames. Imboden reported: 'I saw the aircraft turn over, belly-up, like it was shot down. It turned slowly and then began to crash. Just as it disappeared behind a ridge there seemed to be an explosion.'[7]

Immediately, men on the ground gathered ice axes, crampons and climbing ropes, and set off at pace. Reiser and Imboden headed towards a pillar of smoke they could see rising from the wreckage on the other side of the Pinnacle Ridge, which separated them from the plane. They were the first on the scene, taking 45 minutes to get there at as much of a run as their bodies would allow. From the ridge they could see that the wreckage was scattered over a wide area in difficult, steep country among rocks and snow, between Te Heuheu peak and the lower Pinnacle Ridge. It was a desolate scene. As they approached, they saw the fuselage was still burning. The two men found a wing with a motor still attached, around 200 feet (60 metres) from the main section of the wreckage. Curiously, the wing had very little damage.

Imboden had pushed himself to his physical limits in trying to get to the site as fast as he could. 'Everything was still burning when I got there and I could see there was nothing I could do to help,' he said. 'The remains of the people in the plane were spread out over quite an area.' He and Reiser tramped back and met with Mazey's rescue party coming in.

The newspaper headlines the next day were dramatic: 'WRECKAGE, BODIES ON ROCK FACE', one read.[8] Body parts and debris were found spread over a wide area down a steep, snow-clad spur. The horizontal tailpiece was further away from the main

The wreckage of the Aero Commander in a remote spot on Ruapehu. Richard Waugh collection

site. Cabin insulation was strewn across rocks higher up. Personal effects littered the mountain, including clothing, magazines, books and letters.

The wreckage was initially unrecognisable as an aircraft. One newspaper reported: 'Ashes of fabric could be seen amongst twisted and shattered metal struts and stays, small unburnt bakelite objects, trailing bits of wire, instruments from the dashboard and electrical components from the left engine. A small pair of boy's light blue pants were amongst the unburnt wreckage.'[9]

The sun went down, temperatures plummeted and the scene became bitterly cold. A thin layer of ice formed on the rocks. With such clear skies, the overnight refreeze was extreme, and it was too difficult and icy to recover bodies. Mazey's party camped out at the wreckage that night, prepared to do battle in the morning.

The next day the mountain road was closed to visitors in a bid to assist with the rescue but also to prevent false reports filtering from the area. Four parties brought out the crash victims in a long and gruelling day of relentless wind and ice. The wind was too strong for the chairlifts to operate so the exercise had to be completed on foot, including carrying the bodies over the steep and tricky terrain of Pinnacle Ridge.[10]

Media interest was strong, and journalists found a way around the mountain closure and restrictions. This nearly led to another set of air-crash victims, when a light plane carrying a Wellington press photographer was caught in violent turbulence over the mountain. The plane flipped over onto its back and plunged towards the mountain at terrifying speed, but the pilot managed to regain control a few feet above the rocks. The press photographer's camera was torn from his grasp and badly damaged. Onlookers said the plane missed the mountain by only 20 feet.[11]

Investigators soon arrived on the scene. Wing Commander O. J. O'Brien, Chief Inspector of Air Accidents, was led to the scene by mountain men on 23 November. He observed that the starboard wing, engine and propeller were found as a complete unit at around 7400 feet (2255 metres), while the fuselage and port wing were almost completely destroyed.

A small quantity of mail — first-class letters — was found around the plane and gathered up. It was later weighed to find out how much of the mail was missing. The starboard wing was uplifted and sent to the DSIR for metallurgical examination and evaluation.[12]

Over time, it emerged that this particular plane had something of a history. In 1958 Captain Alf Bartlett had travelled to the US on an aircraft-shopping trip for Bay of Plenty Airways, and had decided to buy the ill-fated Aero Commander for US$70,000. He had it fitted with long-distance fuel tanks, then took it on a lengthy ferry-flight back to New Zealand. Bartlett wrote to his 11-year-old son Russell from the US: 'Dear Rus . . . I've seen quite a few Commanders now. Today I decided to buy this one — it's just like new. I'm sure you'll think it's okay.'[13] The aircraft was used for scheduled passenger flights around the North Island for the next three years.

Bartlett noticed the plane had an odd 'nose heaviness', but he wasn't too worried; other Aero Commander pilots reported the same thing, so it was assumed to be a common characteristic of the model. Engineers working for TEAL (now Air

ABOVE: The wreckage of the Aero Commander on the snow. Richard Waugh collection

BELOW: Photos of the aircraft such as this one were later scrutinised as part of an inquiry. Transport Accident Investigation Commission

New Zealand) evened it out by placing 45 kilograms of lead in the tail. Nobody thought the heaviness was of much significance.

Nor did anyone think much of a heavy landing the plane had made earlier in 1958 at Oklahoma City that required repairs to the fuselage near the starboard wing spar. The aircraft was inspected and no further damage was detected. However, a fatigue crack that later developed in a wing spar was thought to have been initiated by that landing.

Inspector O'Brien later told reporters that a 'particularly comprehensive' 5000-hour structural check had been carried out on the aircraft two months before the crash. 'It is manifestly impossible to design an aircraft in which every single part of, say, the internal structure of a wing may actually be seen,' he pointed out. 'The only method by which the crack might have been detected would have been by x-ray examination. The very successful operation of more than 1,100 Aero Commander planes all over the world has shown no need for making such x-ray examinations either necessary or mandatory.'

O'Brien strongly defended the aircraft's integrity. 'It may well be pointed out that the New Zealand accident was the first in which structural failure in the flight of an Aero Commander had ever occurred.'[14]

The blame game began soon after the accident. Although witnesses had clearly reported seeing the wing come off, then an explosion and fire before the plane tanked, investigators considered it had first struck the mountain and crashed as a result, meaning the pilot was at fault.

It also seemed noteworthy that this was the third plane to come to grief on the same route. As Jock Graham recorded in his book *Ruapehu: Tribute to a mountain*:

> It is curious that all three [air] accidents have occurred to aircraft on approximately the same route from south to north up the centre of the island. The third tragedy brought reports of Te Heuheu as a 'killer peak', generator of unpredictable air currents and fatal turbulence . . . Ruapehu seems to be a mountain to be approached from the air only by those well acquainted with its ways.[15]

The first accident report was released three months after the crash and largely blamed the pilot, claiming that he had decided to fly too close to the summit of Ruapehu, where turbulence or a pilot manoeuvre caused the starboard propeller to hit a rock outcrop. O'Brien had noticed that the propeller tips on the severed starboard wing were bent forward, and therefore concluded that the plane had hit something before crashing. A passenger's camera was recovered from the crash site and the film later developed. Its images showed the approach to the Crater Lake. O'Brien's report concluded that Bartlett had flown into the crater and hit a rock on the way out before crashing on the northern side of the Pinnacles. The rock strike, he thought, resulted in unbalanced propeller blades, and combined with high winds, severe turbulence and defective spar

D
E

caps, this had resulted in the starboard wing separating from the fuselage.[16]

It was also surmised that sudden turbulence had aggravated the long-standing fatigue crack in the wing spar. The Minister of Civil Aviation, John McAlpine, waded in: 'The crack progressed into an immediate fracture, which deprived the wing of most of its normal strength and resulted in the starboard wing becoming separated from the fuselage.'[17]

Ultimately, however, O'Brien concluded that Bartlett was reckless and had broken aviation rules by flying within 500 feet. It wasn't the aircraft itself, the report stated with force: 'The structural integrity of the Aero Commander 680S aircraft as a type is unquestioned.'[18]

To some pilots around New Zealand, the inspector's conclusions seemed incredibly odd and also unjust. There were so many inconsistencies, and the photos showed the plane hadn't been below the mountain crest at any stage. But O'Brien continued to insist on the infallibility of the aircraft's manufacturing. 'I believe this is the first instance in the world of a crash of an Aero Commander resulting in a failure in the wing,' he said. 'There are about 1,100 of these aircraft in the world and I have not heard of any other crashes.'[19]

The media moved on, but the incident stuck in the minds of several experienced pilots. To them, it seemed unfair that Bartlett's name had been muddied when it was obvious a fatigue fault in the aircraft was the main reason for the accident.

In 1969, Mount Cook Airlines pilot John Stokes went to see Canterbury University Professor Les Erasmus, who was a renowned metallurgist. Stokes arrived armed with a box of charred fragments from the wreck, which he and others had insisted be preserved after the inquiry. The bits didn't help, it turned out, but Erasmus read through the accident report and found it supremely fishy. He examined the starboard wing spar and found an old stress fracture that had been there for a long time.

Turbulence was the final straw for the weakened wing, Erasmus determined. What Bartlett and other pilots had attributed to 'nose heaviness' had in fact been the weak wing twisting during flight. Erasmus also examined the propeller blades. If the aircraft had struck rock, as the report claimed, there should have been abrasive score marks on the blades or fine mineral particles embedded in the metal. But the blades showed no signs of damage, aside from the tips, which had been bent back — probably because of the impact with the fuselage.

After further examination and testing, Professor Erasmus became convinced that the crash had been the final stage of the failure of the stress fracture in the spar cap, probably starting with the heavy landing at Oklahoma in 1958. It had caused stress and cracks, he thought, which propagated progressively over a long period. Wing failure was inevitable, and imminent when the plane left Wellington that day, if it ran into turbulence — and above Ruapehu, where hot and cold winds mixed together angrily, it did.

Others were also dissatisfied with the report's conclusions. Aviation historian the Reverend Dr Richard Waugh notes that Forester Linsley and engineering professor Neil Mowbray from the University of Auckland also dissented and joined with

Erasmus and Stokes in trying to clear Bartlett's name. The group examined and tested the photos taken by Irvine Down, the passenger who was in the co-pilot seat, just before the fatal accident. The photos documented the approach to Ruapehu, and the last shot was of the Crater Lake, taken just a few seconds before the plane began to break to pieces in the air. The photos showed that it wasn't below the mountain's summit at any time, nor was it near any summit rocks.

The group was finally successful in having a second accident report, issued in 1962, withdrawn and a new report issued in 1984. However, the new report only partly exonerated Bartlett, concluding that no mountain strike had happened — instead, it was a case of major structural failure resulting from damage initiated by the heavy landing three years prior, and that the plane had been flown too close to the mountain. This second revised report continues to be contested by experts.

Later, in 1995, Steve Swift, principal engineer fatigue evaluation for the Civil Aviation Authority of Australia, presented a paper titled 'The Aero Commander Chronicle', which argued there was a major weakness in the main spar of the Aero Commander design.[20] Incredibly, he observed there had been 24 Aero Commander accidents resulting from wing separation during flight. Tragically, the Ruapehu flight was likely the first, in spite of O'Brien's very public insistence on the aircraft's structural integrity. A further 35 wing spars were found to be cracked during inspection.

Erasmus made some damning remarks following publication of Swift's paper: 'Much of this information must have been available to the Civil Aviation authorities in New Zealand prior to 1984, but was never revealed to anyone involved with the ZK-BWA investigation,' he stated. 'Throughout the period 1970 to 1984 we had minimal co-operation from the Civil Aviation Authority or the Chief Inspector of Accidents, and generally had great difficulty extracting the parts of ZK-BWA which they had retained, and which they eventually "lost". The aircraft manufacturer, Rockwell-North American was equally unhelpful.'[21]

I got access to the archival material held by the Transport Accident Investigation Commission and rifled through a few boxes in the hope of finding some coordinates or other concrete intel on where the wreck lay. I also contacted Richard Waugh to ask if he knew anything about the wreck's position. He was rather trusting of me as a stranger making a random enquiry, and kind enough to courier me all his files about the accident — several kilograms of material, including newspaper clippings and photographs — to look through.

I found maps in the commission's archive and also in Waugh's files, but these were from the era before the switch from imperial to metric, and stylised in a different manner to current maps, which made it hard to pinpoint the locations. Moreover, it appeared that because the wreck had begun to break apart in the air, it had spread over an incredibly wide area of tricky, steep terrain.

I heard on the tramping grapevine that Barbara Morris from the Taupo Tramping Club had been to the wreck site in 1998 and again 10 years later. The tramping grapevine also helped me track down Morris, who confirmed she had been to the wreck but 10 years later it had disappeared.

'A Taupo Tramping Club group went up the Wairere Stream and eventually on to a ridge which I believe lay between Pinnacle and Waihohonu ridges,' Morris told me. 'We were led by John Wheeler, now deceased, a registered surveyor, and we had no trouble finding the site, which leads me to believe that John had done his homework before the tramp, as we climbed to the exact spot.'[22]

Morris and co found various pieces of twisted metal and a copy of *Best Bets*, a racing magazine of the time, along with a torn sleeve from a man's jacket or cardigan. They also found a set of earrings, with possibly a lapis lazuli or opal setting. They buried the remains of the magazine and the jacket sleeve at the site, and stood for a few moments as a mark of respect for those who had died. The earrings had presumably belonged to one of the two female passengers. Some of the group wanted to leave the earrings on site, buried with the other items, but there was a question mark over the idea that the family could potentially be traced. Morris told me she thought the earrings ended up with the police in Taupō but she never heard the end result.

On New Year's Day 2008 Morris returned, as there had been some debate about the location of the wreckage. That trip, she found no trace. 'There was no doubt in my mind I was on the wreckage ridge, both from memory and looking at photos and checking various rock features and so on,' she told me. 'It seemed a puzzle that the wreckage had survived on the ridge for some 37 years but then disappeared within ten. I spent the afternoon searching but found nothing. I built a small cairn for future use, took some GPS coordinates, and had a delightful camp-out under the stars at the bottom of the ridge. I can only think that possibly DOC had removed the wreckage, or that it had broken up and been buried over the course of time.'

In 2013 the Taupo Tramping Club went back to see if they could find any wreckage, but none was visible. They did, however, find the cairn Morris had built five years earlier.

I also found Morris's cairn, but I will admit that it was an easy exercise given that I was armed with her coordinates. My adventure buddy Alex and I tramped to the site via Pinnacle Ridge, where Whakapapa had poled a short walk to the skyline above the Valley T-bar. It was easier than it looked, but getting down the other side entailed finding a path around the expansive patches of hardened leftover snow from the winter. We both had ice axes just in case, but there was enough rock to hop around on. I'll also admit that Alex found all of the pieces of the wreck, not me, although I chalk this up to his superior eyesight and height advantage.

We descended into the valley on the northern side, delighted by terrain we hadn't seen before in summer (I'd skied it in winter and walked out via the Taranaki Falls Track, but summer revealed all sorts of rocky outcrops and features). We checked Morris's coordinates a few times and maintained a path directly to her cairn. Then, when we were about two contour lines away, Alex stooped to pick up something.

'Look at this,' he called (I was catching up). 'This isn't natural, surely?'

It was a small plate, partially rusted, about the size of a large mobile phone.

The wreck in 1998.
Barbara Morris collection

CLOCKWISE FROM TOP: Wreckage in 2023, wedged in the sand and rocks; Alex traverses Pinnacle Ridge to drop down on the northern side of Ruapehu in our search for the wreck; a plate from the radio showing a serial number and location confirmed that the wreck was the Aero Commander.

'Look, there are numbers,' I said. I snapped a close-up photo. 'Serial numbers. "Dynamotor unit", I think. Oooh! It says "Aircraft Radio Corporation". This is it, this is definitely it!' I followed up with some language that isn't fit to print, in my sheer excitement that we'd walked more or less straight to the spot, and the first piece of wreckage had solid identifying details. 'And it says "Boonton, New Jersey" — and we know he bought the plane from the US!'

I hopped about for a bit in excitement while Alex laughed at my enthusiasm. We replaced the plate, snapped some more photos, and started a grid search across the sandy fan, combing the terrain for more pieces. We (okay, Alex) found several small pieces of twisted metal, some of which showed the radical impact. Then I veered left, Alex veered right, and after a spell I realised I'd lost him entirely. I yelled but heard nothing, so I tramped over to where I thought he should be.

'Found anything?' I yelled. He was deep in a gully, where patches of snow hid the stream in places.

'Heaps!' he yelled back. 'Come down!'

The stream contained the bulk of the wreckage we found that trip. In places, large sections of metal were partially encased in the season's hard snow, with water running underneath. The red and blue paint of a lockable hatch was still visible on the outside, and a cam was rusted but still well identifiable. It was enough: we'd found the wreck, and traced this part of history to where it still lay on the landscape.

We returned to where we'd left the plate with the serial numbers, built a small cairn on a flat-topped rock and placed the plate at its base, safely stashed in between rocks. I took a note of the coordinates for future reference. We gazed around. 'It's actually really accessible, isn't it?' Alex said. 'Incredible terrain, too. Next time I'd keep going, down the Wairere Stream and maybe camp out.'

Two hours later we were safely back at the car after puffing up to the ridge again — soft sand is quite the workout on the legs — and kicking steps up a snow slope, now softened enough to be able to pass without crampons.

I emailed Barbara Morris to let her know we'd found it, and she was relieved to hear the wreck was still there.

'That is so exciting!' she replied. 'I'm so pleased you were successful, and I feel much happier knowing it's still up there in its final resting place and not taken for souvenirs or whatever — I couldn't understand why I didn't find any evidence on the second trip, but it's a big mountain and I suspect I wasn't quite high enough.'

Some of the wreckage had definitely disappeared — we failed to find the same pieces of metal that Barbara's photos had shown. But that is likely attributable to the ravages of time, and the never-ending activity of the mountain. Pieces are constantly being shifted and covered, and perhaps uncovered and recovered, but one day they will be finally, fully gone, put to rest like the question of the ill-fated pilot, his name and reputation finally cleared.

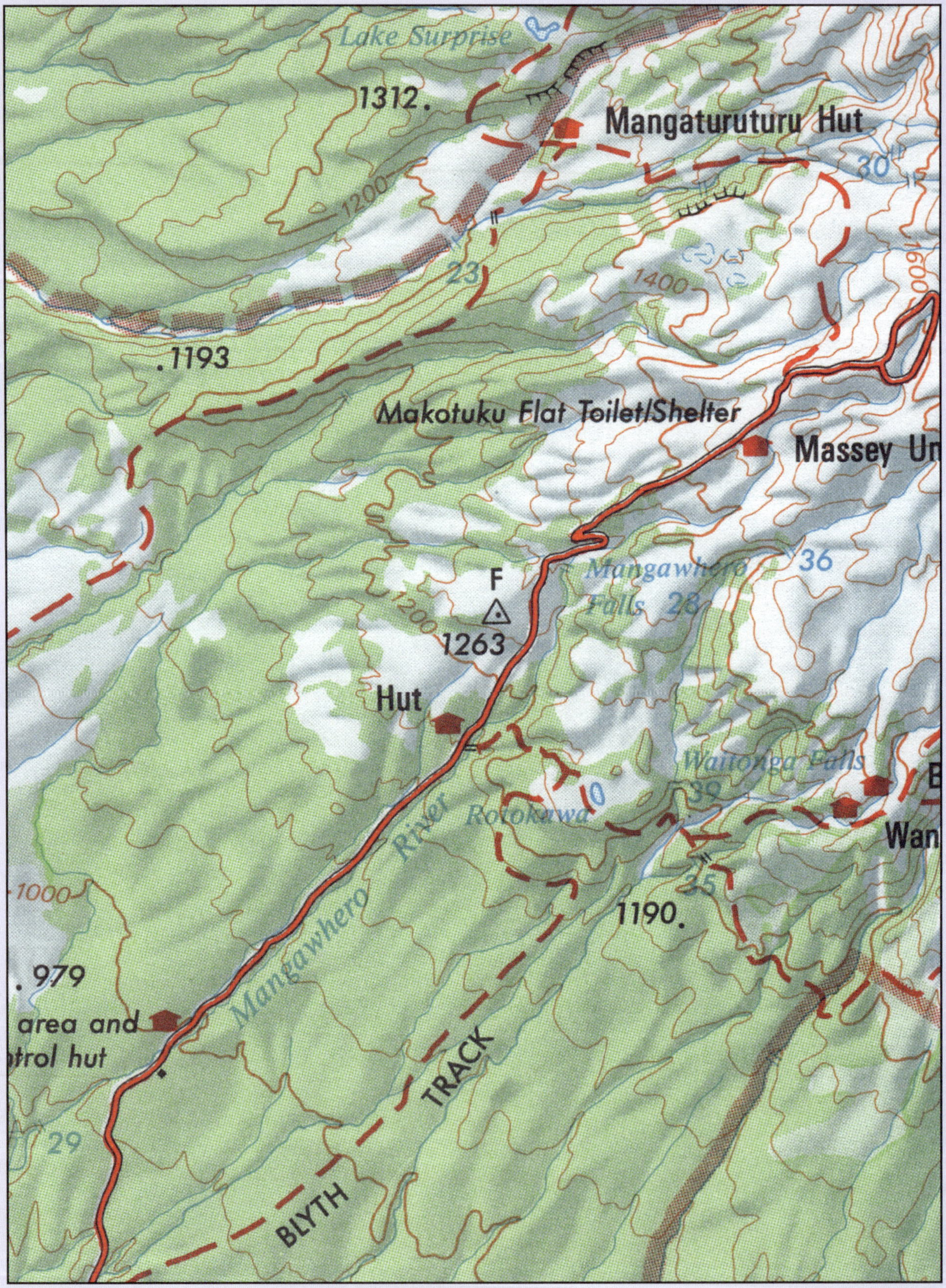

Lake Surprise
1312.
Mangaturuturu Hut
30
1200
23
1400
1600
.1193
Makotuku Flat Toilet/Shelter
Massey Un
Mangawhero
Falls 28
36
F
1263
1200
Hut
Waitonga Falls
39
Rotokawa
Wan
B
1000
35
1190.
Mangawhero River
. 979
area and
trol hut
BLYTH TRACK
29

Map from 1975 showing 'F' trig, in the vicinity of the memorial to those who died in the 1982 helicopter crash. National Library of New Zealand, 37100114_1975

CHAPTER 10

A test flight turns to tragedy

In 1982, five people perished in a helicopter crash while testing out a new spotlight for search and rescue. A memorial exists just off the Ohakune Mountain Road, and Project Tongariro was founded in their memory.

In the summer of 1982, five people gathered for a helicopter flight from Raetihi over Ruapehu. The helicopter, a Jet Ranger, was used frequently in the national park for rescue work, and there were plans to modify it for use as an air ambulance in the next few months. A new search and rescue spotlight had just been fixed to the helicopter by the skids, and the flight that night was to carry out its first test. The group included Ohakune conservation staff Bill Cooper, Keith Blumhardt and Derek White, and the fifth member was park assistant Marie Williams, who'd become engaged to Derek White just a week earlier. Pilot Doug McKenzie was known to be exceptionally talented at flying the machine.

It was 9 December and conditions were excellent — clear weather and good visibility. The helicopter left the Raetihi airstrip at 9.30 p.m. for what should have been a half-hour flight. When it didn't return, the alarm was raised. The flight was formally reported missing just after midnight and a rescue party departed at dawn the next day, with aircraft coming in from Whanganui, Taihape, Taupō and Taumarunui to help search.

At 5.25 a.m. the wreck was spotted just 200 metres from the Ohakune Mountain Road, the bright yellow of the helicopter visible against the tussock. According to the accident report, the helicopter had crashed in a clearing and was on its back in a small crater, the cockpit almost totally destroyed and wreckage scattered over a 10-metre radius.[1]

It was New Zealand's worst helicopter disaster and it hit Ohakune hard — the five were all well known in the small mountain town, which had a close-knit community. More than 300 people packed out the Chateau for a memorial service, marked by stormy weather that seemed to symbolise their grief and anguish. Marie Williams was described as charming, intelligent and vivacious, someone who loved a challenge.

When I tramped into the area, I wasn't looking for a wreck — the accident was recent enough to make that feel pretty inappropriate — but I'd heard that a memorial plaque had been installed somewhere, although I couldn't find much information about it. The only two plaques mentioned in the Tongariro National Park Management Plan were the Stanton Memorial and one marking the park's centennial. But I came across some coordinates in the DOC archives, in an old list using the NZMS 260 maps from the time. These guided me to a spot height just off the Ohakune Mountain Road, aligning with the 200-metre distance mentioned for the site of the accident. Old maps labelled it 'F Trig' (in the past, Ruapehu's trigs were unimaginatively named by letters of the alphabet, although some more interesting names existed: 'Ski', 'Otemoa', 'Tufa').

It was a summer day when I set off in search of the plaque, my legs in gaiters to push through the low scrub. Although the day was hot and dry, somehow the area retained a boggy quality, with deep pools of water in places waiting to trap the unwary. It was off-track travel but not particularly difficult. Soon I was standing directly on the spot height on the map, but there was no trig to be seen. Eventually, after moving to higher ground, I noticed some material just down from the trig site, on the edge of a drop-off, and sure enough, there was the broken and defunct trig station. Either it had been marked incorrectly on the map, or somehow it had moved itself downhill 10 or 20 metres. After hunting around I found some other items, which I took to be rain gauges, and a locked box with a solar panel — I assumed this was either a weather station or a secret underground bunker for former Ministers of Conservation in the event of the world ending. (Probably the former.) But there was no sign of any sort of memorial.

I wrote the idea off mentally; it was likely no memorial existed, given it seemed to be a word-of-mouth thing only and I hadn't found mention of it anywhere else. The subject re-emerged from the murky depths of my mind (always a dangerous place) when I took a trip to Mangaiti Hut one day to meet up with some members of the Tongariro Tramping Club. On hearing about my interest in backcountry history, one of the members produced a flipbook of material from the hut. And there, with photos and instructions on how to find it, were several pages about the memorial to the park employees. I'd still have to hunt around for more intel, but at least this was confirmation that the memorial did in fact exist, and that I had been hunting more or less in the right place. In fact, it was surprising I hadn't stumbled upon it already — I'd just need to go back and hunt more carefully. The instructions noted that it wasn't easy to spot, as it was nestled in the surrounding vegetation. Looking on satellite images and comparing topographic maps from the 1980s with contemporary ones, it also looked as if the vegetation had expanded significantly.

Months later I tramped back in again. This time I had the advantage of knowing that a ground trail existed between the road and the trig, and slightly further on as far as the locked box. My buddy Alex and I made swift work of the tramp in, and soon we were hunting around where the intel told me a 'tongue of bush' extended northwards into the tussock from a stand of beech trees. The site was apparently marked with a stylised wooden memorial. A further plaque bore the names of the whole party.

Alex spotted it first, and I was amazed to see that I'd almost been on top of it on my previous visit. The memorial looked out with a clear view towards Ruapehu, still covered mostly in snow at that time, and it had withstood exposure to the elements well. The plaque was simple: in memory of those lost, with the date they perished. The letters were slowly being taken over by lichen, and I thought to go back at some stage with some 'spray and walk away' to help keep it clear. Alex brushed a few twigs off the plaque.

'That's quite lovely, actually,' he said. 'Brilliant spot too.'

We sat on the rocks at the edge of the clearing for a while. The site felt cloaked with a sense of sacredness and peace, and it was easy to imagine how much it must have meant to the loved ones of the people who had died there.

The accident led to the establishment of Project Tongariro, the Tongariro Natural History Society. The mountain community was grief-stricken, and the idea arose of some kind of tangible memorial. People donated money, and park rangers, colleagues, friends and family of the deceased came together to discuss what form the memorial might take. The idea of a natural history society developed — to establish a network of people who loved Tongariro National Park and would work alongside park staff.

IN MEMORY OF
MARIE WILLIAMS
DEREK WHITE
WILLIAM COOPER
KEITH BLUMHARDT
DOUGLAS McKENZIE
WHO DIED IN A HELICOPTER

ABOVE: The memorial plaque with the names of the five people lost, installed at Easter, 1988.

BELOW: The memorial looks across a clearing and out to Ruapehu. The sculpture represents the life forces of the five people in the crash.

The society, today best known as Project Tongariro, was formally founded in July 1984, and it became a 'living memorial' to the five who had passed away. The money that had been donated went to a memorial fund, which was later used to publish several books — including a geological field guide to the national park called *Volcanoes of the South Wind*. It was written by Karen Williams — sister to Marie Williams — who also co-authored the book that had sparked my Ruapehu obsession, *Skiing on the Volcano*.

Forty years later, Project Tongariro continues to honour the victims of the tragedy and the mountain they loved: 'Arising from a tragedy more than 40 years ago is a vibrant organisation that recognises, in all its endeavours and activities, the spirit of the people who died that night on the slopes of Mt Ruapehu. From despair and sorrow have come fresh ideas and the progressive realisation of an enduring dream. The Tongariro Natural History Society is indeed the living memorial that was envisaged so many years ago.'[2]

The crater area of Ngāuruhoe (2287m). The volcano once erupted regularly, but has been silent for decades. Mike Heydon/ChopperWorx

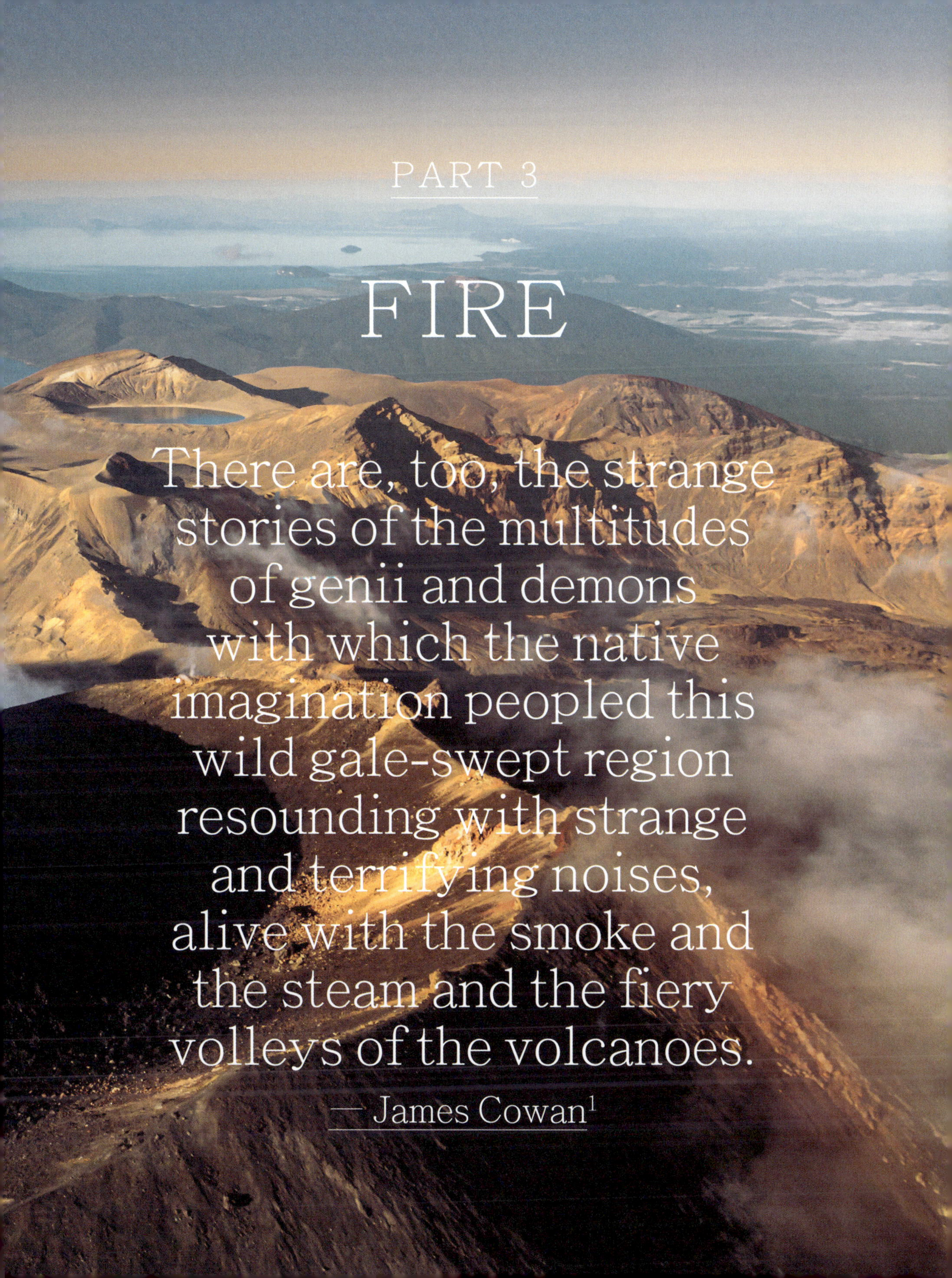

PART 3

FIRE

There are, too, the strange stories of the multitudes of genii and demons with which the native imagination peopled this wild gale-swept region resounding with strange and terrifying noises, alive with the smoke and the steam and the fiery volleys of the volcanoes.

— James Cowan[1]

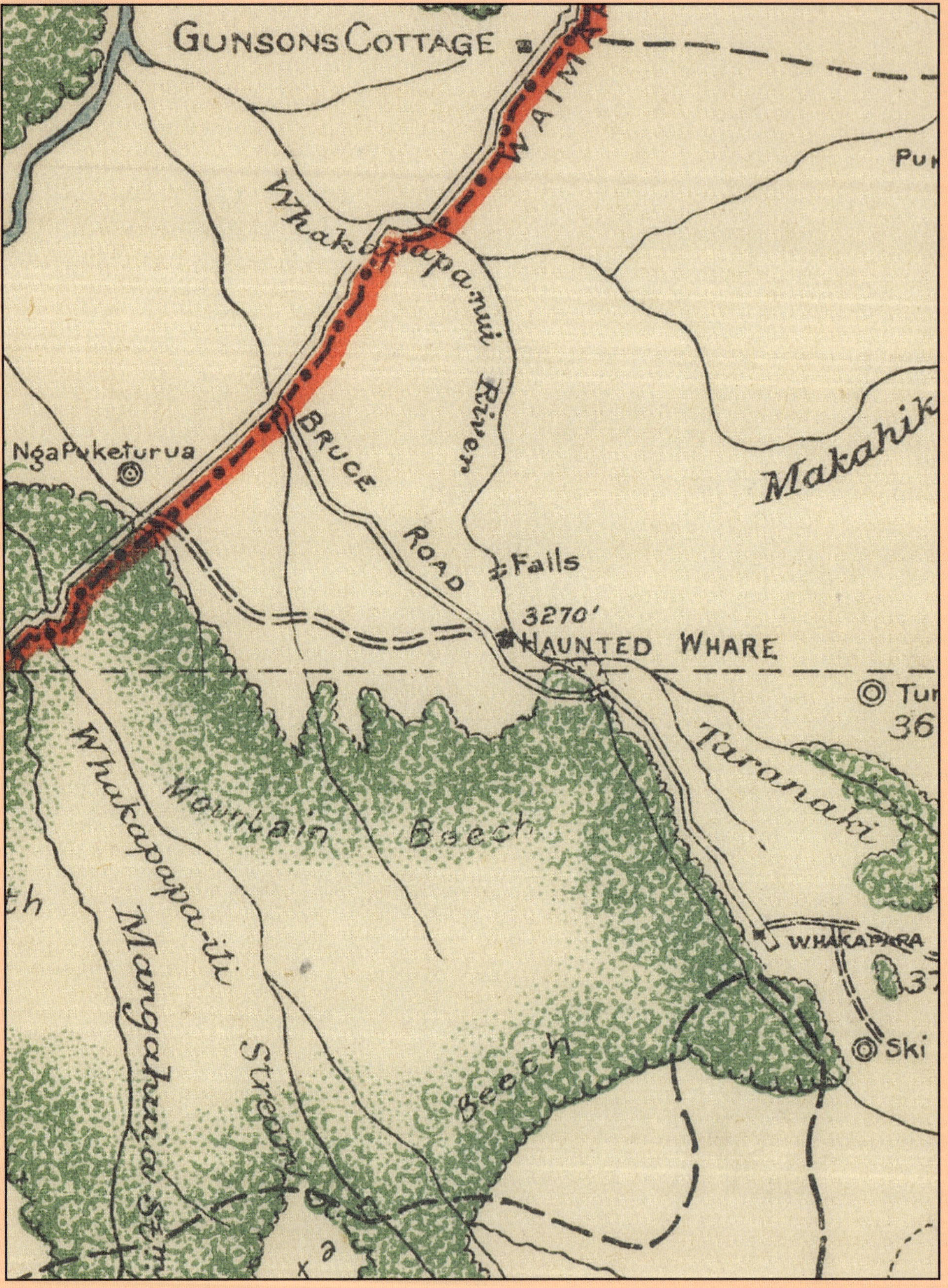
GUNSONS COTTAGE
Whakapapa-nui River
Nga Puketurua
BRUCE ROAD
Falls
3270'
HAUNTED WHARE
Taranaki
Mountain Beech
Whakapapa-iti
Beech

Map showing the Haunted Whare, near the Whakapapanui River. National Library of New Zealand, 35094335

CHAPTER 11

The legend of the Haunted Whare

A small shack near Tawhai Falls below the Chateau was reputedly haunted by the ghost of a woman searching for her lost lover. The whare burned down, twice. Rumours trickled through that a plaque or sign still existed on the overgrown site. Could I find it, and would the ghosts talk to me if I did?

There's a spot towards the top of the Mangawhero Forest Walk, a loop at the bottom of the Ohakune Mountain Road, where the track emerges from the overhanging, clingy bush and breaks out into a short clearing. It's grassy, with a strip for walkers that's mown regularly by DOC. There's thick growth on either side, and one side sports a rough trail I've never had the courage to follow. Whenever I walk through, this spot makes me shiver as I blink rapidly in the sudden sunlight after the dark of the forest, and I get an eerie sensation deep in my bones. I've wondered a lot about the ghosts and spirits that walk the slopes of the maunga, restlessly searching for something they will never find.

One day I walked the trail with a friend. As we emerged into the clearing, we both hurried through the grass strip.

'I always get a really freaky feeling just in this bit here,' he said.

I gripped his arm, staring at him wide-eyed.

'Are you even serious?' I said. 'I'm exactly the same. I get a sort of chill. It's got a weird feeling for me, and not in a good way.'

'I wonder if we could find out what happened here. I know there was a logging camp further up — maybe something really shady went on at this spot.'

The same thing happened again, unprompted and with another friend, except she insisted the spot had a positive feeling, not freaky or creepy at all, but very pure and spiritual.

'This bit, I love it,' she said. 'It just feels really good to me.'

We walked from the little clearing up to cross the asphalt where the Mangawhero track loops across to the other side of the road, and she spoke again.

'A friend of mine reckons she's seen spirits on the road here. They're ancient Māori warriors in full traditional dress, and as soon as you see them, they turn and look at you, then they disappear.'

Over on the Bruce Road, far away from the roaming spirits of the Mangawhero, there's a little bump on the ground above the Tawhai Falls carpark. Tourists stop at the falls to see the 13-metre-high waterfall that plunges into a green pool surrounded by smooth rocks — an ancient lava flow — and wavering forest. In years past the bump was home to the Haunted Whare, a hut that only ever bore that name. Clad in corrugated iron, its sole window was the only eye for its troubled soul.

There's a legend about the Haunted Whare's ghostly status. A young woman fell in love with a man from a poorer background but her family disapproved. Forbidden to continue their relationship, the young couple ran away together and spent the night near Tawhai Falls. The next day the girl's father and brother pursued them, killed the man and threw his body into the Whakapapanui Stream, then dragged the girl back home. She ran away and returned to the spot near the falls, where, overcome with grief, she cried out for her lover but only heard the river flowing. Desolate, she threw herself into the river and took her own life. It's said that her unhappy ghost now roams the tussock-clad plains and the beech and toatoa forest around the Whakapapanui area, searching desperately for her lost lover.

An old information board, completely hidden in the trees, is the only sign that the Haunted Whare ever existed here.

In the late 1800s, sheep farms began to be established around the flatter lower slopes of what would become the national park. In 1880, shepherd Rawiri Ketu, who worked for the large local sheep run, built a slab hut on the hillock near Tawhai Falls, about a quarter of a mile from the stream. Unbothered by ghosts and the sweeping winds that buffeted the plains, 24-year-old shepherd Wi Takerei, of the Ngāti Waewae iwi of Lake Rotoaira, later took up residence in the whare. It was lonely and remote, but the runholders routinely sent out food supplies to Wi Takerei and the other shepherds by packhorse.

In 1927, historian James Cowan recounted the story of the Haunted Whare:

> It was a solitary life for Wi Takerei, in that lone hut in the wilds, the dark wizardly-looking forest on the south, the rumbling volcano smoking its volcanic pipe above him.
>
> Most Maoris avoided that part of the volcanic country. To their minds it was an abode of spirits and mysterious wild people of the bush. There were patupaiarehe there, an uncouth unfriendly tribe of fairy beings, whose legendary chief was a dread, being named Te Ririo. There were spirit voices in the gales and in the creaking of the ancient trees in the bush — voices of 'atua' and 'kehua'. Wi Takerei exhibited more than ordinary courage, unusual indifference to the affrighting sounds of the wilderness, when he agreed to live there without any human companionship.[1]

By August 1882 the area was hit with heavy snowfall and severe storms, and Wi Takerei had not been seen for many weeks. The station manager, R. B. Maunsell, became concerned, and when the weather abated, he visited the whare with another man, Wi Poinga. They found Wi Takerei dead, lying face-down on the floor, clad in only his shirt, with his blanket on a stool next to him. One of his eyes was missing. There were no visible marks of violence, and it was concluded that he had probably died of heart disease. The missing eye, however, remained a spooky mystery, and many thought the ghost had something to do with his death. Wi Takerei's iwi came out from Rotoaira, Ōtukou and Papakai, burned the whare and all its contents to the ground, and took his body away for burial. The cause of death was assumed but never confirmed, and it was said that the ghost, the 'kehua', had plucked out Wi Takerei's eye.

Cowan later wrote: 'The lonely desolate spot on which the whare stood had been regarded by the Maoris as haunted by the ghost of a young woman who had come to a violent end near there, and now the people were disposed to believe that the kehua or ghost had had something to do with the young shepherd's death. Mohoao, or wild men of the woods, too, were believed to haunt the place.'[2] (Mohoao are similar to patupaiarehe, but they are wild and angry, sometimes violent, and dangerous to humans.)

Runholders the Grace brothers rebuilt the hut a little further to the east, close to the bush and accessible to traffic going by on the dirt road. Built of corrugated iron, its

The Haunted Whare, date unknown.
Bagnall Collection, Massey
University Library

simple room had a big fireplace that took up one end of the structure. Although John Grace slept in the new whare often in the 1880s without seeing any ghostly apparitions, its reputation for being haunted spread quickly.

In 1883, a surveyor named Springhall was living in the new hut while working nearby. One night during a fierce snowstorm, Springhall, his wife and another woman were playing cards inside to pass the time. As the wind howled through the trees outside and snow assaulted the corrugated-iron walls, the fireplace struggled to mitigate the chill. Then one of the women screamed. She had seen a ghost at the window, a young Māori woman with her hair in two long plaits that fell down her back and an expression of deep grief on her face. As the dogs outside barked and whined, both women fainted. Springhall bravely went outside and searched around widely but found nothing and nobody — not even any footprints in the fresh snow.

Springhall returned to the whare, where the women were recovering from their fainting attacks. He shut the door securely, hung a thick shawl over the window to prevent any further frightening appearances, and they lit candles to dispel the shadows. The women described the apparition as 'urukehu', referring to fair-haired, fair-skinned Māori people, who sometimes had a ruddy or golden tinge to their hair. Urukehu are believed to be the offspring of patupaiarehe, supernatural beings who live in the mist and avoid sunlight. Woe betide the human being who invades the territory of the patupaiarehe, the deep forests and foreboding mountains. The party in the whare recognised the woman as the spirit of the girl looking for her lost lover.

After this episode the hut stood deserted for a spell, but travellers who camped there reported seeing the same face at the window — a grief-stricken young woman with two long plaits.

From 1885 Roderick Gray took up residence in the Haunted Whare while working as a shepherd. He was wholly unbothered by the ghost, to the point of interacting with her regularly. Regarded as a recluse and an 'uncommon character', Gray was known for his conceptualisation of mountains as sacred. In his 1890 book *Tongariro: The sacred mountain of the Maori*, he wrote: 'I need scarcely say that often a great awe comes over me whilst living here alone, and in the neighbourhood of sudden and violent death . . . always having the mountains in my gaze, any chance occurring is quickly noticed. I have learned to regard them as friends, as they have sheltered me for a length of time.'[3]

Gray had seen his share of international adventure, having spent time in India with the British Army, but he'd been forced to resign his commission because of sunstroke. He then moved to New Zealand for health reasons, and perhaps was drawn to Ruapehu not just for the cold climate but also for the spiritual atmosphere. Cowan described Gray as an educated man, who would spend much of his free time reading the classics beside the fire, listening to the hail on the roof and the gale outside: 'The lonely life suited his studious, contemplative temperament.'[4]

Despite his reputation as a recluse, Gray sometimes visited the other shepherds in their camps and told them of his eerie experiences in the wilderness. He once saw a wild woman near the hut, he told them, but she ran into the bush and disappeared, despite his extensive searching. Then a mysterious 'Mohoao' woman began to visit

ABOVE: The Haunted Whare, date unknown. Department of Conservation archives

BELOW: A 1918 newspaper photo of the Haunted Whare, showing park warden John Cullen and former mayor of Auckland Sir James Gunson. Auckland Libraries Heritage Collections

him. She would come inside the hut, sit by the fire and chat with him. Once, as he went to cross the swollen Whakapapanui Stream near the hut, the woman appeared and warned him not to. He would drown if he did, she said. He ignored her and continued, and she warned him again, then disappeared. Gray looked at the water roaring down the stream and decided to obey the supernatural warning. He returned to the Haunted Whare, and later considered that she had likely saved his life.[5]

The Haunted Whare eventually became an icon of Tongariro National Park. 'The lonely whare peers out at you with its one window as you approach,' Cowan wrote in 1927. The whare's nine-pane window can be seen in the 1925 photo, but in later years it disappeared. 'Sometimes alpine sports campers still use it, though it is nearly half a century old. But they go in parties; no one is anxious to spend a night alone in the Haunted Whare.'[6]

The ghostly happenings tailed off, and Cowan theorised that as the park had become an attractive playground for tourists, large parties of trampers and skiers had driven away the 'last-lingering spirits of the Whakapapanui'. When the Chateau was built in the 1920s the hut, which was right on the road, became a popular stop on the way. Visitors would leave their signatures on every surface available. In 1936, a party reported visiting the hut at midnight but the only 'ghost' they found was a persistent rat under the floor — and later, the 'ghost' (presumably of a digestive variety) of the cheese, sardines and crackers the party had eaten under its haunted roof.[7]

Around the same time, a couple of teenage boys from Taumarunui stayed in the whare in the hopes of a supernatural adventure. The rest of their party sensibly stayed at the Chateau. They conducted an inspection of all corners of the hut, finding nothing more than a few spiders. Then they heard a rumbling noise that ceased abruptly, trees scraping and footsteps outside. The rumble was 'decidedly queer', wrote Jack Tunnicliffe, the 17-year-old ringleader, and the footsteps gave him a prickly feeling running up and down his spine. He became terrified.

Then they heard a voice: 'All right in there, you chaps? Perhaps you'd better come up to the Chateau after all. We'll be able to get an earlier start in the morning if you do.'

It was the leader of their party come to fetch them. The boys hastily agreed.[8]

The original legend of the whare's hauntings persisted in lore, even if the ghost seemed to be gone. 'Nevertheless,' Cowan wrote, 'you will be told that if you care to spend a night alone in the whare, you may be rewarded — if you care for that kind of reward — with the midnight vision of a mournful woman's face at the window, the wan bush girl seeking her lost lover.'[9]

In 1938, the whare came close to being razed by fire. Careless trampers had been starting fires that had destroyed much of the flora in various areas around the national park, and in mid-August that year, a fire caught on in the vicinity of the Haunted Whare. The weather had been dry for a while and the vegetation and trees around the area were completely destroyed. Park warden John Cullen (who, you will remember from the Hauhungatahi expedition, was personally responsible for the heather portion of the flora) reported:

> I am of the opinion the fire was caused by someone in a passing car throwing out the end of a cigar still alight. The winter sports were on at the Chateau at that time, which was the cause of a continuous stream of cars passing to and fro to the Chateau. Luckily, the wind was from the north-east at the time; had it been from southerly or westerly direction the fire would have crossed the road and burned all the area up to the Haunted Whare.[10]

As warden, Cullen looked after the whare and ensured its pecked-out eye was repaired, fixing the broken window and doing maintenance on the roof with the reluctant blessing and funding of the Park Board. Its location on the road made it subject to much vandalism, as road-accessible huts still are today. Unthinkably, in 1936 its six bunks had been pulled out and used as firewood by one group of car campers who wanted to boil the billy.[11]

Then, in 1943, the Haunted Whare once more burned to the ground. In March the following year, the acting secretary of the Park Board sent a memo to 'the Medical Superintendent, care of the Temporary Mental Hospital, Chateau Tongariro', demanding answers: 'I understand that the building at the Park, known as the Haunted Whare, has been destroyed by fire, and I should be glad if you would kindly arrange for police enquiries to be instituted with a view to determining the cause of the outbreak.'[12]

The cause of the fire isn't on record in the newspapers of the day, or in any Park Board archives. I followed the thread of the Haunted Whare from Archives New Zealand to the Department of Conservation and the Alexander Turnbull Library and found no police reports on its destruction — accidental, ghostly or otherwise — aside from the above brief mention. Then I stumbled across the answer in a journal article. At the time, the Chateau was being used as a mental-health facility after Porirua Hospital had been damaged in an earthquake; 300 patients and staff were being housed just up the road from the Haunted Whare. A nurse who was stationed at the Chateau was witness to the hut's negligent burning. 'We were all young and sprightly creatures and we didn't ever see any men,' she said. 'One time a crowd of air force fellows came from Waiouru and we had a party at the Haunted Whare about a mile down the road from the Chateau. It was just an old tin shed really and we lit a fire and sat around. Afterwards the fire wasn't put out properly and the whare got burnt. Nobody knew until the truck went down to National Park the next morning and there was what the driver called "this charred bloody ruin". All the members of the National Park Board came and interviewed us and I've never been so terrified. There is a little plaque there now which says it was burnt down in 1943 but you'd have thought it was Cleopatra's Needle or some such, the fuss there was.'[13]

Local historian Karen Williams wrote a summary of the Haunted Whare's story in a Project Tongariro journal in 2000, and said that there was now nothing left to see: 'And so ends this story of the Haunted Whare. Today there is no sign of the plaque nor of any remains of the old building which was once located about 400 metres to the southwest of the Tawhai Falls carpark on the road to Whakapapa Village.'[14]

I made a mental note: there was nothing left to indicate that the Haunted Whare had ever existed. Still, I'd hunt for it anyway.

ABOVE: A picnic party with the Haunted Whare in the background, date unknown. Bagnall Collection, Massey University Library

BELOW: Trampers at the Haunted Whare, 1931. Auckland Libraries Heritage Collections

I put my research shoes on and began pounding the pavements of Wellington, going from department to department to trawl through archival material in the hope of finding concrete clues to its location. At Archives New Zealand I found several maps on which the Haunted Whare was clearly marked on the road leading up to Whakapapa. It always seemed to be just adjacent to the road, a little square snuggling up to a line, always shown between the road and the waterline of the Whakapapanui. It did occur to me, though, that the road could have changed over the years; it was, after all, just a dirt road for horse and cart initially. Once it was properly tarsealed it could have been rerouted for any number of reasons.

I found mentions of the first whare being 'about 400 metres to the south-west of the present Tawhai Falls carpark' and the current one being 'about 100 metres above the existing carpark'. One document said a suspension bridge across the Whakapapanui existed just below the Haunted Whare and Tawhai Falls was about fifty metres down from the bridge.[15] A Tongariro National Park ranger's report placed it 'on the Bruce Road, two miles from the Chateau and close to the Tawhai Falls', noting that it was of great historic value:

> It is surprising the number of visitors to the Park who are very disappointed to find that this interesting little hut has gone. Many people were so interested in this hut, that they pay a visit to the old site. The interests and ghosts of this hut are still very much alive among the present day visitors and many people would be very pleased to see this building reconstructed.[16]

When construction of the Chateau Tongariro was being planned in the 1920s, there had been some debate by the Park Board and even at parliamentary level over the proposed site. At Archives New Zealand I found old maps showing four proposed sites, one of which was directly opposite the Haunted Whare, on the other side of the Bruce Road. Helpfully, it included details for the proposed site: it was at an altitude of 3220 feet (981 metres), 2.25 miles (3.6 kilometres) to the Whakapapa huts and 1.75 miles (2.8 kilometres) from the junction with SH47.[17] I considered it a wise decision to build the Chateau in its present location at Whakapapa Village, as the Haunted Whare site was fairly underwhelming by comparison.

I also found some letters from the Park Board penned in a state of irritation to the Prison Department, which had apparently installed a stable near the Haunted Whare in the 1930s. 'It has been stated that the smell from the stable yard makes the Haunted Whare itself unsuitable to occupy for camping purposes,' one complained. And another: 'Many who would otherwise have been keen to utilise the Haunted Whare, are now repelled by the proximity and stench of the stableyard.'[18]

At the DOC archives I came across an old booklet about walks in Tongariro National Park, which had consistent directions for finding the site: 'Look carefully for the sign marking the spot because it has been overgrown by the beech forest,' the author advised. 'It is a difficult site to get to as there is no track, but as most people are fascinated by the supernatural I can imagine most readers trekking through the scrub and mountain beech to get to the marker-sign.'

The National Library staff dug out an article for me from 1983, which noted that the Haunted Whare was on a small knoll to the left-hand side of the road. But the writer of this piece, too, claimed there was nothing left. 'In recent years a notice board stood on the knoll stating that this was the site of the Haunted Whare. When I visited the Chateau a few months ago the notice board had disappeared and the knoll stood alone with its trees and shrubs and not even a single plank of the building to bear testimony to anything that man had constructed, haunted or otherwise.'[19]

I concluded that I knew what I was looking for: a site where there was nothing left to indicate that anything had ever been there, next to the Bruce Road, just above the Tawhai Falls carpark. It sounded silly, and I procrastinated about even bothering to go there. Then one day I was up on Ruapehu with Harry Keys, who reckoned there was an old sign at the spot — or if there wasn't, he could at least find the site. He suggested we hunt around in the bush on the way back.

We parked on the road just above the Tawhai Falls carpark. 'There used to be an old road marker here, which was how you'd find the spot, but it's gone,' Harry said. 'It's not far into the bush though, so we can just push in and have a look. It's round about here anyway.'

We found a tiny entranceway in the forest and slipped in.

'How about you go up that way in a straight line and I'll go down this way, and we'll yell if we find anything,' Harry said.

Neither of us had gone far when Harry almost tripped over some number-eight wire on the ground. 'Can't be far away.'

I brushed some spiderwebs off my face and kept tracking upwards, staying parallel to the road and crashing through tree branches. Then Harry yelled. 'Found it!'

'Woohoo!' I yelled back. 'Well done!'

A few seconds later I was at the site. There was an old sign indicating the spot. It stood in a small clearing, tiny but distinctive, and as per the intel I had garnered, it was exactly on the 980-metre contour line. The sign featured a small sketch of the hut, and the text was still very easily readable:

HAUNTED WHARE
About 1881 a shepherds' hut was built on this site.
This hut replaced the first hut built in the Park in 1880 which
was deliberately destroyed by fire after the finding of a dead
Maori inside. HUT BECAME KNOWN AS THE HAUNTED
WHARE AND WAS FINALLY DESTROYED IN 1943.

I peered around the clearing. Apart from the sign, there really wasn't anything to indicate anything had ever stood here. It was hidden from the road, just, not far into the bush, and flat enough to make an excellent camping spot. I decided I'd come back and camp out, and see if the ghost of the Haunted Whare would come and visit me. After all, she wouldn't have had any overnight company since 1943, and she'd probably been through a lonely patch.

I mentioned this idea to a few friends to see if anyone wanted to join me, and predictably everybody thought I was nuts. Reactions ranged from 'No fucking way!' to 'Why would you even want to do that?' to 'What is actually wrong with you?' I knew from past experience that when everybody thinks you're mad, either you've hit on an excellent idea or you should be sure to take a personal locator beacon and extra snacks. It was only by the road, though, so no need for the PLB, but I would pack some treats. It's only polite, if you're entering ghostly territory, to take some sort of offering as an intruder.

I went back a few weeks later, wanting to complete my overnight camping mission before winter hit. For once, I didn't leave my intentions with anyone, partly because it was right by the road, and partly because I knew my loved ones would think that the cheese had finally, thoroughly, slipped off the cracker.

I parked by the Tawhai Falls carpark around 5.30 p.m., leaving enough time to set up my camp before dark but not so much time that I'd get bored before bedtime if the lady ghost didn't show. I took a bivvy bag rather than a tent — figuring it would be swifter to pack up if the going got too ghostly — but stashed a fly in the car just in case of rain. The skies cleared as night fell, revealing stars when I ducked back to the car after forgetting something, and the air suddenly got cold and crisp. I inflated my mattress and stuffed it into the bivvy bag with my thick winter sleeping bag on top, and a proper pillow, plus a thick book from the Ohakune Library rather than my lightweight Kindle. This was luxury!

The clearing was plentiful with bush litter, so I pushed the leaves away from a little spot before lighting my cooker for dinner. No dehy cardboard meals here — I'd brought leftovers of a dahl meal I'd made the night before, and a supermarket naan bread, which I managed to sort-of toast over the cooker's flame.

Night fell as I ate, and the ghost did not arrive to join me. I cleaned up, sorted gear and got into my bivvy bag, regretting not bringing the tent as my head torch attracted swarms of bugs. No matter; I read by the red-light setting.

Still the ghost did not arrive. Tired, I did a final bush wee, executed a set of 20 jumping jacks to get the blood flowing around my body and help me keep warm once I got into my sleeping bag, then decided I needed a properly final, final, just-in-case bush wee, got into bed and switched off my head torch.

I held my breath and listened for the sound of the ghost approaching.

Eventually I drifted off, thoughts swirling of Sir James Gunson having a party with James Cowan and committing arson by dousing the Haunted Whare in petrol and striking a single match while helicoptering their guns around. Why were there no metal remnants at the site, given the whare was made largely from corrugated iron? My tired brain had no answer.

In utter darkness something prompted me awake. Finally! It was the ghost. She had

come to talk to me, in the same way she used to sit by the fire in the Haunted Whare and converse with Roderick Gray. (Did he claim this in earnest, I wondered, or was he regularly partaking of the local electric puha?) Or perhaps — excitingly — it was the ghost of Roderick Gray himself, and we'd be able to talk about our favourite books!

I heard footsteps. Light steps, crushing leaves. I held my breath, listening, hearing my blood pounding in my head. A twig cracked. I fumbled for my head torch and switched it on. This couldn't be real! This couldn't really be the ghost of the troubled lady! If she spoke to me, I'd strike literary gold — it was on record that the ghost of the Haunted Whare hadn't talked to anyone since the 1920s!

As the red glow of my head torch lit up the clearing, I saw the 'ghost': a fat, bumbling kiwi, bless his little brown feathers and pointless wings. He looked pleased to see me, if rather surprised, and dipped his head in a sort of greeting.

'Awww, hello little muffin,' I said, then felt silly. I was on a ghost-hunting mission, in the middle of the night, camped out and talking to a bird in the bush. He poked at something with his long beak, then wandered off, his big bum pushing through small branches, making cracking sounds as he went.

It took me a while to go back to sleep after that, particularly as the chill of the night had set in and my nose felt frosty. But somehow I drifted off again, and woke up in the daylight to find a spider had been hard at work the night before and had spun a web between my cooker and the pot.

Tawhai Falls, where a young woman took her life and her ghost wails for her lost lover. Mandy Rothe Photography

Had the Chateau been built at the Haunted Whare site as it was once proposed, it might have been a doubly ghostly structure, for the Chateau has a ghost, too, known as Charlie. Tales of his spirited exploits began to surface after the Second World War. Generally he hangs out in room 305, and he somehow changes the temperature in the room, so the middle always stays freezing cold and refuses to warm up. Charlie hates the little stool being pushed in under the dressing table, and staff always have to put it back, because he persists in pulling it out. Guests have reported that the kettle boils of its own accord in the middle of the night, and they hear excessive noise, of people in the room above dragging furniture around and jumping up and down on the floor . . . even if the room upstairs has been unoccupied.

One staff member reported: 'I took a school group to the room and the door was open just a little bit, which is really an impossibility without someone holding it open as all our doors are fire doors and close automatically. After a minute or two, the children were about to enter the room when the door suddenly opened itself very wide and then slammed in front of them.'[20]

In the large, opulent lounge downstairs there's a window known as the 'Ngāuruhoe window' because it looks out to that volcano. Staff cleaning it in the early morning sometimes see the reflection of a man coming down the stairs, but when they turn around to ask if they can help him, they find there's nobody there.

Maybe I also needed to camp out at the Chateau in case Charlie was around. It had recently shut its doors, supposedly for good, so it was likely nobody would be around to stop me. I couldn't camp out inside, of course — at least not without risking significant police intervention — but I could camp out on the lawn outside the Ngāuruhoe window. I tucked the idea away for later.

Meanwhile, I turned my attention to breakfast. It was daylight, and although the clearing had been imbued with a 'Blair Witch' sort of atmosphere the night before, the stark sunlight filtering through the trees dispelled any notions of ghosts while I brewed my coffee. Other stories were calling for my attention; I would give up on Ruapehu's ghosts, for now.

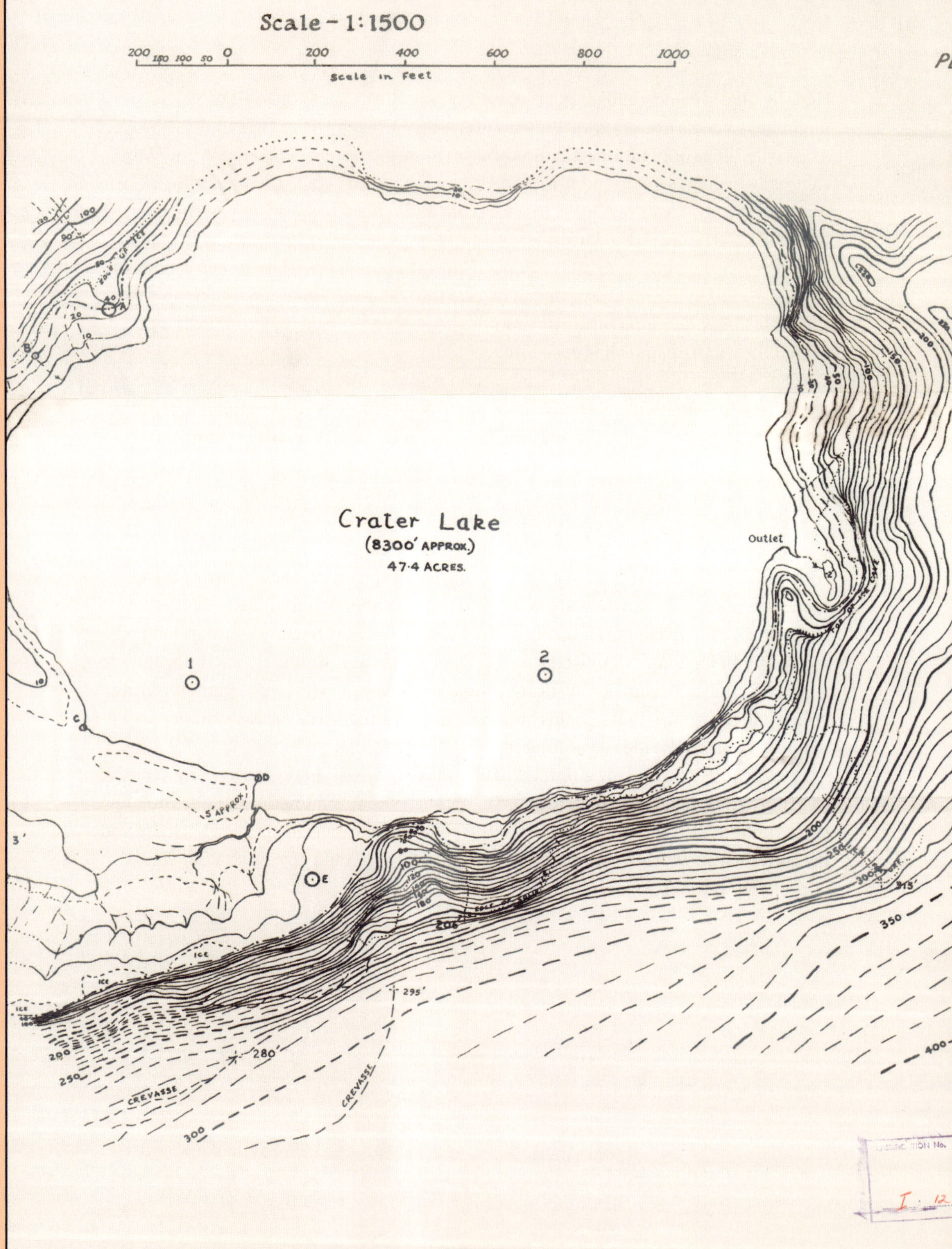
Scale - 1:1500
200 150 100 50 0 200 400 600 800 1000
Scale in Feet
PL
Crater Lake
(8300' APPROX.)
47.4 ACRES.
Outlet
1
2
B
C
D
E
S'APPROX
3'
ICE
CREVASSE
295'
280'
200
250
300
350
400
315'

Map from 1954 showing detail of Te Wai ā-moe Crater Lake on Ruapehu. Lands and Survey Department via National Library of New Zealand, 38313552_1954

CHAPTER 12

Te Wai ā-moe Crater Lake

The Crater Lake has long been a place of fascination. From the 1930s, mountaineers had been trying to verify the link between the lake and the Whangaehu River by exploring ice caves next to the water, and what they found prompted them to warn authorities about the potential risk of a flood from the lake. Then Tangiwai happened.

In Palmerston North, on a still, windless day, dust was falling from the sky. A motorist backed his car out of his garage, gave it a quick clean, and left it standing in the gleaming sun. An hour later, he came out to find the car covered in dust. Other motorists reported the same thing: cars covered in seemingly endless fine dust.

It was 1 July 1945. Ruapehu was erupting, and spreading its ash far and wide. In Ohakune, residents closed their windows. At night they reported a glow above the mountain, now and then lighting up stronger as the activity in the crater reflected on the clouds above. Over at the Chateau a worker swept ashes off the concrete in front of the hotel amounting to 1.6 kilograms, enough to fill a pint glass.

In the following days, tourists flocked to Ruapehu, some ascending the mountain to get a closer look. It was usually safe to view the eruptions from the peak of Dome, just north of the Crater Lake, but not this time; Ruapehu was showering stones and burning sulphur far and wide. Rocks weighing up to an estimated 50 kilograms were strewn across the snow of the Whakapapa Glacier, more than a mile from the lake, cracking as they cooled on the ice. Other rocks the size of houses were seen being ejected and then falling back into the crater.

A group of eight from Victoria University College went up from Whakapapa to see the eruptive action. Six kept going on to Blyth Hut, but two wanted to camp out near the crater. Robin Oliver, having recently graduated, had joined the Geological Survey Department, and he wanted to do some scientific observation and make a few notes. His friend James Witten-Hannah loved adventure.

The two belayed themselves down ice cliffs 50 metres high and into the crater, where they explored the rocks on the empty lake bed. A tholoid, a rounded mass of lava extending above the surface of the crater-lake floor, had formed.

'Where we landed, the tholoid was close to the edge and very definitely alive, particularly on the outside,' Oliver said later. 'The mass was shaking and unstable, and powerful jets of sulphurous steam were bursting out between the rocks. The boulders were hot and as they continually heaved and tumbled about, a red glow came from underneath. Periods of comparative quiet would, without warning, be broken by a deafening report and red hot rocks would hurtle out of the centre of the tholoid, shoot 400 feet into the air, then fall back onto the island. These staccato outbursts would last for two or three minutes at a time and conversation was then impossible. While they lasted, the whole of the centre glowed like an immense brazier.'[1]

Oliver got right into the middle of the action, about as close as you can get into a live volcano without risking immediate death. He attempted to make a closer examination of the tholoid by scaling its trembling 15-foot face, but was foiled due to the heat and the constant movement. Between the tholoid and the ice wall was a pool of grey mud, steaming and bubbling at 58 degrees Celsius, which Oliver took to be the old bottom of the Crater Lake.

He and Witten-Hannah spent about half an hour looking around the crater, then climbed back up the ash-covered ice cliffs and pitched their alpine tent in a crevasse about a metre deep, directly above the edge of the old lake. The activity was becoming

View from Paretetaitonga of an empty Crater Lake following the 1945 eruption. Bagnall Collection, Massey University Library

ABOVE: Crater Lake in the early stages of unrest, 1945. Bagnall Collection, Massey University Library

BELOW: Swimming in the Crater Lake was a favourite pastime of early climbers. Bagnall Collection, Massey University Library

more frequent and violent. They got into their sleeping bags and were brewing tea, just after dark, when the crater blew. The eruption lasted about half a minute. 'Immediately a pretty concentrated deluge of hot rocks showered on to the tent, which collapsed,' Oliver said. 'We could smell our clothing and gear burning.'

Both men were thrown some distance. Oliver was struck on the head and lost consciousness momentarily. Hot rocks seared through their clothes and burned their skin. Witten-Hannah's sleeping bag went up in flames, as did the tent. He dragged the dazed Oliver away from the crater and down the mountain a little way. They struggled on for a while, then Oliver collapsed. Witten-Hannah realised he'd have to go for help. He tucked Oliver into his sleeping bag, which was dotted with burn marks, and set off down the hill. There was no wind, and the night was clear and fine. Lying in his sleeping bag on the side of the mountain, Oliver was treated to more eruptions. 'While I lay there, two subsequent explosions showered me with warm ash, but I curled up and hoped that nothing would hit me.'

In spite of a badly gashed leg, at 1 a.m. Witten-Hannah arrived at Blyth Hut, where he discovered that the rest of the party had had a drama of their own the day before; they'd become lost and only stumbled across the hut by chance.

The group set off to try to reach Oliver, but realised it was too difficult and that they would need help. They turned around, came back down the mountain, and then carried on to Ohakune to alert police. The local constable, R. D. Gardner, and Dr L. E. Jordan, both experienced mountaineers, then mounted a rescue attempt. When they found no trace of Oliver, a rescue party was despatched from the Chateau.

Oliver was eventually found wandering around in a confused state and was brought down the Whakapapa Glacier. The rescue party reported afterwards that the eruption was 'incredible', with rocks estimated at 6–7 tonnes being expelled about a third of a mile from the crater.

Oliver and Witten-Hannah's inspection was the closest made of an eruption during that phase of Ruapehu's activity, but it came at a cost. Oliver had a burned hand and leg, and a moderately severe injury to one shoulder. Their exploits were condemned by local rescuers and police afterwards.

James Witten-Hannah was no stranger to adventure or risky exploits. In August 1937, aged 14, he had tried to climb the steep southern face of Paritutu in Taranaki and had to be rescued from a perch on a ledge. He'd gone up with friends by the usual route, then after descending thought he'd try the harder southern route. He nearly made it but was stymied by a sheer rock face — he couldn't get up, and he couldn't get down either. He sat on a ledge in the shade, freezing, and yelling for help. It took three hours before walkers noticed him and he was rescued — not hurt, just scraped up.[2] Later, he was injured near Barron Saddle in Mount Cook National Park, when a person in a party that was roped up slipped and the whole group was dragged down a steep slope. Two were killed, and four others were seriously injured.

After the crater rescue, Robin Oliver's father wrote to the *Wanganui Chronicle* to publicly thank all those involved:

> I feel deeply grateful to each and every member of these expeditions for their instant and spontaneous response to the need for assistance. I wish to thank Mr Hannah, who, though wounded and dazed by the falling hot rocks, managed to drag his companion away from immediate danger, and then descended the mountain alone and at night to carry word of the accident to the camp. At the same time I very much regret the inconvenience and loss of time caused to members of these relief parties.'[3]

By late July, there was no lake left to speak of. It had reduced from 17 acres (about 7 hectares) down to a tiny, shallow pool of water about a foot deep, perhaps the size of a very small room. The crater was filled with fragmental lava, some of it collected to around 40 feet high, and was piled with shingle, huge rocks and mud. The ground remained unstable, discharging steam and rocks at pace. Ash and coarse volcanic gravel continued to shower the snow slopes down to the bushline. Rocks on the Whakapapa Glacier landed with an impact that embedded them four or five feet into the snow.

Boulders found more than a mile from the crater up to 20 hours after the 'big eruption' were still intensely hot even though they'd been sitting on snow; climbers were able to dry their wet boots by standing on them.

Local mountaineer Joe Blyth said it was certain that the Crater Lake, formerly a great attraction for visitors to Tongariro National Park, would never reappear.[4]

If Ruapehu has a beating heart, it's the Crater Lake, the jewel in the mountain's crown, right in the centre, surrounded by the summit peaks. Its lyrical te reo Māori name, Te Wai ā-moe, means 'sleeping waters', a juxtaposition of the meaning of 'Ruapehu', which translates as 'pit of noise' or 'exploding pit'. Silent and sleeping, but on occasion noisy.

The lake did indeed refill after the 1945 eruption. After the 1953 lahar, when it emptied out again via an ice cave, there was a beach of sorts underneath the Whakapapa Col, allowing bathers easy access to the steaming waters. Now, it's ringed with steep cliffs nearly 80 metres high, although determined climbers can access the lake by circling around to its outlet at the head of the Whangaehu.

The Crater Lake has always had some sort of acidic quality. In 1924, James Alexandre wrote in the Royal Astronomical Society of Canada's journal that it was quite possible to have 'an enjoyable bathe' in the Crater Lake at times, 'even if it does tend to remove all the dye from one's swimsuit'.[5]

It's accepted that Hugh Girdlestone was the first person to swim across the Crater Lake, probably around 1912. Joe Blyth followed suit about 10 years later, and made it a habit during his regular climbs to the top. Then, in January 1932, two Aucklanders, recorded only as N. and K. Sylow,[6] swam across the lake and an account of their experience was published in the press.[7] N. Sylow was a powerful swimmer who had broken the New Zealand salt and freshwater records for 200 yards breaststroke, and presumably he wanted a new challenge. He was known to be a 'dark horse', coming out of nowhere as a newcomer to the sport of swimming to suddenly win big competitions. It took the pair 50 minutes to swim across the lake, a distance said to be three-quarters of a mile. They experienced sudden alternating currents of hot and cold water, and reported that the water was bitter and had similar characteristics to a copper sulphate solution.

Because of the publicity surrounding the Sylow swim, later that year the Park Board began to discourage swimming in the lake. In its 1932 annual report, the Department of Lands and Survey drew attention to the dangers, including cramping in cold water or meeting gas of an 'overpowering nature' discharging from patches of the lake:

> It was reported that two swimmers encountered considerable difficulties owing to the excessively cold and warm patches of water met with. The Manager at the Chateau has been instructed to warn visitors of the dangers referred to, but the Board desires to give as wide a publicity as possible to the matter, with a view to preventing adventurous spirits from embarking on such a foolhardy exploit.[8]

Never mind that the Sylows were accompanied by a very experienced guide, Olaf Pedersen, who was based at the Chateau.

After the 1945 eruption, there was little activity in the 1950s and early 1960s, and swimming in the Crater Lake became a tourist attraction of sorts. Occasional rain and melting snow kept the lake levels topped up, and heat came through via steam underneath. But after 1965, volcanic activity raised the acidity of the lake, and the practice of swimming tapered off.

People still swim there, or so locals tell me, even though it's offensive to tangata whenua. DOC's management plan is clear that the Crater Lake and its surroundings are tapu, and an important cultural site for many mountain users. I've seen photos taken fairly recently of young guys getting dressed after reportedly swimming in the lake, and have witnessed social media threads arguing that you can do it, you just need to wash off properly afterwards in snow or fresh water to remove the acidity, and/or indulge in the unusual practice of slathering yourself comprehensively in Vaseline first.

Photos exist of hijinks in the Crater Lake; university tramping clubs have long thought it hilarious to stage photo shoots of fishing successfully from the lake or canoeing across it. Indeed, the lake has housed watercraft doing scientific work; in 1950 members of the New Zealand Canoeing Association took it upon themselves to sound the depth of the lake (264 feet), following its eruption five years earlier.[9] I've also heard persistent rumours — which I have not been able to substantiate — that there was even a jetty at one point.

Knowing about the existence of the Crater Lake is a vastly different thing to the experience of actually seeing it. The first time I saw the beautiful and imposing Te Wai ā-moe, I'd ascended in a long day from the Whakapapa carpark with my friend Percy. We were both junior snowcrafters, tentative on our crampons and clutching our ice axes

ABOVE: One of the Sylows during their swim across the warm lake. Canterbury Museum

BELOW: Whangaehu Glacier after a lahar. Note the collapse of the ice as the water has run under and over it. Air Force Museum of New Zealand

nervously. I'd been up to the Summit Plateau before with another climbing buddy but had only reached the Te Heuheu/Tukino ridge that borders the flat ice before descending again, hyperventilating mildly at the exposure and the new experience.

Percy and I walked up the west part of the Whakapapa ski field, found our way up to the Notch, a low saddle that gives access into the Summit Plateau, and cramponed up the ridge to Dome (2672 metres), one of the smaller summit peaks. Dome overlooks the Crater Lake directly, looking across the waters to Tahurangi, the highest point, and up on the right to Paretetaitonga, a much more intimidating peak for beginners. From the Dome viewpoint, you can't see a way down to the waters of the lake. A small shelf or 'beach' used to exist here, but now it's a sheer drop — maybe 40 metres, according to the topo map, so it's a long way down. Percy and I took turns snapping photos of each other with the lake in the background, had a look at Dome Shelter, which was frozen over entirely with thick and impenetrable rime ice, and gazed at the mesmerising Crater Lake until we grew too cold to remain. Shivering madly, we added more layers and started to descend.

More recently, I took a group of women up to the fringes of Dome to see the lake. Some of them were there for the first time. Taking 'newbies' up there brings me a fresh realisation of the wonders and delights of seeing a lake in the middle of a volcano surrounded by snow, tephra — volcanic material — marking lines of age in the ice and telling a long story.

Popping up to pay my respects to the Crater Lake is one of my all-time favourite Ruapehu activities, and I don't think that'll ever change. It's my regular ski-touring route, leaving the top of the Far West T-bar and slowly skinning up the Whakapapa Glacier, walls of the glacier acting as a soundproof space, heat reflecting, often protected from the elements. You get the sense you're in another world entirely. I almost resent it when spring fully pops and there's an ant trail of humans plodding up the glacier with me. But I realise that's an elitist view of a mountain experience, to want to have it all to yourself.

It's always hard to leave the beating heart of Ruapehu, and I get a sense some days that the mountain is only just tolerating us up there for a short window of time. More and more, I'm becoming acutely aware of its specialness, and that — just like Joe Blyth's assumption in 1945 that the lake would never reappear — nothing is ever guaranteed.

The first known European person to see the Crater Lake was George Beetham. Born in England, Beetham came to New Zealand with his family aged 15, arriving on the ship *William and Jane* in 1855. He and his brothers built up Brancepeth, a sheep station in the Wairarapa that eventually covered 24,000 hectares, and in 1873 he won the parliamentary seat for Wairarapa. It's said Beetham engaged with local Māori, who knew him as Hori Pitama.

In 1878 Beetham travelled to Ruapehu to make the first of several attempts to get to the top. This first was scuttled by the weather, and on the second he also faced bulletproof conditions, describing the glacier as covered in 'a glittering sheet of ice as slippery as glass'.[10] Accompanied by one of his station hands, Michael Ruddy (aka 'Micky'), Beetham cut steps across the glacier, determined to make it to the top. He approached from the east, having long suspected that the chemical waters of the Whangaehu River started from the lip of the 'extinct' (as it was then thought to be) crater of Ruapehu. Taking a break, Beetham sat down to admire the view, and opened a tin of sardines using his tomahawk. He laid the tool down on what he thought was a level piece of ice, but 'away the confounded thing slipped as if it had been endowed with life', and disappeared over the rocks.

Rattled by the icy conditions, exposure and Ruapehu's habit of cloaking himself in cloud mid-morning, Beetham decided to turn around, but first he left a sign that he had been there. He pitched a flag by cutting a hole in his sardine tin and forcing it into the crevice of a rock, then inserting his alpenstock with the flag attached. He took nails out of his pocket to fasten the flag to the alpenstock, laying them on the ice, where they froze so firmly he couldn't pick them up again. He then put his knife down while he fastened the flag, and when he looked again, it too was gone. It had slipped into a crevasse and slid down the hill where his companion Micky was waiting. It was too much for them both.

Beetham wrote: 'This mysterious disappearance of tomahawk and knife, and the peculiar mournful roaring of the wind that was bringing heavy clouds over the mountain, made me wish to be off the ice and again down the mountain-side, and Micky was particularly anxious to leave such a weird and mysterious place.'[11]

The next year Beetham returned, this time accompanied by Joseph P. Maxwell, another gentleman from Wellington. After two days of trying and failing because of the tricky terrain, they successfully climbed the highest southern peak. This involved crossing from a lower peak via a snowy saddle 'which might be compared to the ridge of a house, a slip from which would mean a slide of some thousands of feet sheer on either side'.[12] From Tahurangi they could see the Crater Lake, although they didn't descend to it and had no idea it was warm. 'From this point, hitherto untrodden by human foot, a splendid view of the surrounding country was obtained.'[13] It took them 13 hours in total to return to their low camp.

Crater Lake has been known to freeze over, although not in recent decades. In 1886 James Park of the Geological Survey Department saw it covered with a sheet of ice, but just four months later surveyor Laurence Cussen saw it violently boiling.[14] In 1913, a mountaineering party reported that the lake was frozen (in January, no less) and another in 1926, when a 'thick coating of snow' also covered the ice.[15] The lake had generally been around 26 to 38 degrees Celsius, hot enough to bathe in.

Joe Blyth regularly observed temperatures in the lake, but his data was considered to be unscientific. When he bathed in the lake in 1920, he warned the less experienced members of the party against staying in too long because of the water's 'enervating influence'. From his observations, Blyth believed the lake's temperature peaked in 1922.

FOLLOWING PAGES: Te Wai ā-moe Crater Lake before the downwasting of the glacier underneath Tahurangi. Now an outlet exists on the opposite side. Auckland Libraries Heritage Collections

What was perhaps the first recognised lahar from Ruapehu in recorded human history occurred in April 1889. Locals reported that the Whangaehu River suddenly rose to become a swollen, raging torrent, filled to its banks and inky black. It hadn't been raining, and the phenomenon seemed to stem directly from the mountain. A newspaper reported: 'There has been no such outbreak previously in the memory of Natives or Europeans who live near its locality, and it is a source of wonder and amazement to them.'[16] A local sheep musterer in the Kaimanawa Range reported he had seen a huge column of steam ascending high above the mountain for about half an hour, something he had never seen before despite living in the area for some time.[17]

When George Beetham reached the Whangaehu River during his explorations he was surprised to see that the colour of the water 'was just like milk, but the taste was far different', like 'sour sulphurous sea water'. Although his horses were thirsty, they wouldn't touch it.[18] In 1858, when a party of young survey cadets came across the Whangaehu River as it cuts across Te Onetapu (formerly known as the Rangipo Desert), they too sampled the water, reporting a combination of rusty iron, alum and zinc.[19] Delicious! During an eruption in 1895, it was reported that the water tasted 'as strong as a saturated solution of alum, with a twang of iron also — someone said like ink'. People took tumblers of the Whangaehu water to see if it would settle overnight, and whether the opaque milky colour would dissipate once given a chance to calm down.[20]

During the 1895 eruption, surveying cadet Walter Dunnage took a great risk in approaching the lake's edge, in a bid for scientific information. The lake was a milky colour and boiling violently, he wrote, and the noise was a deafening roar. Great jets of sputtering sulphurous steam were being ejected from the lake. Despite the danger, Dunnage took a temperature reading — 53 degrees Celsius. He also attempted to take a water sample by lowering a bottle on a cord from the top of an ice cliff, but the contents spilled as the bottle bumped against the cliff on the way back up. It eventually jammed in a crack, and Dunnage broke the cord as he tried to free it.[21]

There was speculation from early on about the source of the Whangaehu River. It was generally thought to be the Crater Lake, but how? Benedict Friedländer, an early surveyor, wrote in 1898:

> It may be asked, What becomes of the water of the lake? A part, doubtlessly, evaporates; but it seems very probable that the River Wangaehu receives water from the lake by percolation . . . the Wangaehu River starts from the eastern slope of Ruapehu, and its waters, as well as the waters of the lake, are turbid, and have a smell of sulphuretted hydrogen. Taking these facts into consideration, there can, I think, be but little doubt that this is the way the water takes.[22]

Still, Friedländer thought the water only ended up in the Whangaehu Stream from the Crater Lake by 'percolation' rather than direct flow. At that time, the Whangaehu Glacier was so much bigger and longer that it was impossible to trace a direct line from the Crater Lake down into the catchment — the water flowed under the ice. Today, it's easy to see.

A Department of Lands report of 1908 seemed to support Friedländer's theory: 'It is highly likely that the water percolates through the porous walls of scoriaceous rock on the eastern side, and perhaps forms the true source of the Whangaehu River.'[23] In 1929, Joe Blyth traced the Whangaehu up to its main source in a ravine at around 2100 metres, where milky pale-yellow water issued from a rock. The source, he said, was about as big as his body, and smelled very strongly of 'sulphuretted hydrogen'. Blyth theorised that the water percolated through the scoria from the Crater Lake because the surrounding glacier would not melt at a rate that could produce such a large flow of water.[24] It was generally thought that the water from the Crater Lake somehow seeped down through the scoria and then sprang out much further down to form the Whangaehu.

In 1935, Roy Sheffield, who was chief guide at the Chateau, and John Bryan, an enthusiastic mountaineer from Taumarunui, went exploring at the source. They discovered a 25-foot-high cave in the ice walls around the Crater Lake, out of which a stream flowed. Snowfall had been thin that year, and the glacier ice hadn't encroached

upon the lake as much as it usually might. The *Poverty Bay Herald* reported that the Crater Lake was like a 'huge bowl of thick green turtle soup, with steam and bubbles frequently rising in the centre, and discoloured chunks of melting ice like lumps of fat, floating near the edges'.[25] The pair got into the lake, swam through the turtle-soupy waters, and went into the mouth of the cave, but they lacked equipment and didn't go any further.

Two years later Sheffield and Bryan went back, taking three others with them. It was March, the time of the year for maximum snow melt. The group ascended the mountain with the express purpose of exploring the ice cave, but they found the ice was too thick and the cave hadn't formed. Instead, a stream of sulphurous water was flowing under the ice, with about six inches to spare between the water and the roof of the tunnel. Bryan and Sheffield roped up, and Bryan belayed Sheffield as he dived underwater and swam into the tunnel. Sheffield reached a small ice cave where the roof was higher and he had room to breathe, and then crawled and swam a little further. He heard a roaring, booming noise, and realised he was approaching a high waterfall.

Sheffield discovered that the water from the Crater Lake dropped out of sight over a rock ledge. He'd come as far as he could without descending over a cliff into darkness and turned back. The pair intended to go back and run tests by tipping confetti into the stream and watching the Whangaehu 'spring' further down to see if it really was the source of the river. While there's no evidence they ever carried out this colourful activity, they did continue to return to the lake to explore the ice cave, which abruptly disappeared after the eruption period of 1945.

Sixteen years later, in March 1954, Bryan and Sheffield gave evidence at the inquiry into the 1953 Tangiwai disaster. On Christmas Eve, 151 people lost their lives after a flood from the Crater Lake wiped out the rail bridge over the Whangaehu. Sheffield told the inquiry that all the water that had gone down the Whangaehu River that night had come from the Crater Lake, which had drained a huge amount. He had gone up to the lake on 14 January to swim, and had found a huge cave shaped like a concert soundshell, 30 feet high, 50 feet wide and 50 feet deep. He began exploring. Large slabs on the roof of the cave were cracked through and ready to shear off, and the floor was littered with broken ice. He could see to the back of the cave, where water was flowing through an opening towards the Whangaehu Glacier. There were two ice falls while he was outside the cave, he said, and one while he was inside. Rattled, he had turned and left.[26]

On 25 January, Sheffield went back and traced the Whangaehu up the flanks of Ruapehu to its known source at the foot of the Whangaehu Glacier, which then extended down much further than it does now. He could see high-water marks, but nothing to indicate that a dam had built up. He tasted the water in a couple of different spots and noted it was as sulphurous as the Crater Lake water, and he took this to mean that there was a constant flow into the Whangaehu from the lake. Like Joe Blyth, he thought that the flow was too great to have come from glacier melt alone. The ice cave, Sheffield told the inquiry, was the same cave he'd explored in the 1930s, but it was now very much bigger.

John Bryan also appeared at the inquiry, and spoke of a 'river flood' down the Whangaehu in 1925. He had concluded then that the outlet at the Crater Lake had become blocked, increasing the lake level, and a subsequent collapse of the blockage had given way to the flooding. Bryan reckoned the same thing had happened in 1953; earth thrown up in an eruption had blocked the outlet, and it had finally given way. He'd been so sure of this potential danger that he'd reported it to an officer of the Department of Scientific and Industrial Research, who told him that dye would show him where the water ran, and offered some, but Bryan and Sheffield already knew where it ran. 'Having reported to him, I felt that if he decided to take the matter further, he could,' Bryan said. He assumed the Railways Department knew of the risk, but he never imagined a disaster on the scale of Tangiwai. If the lake was checked every week or so the situation could be monitored, Bryan suggested.

Bryan's theory was confirmed by the Chateau's current chief guide, Willis Turton, who had inspected the lake on 27 December, just after the disaster, and had observed that the level had dropped by almost 25 feet; it had drained enough to expose a mud

ABOVE: The Tangiwai disaster killed 151 people. Graham Stewart

BELOW: A hole appeared in the ice next to the Crater Lake following the lahar that caused the Tangiwai disaster. Air Force Museum of New Zealand

EW 8506

Tourists once rode up to the Crater Lake in a modified 'snowbus', swam in the lake and skied down. Department of Conservation archives

flat. Across the lake, Turton saw an ice cave where the water had escaped. He'd never seen the cave before. The connection between the Whangaehu River and the Crater Lake was 'common knowledge among Chateau guides', Turton said.[27]

John Bryan regularly went back with others who were interested in exploring ice caves. On one occasion this included students from the O'Rorke Hall Speleological Group at the University of Auckland, accompanied by Wellington mountaineers, all armed with helmets, a ladder and head torches.

'We stood on crumbling rock,' caver 'A.J.D.' wrote later. 'Around us swirled steam and poisonous fumes. On our left a grey stream crashed fifty feet down a yellow waterfall. Above us an arch of ice swept up from mist and darkness to a patch of brilliant sky. Silhouetted against the sunlight, a naked speleologist capered in and out of a gush of ice-water, with animal cries!'[28]

The flooding that caused the Tangiwai disaster had left behind a cave with an ice roof, a floor of solid rock and rubble, and the sound of a rumbling waterfall. The group descended a small 15-metre cliff by ladder, but had to retreat when the cave narrowed and the sulphur fumes became too strong. 'Mist and fumes hid the recesses of the hemispherical grotto, but we could see the black opening where the stream disappeared. A rainbow hung in the air, and our shadows, cast on the mist, had haloes of multi-coloured rays . . . we watched the sunbeams pouring down from the entrance like a huge floodlight to strike a heap of fallen ice.'[29] They swam out into the lake, whose acidic water was at 27 degrees Celsius, and then showered and scoured themselves under almost freezing pure melted glacial water.

So how did people get up to the Crater Lake to bathe in its waters? Did they walk from the top of the chairlift, or plod up from the carpark at the base of Whakapapa ski field? Well, many did both those things. But others did it the easy way, buying a £1 ticket for a ride on a snowcat especially designed for the purpose of shuttling skiers uphill.

The Whakapapa snowbus, known as the 'Whakapapa Cat' or the 'Whakapapaka' ('Whakapapa Car'; it even had fake number plates with that name), was introduced in 1961, when two mountain enthusiasts, Ron Manning and Tom Bates (a brother of the man who helped Edmund Hillary get his tractors to the South Pole), cobbled together a tracked snow vehicle using parts of a tank, tractors and other mechanical material. It was able to travel on terrain even at strange angles, and after much experimentation and some frustration over the course of a season they managed to get it working in a reliable fashion. The Whakapapa Cat carried up to 20 people at a time from the top of the chairlifts to the Crater Lake, a journey that took about 20 minutes.

Jock Graham wrote that this invention 'opened the wide upper slopes to those of less hearty constitution and even to casual visitors unprepared for strenuous exertion'.[30] Graham's choice of vocabulary is revealing of how the mountain was seen in that era: as something to be conquered rather than revered, or somehow overcome, more than respected and honoured:

> Within the last two years even the final lap of the glacier climb has fallen to man's mechanical ingenuity. The 'Whakapapa Cat' now plies up and down the Whakapapa Glacier. Now the least athletic of visitors can reach the summit plateau of the highest mountain in the North Island with no more exertion than that required to transfer from car to chairlift and from chairlift to snowcat.[31]

Foot power still has its place, though. For me, the Crater Lake is the sudden reward at the end of a long slog up the hill. The Whangaehu, though, was less familiar terrain.

In 2018, I set a goal of visiting all the summit peaks of Ruapehu in one season. I'd been 'finger tramping' on Ringatoto (2591 metres) for years before I actually went there. Formerly named Mitre Peak (an underwhelming name, as there are at least five other Mitre Peaks on New Zealand's maps), Ringatoto has thankfully been restored to its te reo Māori name. Intel online indicated it was big, steep and loose, and that stuck scarily in my head. The East Ridge and North Buttress were both, I was informed, Ruapehu classics. A friend attempted an axe-and-crampons grade 1+ climb of the East Ridge, approaching from Rangipo Hut, but pulled the plug after getting the willies due to exposure, and before roping up.

Both these 'classic' routes seemed a bit, well, intimidating. I theorised that there might be an easier way to get to Ringatoto: perhaps skinning up to Whangaehu Hut, slipping into the Whangaehu Glacier, then following a line up the true right, gaining the saddle between Ringatoto Peak and Tahurangi that separates the Whangaehu from the Wahianoa. It would surely be an easy plod from there to ascend three contour lines to the summit.

Even that sounded dicey. As well as being 'big, steepish and loose', a climbing information database informed me: 'Access to the Mitre [Ringatoto]–Tahurangi col is more difficult since the eruptions of the mid-1990s. Take care picking a line through the steep section just below the lip. Without snow cover these slopes can be dangerously unstable.'[32] Yeah, so: big, steepish, loose, difficult, and dangerously unstable. Sounds like all the necessary ingredients for a fun day out.

'That'll work,' said my old mate Ron Thomas, when I asked him for info. 'So long as the snowbridges are all still in. If they're not in, you won't get up.'

Access sounded uncertain in late spring conditions but a buddy and I went anyway, leaving at the crack of dawn from a lodge on Tukino and striking out into a clear, still and eventually roasting-hot day. Getting up to Whangaehu Hut was straightforward, and by the time we reached the hut we were peeling layers off and applying sunscreen. Then we switched from skins and skis to axe and crampons to get into the Whangaehu catchment. There's a section of hard ice there that sits in shade most of the day, if not all of it, and is always rough. I deemed it too risky to try to ski in, even though fiddling about with crampons took longer. I felt silly about an hour later when, from a distance, I saw another party traverse in on skis without incident, but you make the decisions you think are right at the time. They made it, but it still looked pretty ropey.

We transitioned back to skis and skins to ascend the true right of the Whangaehu, and there were plenty of 'Will it go?' moments, followed by 'Holy smokes, it does'. The snowbridges were all still in place — in fact, the whole Whangaehu River was basically one big snowbridge — and we did our next transition around the 2340-metre mark, where cliffs were shedding rocks and ice in the heat of the day. Thankfully we were far enough away to avoid that danger.

When we reached the saddle, skis on packs once more, I understood the 'difficult access' description. A lip of sorts had formed from volcanic rock and some of it was poking through, but enough snow still clung to the edge to give us passage. From there it was indeed a snow plod to pay our respects to the peak itself. The summit ridge of Ringatoto allows expansive views into the Wahianoa, an area I'd passed across while tramping the Round the Mountain Track, but one otherwise totally unknown to me. The Wahianoa gorge looks small on the map when you're finger tramping across it, but it's much more colossal and imposing in reality. We stared and pointed, discussing possible routes we could take down the Wahianoa catchment then exit via the track, but that was a mission for another day.

The ski back down to Tukino took around 20–25 minutes. I had the willies skiing off the saddle, but just held my cookies on the traverse in and then gave it heaps on soft snow. It was like skiing on ice cream. The snow was dotted with small rocks that had fallen from the bluffs above and were sitting about 5–10 centimetres underneath the surface. I couldn't see them until I was right on top of them, but I couldn't hear or feel them making contact with my skis, so I assumed the creamy snow was covering them and pushing them around in its softness. (It's good not to be precious; skis are tools, not jewels.)

We managed to traverse neatly back up to a knoll above Whangaehu Hut, the same traverse we'd elected to crampon down rather than ski earlier in the day. It was hairy, I was purely a passenger, and I managed to scar one ski properly with a rock as I reached the knoll. We enjoyed a cruisy, wide open hoodle back to the Tukino carpark.

'Snowbridges were all in,' I reported back to Ron. 'Well, it was one massive snowbridge really.'

Ron laughed. 'I never had any doubt you'd make it.'

I went back in summer with my friend Christy to see what the Whangaehu was like with its magical snowbridges gone. We tramped up from Tukino to Whangaehu Hut, maybe a two-hour trip, easy but off track with a little bit of navigation required. Occasional poles showed the route, but there was no track as such — just occasional patches of snow to stand in and be excited.

The Whangaehu gifted us another windless, clear day, the horizon adorned with a line of clouds with flat bottoms, the sort a child would draw. A sweep of dark rock led up to the Watchtower, a craggy peak on the ridge between the Whangaehu and the Mangatoetoenui, but looking downhill the rock was beige to ochre. We popped over a ridge and the hut came into sight, light-grey corrugated iron with a roof sloping more

Whangaehu Hut at sunrise.

on one side than the other. Its water tank would hopefully be full, and its longdrop was fixed firmly to the rock with long wires. The hut is perched exactly on top of a rocky knoll, basically on a cliff. If you sleepwalked with any measure of enthusiasm or speed, you could end up in a ravine.

Although it was midsummer, as soon as the sunset faded the chill set in. A snake of snow persisted in one of the deep gullies. Christy and I paced up and down the cliff edge, looking into the Whangaehu's great gash in the landscape, snapping photos and drinking hot chocolate to stay warm.

'I'm really taken with the different rock colours,' I said to Christy. 'Look at how that changes from here to there, and again just there.' Angry red rocks mixed with reassuring creamy clay cliffs, dotted with dark grey-brown moraine.

'Must be different eras of eruption maybe,' Christy said. 'We need a geologist here to give us a guided tour. There's silica in the water, though, I think — see how the rocks are white where the water flows down.'

The landscape of the Whangaehu in summer was a world away from its easy winter blanket. Now, I could understand Ron's caution about snowbridges — it would be difficult, if not impossible, to get much further up the stream bed on the true right, where the water flowed over cliffs and fell down behind piles of snow, and rock obstacles blocked the way. On the true left, the going looked easier. The glacier proper had shrunk hugely from the time of Joe Blyth's exploration of the Whangaehu's source and was a small snowfield high up towards the summit plateau, pockmarked by moraine.

The next morning we woke early, the hut lit up by an attention-seeking sunrise. The fireball sky was blazing with displays of changing colours — blue, orange, red, pink, purple — and was reflected in the hut windows outside. The whole Whangaehu catchment became bathed in orange, and the rocks lit up as if they were glowing hot with volcanic energy. The river below the hut was a thread of silver cutting through brown.

And there we were, perched on the edge of the world, staring into a bare lahar path of history, in the box seat if Ruapehu decided to erupt. Which he might, at any given time, without notice, we are reminded, spreading fire and ice simultaneously, and relentless heat from the centre of the earth.

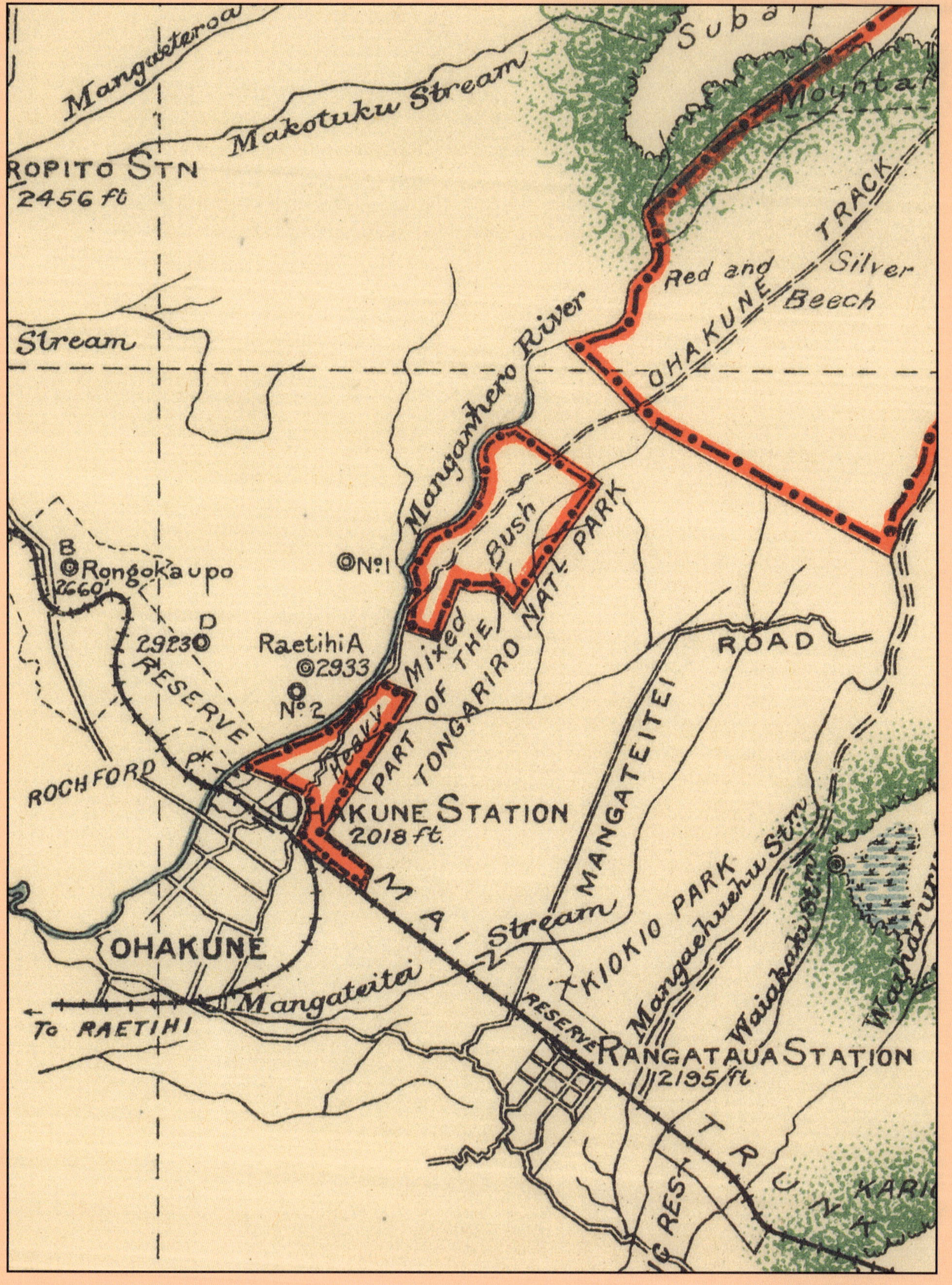

Mangakteroa
Makotuku Stream
ROPITO STN
2456 ft
Stream
Mangawhero River
Red and Silver Beech
OHAKUNE TRACK
Mixed Bush
Heavy
PART OF THE TONGARIRO NAT'L PARK
B
Rongokaupo
2660'
D
2923
RaetihiA
2933
No. 1
No. 2
RESERVE
ROCHFORD PK.
OHAKUNE STATION
2018 ft.
OHAKUNE
To RAETIHI
Mangateitei Stream
MANGATEITEI ROAD
MAIN TRUNK
KIOKIO PARK
Mangaehuehu Stm.
Waiakaki Stm.
RESERVE
RANGATAUA STATION
2195 ft.
RES.

Map showing Ohakune Station and the Main Trunk Line. National Library of New Zealand, 35094335

CHAPTER 13

Sly groggers and a booze ban

The King Country was a dry area until 1953, but that didn't stop the thirst. Sly groggers used backcountry tracks and sneaky tricks to smuggle alcohol in and out of Ohakune and around the mountain. But sometimes, they got caught.

Carrot-themed fancy dress for the unveiling of Ohakune's 'big carrot' in 1984. Robert Milne, Ruapehu Bulletin

Ohakune is a little town with a big carrot. Nestled at the foot of the southern slopes of Ruapehu, it stretches in an oblong shape, curiously, between the railway station in the northern end — the 'Junction' — and 'town' in the southern end, where the Mangateitei Stream flows through. Ohakune sprang up partly because of the public works on the railway in the early 1900s, and it seems to have hung on with the tips of its fingernails while other towns along the Main Trunk Line petered out.

It's famous for carrots — although other vegetables grow there perfectly well, swedes, parsnips, potatoes, to name a few — because of the Big Carrot, an oversized cheery orange fella who greets visitors as they enter from the south. He (I am assuming 'his' pronouns here) was installed in 1984 after ANZ Bank used him in an advertisement about an incentive saver account, then wondered what to do with him.

At the time, the locals' views of the carrot were mixed. Some thought it an eyesore, as so many of these giant icons tend to be (Tīrau and the corrugated-iron sheep, I'm looking at you), while others saw it as an amusing novelty. Several ladies wrote outraged letters to the local newspaper condemning the phallic object as a tool of the patriarchy and suggesting two melons would be more appropriate. But the carrot stood, and today it's accompanied by an entire 'carrot park', with a carrot racing car, a carrot rocket and an assortment of other anthropomorphised vegetables. The standout character is Muncho Manchester, a new but smaller carrot with a face, who gets roundly abused on the regular by local hoons and has to be carted off on the back of a trailer for delicate repairs. There's also Panorama Parsnip, a vegetable creation that transcends gender boundaries in the most modern of ways. I exhort readers to visit the parsnip for themselves.

The Ohakune carrot preoccupation has not been without personal conflict. In 1936, a consumer took a Chinese market gardener to court for unfair carrot representation. 'They looked very well on top, but underneath there was a lot of rubbish,' a Mr Talbot said, accusing Mr Chee of Ohakune for deceptive packaging. The magistrate jumped on board, grabbing a split carrot and waving it around. 'Here, what do you think of this?' he said triumphantly. Mr Talbot showed the court a typical paper bag of carrots, with healthy, large ones on top and then very small ones underneath. Those present in the courtroom laughed at Mr Talbot's tiny carrot. At that point the magistrate declined to hear further evidence, and fined Mr Chee five pounds plus costs.[1]

Vegetables aside, Ohakune has a strong history as a den of iniquity, a hotbed of filth. In 1907, the newspaper *NZ Truth* claimed it was mostly populated with 'the scrum [sic] of New Zealand' — jailbirds, thieves and spielers (gamblers). 'Ohakune is on the Main Trunk route, and it has been a very rorty place in its time, so rorty indeed has it been that "Truth" seriously considered whether it should not rank with Sodom and Gomorrah.' *Truth* admitted, however, that Ohakune 'seems to desire to live down its wretched past — a past of drunkenness and debauchery, a camp of sly-groggers and wickedness generally'.[2]

I worked for *NZ Truth* not once, but twice, first as a reporter when I was quite young, and later on as a layout subeditor on better pay. I have no claims to fame

ABOVE: Ohakune got its start as a collection of tent camps for the building of the Main Trunk Line. Alexander Turnbull Library, 1/2-017097-F

BELOW: Prime Minister Sir Joseph Ward hammers in the last spike of the Main Trunk Line, 6 November 1908. *Appendix to the Journals of the House of Representatives*, 1909, D-2

from my second stint at the notorious newspaper (now defunct; RIP *Truth*), but as a cadet journalist I helped the West Auckland police solve the pressing case of the Henderson Panty Thief, a chap who'd been helping himself to women's knickers off their washing lines for some years. (In a separate incident, a lineup of large black plastic sacks full of women's underwear, all shapes and sizes, was found in the basement of a deceased estate, and as a canny young reporter I put two and two together and got a g-string.) My greatest regret is that while working there and constructing stories about panty thieves and alien abductions ('PROBED: RANUI WOMAN'S REPORT FROM ON BOARD THE UFO') I was never acquainted with the word 'rorty', and hence feel I've been denied the opportunity to properly put the term to work.

Anyway, back to Ohakune, a place of drunkenness and debauchery, rife with sly groggers and purveyors of wickedness. When I moved to Ohakune several years ago, I discovered it was in fact rather quiet. There were fewer carrot wavers than I'd anticipated, although the yearly 'carrot festival' seems to bring them out of the woodwork quite effectively. But the town did seem rather, erm, 'herbaceous', if you catch my drift (my drift is that a lot of people partake of the Devil's Lettuce). At certain times of the year, the pungent smell of wacky baccy wafts around the streets as residents hold their 'trim parties' (this, I have learned, is a sort of harvest gathering where willing helpers clip unwanted leaves off the buds, and for their troubles get to take away some of the booty for themselves).

I heard various rumours about the place. One of the local pubs was a front for Mr Asia! The abandoned building where the old bar Hot Lava used to be had secret canals underneath it! A local man, always thought to be a loose unit, turned out to be finally completely, entirely off his banana and had been burrowing tunnels underneath someone else's house, convinced he could physically mine for Bitcoin! I even heard of a motel in town that was rumoured to have historic stashes of cocaine hidden in the walls. The property sold quickly when it went up for sale, and the new owners swiftly set about doing 'renovations', mostly consisting of knocking the inner gib board off the walls in strategic places.

There were layers upon layers of secret activity. Ohakune seemed to be heavily populated with hermits and dope smokers, and sometimes the two circles overlapped in a simple Venn diagram, coming together to create a new category: hermit stoners. I ran only in the hermit circles, and by nature these circles were very quiet.

My neighbour Jono was an iconic Ohakune resident, the ultimate representation of the laid-back Ruapehu lifestyler type, and fiercely loved by everyone in town. He sported an unwieldy beard, hair that I would describe as 'creative' and an Australian accent, and late of an evening when I looked into his eyes I got the occasional feeling that somebody else was driving. He owned a loud subwoofer, a machine he employed enthusiastically. I took to knocking on his door at 2 a.m. with politely framed requests to lower the thumping, which resounded through my walls and shook the glassware.

OHAKUNE. A707.

(Those lovely, fragile Spiegelau glasses, which I'd acquired after assiduously collecting the New World stickers during the 2020 lockdown, shook themselves right off the shelf and smashed in the sink.)

If Jono didn't answer the door, I'd pop in and check on him. He'd be curled up next to the subwoofer on the couch, remote control in one hand, vape stick in the other. I'd just need to lean in through the ranch slider door and click off the subwoofer at the source. I started to worry about him, so I took to covering him up and tucking him in so he didn't get cold. He never woke up, not when the music was switched off, and not when I tucked the blankets around his neck. He once told me, apropos of his desire to pass his love of loud music on to his toddler daughter, 'My earliest memory is being put behind the subwoofer at a Midnight Oil concert', and I felt this explained a lot.

Once, he was upstairs on his DJ decks but hadn't properly plugged his headphones in so the sound was loose in the airwaves. I assumed he wasn't home, so I crept up the stairs and we both gave ourselves a dose of alarm. He had reasonable cause to be angry at me for intruding into his home — though I had of course knocked, to no response — but he just gathered himself and grinned, always pleased to see another human being.

'Hey, Heather, hey man, how's it going?' (He always called me Heather and I hadn't had the heart to correct him. I also liked to fly under the local radar, and Hazel is far too distinct a name.)

'Hey Jono, yeah good, how are you doing?' Was he going to be angry at me for intruding?

'Yeah man, good eh. Real good. How are you going?' Nope, he wasn't.

'Yeah, great, eh. Yeah. How are you going?'

This exchange, reminiscent of tennis over the net, went on for some time, while Jono swayed precipitously. Eventually I cut it off.

'It's a bit loud, eh.'

'Nah man, I've got the headphones on.'

'Oh yeah they're on, but they're not plugged in,' I said.

He looked around in surprise. 'Mate, so sorry, I had no idea.' He undertook to plug them in, and I left, one of the few times in those days I didn't have to tuck him in.

Jono was for sure one of Ruapehu's local treasures. He had always just come from helping someone on the tools or was just off to take petrol to a motorist who had run out and was stranded on the side of the road. I had a lot of respect for him, and I did begin to wonder if he was Jesus himself, come once again to earth after a 2000-year hiatus, only in a stealthier, but more hairy and liberal form.

I've long held a theory that you can learn something from everyone you meet in life. One day I went over to ask Jono for help to shift a piece of heavy furniture I couldn't lift on my own. He was in his front yard, lying on a giant inflatable doughnut, roll-your-own in one hand, Panhead in the other. The music was pumping, and Jono was staring out at the sky. You get a glimpse of Ruapehu from his place, and the mountain was peeking out above a line of cloud.

'Hey Jono, how you going?'

'Hey Heather, man, I'm great eh. I'm building some trellis.'

I looked around the yard. There were signs of trellis building, for sure — various tools and thin pieces of wood — but it didn't look like the trellis had got very far, nor was it progressing in any meaningful sense of the word.

But that was my lesson from Jono. I know I'm uptight a lot of the time and I need to learn how to chill out more in life. How to lie back and stare at the sky. How to derive peaceful pleasure in the moment, and set aside whatever KPI of the day is pressing on you from every direction.

How to relax on the doughnut.

In 1884, the King Country, covering a large portion of the western and central North Island, was declared dry after requests from Ngāti Maniapoto.[3] Prohibition in the King Country was aimed at 'protecting the natives, who fell easy victims to the "fire-water" of the early European traders', and while this retrospectively seems somewhat condescending, many Māori wanted government intervention and access to liquor tightly controlled.[4]

Although prohibition was ineffective, the ideology persisted. But in 1900, Māori MP Hone Heke publicly stated that sly grogging was prevalent throughout the King Country, that prohibition had been 'a complete failure', and that 'indiscriminate drinking' was worse there than in any other district in the colony. Heke recommended granting licences in the principal centres.[5]

Ohakune remained a dry area until 1953. The nearest pubs were at Tokaanu in the north (in the days of horse travel, at least a full day's journey) and Taihape in the south. Smuggling liquor in on the train was a tricky, risky proposition, as luggage was often checked, but packhorses could slip through unnoticed — especially after dark. Often, sly groggers would leave the pub at Taihape as soon as darkness fell and arrive at Ohakune before daybreak.

Although many agreed with prohibition, there was also a general sense of admiration for those who smuggled alcohol into the area, or perhaps a desire to shake off the restrictions. A nationwide poll held in 1914 showed the overall population neck and neck, for and against prohibition (for: 199,763; against: 198,353), while by contrast the local Waimarino area voted much more strongly against it (for: 827; against: 1688).[6]

In the early 1900s, the Main Trunk Line was being built through the middle of the country, and tent camps were mushrooming. Ohakune sat at the head of the railway's southern extension and took on the air of a gold-mining town during a rush. Its population was predominantly male railway workers, and there wasn't a lot to do except drink, gamble and talk crap. A journalist visiting Ohakune in 1907 reported that:

> Sly grog-selling goes on in spite of vigilant police supervision; in fact, the increased element of risk is a cause of much extra profit to the sly grog shanty keeper. Whisky of unknown brands, merely labelled 'Best Old Scotch' or some other such general description, changes hands at 15/ to 25/ a bottle. This 'Best Old Scotch' is more often called 'Chained Lightning' by its consumers.[7]

Police stationed at Ohakune checked the trains for incoming booty, and often chaps got caught. Local policeman Constable Snow went undercover, popping up in sly grog circles under the name 'H. Barker'. After about a year of intensive detective work, he gave the nod and police swooped in to raid houses where liquor was being illegally peddled.[8] When several smugglers appeared in court in 1910 one after another, Constable Snow's undercover work was acknowledged as having been instrumental in unmasking these devious sly groggers.[9]

Whisky was the drink of choice, and it was sold at very high prices along the Main Trunk Line. It could often be bought at £1 per bottle in Taihape or Tokaanu and smuggled into Ohakune to be sold for three times the cost, and even up to £6 per bottle. (According to the consumer price index, a cost of £1 in 1910 would equate to roughly $200 today.)

The Public Works Department, which was in charge of the railway construction, was also on constant watch for liquor changing hands. Suspicious-looking swags or goods that had no discernible owner were snatched. Whisky bottles were often rolled up in blankets and tents. A story goes that a businessman sent himself liquor labelled 'Drapery' and it had a mishap along the way, so it arrived with a note attached: 'Drapery Leaking'. Owners of goods gone missing didn't ever front up to make enquiries, of course, and anything seized was sent to the constable in Taihape — who presumably had a *lot* of friends.

By the late 1920s, the prohibition cause was losing ground. Polls showed Kiwis had no appetite for prohibition, with 'continuance' — i.e. of the status quo — well in the lead.[10] Ohakune remained dry, however, with some residents supporting the cause. One local, a known prohibitionist, owned a car he couldn't afford due to petrol taxes, registration costs and other expenses, so he kept it in the garage for more than nine months. Eventually he sold the vehicle, and instructed the purchaser to take it from the garage. The amazed buyer — who was silly enough to open his mouth — found 80 bottles of whisky concealed in the back seat. The seller's public prohibitionist stance saved him from prosecution, but the unused car had made an ideal hiding place for an enterprising sly grogger.[11]

Ohakune is known not just for its tasty carrots, but also for its chocolate eclairs. Topped with sugary chocolate icing and oozing with fresh whipped cream, they're touted as one of the town's must-do attractions. The bakery where they're made boasts a sign declaring it 'Johnny Nation's Chocolate Eclair Shop', and although it changed hands in recent years, the eclairs — and their quality — continue to reign. As a local I try to avoid them, out of fear of excess consumption, and I have a hard and fast rule, never broken, that I only eat them if I'm alone or with somebody. There's nothing quite like stuffing your face with a chocolate eclair after a massive day out on the mountain, particularly if it involved majority uphill travel rather than hot laps on a chairlift, and especially if it involved the classic backcountry ski traverse from Whakapapa across to Tūroa. Today the eclairs are rivalled by toasted sandwiches and cream doughnuts as other culinary treats in town that are gaining prominence thanks to word of, erm, mouth. Close your eyes and sin!

In the early 1900s, when Ohakune was a dry area, soft drinks were the local attraction, and 'soda shops' or 'cordial shops' popped up all over town. Some were legitimate, of course, but others were simply a front. Constable Carey busted people selling bottles of 'cold tea' for £1 each. Like Constable Snow, Constable Carey was always on the case, and those stung for violating the law found themselves in court for sly grogging.

So-called 'temperance drinks' could contain no more than 3 per cent alcohol by law. Ohakune locals were peddling ginger beer that was 'accidentally' alcoholic at 11.63 per cent, 'medicated health wine' with a whopping 21.95 per cent alcohol, and 'overproof' hop beer. The editorial writer at the nearby *Manawatu Times* appeared shocked by Ohakune's debauchery: 'Temperance drinks on the Main Trunk line must be strong enough to stand alone. It is a no license area and possibly the absence of legitimate alcoholic competition induced the innocent "soft" drink to put forth a special effort. This sort of thing is evidently a recreation of Ohakune where the Court was crowded for sly grog selling cases.'[12] A sentence of three months' hard labour wasn't uncommon for those who failed to front up in court to answer for their crimes.

One crisp night in September 1907, John Nation — whose name lives on in the great chocolate eclair — met up with his mate Hugh McLean in town. Nation was working as a labourer at Ohakune, and he had his eye on a local lady, Miss Cartier, who ran a fruit shop in town. Nation and McLean met at Miss Cartier's fruit shop, where they had a ginger wine together. So far, so legitimate. They got talking, and whisky was discussed. The two men retired to McLean's own 'cordial' shop, where he retrieved a bottle of whisky, and Nation handed over 15 shillings. Then the two left, and it's here that the wheels came off the trolley. Walking along the street, Nation stopped to wait for two mates while McLean kept going. To their misfortune, the ever-vigilant Constable Carey came along just at that moment.

''Ello, 'ello, 'ello,' said Constable Carey. 'What do we have here, then?'[13]

It was dark enough to cause confusion. Nation handed the whisky to one of his friends just as the other struck a match to light a cigarette, illuminating the act of the bottle of whisky changing hands. The constable demanded they hand over the whisky. Nation — thinking it was a mate pulling a practical joke — gave it over, and the jig was up.

On cross-examination in court, it emerged that McLean and Nation had been on the lash properly the night before. They'd had a bottle of whisky between them and a third chap, and when they went to fetch another bottle Nation fell into a nearby creek. Nation protested, saying he wasn't drunk, just that he had slipped over when going across the plank that bridged the waterway. Still, the prosecutor accused him of being drunk, and pointed out he'd gone to the fruit shop to apologise to Miss Cartier for his drunken behaviour the night before.

'Yes,' Nation said. 'But I knew I was sober that night, and I really wanted an excuse more than anything else to have a talk with Miss Cartier.'

Early maps of Tongariro National Park often showed bridle tracks, which were used to smuggle alcohol on horseback. Archives New Zealand, AECB 8615 199 52/52

Constable Carey had been watching Miss Cartier's fruit shop (or was it the alluring Miss Cartier?) and McLean's cordial shop with his usual persistence. 'When you see men in there till 11 o'clock you can be sure it's not lemonade, squash or lager beer that is keeping them there,' he told the judge.

Sadly for Nation, in court McLean threw him under the bus somewhat, claiming he went into the cordial shop to get a lantern for Nation, who wanted to head up to the railway viaduct. Nation, he said, must have gone into 'a certain shop' after they parted ways. The judge was having none of it. 'There is no doubt whatever that the case is proved up to the handle,' he said. 'It appears that Constable Carey has succeeded in breaking up a sly grog shop.'

McLean was given the maximum penalty because of the porkies he had told, and was fined £50 plus costs, and if he defaulted, three months' hard labour. His lawyer protested: McLean was a working man, and he couldn't be expected to come up with that sort of money — about $10,000 in today's terms — just off the cuff. 'He has probably made the money over and over again,' the judge retorted. 'It must be found at once.' The unfortunate McLean was unable to pay the fine the same day as the court appearance, but it was produced promptly thereafter.[14]

The same year that John Nation ran into trouble with his whisky, the railway reached Ohakune as construction on the Main Trunk Line pushed forward. But a gap of 39 kilometres between the southern and northern railheads remained. Horse traffic took a well-benched route that cut around the lower reaches of the southwestern side of the mountain, following a similar line to the one the railway would eventually follow, joining Ohakune with nearby Horopito. It's thought the bridle track was initially completed in 1886, then upgraded in 1895 to a dray road, and again in 1906 to a road used by coaches that transported passengers and goods between the two railheads. The latter round of upgrading included putting in 'setts' (rock pavers, a sort of cobblestone), creating an all-weather road with less mud.

No surprises, then, that the route became a popular one for sly-grog sellers, not only to transport their booty north and south but also to peddle it to the men working on the railway, who were housed in the tent camps that proliferated along the route. These shelters were made of canvas with timber components and corrugated-iron chimneys, but sometimes they were incredibly primitive, with bunks fashioned from bush vines and tightly stretched sacking. Provisions were sparse, so the men grew vegetables on site and killed native birds for fresh meat. Hard liquor was therefore a welcome sight along the construction route, where there was no entertainment and little else to spend money on.

After the railheads met in 1908 and State Highway 49 was constructed, the route fell into disuse. It sat untouched until the early 2000s, when a group of locals took the initiative of reopening it to create a walking and mountain-biking track, the Old Coach Road. The project's conservation plan noted that the route was essentially an untouched time capsule: 'The end of the road's useful life froze it in time and,

By Authority: Marcus F. Marks, Government Printer, Wellington

M. Crompton-Smith, Chief Draughtsman, Head Office, Lands and Survey Department, Wellington

other than the natural deterioration it has undergone since its use stopped, it is in remarkably good condition.'[15] It was covered with nearly a hundred years of forest litter and loess (dust and silt), which had almost completely hidden the original surface.

Ohakune local Dave Scott, who chaired the restoration committee, was among a group of enthusiasts who went on a mission to see if they could follow the route, bush bashing where necessary. Scott commented that the grog bottles they found along the route were 'an interesting reminder of one of the reasons the coach road got such a lot of use. This was a dry area and those bottles were from the old Taihape Brewery. Obviously it was a sly-grog route as well as a link between the two railheads.'[16]

And so the sly groggers navigated the obstacle of Ruapehu by skirting around the Old Coach Road. But Ngāuruhoe and Tongariro remained as obstacles — or perhaps, opportunities, as the mountain terrain afforded them places to hide.

In his book *Memories of a Mountain and a River*, Bill Mead tells of a secret track between Hauhungatahi and Ruapehu that was used by sly groggers at a time when police in plain clothes were frequenting the usual, easier routes around the central plateau. Mead managed to find the track's northern end, near the current Bruce Road, but it took him some years before he found the southern end.

After the Tongariro Tramping Club built Mangaiti Hut on the southern slopes, with access from Ohakune, Mead began hunting for a shortcut from the hut towards the Mangaturuturu Valley and on to Lake Surprise. From there, the scrub gives way to open country and travel is much easier. Near the Cascades waterfalls in the Mangaturuturu (Mead calls these falls the 'Cataracts'), he found small clearings that could be connected by blazing short trails through bush. When he set out one day with a machete, intending to cut a route through, he discovered a clear track that led into the bush and on to an old formed pack track down into the Mangaturuturu Valley. Mead had lit upon the old sly-grogging track.

'Pack horses, each with two kegs of whisky on the pack saddle, could come in from the Desert Road, over the old horse track past Tama Lakes, and on by the old secret track behind Hauhungatahi,' Mead wrote.[17] From there it was easy to get down the stream to Pokaka, a small settlement on the western side of Ruapehu. If the cops were known to be lurking in Pokaka, another track led to Horopito.

Well-meaning people often put a macron on the 'O' in Ohakune. In 2019, the Powers That Be (well, the New Zealand Geographic Board) decided to allocate Ohakune a macron: Ōhakune. Ngāti Rangi protested.[18] The board hadn't consulted on the change and was forced to backtrack rapidly. The name Ohakune comes from the saying 'e oha, ka oha, he Ohakune ki te ao', translating to 'an opening to a new world'. The name is a nod to the fact that sometimes it can be good weather up on the maunga and bad down below, or vice versa, and people come down off the mountain to a whole new world, descending through the forest of Ruapehu to the grassy land and swamps below.

Currently, the Ohakune community and other townships around Ruapehu find themselves in tricky times. Ruapehu Alpine Lifts went into voluntary administration in

2022 and at the time of writing is in liquidation, and the Chateau Tongariro has closed, faced with the need for earthquake strengthening. In May and June, it's particularly quiet, as local businesses often shut up shop for a spell before the winter snow arrives, and howling winds sweep the township and mountain tops.

On 6 November 1908, the last spike was driven into the Main Trunk Line, the honours being handed to Prime Minister Sir Joseph Ward, who wielded a brand new hammer for the job. Dignitaries and guests arrived on trains that ran from Wellington north and from Auckland south to the location between the Manganuioteao River and the Makatote River. The final spike was adorned with a silver top, and immediately after the crowd had dispersed it was swiftly taken as a memento by a savvy bystander and replaced with a spike of the common-or-garden variety.[19] Sir Joseph was presented with an additional engraved silver spike as a souvenir, and the trains departed again amidst a violent hail shower.[20]

Since the first sod had been turned in 1886 in the Manawatū, the railway project had taken countless men and resources. It was widely expected that Ohakune would die off as a township, now that the railway works were no longer an economic driver in the region, but — probably thanks to the ski field — it never really did. The canvas towns that had sprung up all along the railway line soon shrank away, but Ohakune persisted, somehow, and maybe it will persist yet, driven along not by a rail engine but by the love and enthusiasm of the carrot wavers who stick to its southern side.

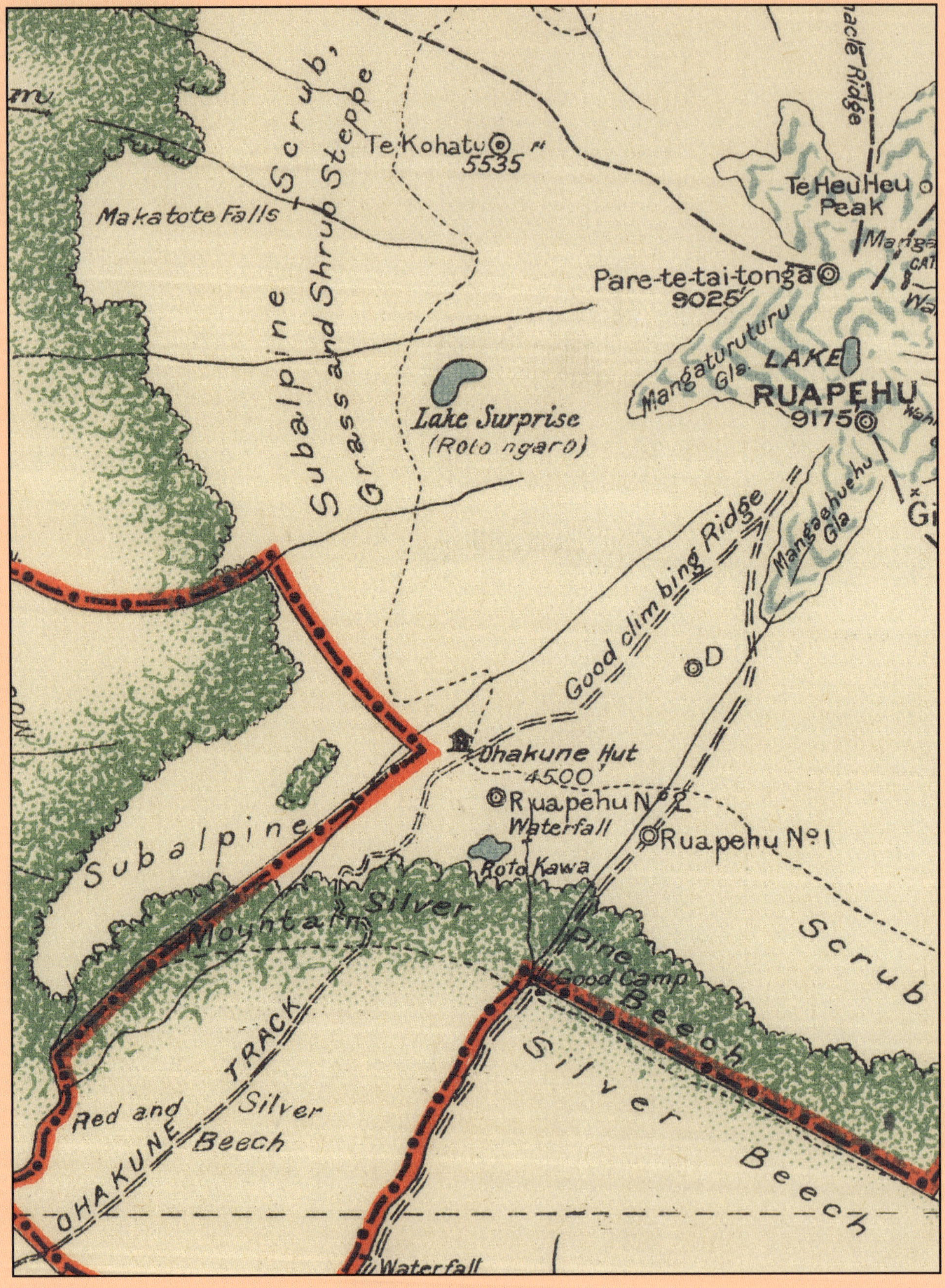

Te Kohatu
5535
Makatote Falls
Subalpine Scrub,
Grass and Shrub Steppe
Te Heu Heu
Peak
Pare-te-tai-tonga
9025
Mangaturuturu
Gla.
LAKE
RUAPEHU
9175
Lake Surprise
(Roto ngaro)
Good climbing Ridge
Mangaehuehu
Gla.
D
Ohakune Hut
4500
Ruapehu No. 2
Waterfall
Ruapehu No. 1
Roto Kawa
Subalpine
Silver
Mountain
Pine
Good Camp
Beech
Scrub
Silver Beech
OHAKUNE TRACK
Red and Silver Beech
Waterfall

Map showing Joe Blyth's Ohakune Hut, before the Ohakune Mountain Road was built. Access was by foot or horse. National Library of New Zealand, 35094335

CHAPTER 14

Joe Blyth's Ohakune Hut

Old Joey Blyth was known for his love of the mountain and for guiding people on his classic 'summit, swim, slide' trips. What started as the Ohakune Hut became Blyth Hut in his honour, but when the hut fell into disrepair the Park Board chose to burn it down. I went on the hunt for the old site, with its stunning open views to the mountain that Blyth loved so much.

Joe Blyth outside the Chateau Tongariro. Bagnall Collection, Massey University Library

My favourite hut is tucked into the beech forest, on the top of a sloping ridge. Cold, clear streams run on either side. The first time I ever visited it, snow blanketed the ground all around, topping trees as if someone had passed overhead with a sieve, giving the area a heavy-handed dusting. Inside, all the bunks are doubles — upstairs/downstairs affairs — except one, a single bunk without an overhead bed that's attached to a large window on the eastern side, facing slightly uphill. Don't tell anyone, but this is the best bunk at Blyth Hut. The view from the window is dotted with stars on a clear night and sometimes the moon passes by, and before dawn a blazing sunrise lights up the landscape. The tiny lights of Karioi mill and Waiouru twinkle in the distance.

I like to visit Blyth Hut on a weeknight, when it's almost guaranteed to be empty, to take up residence in my favourite bunk and watch the night sky put on its show. It's my favourite bunk in my favourite hut on my favourite mountain. Now, there's nothing particularly special about Blyth Hut that makes it my favourite hut — just that it's special to me. Blyth and I have a 'thing' going on.

I did my first ever proper overnight solo tramp to Blyth Hut simply because I felt comfortable going there. I've tramped in with friends to light a fire and roast marshmallows at what we think of as our 'bach' while snow falls softly outside. I've been there in silly winter conditions, battling knee-deep snowdrifts, in sideways hail just because I needed a trip to debunk my cabin fever, and in glaring hot sunshine. Everyone visits Ruapehu in winter while the chairlifts are going and then abandons the area, but the big secret is that summer has just as much to offer.

The area around Blyth Hut is dotted with perfect swimming holes, and contrary to expectations of mountain, they're not that cold. I discovered this one day when I stopped to drink from one of them, expecting a refreshing icy temperature, only to realise it was lukewarm, like bath water. I stripped off and got in. There are a few swimming spots just below Blyth Hut, where you last cross the stream, although in high summer they tend to dry up completely. The locations of the others are secrets I'll take to the grave, but those who elect to wander up and down the mountain's catchments will be amply rewarded.

Over the years I became more curious about the name, and why this hut sits off the main track. There are two information boards inside the hut about the man called Blyth. Initially I ignored them — who cared about some old dude who cut some tracks, I thought — but one day I began to read about the local legend who was Thomas Arthur ('Joe') Blyth.

Joe Blyth had two typical appearances in the old photos. In one, he sports a cap and bow tie and holds a smoking pipe — ready for his job teaching at Ohakune School. In another, he wore hobnailed boots, old trousers tucked into his socks, no collar, an old coat and an old felt hat pulled well down on his head. He was ready for the mountains.

Blyth was born in Whanganui and came from Scottish farming stock. He excelled at school but intended to go into farming like his relatives, so his first job as a teacher was only ever intended to be temporary. But it stuck, and he was headmaster at Ohakune all his life. He and his wife Jane had three children, and three horses — Cocky,

Ohakune Track, built by Joe Blyth and intended to withstand horse traffic. William Bower Black via Canterbury Museum

Polly and Betty — all of whom, horses and children, helped Blyth in constructing a 14.5-kilometre track up the southern slopes of Ruapehu in the days long before the Ohakune Mountain Road was built. Blyth was a family man, for sure, but he was a mountain man, too. His son John, known as Jack, said that when Jane passed away in 1915, the track-building helped him grieve: 'After my mother's death, and his return from the war, the mountain and especially the track, was a solace to him. He spent years of hours between after school and nightfall, hours of days, weekends, school holidays, Christmas holidays, even winter holidays, when prior to pitching a camp in the dark at the Six Mile Peg, one foot of snow had to be cleared away before work could be started. I was his co-worker over weekends and holidays when other, more fortunate boys (as I thought then — now it is different!) went swimming, playing games or on holiday. The track for me became a living, hated thing: but it was built and I grew up in the best company possible.'[1]

Blyth was separated from Ruapehu during the Second World War, in which he served just over three years in New Zealand and abroad, and was awarded the British War Medal and the Victory Medal.[2] His biggest war injury was a badly sliced finger; he cut himself with a table knife in fright when a shell landed in a trench alongside him. Luckily, it didn't explode. He returned to Ohakune and took up his old position as headmaster, and once again found peace working on tracks on and around his beloved Ruapehu.[3]

He loved to take people on his guided tour of Ruapehu, up the track to the bushline, a stay overnight at Ohakune Hut, then straight up to Tahurangi Col. They'd have a dip in the Crater Lake, then slide down the wide glacial snow slopes known as Gliding Gladys on gunnysacks. The fibre sacks weren't waterproof, but the fabric gave the slider a sensible balance between grip and speed. It was well known that torn trousers were the only major damage from a trip with Joe Blyth.[4]

Jack Blyth said his father was instrumental in introducing his students to the delights of the mountain. 'Altogether, my father took about 500 pupils on mountain excursions without other than the loss of some trouser seats from contact with "Gladys". If none of these pupils developed a love for nature, all must have glimpsed something of its grandeur, all at least had one interesting experience.'[5]

When the party returned to Ohakune Hut, Blyth would create a hearty dinner and stoke a roaring fire. One tramper recalled: 'As night fell we would make the hut where there would soon be a huge fire blazing, while the welcome aroma of frying chops, onions and tomato assailed our nostrils. Nothing was forgotten to give zest to the meal or the enjoyment of the trip.'[6]

Gunnysacks may have been the usual sled of choice, but Blyth once put the hut's frying pan to good use. Tramper Ashley Cunningham remembered summiting with Blyth in 1928 and getting ready to slide down the snow on sacks as per the usual practice, when Blyth pulled out a frying pan from the hut, sat down on it, and with the handle between his legs, he took off and beat everyone down the slope.[7]

Joe Blyth's beloved track still bears his name. What's left of the track, anyway. Some of it became lost and has been rediscovered; some of it is now under the Ohakune Mountain Road. But it's easy to see the line Blyth chose, cutting straight up the southern slopes of Ruapehu from Ohakune to the bushline. He cut rounds of wood and laid them across the pathway, a technique designed to stop horses from creating mud pits. What's left of the track today, referred to as the Old Blyth Track, is an unrelenting mudfest. It departs from a corner where the road curves to the left and gradually slogs up several hundred metres of elevation, suddenly ducks left to avoid a steep section and then emerges near the Rotokawa tarn. I've only ever walked it a few times, not for fun but in order to tick the box and pay homage to Blyth and his early work. The existing track amounts to about a third of the original; from the Rotokawa tarn there's some 'lost' track through the bushline to where Ohakune Hut stood, and an occasionally poled route leading higher.

For a long time I'd assumed that Blyth Hut had replaced an older hut of the same name. I'd also read of Ohakune Hut, Ohakune Mountain Hut and Mangawhero Cottage. A bit of research led me to realise they were all the same thing, but the original hut was built on a totally different site to today's Blyth Hut. Ohakune Hut was nestled just above the bushline, with an arresting view of the maunga. It had three rooms, one of which was often used as a private room by Blyth as he was the custodian. Made from corrugated iron and matchlined, the hut had a deck, two fireplaces and 22 bunks. A horse yard was nearby and a spring provided a water source. It was kept unlocked and the public could use it but were expected to pay fees towards its upkeep. As custodian Blyth presided over supplies such as cutlery, crockery and cooking items (including the famous frying pan).

In 1922, after two years of construction, Ohakune Hut was the first hut on the track to open. Bill Salt of Ruapehu Ski Club, who had built the Whakapapa huts on the northern side, was contracted to do the work, and Ohakune Hut followed the same design.

That year, Blyth, who visited the hut regularly to ensure all was in order, was appointed a founding member of the Tongariro National Park Board.[8] The Ohakune Hut was well patronised by enthusiastic skiers and climbers, and early photos of the hut often show skis standing up outside and the ground blanketed in snow.

After Joe Blyth died, there was local pressure to change the name of Ohakune Hut to Blyth Hut in his honour. The Tourist and Publicity Section of the Department of Industries and Commerce, Tourist and Publicity (what a name!) agreed with the Park Board's decision to rename it. Some were keen on a memorial tablet but the board decided that any tablet should go in the hut and not be erected on the mountain.[9]

I'd heard rumours that the old Blyth Hut had been burned down by hoons and vandals, and I went in search of details. At Archives New Zealand I found a file of old correspondence and pieced things together. In 1961–62 the newly constructed Ohakune Mountain Road reached Mangawhero Falls, meaning Blyth Hut could be reached within a 10-minute walk from the road rather than by a long horse trek from Ohakune. This improved accessibility led to increased usage but also to increased vandalism — much like the Haunted Whare. The Park Board had problems on its hands with ongoing costs for the hut's repair and maintenance. By the early 1970s, people were calling for the hut to be rebuilt or resited further away from the road.

Word got around and citizens wrote in to have their say on Blyth Hut. A group of Venturer Scouts from Taihape offered to take over the hut and make sure it was shipshape for the public to use too, but the board hated the idea of private ownership of huts and their application was declined with polite thanks.[10] The Waimarino chapter of the Deerstalkers Association also protested vociferously about the proposal to remove the hut, which led to a respectful response from Chief Ranger John Mazey: 'The Board is deeply concerned about every aspect of the Park including the history of the area . . . Blyth Hut as at present constructed and located does not fit into the Round the Mountain Hut and Track System.'[11]

Mazey wanted the hut replaced on the same site so that it stayed on the Ruapehu circuit, providing a base for climbers and trampers and shelter for people travelling from Mangaehuehu Hut to Mangaturuturu Hut in one day. He also wanted Lupton Hut (owned by Whanganui High School) to be moved to a new site near the Wahianoa River for pine control work, and wanted the Tongariro Tramping Club's Mangaiti Hut removed (frankly, he wasn't the first to object to Mangaiti Hut). Mazey didn't like club huts or privately owned huts in the national park, and thought the Park Board should also take over Mangaturuturu Hut, the Wanganui Tramping Club hut. Lupton Hut was too close to the new Blyth Hut, he thought. This was all a logistical exercise: 'All in all I do not find the situation as being a sensible tidy arrangement,' he wrote.[12]

But the demolition of Blyth Hut was the biggest itch in Mazey's breeches. 'From time to time some of the residents of Ohakune have expressed concern about any possibility of the existing hut being demolished,' he wrote. 'It would appear that many people are of the opinion that the original hut known as the "Ohakune Mountain Hut" was erected by the late T.A. Blyth and because of his great interest in the mountain that it would almost be sacrilege to demolish the hut.'[13] With such strong public sentiment, Mazey recommended robust public consultation before any decision was made, and called a public meeting in Ohakune in April 1974.

I found a memo in the file at Archives New Zealand detailing the outcome. The Park Board, along with the mayor of Ohakune, called a public meeting for 8 p.m. on 3 April. By 8.15 p.m. the only people at the meeting were Mazey, another ranger and the mayor. For the sake of process, Mazey explained the issues and various proposals to the mayor. At around 8.45 p.m., one other person arrived at the meeting.

'In brief I went over the same grounds again for the benefit of this person,' Mazey recorded. 'No objections were raised to the possible demolition of the existing Blyth Hut.'[14]

A few months later, in October that year, the board decided to demolish the (admittedly almost derelict) hut and build a new, larger one further from the road. Once the new Blyth Hut opened in 1975, the Park Board burned the old one down. It was decided that one of the old planks with names engraved on it would be preserved and incorporated into the new hut,[15] but unfortunately that never happened — the whole

ABOVE: Ohakune Hut with Ruapehu in the background. Department of Conservation archives

BELOW: Ohakune Hut, a mecca for explorers, in snow. Ashley Cunningham collection, Ohakune Library

hut went up in a grand blaze in what was essentially Park Board-sanctioned arson (imagine DOC setting fire to, say, Mangatepopo Hut in a contemporary context). The great fear that Blyth Hut would be destroyed was realised, but at the hands of officials rather than hooligans.

A book about the construction of the Ohakune Mountain Road contains a photo of the old Blyth Hut. 'The burning was not popular with the locals, many of whom had built and maintained it,' author Karen Hawke Grimwade wrote. '[Historian and ranger] John Lythgoe made the suggestion it could have been moved off-site as a museum — perhaps that would have been a good compromise.'[16]

The new Blyth Hut, my beloved hut with its sunrise window, isn't on the Round the Mountain Track and perhaps that's what makes it special, quietly tucked away as it is higher up on the slopes. The final decision of the Park Board ignored Mazey's recommendation to keep the replacement hut as a Round the Mountain asset, and instead it was built elsewhere in the style of Joe Blyth, as a structure to serve the people who came to explore the higher slopes on the mountain. A poled route exists above the hut, leading further onwards, luring us to explore.[17]

Once I knew the history of the original Blyth Hut, I felt the urge to go on a mission to find the old site. I'd found coordinates from a list of historical assets in the archival material at DOC and plugging those into the old S20 maps gave me a good indication of the area. Then I looked on other old maps; some showed the hut possibly in the vicinity of Rotokawa, yet others showed it on a ridge not far from Mangawhero Falls. I had enough information to go on that would put me in the general area. I'd need, of course, to have a thorough poke around.

I set out on a still day from the Massey University Alpine Club hut below Tūroa to gain the upper part of the ridge, above any scrub, and descend down on the ridgeline to the old hut site. I battled scrub occasionally but I won, and after a short puff and grunt I gained the ridgeline. I began to pick up old marker poles and tracked them on my topo map app with a pin for each one; I'd be able to see the line of the old track on the map later, although the ground trail was now only very faint in places, and totally gone in others. I'd lit upon the upper part of Blyth's old track, the route he would have taken to lead people up the mountain on his 'summit, swim and slide' trips.

The marker poles ran out near a small stand of beech forest. I peered inside but saw nothing that provided a clue. No water sources trickled nearby. I knew there was supposed to be a spring, although that could have dried up or been diverted long ago. I walked around, conducting a grid search in each direction within the small U-shaped clearing. I blazed a line south, and found the site.

A smooth layer of moss had grown back where the base of the hut had denied the ground sunlight for so many years, but other plants and grass hadn't taken hold. Tussock waved its hands around the edges of the hut's old footprint. I identified tiny fragments of charred timber from the sanctioned arson, and diamonds of shattered glass from the former windows. A few rusty, decaying nails punctuated the remnants.

CLOCKWISE FROM LEFT: Joe Blyth's grave at the Ohakune Cemetery; the sign that still stands at the site of Ohakune Hut; the one-time site of Ohakune Hut, in 2023.

I picked up something that caught the sunlight; it was half a round from the bottom of a glass bottle, bent and warped in the fire. A sign on an old wooden post informed me of the way: Chateau, nine hours in one direction; Mangawhero Falls and Mountain Road in the other.

Further down from the hut I found long loops of wire, which I later found out were from the horse yard. I tried to follow the track further down the hill to see if it would meet up with the existing track past Rotokawa, but I lost the thread of it and the beech forest had taken over. I tracked the last remnant of it on my app with the note: 'Last marker pole before potentially significant bush bashing stupidity.' The area was boggy underfoot, a condition I'd read about in the old correspondence, but I couldn't find the spring they used to drink from. Any water sources in the area were very minimal.

I turned around and drank in the view, the same view I'd seen in the historic images of Blyth Hut, only they were always snowy and today abundant sunshine was baking the mountain's bare, rocky slopes. Imagine, just imagine, if Joe Blyth's hut had been preserved like the Old Waihohonu Hut on the eastern slopes of Ruapehu, rather than going up in a blaze. A fire to erase the problem of vandalism.

Joe Blyth made 147 summit trips in his lifetime, leading other people and sharing his extensive knowledge of mountain flora. He was known for being a walking visitor centre full of knowledge, often exercising his talent of telling a yarn with a wealth of detail. He'd arrive at the hut with horses laden with supplies for a trip, calling out with a cheery laugh and an inexhaustible supply of anecdotes at the ready. As headmaster at Ohakune he was known for teaching the four Rs: reading, writing, arithmetic and Ruapehu. But in spite of his love of the mountain, he never liked to close school early on break-up day and was known to exhort his pupils with: 'Keep up the pressure.'

I found an entry from the old Ohakune Hut book in 1924 written by Blyth to celebrate his fiftieth ascent: 'Having on sundry occasions during the past fifteen years had to acknowledge defeat and discomfiture in divers assaults on the snowy fastnesses of Ruapehu, it is with some satisfaction that I record on this 11th day of January, the fiftieth occasion on which I have placed my jaded heel on the hoary brow of my venerable opponent. T. A. Blyth.'[18]

He died after a brief illness on 3 February 1940,[19] in the shade of the mountain he loved and having managed his last ascent just a fortnight before his death.[20] Blyth was laid to rest in a beautiful spot overlooking the Rangataua Lakes, whose view is out to the mountain he loved so much. I found his grave, a family tomb with his wife Jane Elizabeth and their children Gordon, Marguerite and John. Two ferns are engraved at the top of the tombstone and there is a short inscription: 'I to the hills will lift mine eyes.'

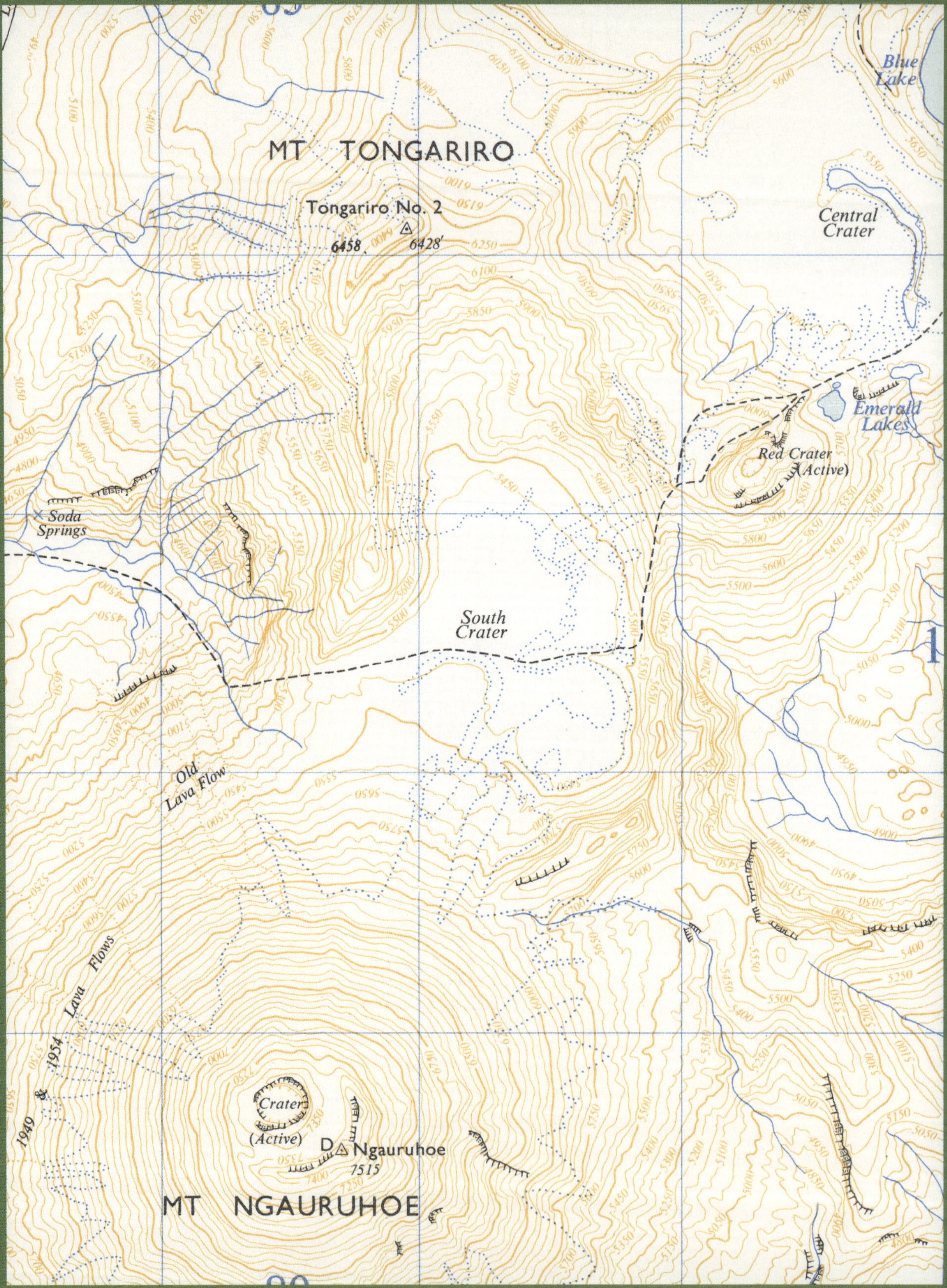
MT TONGARIRO
Tongariro No. 2
6458
6428′
Blue Lake
Central Crater
Emerald Lakes
Red Crater (Active)
Soda Springs
South Crater
Old Lava Flow
1949 & 1954 Lava Flows
Crater (Active)
Ngauruhoe
7515
MT NGAURUHOE

Map of Ngāuruhoe and Tongariro from 1963, showing the old snowline. National Library of New Zealand, 23362514

CHAPTER 15

Skiing Ngāuruhoe

In 1968, ski-filmmaker Warren Miller shot famous French skier Jean-Claude Killy on Ngāuruhoe as the volcano erupted. After organising a food and gear stash at the eastern base of Ngāuruhoe, I set off to see if I could recreate Killy's line (only without the eruption).

In August 1968, French skier Jean-Claude Killy and filmmaker Warren Miller arrived in New Zealand with a crew of 12 to film the 13-part series *The Killy Style.*[1] Warren Miller was an up-and-coming filmmaker and ski bum who combined these two passions to create a legacy of ski films. Killy was known to be something of a reckless skier. In 1962 he fell while racing to qualify for the world championships (unaware he'd already been selected), but immediately got up again and crossed the finish line on one ski. The other leg was broken, but Killy still managed the fastest time. He had three Olympic gold medals and a sponsorship from champagne company Moët & Chandon, which required him to tote a bottle around and place it strategically in any shot if he was photographed.

The crew had been sitting in rain on Ruapehu for nearly two weeks, unable to film anything of note, and they were getting itchy. Meanwhile, Ngāuruhoe gleamed in the sun, beckoning them over to film and ski. Just getting to this point had taken them six months of planning, logistics, production and negotiations.

During the fortnight Ngāuruhoe had been regularly active with small eruptions, and Miller noticed they seemed to happen regularly between 3.30 p.m. and 4 p.m. 'as though triggered by some geological time clock'. He got to thinking they should hire a helicopter to fly the group to the summit in the morning. If they could ski and film before 3.15 p.m., then they'd be clear of the danger zone before the 'daily eruption' began.

They lifted off at 7.30 a.m. and after a 10-minute flight were dropped off on the rim of the smoking crater of Ngāuruhoe. The noise was overwhelming, the sulphuric smell penetrated their nostrils violently, and the ground shook and rumbled beneath their feet. The mountain was alive, and not that happy about their presence. When the crew threw rocks into the crater they seemed to fall forever.

'It was awesome to stand on the lip of an active volcano and look down into the steaming crater and see pieces of earth moving,' Miller said. He and another cameraman filmed all day as Killy skied aggressively and the volcano continued to smoke.

About 2.30 p.m., the ground started shaking. The cameras were moving so much they couldn't get a steady shot, and they had to discard their tripods. 'Relying on my full semester of Geology 101 in college, I made the decision to stay, noting, "I think it'll be an hour before its daily explosion",' Miller said.

Killy skied down the 'previously unskied eastern slopes' of Ngāuruhoe, clocking up speeds of 160 kilometres per hour on the way, on mostly 35-degree slopes. But he fell on the first run and cloud cover spoiled the shot, so Miller asked him to do it again. They flew to the top and set up for a second run. The pilot looked over and gave the team a thumbs-up. Then Ngāuruhoe blew, properly, far more violently than before, its ash going higher than 3500 metres.[2]

'Precisely at that moment, the biggest eruption we had seen all week blew out of the crater where we had been filming less than 25 minutes earlier,' Miller said.

After finalising the series, Miller presented the episode to the network, but they refused to screen it, claiming nobody would believe the someone would be 'dumb enough' to ski down the side of an active volcano. Miller had financed the entire series

Jean-Claude Killy, who clocked up speeds of 160 kilometres per hour on Ngāuruhoe. Getty

himself and gone over budget. The network refused to pay and dared him to sue, and he lost about US$160,000 on it.[3]

'For years I have said skiing is like dancing with the mountain,' Miller said. 'That day, we were all dancing with death.'[4]

I tracked down Bruce Jefferies, who was with Miller and Killy that day. Jefferies got his start in the national park after helping with the search for Anek Chelling in 1965. In 1968 he was running the ski patrol on Whakapapa and was assigned to the ski expedition as part of the park's safety services. His recollections differ from Miller's narrative — Jefferies reckons they skied the northern slopes directly down into South Crater, not the eastern slopes.

'The eastern-facing slopes of the park are all fantastic spring skiing,' he told me. Jefferies had skied most of them, including the classic line from Te Heuheu summit down Waihohonu Ridge to the old Waihohonu Hut, and over the Tongariro Alpine Crossing and down to Ketetahi. He hadn't skied Ngāuruhoe before but he went on to ski it many times after that.

'It's an amazing feeling, skiing down the mountain into South Crater with nobody around, then getting back into the helicopter and 15 minutes later you're having a beer at the pub.'

Jefferies also doesn't remember the eruption that day in the same way Warren Miller described it. 'I'm intensely interested in volcanoes and I would've remembered it. I found some of his recollections a bit exaggerated, but I'd also accentuate the fallibility of my memory going back all that time, too — I wouldn't swear an affidavit on it.'

I pointed out that he'd done something — heli-skiing Ngāuruhoe — that nobody ever will do again; the park management plan now only allows helicopter use for management purposes.

'Of course, you become a hypocrite but that's something you've got to live with. I'm a strong advocate for the wilderness values of the national park and the sacredness of it.'

Jefferies, who went on to become chief ranger, had a personal view that park rangers should know the national park in the most specific of details. 'I had a mantra that no one should know this place better than us — and I mean no one. I encouraged everyone to get out there and explore everything. I'd been down all the catchments, all over the place. It's something that's become sort of lost, that commitment to get out and know the land. It was quite important to me and a lot of fun, to boot.'

Paul Green, former Regional Conservator for Tongariro-Taupō, recalls a lot of pressure to offer or allow heli-skiing in Tongariro National Park. 'That was not surprising given that a three- to five-minute ride from Iwikau Village carparks could get four people to the Crater Lake,' Green said.

Skiers on Ruapehu with Ngāuruhoe smoking behind. Bagnall Collection, Massey University Library

The Tongariro National Park Management Plan was being reviewed in 1976 and the Park Board was very divided over whether or not heli-skiing should be allowed. They decided on running a trial of one helicopter from the Iwikau carpark during the winter of 1976. It was, Green said, very successful from an economic perspective, and skiers were enthusiastic, but Tongariro National Park ranger staff were strongly opposed because of the potential impact on a sacred, remote and special area — the Crater Lake. The Park Board debated the trial extensively but finally resolved by a majority of one not to allow the recreational use of helicopters, and the subsequent management plans all reflect this.

'In my view at the time and since, it was an odd trial as the demand was obvious, as was the impact on backcountry users,' Green told me. 'It was one of the early discussions about intrinsic values and cultural values. Curiously, at the time Ngāti Tūwharetoa supported the use of helicopters but I don't believe Ngāti Rangi or Uenuku were ever consulted. From that day forward we regularly received requests from helicopter operators for heli-skiing or other recreational uses and the firm policy of the management plan gave certainty and clarity.'

Green recalls seeing Warren Miller's series and notes that things in the 1960s were a lot more relaxed about helicopter usage, as they were new and small in number. He took over as chief ranger in 1986 and had to decline a lot of tourism filming applications involving helicopters — something that might seem unthinkable to anyone who isn't familiar with conservation values or the management plan.

'Pressure to allow helicopters continued for the next 26 years with extreme pressure coming from the *Lord of the Rings* filming, which I declined. That decision was questioned by the DOC CEO but ultimately supported by Prime Minister Helen Clark after review by her "minder" Heather Simpson.'

Green also declined the use of dogs and horses for *Lord of the Rings* filming and required battle scenes to be practised at Iwikau Village carparks rather than on tussock in Happy Valley and at Meads Wall. Temporary boardwalks were installed to limit impact to sites and second-hand carpet placed over tussock for final film practice before being removed for final shots.

'With these measures in place — developed and supervised by my staff — it was great that filming was completed with great outcomes and no damage to the World Heritage Site.'[5]

In 1976, when the review of recreational helicopter usage was taking place, New Zealand actor Sam Neill was filming content for a homegrown ski film called *Flare: A ski trip*. Neill was familiar with the Kiwi content in *The Killy Style* and wanted to emulate it in *Flare*, which he'd been commissioned to film for the New Zealand Tourist and Publicity Department.[6] Among other locations, the ski team filmed on Ngāuruhoe in the style of Killy eight years before. There was steam, but no eruption, and the sulphur smell was almost unbearable to the skiers. They managed 19 laps of Ngāuruhoe in a day of filming.

The videography still makes it look extreme, though — skiers stand on the lip of the crater, steam billowing out, then fly over the ice and snow, past exposed scoria.

The mountains of the central plateau have long captured the imagination of filmmakers, including these early film enthusiasts. Department of Conservation archives

At one point the cameraman is downhill, filming the skiers as they emerge from fog and steam, wiggling and hopping their retro turns side to side. They ski almost on top of each other, with disregard for any potential consequences should the slope avalanche. There's a bushy beard, skinny lycra pants, a paisley headband and duct-taped sunglasses. And there's plenty of stoke.

'Ngāuruhoe, one of the three great skiable volcanoes in the North Island,' the British tones of the narrator enunciate carefully. 'But unlike the others, this one is alive, and thus undeveloped. So, once you're there, you can realise a dream: to have the mountain all to yourself.'

It would have worked well as promotional content if heli-skiing had subsequently been allowed. But Ngāuruhoe has never had recreational facilities or lift-accessed skiing. If you want to ski it, you've got to do it the hard way.

And I was of a mind that I'd like to make it even harder. I wanted to recreate Jean-Claude Killy's ski line on the 'previously unskied eastern slopes' — these days, I'd think of them as 'seldom skied', as most people stick to the northern face because it's closer to the access point in South Crater and hence involves less walking. I decided also to turn it into an overnight trip. I'd climb and ski the eastern face, walk to a prearranged overnight camping gear drop site, bivvy out and walk out to the road the next day. That way I'd get to contemplate the mountain from a whole new angle.

I waited (and waited, and waited) for two clear days to crop up in the forecast, with enough snow to ski the whole line, low avalanche risk in the daily avalanche reporting, and a high enough freezing level that it wouldn't be a block of ice. Finally, a lineup of sunshine icons winked saucily from my computer screen. I dropped everything, drove to the Desert Road entrance to the Waihohonu Track on the eastern side of the mountain, and tramped in furiously, bearing an old overnight pack I was happy to leave exposed to the elements on its own for a few nights.

I bypassed Waihohonu Hut and headed up the track towards Oturere Hut, departing from the track at the top and taking the ridgeline in a northwesterly direction. Then I dropped off the ridge, heading towards point 1212 at the foot of Ngāuruhoe, where the Waihohonu Spring issues from the base of a small hump. I stashed the overnight bag safely in the scrub, put a pin on my topo map to record where I left it, and hightailed it out again to the car. I hoped like hell it would still be there when I next reached the spot.

Two days later I left the Mangatepopo carpark and walked up the Mangatepopo Valley with my skis and boots racked on my pack. I crawled slowly up the so-called Devil's Staircase, which I was becoming hardened to thanks to regularly guiding clients on the Tongariro Alpine Crossing that year. I'd been told the name 'Devil's Staircase' was inappropriate (it's also inaccurate), so I'd started referring to it as the Stairway to Heaven or just 'the staircase'. Clients got intimidated by the name, so I'd learned not to point out where we were climbing to unless they specifically asked, lest they get the wobbles. We often turned people around at the 6-kilometre mark, just at the entrance to South Crater, if we thought they weren't fit enough to get over the top of Red Crater and down to Ketetahi in reasonable time ('reasonable' time being sometimes nine hours).

I hadn't yet had to push someone to turn around, because usually they'd ask to go back. Sometimes they'd beg. More than once, I've had to console crying clients on the staircase. Once, I cut steps into the ice back down from the 5-kilometre mark for a couple of young girls from Japan, who then teared up with relief when we got back to the flat ground at Soda Springs in the valley.

'How can we thank you?' one asked.

'Five stars on TripAdvisor,' I reminded her.

Indeed, I'd become hardened to the staircase, and now I was thankful, carrying a heavy load of ski gear. I stopped briefly at the far side of South Crater to switch from my lightweight tramping boots into ski boots with crampons, and to get an ice axe ready. Then the work proper began. I zig-zagged up the side of the cone until just over the 2200-metre mark, sweating furiously at times. The day was cloudless and I could see the snow-touched tops of the Kaimanawa across the other side of the Desert Road. I angled around the mountain slightly at the top so I was directly sitting on an easterly ridge as my line down. The snow was releasing nicely but still icy in patches and I used my ice axe to dig out a platform for my skis.

Shaking slightly from the effort, the exposure and the thought of Miller and Killy, I undid and stashed my boot crampons, did up my ski boots, put my pack on, and stepped into my bindings. I have a superstition about my ski bindings. They're technical bindings for ski touring, different from regular alpine skiing bindings. They have two pins at the top that snap into the toe part of the boot, and you don't always manage to click in successfully the first time. Sometimes it can take embarrassingly long to get into them, to the point where a gun skier friend of mine once had a little old lady in 1980s gear offer to help him. Anyway, I hold a silly superstition that if I can click in on the first go, it'll be a good run.

I managed to click in on the first go. It was steep, and challengingly so, and like skiing on ice cream with ice cubes mixed in. I could hear the snow making a 'shushhh' noise with each turn. Every few turns, I stopped, shaking with excitement, and tried to calm myself, but soon took off again. It was far too quick when I reached the end of the snowline just under 1600 metres, underneath Half Cone, point 1727, and deep into the eastern rifts of the Waihohonu valley.

I had to sit down for a spell to stop shaking. Then I transitioned again, back to tramping boots with skis on the pack. And the next phase began, down the flanks of Ngāuruhoe and south to my bivvy stash. I knew that a discernible ground trail existed over the top of point 1212, which would save me from trying to cross the Waihohonu Stream, a feat that would be likely impossible due to the strength and volume of water that issues from the springs.

My stash was exactly where I'd left it and thankfully undisturbed by possums, mice or other hungry critters who may have sought to snack on my dehy dinner. It was still relatively early in the day, but I unpacked, set up a camping site by pitching my fly, inflating my mattress and putting it along with my sleeping bag into a bivvy bag. I'd

ABOVE: The author guiding a group on the Tongariro Alpine Crossing, 2023, with Ngāuruhoe silent behind.

BELOW: The smooth eastern slopes of Ngāuruhoe.

taken my winter sleeping bag, rated down to something silly like minus 20 degrees, but I knew it'd still be a cold night.

For a while I baked in the sun while staring at Ngāuruhoe's glistening arms. Then the sun suddenly went off me as it dipped behind a nearby ridge, and I shivered. Dinner was brief: boiling water into a dehy packet, then shoved into my face. The night was appropriately starry, with later incoming cloud cover that helped to keep me warm. I'd also chosen a camping spot that was as nestled into the shrubs as I could reasonably achieve, so it was real bug-in-a-rug stuff.

The next day dawned clear with hoar frost emanating from clay pans nearby. I destroyed the crystals with my foot occasionally, a deeply satisfying action. My pack was heavy, with the overnight gear inside, skis and boots on the outside, and my other day pack from the climb the day before also tethered to the back, and it took me longer to gain the ridge than I'd anticipated. I stopped at Waihohonu Hut and treated myself to a second coffee thanks to someone offering their boiling water. He looked at me, bug-eyed, as I wombled up to the hut with skis poking out the top of my pack.

'I didn't know there was a ski field around here,' he said.

'Oh, there isn't,' I said cheerfully. 'I climbed Ngāuruhoe yesterday and skied down.'

We did the usual dance of him saying 'that's insane' and 'you must be crazy' and me garbling about this French guy who skied down it once and it erupted. I don't think I was that coherent, but the billy then reached boiling point and took all our attention.

I waved him goodbye and trudged out to the Desert Road to hitchhike back to the car, answering the same questions several times along the way. Yes, it was cold; yes, it was difficult; yes, it was scary; and yes, yes — I was completely, thoroughly unhinged.

I contacted Warren Miller Entertainment in the hope that they had footage still in an archive somewhere, although I knew it was unlikely. A press representative replied initially, then went quiet, despite me chasing repeatedly. My own iPhone, which I relied on to snap pics and selfies on missions such as these, had frozen from the early morning cold going up the Mangatepopo Valley in the semi-darkness and refused to switch off or on, then died entirely until I got it home and plugged it in. But I had the memories inside my own head of an outing not many other humans would experience in their lifetimes. As Warren Miller had said, 'Skiing Ngāuruhoe in 1968 was one of the nicest experiences of my life.'[7]

I guided on the Tongariro Alpine Crossing that year about once a week, navigating around my four day a week 'normal' job driving a desk. I did get a bit tired of hearing Ngāuruhoe being referred to as 'Mount Doom' by clients, usually foreigners who were on the *Lord of the Rings* circuit. One woman showed me how she'd dressed up as a hobbit in Matamata, and another wanted to be photographed in places and positions that were somehow relevant to the action in the film. Clearly it's done wonders for bringing people to New Zealand; it's just a shame they're not particularly interested in the culture and history of the landscape beyond the fantasy they've seen on a big screen.

John Bidwill, Sydney merchant and occasional botanist, was the first known

PETZL

European to ascend Ngāuruhoe, on 3 March 1839. Bidwill hired several Māori guides (early European explorers referred to them as 'natives', often 'my natives') and spent the night below the base of the cone. During the night, the party heard noises from the mountain, and the next morning the guides refused to go any further. Bidwill continued alone, and was toiling up the steep slope when black smoke went up and spread out in a mushroom-shaped cloud. He heard a hissing noise — the steam venting. Several eruptions followed and the smoke continued to billow out. Bidwill was not deterred from his mission, but later admitted: 'Had it not been for the idea of standing where no man ever stood before, I should certainly have given up the undertaking . . . It was lucky for me another eruption did not take place while I was on it, or I should have been infallibly boiled to death.'[8]

He got close enough to peer over into the crater, which he described as 'the most awful abyss I ever looked into or imagined'. Its sides were so steep they were impossible to scale, and the stones he threw in took seven or eight seconds to hit the bottom.

Bidwill ascended surreptitiously, and in the knowledge that the local Māori considered Ngāuruhoe tapu. In doing so, he offended tangata whenua, but reportedly placated Te Heuheu with a generous gift of tobacco. Later, other similar explorers such as Ernst Dieffenbach and Ferdinand von Hochstetter sought to climb Ngāuruhoe but were denied permission, and respected the denial. Dieffenbach wrote in *Travels in New Zealand*:

> Here, after having reached the foot of Tongariro, to ascend which we had come so great a distance, we met with an obstacle which quickly put an end to all our gratification. We could not persuade the natives to allow us to ascend the principal cone, which we might have accomplished in four hours. The head chief of the Taupo tribes, Te Heuheu, was absent on a war excursion to Wanganui, and before he went he had laid a solemn 'tapu' on the mountain, and until his return they could not grant us permission to ascend it. This 'tapu' was imposed in consequence of a European traveller of the name of Bidwill having gone to the top without permission, which had caused great vexation.[9]

Hochstetter wrote of Tongariro being tapu as it was the resting place for Tukino Te Heuheu, who had been disinterred and preserved in a 'magnificently carved coffin'. His remains were taken up to near the foot of Tongariro to be his final resting place: 'For the deep crater of the volcano was intended to be the final grave of the hero, with the heaven-ascending pyramid of scoriae and ashes for his monument.' However, the remains did not make it into the crater.

> The grand idea was but half carried out. As the bearers were approaching the top of the ever steaming cone, a subterraneous roaring noise became audible, and awe-struck they deposited their heavy load upon a projecting rock. There the remains still lie. The mountain, however, is most strictly tapu, and nobody is allowed to ascend it . . . I made no attempt to extort a permission, or to elude the natives.[10]

Hochstetter observed that the only two Europeans who were said to have been to the top of Ngāuruhoe did so surreptitiously. One of them was climber H. Dyson, who ascended secretly in 1851. Dr A. S. Thomson wrote of the mountain that 'the only way to get over this difficulty [of tapu] is to ascend the mountain unknown to the natives of the place, or even your own natives.' Dyson did just that, but was discovered by 'a curious accident', Dr Thomson wrote.[11] While Dyson was ascending he took a path along the base of Tongariro towards Whanganui, a route that was used enough to be well known. He followed it for a time, then departed from the track.

A local Māori man returning along the path saw Dyson's footprints and recognised them as European. He saw the spot where the footsteps departed from the path, and when he arrived home at Rotoaira, let others know that a European was out wandering alone on Tongariro. Dyson was immediately suspected to be the culprit, and it seems he was somehow punished over the matter via confiscation of his property, but he himself did not publicise the fact (Dr Thomson happily did that for him).

In recent years the old poled route up Ngāuruhoe from the entrance to South Crater has been taken out and the track washed off maps. In 2017 the Department of Conservation asked people to stop going up Ngāuruhoe, and removed access signs to the peaks.[12] People were advised that it was a culturally significant area, and that it was time to show respect for the sacred land. The peaks and waterways are sacred to the local hapū, Ngāti Hikairo ki Tongariro.

I endorse a general practice of discouraging unsuspecting hikers from ascending Ngāuruhoe, but mostly for safety reasons. During that winter of 2023, several people were plucked off Red Crater and Ngāuruhoe because they'd somehow ascended without ice axes and crampons, and had then got stuck when it got steeper and icier, or when the refreeze happened in the afternoon. During my guiding days I witnessed far too many people who were a whisker away from sliding on ice to their deaths, although they probably didn't know it.

At the same time, I hope we can reframe our relationship with mountains away from a very European settler mindset of 'conquering' peaks for the sake of the summit and towards something more concerned with engaging with the environment and truly knowing it, understanding its history. One of the reasons Ngāuruhoe was sacred, historically, was that the mountain was a food source. Ngāti Hikairo ki Tongariro representative Bubs Smith told me people used to procure tītī and tāiko from its slopes. The last cultural harvest he knows of happened in the early 1940s.

I had ascended Ngāuruhoe, albeit not to the top, and I was acutely aware of the tension between the tapu peak and the very Kiwi principle of freedom of entry and access to a national park, a right enshrined in the National Parks Act, 'so that [people] may receive in full measure the inspiration, enjoyment, recreation, and other benefits that may be derived from mountains, forests, sounds, seacoasts, lakes, rivers, and other natural features.'[13]

The cold, swift Whakapapanui Stream, from just above Mahuia Rapids, with Ruapehu's northern peaks watching over. Some of the North Island's major rivers start on Ruapehu and Tongariro. Conrad Smith/ Alpine Jesus

PART 4

WATER

Glaciers may be scaled, and volcanoes explored, but unless an exact record of changes and movements can be kept it is useless to expect results of any permanent scientific value.

— H. Hill, F. G. S.[1]

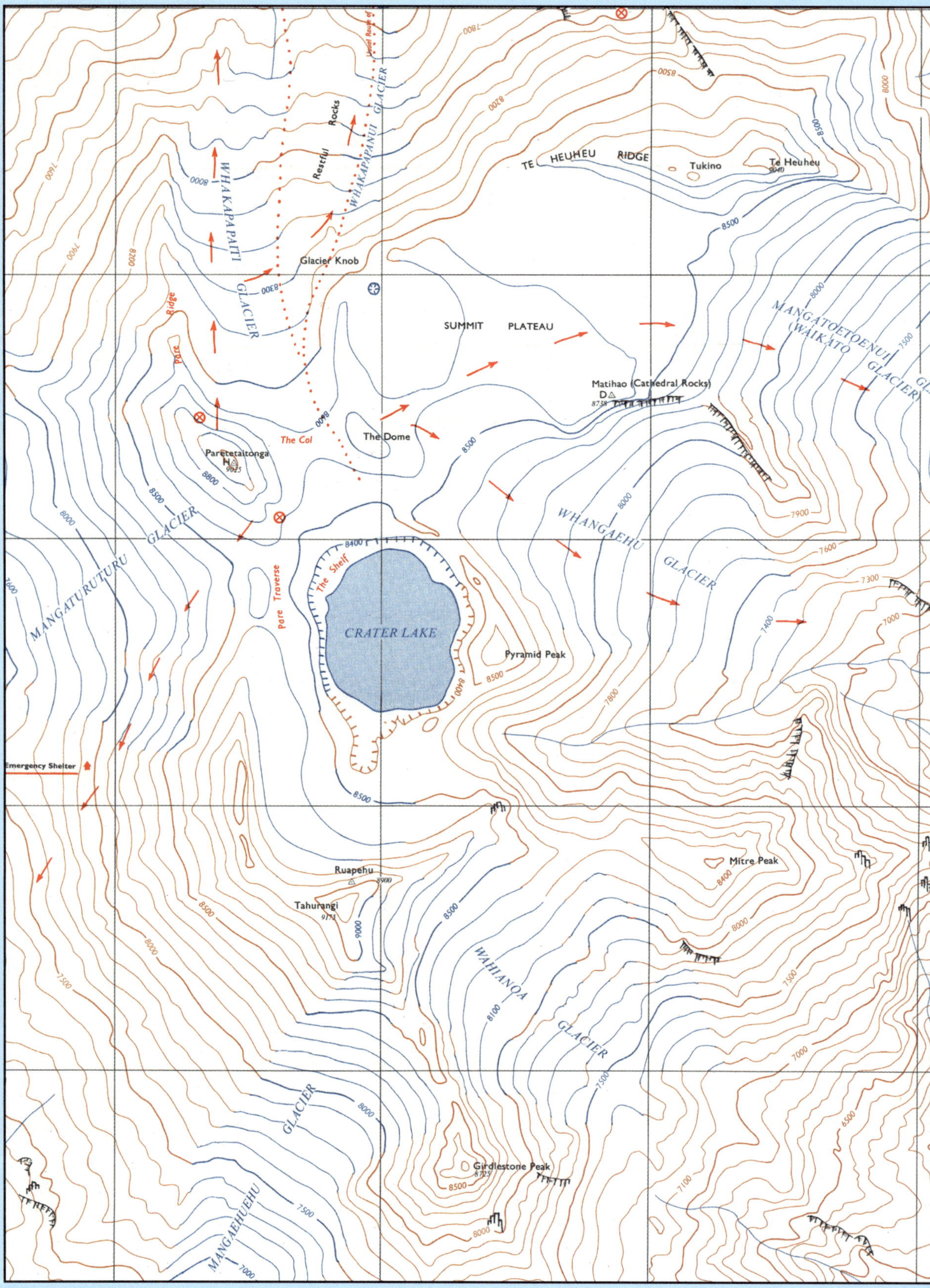

Usual Route of Ascent
WHAKAPAPANUI GLACIER
Restful Rocks
WHAKAPAPAITI GLACIER
TE HEUHEU RIDGE
Tukino
Te Heuheu
Glacier Knob
SUMMIT PLATEAU
MANGATOETOENUI (WAIKATO GLACIER)
Matihao (Cathedral Rocks)
Pare Ridge
The Col
The Dome
Paretetaitonga
MANGATURUTURU GLACIER
WHANGAEHU GLACIER
The Shelf
Pare Traverse
CRATER LAKE
Pyramid Peak
Emergency Shelter
Ruapehu
Tahurangi
Mitre Peak
WAHIANOA GLACIER
MANGAEHUEHU GLACIER
Girdlestone Peak

Map showing Ruapehu's glaciers, 1969. National Library of New Zealand, 38239634

CHAPTER 16

Disappearing ice

Ruapehu once held 18 glaciers within its arms. Now there are just nine, and we'll probably lose many of them within our lifetimes. One summer I convinced scientist Dr Harry Keys to come with me on a trip to the Summit Plateau to check on their retreat and an ephemeral lakelet, explore ice caves and conduct a Mallowpuff Test.

On 7 September 1939, Austrian mountaineer Ludwig Krenek stood on the summit of Mulkila (6516 metres) in the Himalaya alongside his friend and climbing partner Fritz Kolb and four British students they were guiding. It was a first ascent for that peak, and the party celebrated, unaware that their respective countries had declared war a week earlier.

The pair had been climbing on a shoestring budget. Determined to climb and survey among the 21,000-foot peaks of India's Lahaul, they planned, trained and saved every penny they could. They knew it was a long shot that either of them would be selected for an official expedition for the Third Reich, so instead they teamed up with young English students who would be happy living on a budget for the sake of climbing.

Krenek and Kolb achieved the summit of Mulkila alongside Hilda Richmond, Donald Comber, Frank Hollick and Robey Johnson, and under the sponsorship of the National Union of Students. On returning to base camp, Kolb tried to find a newspaper to see whether Italy had entered the war. 'This was of great importance for our English friends,' Krenek wrote. 'It would make no difference to Kolb and myself — holders of German passports. We knew what was in store for us.'[1]

More immediate tragedy awaited: Richmond died soon after they got back to camp, killed by a falling stone while washing in a brook. The base camp spring had frozen the previous night and she'd climbed a little higher to search for water. Richmond had been alone, and it was only after a considerable search that the team managed to find her. The climbing team buried her at its base camp site, with a memorial of rectangular stone slabs to mark the grave.

Three days before the expedition was due to end, a runner arrived at the camp to confirm war had broken out. As Austrians, Krenek and Kolb were considered to be part of the Nazi regime, and as such were at war with Great Britain and her colonies. A policeman was waiting for them at the first village they came to.

Krenek and Kolb were swiftly sent to an Indian internment camp at Ahmednagar, where Kolb founded a mountaineering club and used the rough stones of the barrack walls as a climbing wall. They were afforded much leniency at the camp. Most British officers with any talent were off contributing to the war effort in more strategic places, and those with less to offer were put in charge of internment camps in the colonies. The head of the camp was happy to allow Krenek and Kolb to indulge in their climbing obsession on the weekends, provided they promised not to escape while they were adventuring. The climbers soon found they could convince their minder to sleep under a nearby tree instead of expending physical effort by accompanying them on their climb. All they had to do was wake him up when they got back.[2]

The two men were later transferred to camp Dehra Dun, and took up teaching appointments in India on their release in 1944. In 1947 they went adventuring again, in Padar, near Kashmir, and in the mountains further east, using basic equipment they had salvaged from their original climb.

Eventually Krenek emigrated to New Zealand, convinced to do so by Heine Schmidt,

ABOVE: Ludwig Krenek, his son, Steve, and his daughter, Gita, climbing on Ruapehu circa 1957–58. Ngā Tohu/Pinnacle Ridge is behind them. Krenek family collection

BELOW: Glacier enthusiast Ludwig Krenek with sherpas. Krenek family collection

a friend of his wife Lisl, who had mentioned that the skiing was good there. The Kreneks settled in Whanganui and Ludwig took up a teaching position at Whanganui Girls' College. He joined the New Zealand Alpine Club and began to explore his new local mountains, the central volcanoes of the North Island.[3]

Krenek became interested in the glaciers of Ruapehu, and began tracking the size and volume of the Whakapapa Glacier from 1952, later publishing his findings in the *New Zealand Journal of Geology and Geophysics*.[4] Walkers heading to the Crater Lake generally passed by the snout of the glacier, and no change to its size had been noted in the past 25 years by regular visitors, including Bill Mead, author of *Memories of a Mountain and a River*. Then, in February 1955, Krenek noticed extensive downwasting and retreat — a whopping 94 metres that year and another 65 metres in 1956, both years with warmer and wetter than average summers. Then it slowed, with just 6 metres retreat in 1957, and went back to being stationary again in 1958.

The changes of 1955 were not just noticeable, they were remarkable. The Whakapapa Glacier, usually smooth with no crevasses, suddenly had become so heavily crevassed that it made travel up the glacier impossible, and getting from the rocks onto the ice became very difficult. The ice had become so thin from downwasting that the underlying rocks and moraine could be seen through the crevasses, which were only 10 metres deep in places.

'Large areas of rock emerged nearly every day,' Krenek wrote, 'which shows both how surprisingly thin the glacier was and how fast the downwasting occurred.' He included several sketch maps, one of which shows the glacial ice stretching down into the Gut opposite the Knoll, as low as 2220 metres.[5] Today, the idea that the glacier ever stretched that far is frankly unthinkable.

Krenek wrote to a colleague that he hadn't seen anything like the decay of the Ruapehu glaciers anywhere else.

> The glaciers of Ruapehu are simply collapsing. The Whakapapa has receded 75 yards since last year, and enormous areas of rock have emerged. Hundreds of crevasses have opened up and the area is so badly crevassed that it is difficult to find a route to the Crater Lake. Over a considerable part of the glacier the ash of the 1945 eruption is now exposed, often one foot deep. The melt waters cut this layer of ash into longitudinal ridges; the horizontal crevasses, which open up everywhere, cut these ridges at right angles, so that hundreds of black hummocks are formed. A little further downstream ablation has proceeded far enough for the development of dirt cones. There are hundreds and hundreds of them.[6]

Krenek also kept tabs on the outlet of the Crater Lake and other glaciers on Ruapehu, and arranged for photos of the Mangaehuehu Glacier to be taken from the same point at certain intervals so the glacier's behaviour could be tracked. His astonishment was clear. 'I really think the development is quite unique, because it came so suddenly,' he wrote in the *Journal of Glaciology*.[7]

The first time I ever went up to the Summit Plateau outside of snowy winter conditions, I did so with a specific purpose. I'd seen photos on Instagram by a local photographer and mountain guide, Zhi Yuen Yap, who had found a little meltwater lake at the intersection of the plateau and the Mangatoetoenui Glacier. The lakelet was bright blue and mesmerising, and he had snapped it when the outlet was partially frozen on the surface, creating an aura of crystal with pure, clear-flowing water underneath. It looked like an impossible creation, and I wanted to go and see it for myself. I became even more fascinated when I discovered the Mangatoetoenui Glacier had once also been referred to as the Waikato Glacier — so to find the meltwater lake would mean finding the very highest headwaters of the mighty Waikato River. My brain fairly exploded.

'The hot summer so far has resulted in the early formation of this glacier meltwater lake on Mt Ruapehu,' Yap wrote on his Instagram post. 'Thanks to the freeze-thaw cycles, there are numerous intricate ice formations, some of which are like the corals in the tropical seas.'

I roped in Mike Heydon, one of my climbing buddies and the best photographer I know.[8] We'd been warned about potential sinkholes on the Summit Plateau. I'd been told that ground that looked stable and firm could at any time give way to gaps that would eat us for breakfast. To mitigate the risk of disappearing into a crevasse on Ruapehu (although this has never happened to date, not that I can find anyway, and believe me I have really, really searched), we took not only ice axes and crampons but also a snow stake each, a short rope and enough gear to do crevasse extraction, if it came to it. We'd make a call when we got to the plateau as to whether or not we needed to rope up. In retrospect, this was mad overkill.

The weather for our chosen day was looking doable, and we headed up directly from the Manawatu Tramping and Skiing Club lodge on Whakapapa, where we had spent the night. The main part of the ski area was closed for the installation of a new gondola, a piece of infrastructure that was installed to increase summer tourism and boost the coffers of Ruapehu Alpine Lifts, the ski area operator.

The blue sky beckoned us, and a gusty wind was inconvenient but not cold enough to turn us back. We cut a line up the skier's right of the Amphitheatre then scrambled up from the NZAC hut at Delta Corner straight onto Restful Ridge, also known as Restful Rocks (the ridge that separates the Knoll T-bar area from the 'west' area of the ski field). The snow was only patchy until the upper parts of the ridge, but we didn't need axes or crampons to ascend.

'We're probably the highest people in the North Island right now,' Mike mused as we neared the top. But no: we saw one or two other stragglers higher up, just on the Whakapapa Glacier ridge, and later encountered two Dutch trekkers who embodied all the usual stereotypes of clueless tourists. And certainly they were not carrying enough gear to perform crevasse extraction, should it come to it.

Arriving at the entrance to the Summit Plateau, we struck patches of ice and donned crampons. The residual snow patches were mixed, dirty and not to be trusted, as every step encountered a different type of snowpack. Still, there was enough of a thick and robust snowpack that we opted to leave the rope in the pack.

We struck out across the Summit Plateau and after a short section of plodding and gaining a contour line, suddenly a bright blue patch came into view. The lake had looked quite substantial from the photos we'd seen on Instagram and I'd seen similar snowmelt lakelets on Google Earth; however, this lake was miniature, not really even big enough to properly swim in.

Mike took advantage of the photo opportunity and we spent a good hour there, just watching it and being astounded by it. I was fascinated by the meltwater tumbling out of the ice and down the hill, snaking beneath the Mangatoetoenui Glacier. It was hard to look away.

Zhi Yuen Yap later told us he had photographed the lake just in time. He went back shortly after our trip and deemed it to have shrunk in height by 80 centimetres, simply by dint of the ice terraces having collapsed and melted. My mate Papa Smurf went up a couple of days after my outing, and thanks to a day of snow, rain and low temperatures, the lake was almost completely frozen over again, and he missed out entirely.

Mike and I eventually tore ourselves away from the ephemeral lakelet, recognising that clouds were coming in and the clock was marching on. We retraced our steps across the Summit Plateau and half-slid, half-glissaded back down off Restful Ridge and through the Gut near the Knoll T-bar. An abundance of rock fall, including several sizeable boulders, cautioned us to keep trucking along at pace, and mind as you go. The last part of our retreat involved crossing a tumbling stream down the Delta area near the NZAC hut, and picking up a well-worn track to descend on the skier's right of the Amphitheatre and back to the ski club lodge.

I spent most of that evening researching the Waikato Glacier. An article on the Waikato River in the *New Zealand Herald*, from March 1928, went to town on describing the river, including its high sources:

> It is practically impossible to describe the Waikato in comprehensive terms. It must be dealt with in sections. First of all is that portion that flows between its primary sources and Lake Taupo. This is only a short section of between 30 and 40 miles, but how wonderful it is! On its left bank here rise three huge old volcanoes, Ruapehu, Ngauruhoe and Tongariro, and from their steep slopes tumble innumerable tributaries, some from the high snow fields.[9]

I discovered there had been another meltwater lake on the southern side of the summit plateau, just under Tahurangi. A newspaper story from 1926 reported on some earlier explorations by Joe Blyth and Mr A. J. Ford, a fellow Ohakune mountain enthusiast. They climbed the mountain and went to the Crater Lake for 'the usual bathe after the climb'. Blyth mentioned he had discovered a lakelet in 1920:

> Some time ago, on the snow and ice field in the crater, on the south side of the Crater Lake, Mr Blyth noticed a circular depression, and when he was next on the mountain, cracks had formed in it, and through them he heard the sound of running water. About the same time, Mr Ford saw what he is certain was a second lake, circular and extremely blue. Owing to the lateness of the hour he did not have time to go down to examine it closely. The site is precisely that of the depression noticed by Mr Blyth. Later in the same season lake and depression had disappeared and the ice and snow lay at the original level.[10]

Around the time this was published, the Crater Lake had gone cold — completely, stone cold — while activity in the crater of Ngāuruhoe had increased, leading locals to theorise that increased activity in one volcano had somehow 'cooled off' the other. (This is false — an age-old myth with no basis in fact. The two volcanoes are not connected, and their eruptive histories are unrelated.)

Ruapehu's landscape is always changing, and you simply don't know what you're going to get. He's alive, and it's always sensible to keep that in the back of your mind. Thankfully, he didn't swallow us down a sinkhole that day.

I wondered if the melt lake on the northern side was a marker of climate change, or if it had been a feature for some time. Just as Zhi Yuen Yap visited it several times and has tracked it over time, even back in the 1950s locals were keeping a close eye on ablation on Ruapehu's snowfields.

I intended to track it myself — not only was it fascinating, it was also excellent exercise ascending 1000 metres to reach the lakelet. I resolved on that trip to return in autumn to see what state it was in, but life got in the way and I didn't go up in summer conditions for four years.[11] Looking back, my absence from this special place feels, to me, unthinkable. How could I have abandoned it for so long? What had happened during that time? I had neglected this part of Ruapehu, and now I'd never know.

'The Mangatoetoenui Glacier is one of the highest, and most spectacular, sources of the [Waikato] River,' Sue Miles wrote in the 1984 book *The River: The story of the Waikato*. 'Stand here, amid the snow and ice, looking out across the dark, treeless wasteland that stretches across to the edge of the distant Kaimanawa Ranges and it is not difficult to understand why the Māori regarded this land with awe and terror.'[12]

In 1919, British climber Noel Odell stood on top of Foel Grach, a small peak in Wales, at 975 metres, with his wife Mona, when a man surprised them by arriving on a motorcycle. It was Andrew Irvine, and the two men later met on a climbing expedition. When the 1924 Everest expedition gathered steam, Odell recommended Irvine, who was then 21 years old and was considered to be the 'superman' the expedition needed to succeed.

On 8 June 1924, Odell watched George Mallory and Andrew Irvine leave Camp Six for the summit. Odell was consigned to duties as oxygen officer and had moved up in

support from Camp Five. He saw two figures near the rock steps, going strongly for the top. Then mist clouded his view, a storm followed, and Mallory and Irvine vanished into history. Odell was the last person to see them alive.

'I saw the whole summit ridge, and the final peak of Everest unveiled,' Odell said.

> I noticed far away on a snow-slope leading up to the last step but one from the base of the final pyramid a tiny object moving and approaching the rock step. As I stood intently watching this dramatic appearance, the scene became enveloped in cloud. Mallory and Irvine had but another 800 feet to go to reach the top. If no particular difficult obstacle presented itself on the final pyramid they should have got there. It is very probable that Mallory and Irvine succeeded.[13]

Odell spent 12 days and nights at over 7000 metres without oxygen, and climbed twice, alone, to more than 8200 metres to search for them, setting new standards

for human endurance at altitude. Opinions were divided on whether or not the pair had summited; climbers generally hold to the idea that a successful summit can only be claimed when you are safely back at camp. Indeed, Sir Edmund Hillary himself asserted: 'If you climb a mountain for the first time and die on the descent, is it really a complete first ascent of the mountain? I'm rather inclined to think, personally, that maybe it's quite important, the getting down. And the complete climb of a mountain is reaching the summit and getting safely to the bottom again.'[14]

Odell thought it likely the pair had succeeded in reaching the top. '"Has Everest been climbed?" will ever be a mystery,' he said. 'Considering all the circumstances and the position reached, I am personally of the opinion that Mallory and Irvine reached the summit.'[15]

He later completed his PhD in geology and turned to academia, although it was widely accepted that he tended to put 'other interests' ahead of study. In other words, Odell preferred climbing, and had a reputation for only being interested in geology so

PREVIOUS PAGES: The ephemeral lake at the top of the Mangatoetoenui Glacier in the summer of 2019. Also known as the Waikato Glacier, this pool of water is technically the headwaters of the Waikato River, when it appears during the summer melt.

ABOVE: Glacier ice on the Summit Plateau of Ruapehu showing layers of tephra — eruptive material — from the 1990s.

BELOW: The crevasses of the Whakapapa Glacier used to be large and distinctive. Now, there's almost nothing left. Harry Keys collection

far as it allowed him a way to get onto exciting expeditions. Good on him.

Odell socialised with the likes of iconic British climbers Eric Shipton, Howard Somervell and Frank Smythe, and was considered a 'gentleman mountaineer'. He was tall, lean and striking, and wherever he arrived on the Otago University campus, where he was professor in geology, he did so with a strong stride. With his British stiff upper lip firmly in place there was little emotion. In fact, in 1936 when he and Bill Tilman achieved a first ascent of Nanda Devi (7816 metres) in India, at that time the highest peak to be climbed, the pair were so overcome with emotion that they 'actually shook hands!'.[16]

Odell and Krenek corresponded about Ruapehu's glaciers, and Odell's much-cited 1955 journal article, 'Mount Ruapehu, New Zealand: Observations on its Crater Lake and Glaciers', is often mentioned in the same breath as the work of his contemporary.[17] Odell primarily focused on the collapse of the Crater Lake dam as causing the 1953 Tangiwai disaster more than the shrinkage or changes in Ruapehu's glaciers. Odell hadn't quite scrutinised the glaciers in the same way Krenek had, and although they were doing field work at the same time, Odell published first. He did, however, note 'the sluggishness as well as the thinness of these névé, rather than true glacier, masses on all flanks of Ruapehu', and observed, like Krenek: 'During the past Summer — a season of exceptional dryness — the process of ablation and wastage has been greatly accelerated, so that immense areas of rock and ash have freshly emerged, and crevasses and dirt-ridges have taken the place of smooth névé or glacier surfaces.'

Odell's field work on Ruapehu only consisted of three ascents, whereas Krenek was a proper enthusiast for the maunga. I tracked down Krenek's children, Steve and Gita, thanks to the uniqueness of their last name combined with the search possibilities of Facebook. Steve told me that his father would periodically walk up from the Wanganui Ski Club hut on the Whakapapa side, past the Crater Lake and down the Tūroa side, in order to track the progress of the Mangaehuehu Glacier on Ruapehu's southern slopes. Then he'd climb back up over the top and ski home. His last visit was February 1954, and he painted 'Feb 54' on a large rock at the furthest extent of the glacier at that time. Sadly, Ludwig Krenek became affected by arthritis, which put a handbrake on things.

Odell's enthusiasm for adventure over academia was clear from the lazy inclusion at the end of the journal article of three fat paragraphs from a letter written by Krenek, giving details of the glaciers' collapse in recent years. And yet, in 1952 Odell publicly cracked the whip on New Zealanders and what he saw as their 'laziness'. Speaking at a Victoria University College graduation ceremony, he criticised New Zealanders' lack of the spirit of adventure, arguing that Kiwis were losing their grip on the more vital aspects of life. 'New Zealand should be warned against the insidious dangers which lay in the sense of laziness and complacency which seemed to obtain under the so-called welfare State,' he thundered. 'There should be a fuller realisation of the opportunities awaiting the adventurous.'[18]

Before Odell and Krenek — many decades before — Dr Benedict Friedländer also wrote of Ruapehu's glaciers. 'Dr Benedict Friedländer, of Berlin, who is visiting the colony in the interests of natural science, is now in this City,' the *Evening Post* announced in its 'Personal' column on 5 February 1897. Friedländer, who had a long, hairy beard and piercing eyes and wore his hair slicked back in a man-bun that was before its time, was a German volcanologist and physicist, and, curiously, also a sexologist. He was also something of an activist, and crusaded for social change and gay rights at a time when it was a dangerous position to take. In his native Berlin, as in New Zealand at the time, the law criminalised the so-called 'unnatural vice' between males. Friedländer founded a breakaway organisation named the 'League for Manly Culture', which folded after he unfortunately ended his own life in 1908, aged 41.

Friedländer visited the central plateau volcanoes and inspected Ruapehu's glaciers. At the time, the perennial snow came much further down the mountain than it does today — indeed, from the northern side, when viewed from National Park in high summer, Ruapehu appears to have no snow at all these days. Friedländer wrote that Ruapehu surpasses the snowline considerably — 'i.e., that height above which more snow falls than can be melted'. Based just on what he saw in front of him, Friedländer believed Ruapehu to be as fully active as Ngāuruhoe (which, then, was much more active than it is today), but without openly appearing so.

After describing the various areas of snow and ice he found on the upper parts of the mountain, he also concluded that the result of the conflict between volcanic steam and the névé of the crater glacier(s) was the formation of the lake, which acted as a 'steam condenser', hiding to some extent Ruapehu's activity.[19]

Ruapehu's glaciers have long attracted a particular brand of adventure-scientist. Nearly a decade after Odell's publication, in 1963, Arnold Heine — polar explorer, glaciologist, scientist — published an article on the central plateau ice, proposing a system of places from which the glaciers should be regularly photographed.[20]

Heine had been tracking the glaciers in the 1950s, and noticed the retreat and ablation of the Whakapapa Glacier. Notably, the 'thinning' of the glacier had 'exhumed' the ridge now known as Restful Rocks, or Restful Ridge, and the emergence of this ridge began to disconnect the two 'terminal lobes' or origins of the Whakapapa Glacier. According to Heine's tracking, the Whakapapa Glacier had split and become two separate glaciers by 1958. From that time, the ice directly uphill from Knoll Ridge was referred to as the Whakapapanui Glacier, while the main glacier that originated underneath Paretetaitonga was named the Whakapapaiti Glacier. A curious legacy of this naming (which merely aligned with the Whakapapaiti and Whakapapanui waterways further down on Ruapehu's slopes) is that the now much bigger Whakapapaiti Glacier has the suffix 'iti', meaning 'small', while the almost non-existent Whakapapanui Glacier has the suffix 'nui', meaning 'big'.

Today, most people refer to the Whakapapa Glacier, and know it to be the huge expanse skiers and snowboarders trudge up in spring to gain a view of the Crater Lake, and most people assume Restful Rocks to have always existed as such. It's now a seasonally snow-covered valley. There's no glacier left on the valley floor except a few small areas of relic ice buried beneath lahar and tephra debris. Whakapapa Col, and some of the upper slopes of Paretetaitonga, do contain areas of perennial ice and snow.

Heine, our adventure-scientist, was awarded the Polar Medal among other accolades, and unsurprisingly spent a lot of time in Antarctica during the time when Scott Base was being established — in fact, he spent 17 seasons on the ice.

In August 1957, in an era before avalanche transceivers existed, he had a brush with death on Whakapapa. Heine was leading a snowcraft course with the Hutt Valley Tramping Club. The group was on the Yankee Slalom area of the mountain in a blizzard, with driving snow hurling all around and pelting them sideways. Powder stashes — actual powder, not so-called 'Ruapehu powder', otherwise known as milled ice — built up in pockets and on lee slopes. Heine was glissading down a steep slope when he heard a crack-bang noise.

'The slope exploded, and I was engulfed,' he later told reporters. 'It was like being caught up in a big ball of cotton wool which pressed tightly in on me from all sides. I remembered that old saying about avalanches, that going through a swimming motion is supposed to bring you to the top. I tried, but I could not move my arms.'[21]

The snow slope, totally collapsed, was moving at 110 kilometres per hour downhill like an arrow. Somehow hanging on to his ice axe, Heine was hurled more than 100 metres down the slope and buried almost completely in an area of avalanche debris 30 metres wide and nearly 3 metres deep. (He was lucky: if an avalanche victim is buried more than 2 metres deep, it's very unlikely they'll survive, simply because of the time it takes to dig them out.)

Incredibly, although he couldn't move his limbs Heine managed to shake his head free and push it up out of the snow. His companions, back on the ridge, had also heard the noise and felt a jolt as the slide began. They later reported that they saw the crack open, the slope explode, and Heine simply disappear. They were more scared than Heine was, partly because it happened so fast. They wasted no time in digging him out.

Heine later tried to dispel the myth that Ruapehu's snowpack is so locked up with ice that it doesn't tend to avalanche. Even today, many adventurers go into the backcountry without avalanche gear or training in companion rescue, meaning that if someone does get buried, they will probably not survive.

'Ruapehu has a reputation for not having avalanches,' Heine said. 'The hard southerly wind and heavy snowfall showed that under certain conditions, snow will accumulate on steep faces and form at unnatural slopes, waiting for the first shock to dislodge it. Ruapehu can have avalanches and they can be dangerous. I feel more people should know about them.'[22]

In 1988, more than two decades after Heine, adventure-scientist and glaciologist/volcanologist Dr Harry Keys published a survey of Ruapehu's glaciers, establishing a baseline for detecting effects of climate change.[23] Keys wrote that Ruapehu had nine glaciers, most of which had thinned by between 5 and 30 metres and retreated by an average of 240 metres since 1961. He predicted that climate warming might accelerate the recession of some of the glaciers but shouldn't make them all disappear.

Keys noted the remarkable retreat of the Whakapapa Glacier: 'The Whakapapa is

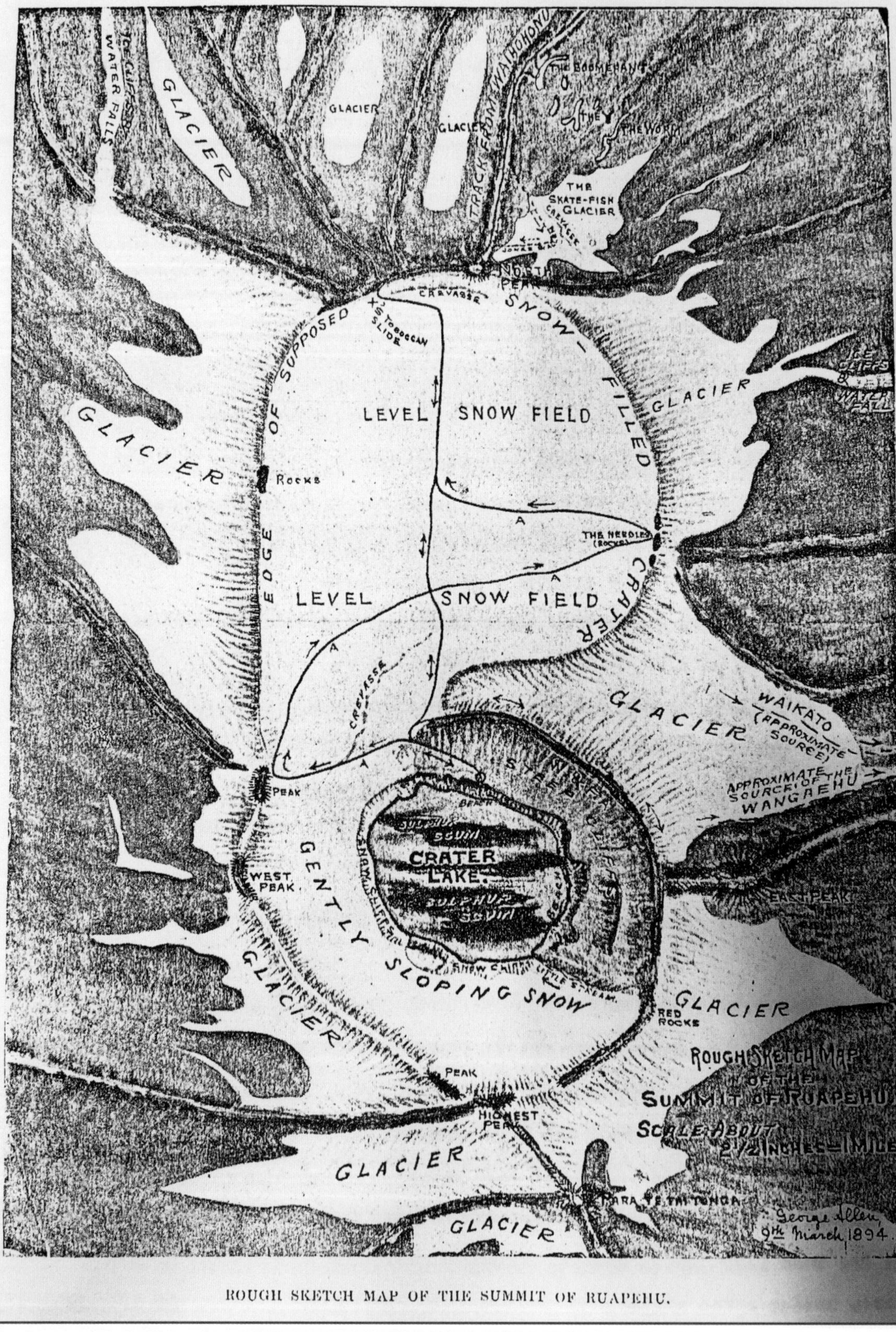

ROUGH SKETCH MAP OF THE SUMMIT OF RUAPEHU.

A sketch of the summit area of Ruapehu by George Allen, 1894. He labelled Girdlestone as Paretetaitonga. Bagnall Collection, Massey University Library

most noticeably affected — the whole of its trunk has thinned by 20–30m and now large areas of bedrock are "emerging" as far up as 2600m above sea level. Rapid retreat of its terminal appears to be imminent.' More recent study by other scientists has quantified this ongoing retreat.

Keys also wrote about 'glacial striations' — scratches left on bedrock by the movement (retreat) of glacier ice — and how long it took for weathering to remove them. Restful Rocks had noticeable striations, and photos by Heine showed that the area was exhumed from the ice less than 27 years previously, around 1961. Striations could give us an idea of how recently glaciers had retreated from a particular area, Keys said — they suggested that much of Knoll Ridge had been covered by ice within the past century.

I came across the Keys report while researching the Mangatoetoenui Glacier and the meltwater lake; I'd wanted to know how fast the ice moved (according to Keys, 24±5 metres per year, using the wreckage of the Oxford aircraft as a reference). Then I fell down a research rabbit hole (from which it is often difficult to extricate oneself) looking for photos of crevasses on Ruapehu. If we had glaciers, I figured, surely we had crevasses? Or at least sinkholes on the Summit Plateau, which one could fall down much like a rabbit hole.

I found photos of both — crevasses and sinkholes, of a sort — and unthinkably, a photo of Harry Keys standing next to a sinkhole, or at least what looked like a sinkhole, but which was labelled an 'ice doline'. These, I discovered, are round sinkholes caused by water melting within the ice, which then caves in if the water drains suddenly, leaving behind a small, round crater. The photos, published on a Swiss website about glaciers, also showed gaping crevasses underneath Paretetaitonga, big enough for Keys and other researchers to get into and walk up and down.[24]

I revisited the website many times, fascinated with the idea of these interesting formations living on the top of Ruapehu, changing each season, and spending their winters blanketed in the snow that would cause them to change. I thought that one day, maybe, I'd meet Harry Keys and go for a walk up Ruapehu to clamber into crevasses and ice caves.

Then a ranger at the DOC office at Whakapapa, possibly fatigued by my endless requests for historical information about the area (and I don't blame them), introduced me to Harry, indicating that he was the man who'd have all the answers. This was a hospital pass if ever I saw one, for now my enquiries and obsessions would be targeted at Harry rather than a government department. But he agreed — enthusiastically, even — to taking a walk up Ruapehu with me to look at all the things.

Harry and I shared a couple of interests. Firstly, Harry had been tracking the meltwater lake on the Summit Plateau since 2016, measuring its size and noting its features and dates. I hadn't realised that the lake had a habit of draining in autumn — I'd assumed it simply formed as meltwater and then somehow turned back into ice — and that it sometimes left ice caves in its wake.

Secondly, Harry had pioneered the Mallowpuff Project.[25] His party had been working high up the mountain beside the Crater Lake digging a 2.5-metre-deep hole to replace batteries for the lahar warning system installed before the March 2007 lahar, when the team discovered their morning tea had broken — every single Mallowpuff in the packet he'd carried up there had cracked. Was it damage from the trip up inside a pack, or the altitude, or some other cause? Harry contacted Griffins, the manufacturer, which sent through some samples for further field testing. Harry et al. (2006) discovered that 30 per cent of biscuits tested cracked by the Whakapapa carpark (1600 metres), 86 per cent by Knoll Ridge cafe, and 100 per cent by the Summit Plateau (2600 metres). Speed of ascent didn't seem to make a difference, and the team even tried different combinations of holes melted through the chocolate so the Mallowpuff could 'vent'. The research team concluded that the cracking had no effect on their taste. As an arts graduate, this is exactly the kind of science that I can get behind.

Our diaries aligned, the weather cooperated, and I emailed Harry: 'See you tomorrow, 10am at the Sky Waka. I'll bring the Mallowpuffs.'

We ascended on a clear autumn day in April, with a cool breeze blowing. I acquired Mallowpuffs from New World in Ohakune, stopped to check them at National Park (none dead yet), and again at the Whakapapa carpark (several soldiers down).

'I'll be a bit slow, Harry,' I warned. 'I was out yesterday on a big mission.' I'd done an eight-hour day out to the southern base of Ngāuruhoe on another trip.

'I'm relieved to hear you say that,' he said. 'I thought I might not be able to keep up with you.'

As it turns out, Harry is a mountain goat, probably from having spent so much time on Ruapehu chasing glaciers and running away from eruptions. The best pace is the one you can do without stopping, he said, and too right. Harry led me up a way I hadn't been before; I was used to using the Gut, which was currently completely devoid of snow, requiring significant scrambling. We went the way the guides use, crossing over just below the Gut, above 'Jabberholes', and ascending via Twin Rocks and Restful Ridge, which proved much swifter and more solid than the more erosion-prone routes I'd taken in the past.

About halfway up Restful Ridge we stopped at a rock with obvious striations. Ice scratches, Harry called them, because he likes to use terms people will understand. We talked a little about Odell and Krenek and their early research, and how the Whakapapa Glacier once came all this way down the mountain.

At 2300 metres we stopped for a Mallowpuff check. All were now cracked, and he ate one. I was shocked — Harry was eating the experiment! I'd had it in mind that we'd carry them up to the Summit Plateau at 2600 metres to see what happened to them all before snacking on any of them.

'I haven't studied fracture development,' Harry said unapologetically. 'Only fracture initiation.'

Harry's Mallowpuffs had cracked across the top, a satisfying shear in the chocolate shell as the marshmallow expanded. These, however, had cracked on the bottom, usually breaking the biscuit base but sometimes creating a perfect circular cut right around the Mallowpuff between the base and the mallow. Further experiments would clearly be required.

We reached the Notch in under two hours from the cafe, making good time. We

ABOVE: Scientists Harry Keys and Noel Sissons on Whakapapa in 1969. Harry Keys collection

BELOW: Scientists searching for the source of sulphur gas in ice caves underneath the Summit Plateau. Karen Britten, GNS Science Te Pū Ao

stood at the edge of the plateau, once again snacked on the experiment, and peered around. It didn't look as if there was much happening in terms of ice caves, and any ponds had disappeared. We tramped down and wandered into the ice and moraine. Harry pointed out the difference between what was just residual snow from this season and true glacial ice, which had tiny bubbles of air in it. We walked through ice formations sometimes twice my height. One had a line of ash through the middle, which Harry pointed out was tephra from the 1995 eruption on one layer, then glacial ice, and more tephra from the 1996 eruption on top of that.

I thought about the warning Mike and I had received about sinkholes in the plateau when we'd come up to visit the lake.

'Is there any danger of crevasses or sinkholes up here, Harry?' I asked. 'I'd been told once to watch out for them.'

'No, sinkholes aren't a problem,' he called back. 'Crevasses only form when the glacier stretches over something — it needs some sort of stress to become crevassed, and the Summit Plateau is just downwasting, it doesn't travel anywhere.'

Over at the site of the ephemeral lake, close to the Mangatoetoenui Glacier, there was no water to be seen, just fractured ice coated with snow. The plateau level was about 12 metres lower than the rock rim where I'd stood when the lake was overflowing into the Mangatoetoenui, reflecting a significant seasonal change.

Harry spotted a potential cave, where a crack existed next to a large block of ice. We put on crampons and grabbed ice axes, and downclimbed into it. Harry got in easily, but as a shorter human I struggled. There was a drop from the ice down to a small waterway and my leg dangled in space. 'You're nearly there,' Harry said. 'You've got another ten inches to go . . . six inches . . . two inches . . .' and then I was there, standing on a block of ice, in the bowels of the earth. Water rushed past our feet and ice stalactites dripped from the roof of the cave. We couldn't see where the water went to, but it was clear we'd found the drainage hole for the lake. Cold wrapped its hands around me.

Harry swiftly ripped up the ice wall again to the sunshine, but I had some trouble getting up onto the ice initially. A hollow had been carved out lower down, requiring an awkward leg move and a lot of clinging and trusting of crampons. I was just a whisker too short to do it easily. I fell once and began to feel a sense of rising panic: what if I couldn't get out? I distracted myself by chipping a small platform on the ice for my left foot to get onto.

Harry handed his axe down to me, and with one axe in each hand I managed to get purchase on the ice. For extra certainty, Harry reached down and grabbed the hood of my jacket for greater leverage, and with a bit of effort I managed to get up and out of the stream, then up the ice slope to the sunshine. (That night I woke up in a cold sweat, dreaming about ice caves collapsing on me, and having to be rescued by the Ruapehu Alpine Rescue Organisation because I couldn't climb out, and the media headlines read 'Stupid writer who can't climb rescued after getting stuck in ice cave.')

We took a different route down the mountain, dropping directly off the crater rim and down to the top of the Knoll Ridge T-bar, digging into soft scree that was much kinder on the knees. I checked the Mallowpuffs (or at least, the survivors). Some had

ABOVE: Harry Keys beyond an ice arch on the Summit Plateau in 2023.

BELOW: The ephemeral lake that forms on the Summit Plateau, just under Te Heuheu peak. Paul Stevens

ABOVE: Cracked Mallowpuffs at the Notch, looking into the Summit Plateau.

BELOW: The author in an ice cave underneath the Summit Plateau, near the top of the Mangatoetoenui Glacier. Harry Keys

cracked further across the tops as well as the bottoms, so perhaps extra time spent at altitude had accelerated their destruction. At some point, Harry had spoken to Griffins, which had acknowledged that they ship their Mallowpuffs by road, not by air, otherwise they'd all crack with alacrity. I wondered if they'd found out the hard way.

I convinced my friend Garth, who had access to a commercial kitchen, to help me further the Mallowpuff experiment. First, he put one into a vacuum packer and took it up to the equivalent of 20,000 metres. It cracked, but not dramatically — he'd hoped for a proper explosion. He then repeated the process with a fridge-cooled puff (similar results) and a frozen one (it stayed intact).

'As marshmallow is chilled, it crystallises and hardens, losing its fluffiness,' Garth said. 'Not helpful if you want a cracking good time but a handy tip if you want them whole on summits.'

Later, he vacuum sealed two puffs individually into plastic bags and dropped them down to 40 metres off his boat into Lake Taupō. One puff had an air cushion around it, while the other had been sucked out. The puff with the air cushion survived intact, while the other was crushed.

The Mallowpuff Project captured Garth's imagination, as it had mine. 'Got the bug now, thanks Hazel,' he wrote.

I contacted Griffins and explained the Mallowpuff Project in the current day, hoping that they might help. 'I realise this is a bit weird,' I wrote at the end of my summary. 'But call me any time.' I got a carefully worded response from a customer service representative politely asking me to go away.

I returned to the Summit Plateau a week after my trip with Harry, this time with some friends. We'd had a week of rain, some of it quite heavy, and the section of the plateau where Harry and I had been into the ice cave had downwasted by 3–4 metres. A block of ice had tilted onto its side and was sticking up in the air like the Shark's Tooth on Taranaki. I stood at the edge, listening to the roaring of running water, which I'd scarcely been able to hear on the previous visit. Everything was cracked and shattered. I wasn't going near it — the ice could be a total death trap. It stunned me how much the environment changed in such a short time, which made it feel as if Ruapehu was impossible to properly know.

We rushed down, short on time as one of the group wanted to descend via the gondola rather than walking the knee-crunching descent. I wanted to linger, but perhaps I'd need to come up solo another time and linger alone. Noel Odell once described how, on a night-time descent of Ruapehu in failing light, he'd begun to appreciate the different vistas afforded by the night: 'As I passed along the ashy and snowy crest, the moon was rising, and soon through a clear sky its light afforded all that was necessary for rapid progress. Whilst making my way down the Whakapapa Glacier, its surface sparkling in the moonbeams, I fell to wondering why climbers are so prone to rush early from their summits and thus miss the glories of sunset dissolving into moonlight upon the mountains.'[26]

6100 FT
6220 FT
West Crater
5530 FT
Wanganui River
TONGARIRO
6458 FT
Central Crater
5690 FT
5570 FT
ROTOPOUNAMU
SULPHUR LAGOONS
6140 FT
(QUIET)
RED CRATER
6050 FT
South Crater
5420 FT
4810 FT
SODA SPR.
5720 FT
Mangatepopo Str.
7515 FT
NGAURUHOE
(ACTIVE)
4780 FT
5190 FT
RIFT
Waihohonu Str.
3880 FT
4695 FT
4240 FT
Nga-puna-a-tama
4770 FT

1891 sketch map of Tongariro and Ngāuruhoe, showing the 'Great Rift', the location of Holl's Rock, above Upper Tama Lake. National Library of New Zealand, 38314409

CHAPTER 17

Holl's Rock

In 1927, Horace Holl, who had an uncanny ability to read the weather in the mountains, died while crossing the Mangaturuturu River. The national park management plan named Holl's Rock and Holl's Cairn as significant, but passively managed, assets. Only, where were they? And what were they all about? I roped in a buddy and went to re-enact Holl's 'classic climb', off track at the base of Ngāuruhoe.

Peretini/Girdlestone Peak was one of Horace Holl's favourite climbs. Note the crevasses of the Mangaehuehu Glacier. Auckland Libraries Heritage Collections

On the southeast buttress of Girdlestone there's a spectacular rock hole in the lower ridge known as 'The Window'. It's described by climbing-guide website *Climb NZ* as 'an adventurous summer line on variable rock' (in other words, 'choss' — unstable and crumbly). One user reviewed the route as a fun climb and good adventure, one that was relatively remote for Ruapehu. 'Look, if you come into this climb expecting "sound rock" you will be severely disappointed,' they wrote. 'Delightful glacially carved slabs? Nope. Basalt columns? Nope. Try glued moraine, barely stuck together conglomerate and ridiculously precariously stacked boulders of varying sizes. The "Window" is cool though, if a giant pile of choss surrounded by slightly worse choss.' Climbers should expect some exposed and 'largely unprotectable' crux sections: 'Know what you're getting yourself into.'[1]

Mountain enthusiast Horace Arthur Holl loved Girdlestone and had climbed the peak many times in his 50 or so ascents of the mountain, including the first ascent of the southeast ridge, which was one of his favourite climbs. Nobody knew the central plateau mountains better than Holl; he was considered an authority on Tongariro National Park and an intrepid alpinist who pioneered rock climbing in the area.

During the 1927 summer holidays Holl led parties of trampers and climbers on and around Ruapehu, including a trip up Girdlestone. He took his group up the southeastern arête, the ridge that borders the Wahianoa Glacier on the northern side of the peak. The climbers met with unpleasant weather and incredibly hard climbing conditions, but they pushed on. Thunderstorms came over and soon they were unusually heavy, pelting the climbers with painful stinging rain. Thunderclaps close by and lightning strikes illuminated the dark skies.

The party managed to summit and descend successfully regardless — in stark contrast to the men who attempted to place the plaque for Hugh Girdlestone in 1921, and possibly simply because it was summer, and hence marginally warmer. An account based on information provided by the party was published in the *Dominion* newspaper.

'Startling accounts of the effect of the electrical disturbance are given by the party, and only a strong spirit of intrepidity could have inspired the climbers to complete the ascent,' the newspaper account read.

> The lightning, it is reported, appeared to be striking the peak and when within 150 feet of the top, shocks were experienced by every member of the party. A further phenomenon to test the mettle of the mountaineers came in the way of an extraordinary buzzing from the steel parts of the ice axes, while on reaching the summit, the rocks, which apparently were charged with electricity, were hissing like gas-jets.[2]

It's fair to say that Holl would have relished the challenge.

Holl was born in England and emigrated to New Zealand, where he established the University Coaching College, a private tutoring business, in Auckland in 1912. He

was quickly taken with New Zealand's impressive landscapes and became a regular visitor to Ruapehu whenever he could get away, sometimes for several weeks at a time. Sometimes he'd take a tent and simply set up camp wherever fancy took him.

He loved any place that afforded him the opportunity to go rock climbing, and he quickly became known as an expert climber. Although he scaled impressive columns of rock and eventually moved on to climbing extensively in the South Island — including the feat of summiting Aoraki Mount Cook twice within a fortnight, something no other amateur had done — he always took pains to climb with a tested rope and an ice axe.

Few amateur alpinists in New Zealand had more knowledge of climbing than Holl, who had also climbed in the UK and Switzerland before emigrating. And he began passing on his love of climbing, introducing people to the national park and informally guiding parties on the mountains of Ruapehu, Tongariro and Ngāuruhoe.

At the southern base of Ngāuruhoe is an area with a distinctive chasm of sorts, in between two ridges, with spot height 1584 metres on the west and 1562 metres on the east. The map shows a tarn at the southern end, though it's often dry, and at the base of this tarn a precipice drops down to Upper Tama Lake. The area is seldom visited except by off-track trampers, although several ground trails exist. In 1931 surveyor Laurence Cussen named it the 'Great Rift Valley', and writer James W. Alexandre observed the valley's constitution of a 'tumbled mass of stony hills, split by a remarkable explosion chasm'. The Great Rift, Alexandre wrote, was a mile long and half a mile wide, and its eastern precipice was 496 feet (about 150 metres) above the valley floor. Crucially: 'At its northern end there are some remarkable forms of columnar andesitic lava which provide plenty of work for that peculiar fraternity known as rock-climbers, there being several fine chimneys with difficult capstones.'[3]

Horace Holl was not only a member of that peculiar fraternity, he was also its president and most enthusiastic publicity officer. So much so, in fact, that the Great Rift's most exciting precipice became known as Holl's Rock. Holl was the first to climb it, and whenever he could find any potential new recruits to the peculiar fraternity of rock climbers he would take them to the rock to test their mettle.[4]

Bill Mead wrote of Holl's contribution to the Ruapehu community in his book *Memories of a Mountain and a River*, noting that he was also an early member of Ruapehu Ski Club, the first club to introduce the sport of skiing to the North Island. Mead and his companion Bernard Drake were the founders of Ruapehu Ski Club and roped Holl in for ski touring on the lower slopes around Tama Lakes. It was on these early ski-touring occasions that Holl first spotted the precipice that would later informally bear his name. Mead wrote:

> His greatest interest in mountains was in rock climbing, which had fascinated him since he had been introduced to it in England when on a tramping trip to the Lakes District. When skiing, he was always on the lookout for 'nice black rocks' and a cliff of fifteen or twenty feet would tempt him to take off his skis and try it out if it was not absolutely smooth. In this case the big cliff of Tama showed no holds on the lower part, but a little to the left of the direct line there were hand and footholds for about 100ft then a horizontal crack across to the main cliff line, and above that there appeared to be sufficient holds for the climb to the top. This became one of Holl's favourite climbs on summer trips.[5]

Holl's Rock is essentially a collection of vertical rock columns, but this horizontal crack permeates them — in fact it shatters them, in places — and runs from bottom right as you're looking at the crag to the top left, where it disappears around the corner. This was Holl's classic climb, the one he became really well known for. It was the first proper 'crag' in the park, much later followed by renowned spots such as Whakapapa Gorge, which — the now out-of-print New Zealand Alpine Club Tongariro guidebook informs us — was 'sniffed out' by 'inveterate crag hound' Paul Rogers while on a 'tour of duty' at the region's Sir Edmund Hillary Outdoors Pursuits Centre.[6] Whakapapa Gorge is a few minutes' walk from the carpark and its easy access meant Holl's Rock became forgotten over time.

Horace Holl, in an era when smoking during a photography session was acceptable.
Alan Graham collection

I came across Holl for the first time while journeying through the Tongariro National Park Management Plan 2006–2016. It contains a list of 'actively managed historic resources' (such as Waihohonu Hut, the Chateau, Glacier Hut and the Old Coach Road) and 'passively managed resources'. Here I found 'site of the Haunted Whare', 'Stanton Memorial plaque', 'Mangaiti Hut', 'Ketetahi Bridle Track' and, very curiously, an entry that read: 'Hollis or Holls cairn, true right bank of the Mangaturuturu Stream'. Holl's Rock and Holl's Cairn appeared to be the same thing, but the Mangaturuturu Stream is nowhere near the Great Rift and Holl's Rock — in fact, they're on entirely different sides of Ruapehu.

How do you find a needle in a haystack? I googled 'Hollis cairn' and 'Holls cairn' without any luck, so I went straight to the source and sent a query to DOC, asking what was the Hollis or Holls cairn and why was it of significance. I wondered, was it even the same Holl, or was Hollis someone else entirely. They told me Horace Holl was an early adventurer who died while crossing the Mangaturuturu in flood. So far, so good. I asked where it was, and got no response. I heard second-hand that the staff at DOC Whakapapa think I'm a bit mad, and honestly I don't blame them. They have other things to do than respond to my fishing expeditions such as deploying hungry heather beetles and tracking down the butterwort crim to bring him to justice.

Once I found his name — full name Horace Arthur Holl — I managed to dig deeper. I discarded 'Hollis' as likely to be a typo, but also found mentions of Holl's Rock as well as his cairn, which could well have been the same thing. I put in a request to the National Library (whose staff are also probably questioning my sanity by now, only on a bigger scale than DOC), and their research experts unearthed many treasures. Notably, a *Wilderness* magazine article from 2002 showed early climbers Malcolm Ross and his badass lady-climber wife Forrestina (aka Bessie) at the Great Rift, staring at Holl's Rock, and gave some basic details about Holl as a pioneering climber. Holl wanted national parks to be accessible to all New Zealanders, and was particularly encouraging to women, I read. Separately I discovered that one of his group adventure trips, in 1917, was responsible for introducing Ronald Algie and Helen Adair McMaster, who later married and did many climbs together.[7] Old chap Ronald must have been special to Holl, as he was named executor in his will (which is digitised, I discovered, and available via Archives New Zealand).[8]

Finally I hit upon the exact location of Holl's Rock in the Tongariro climbing guidebook.[9] I realised I'd walked right past it on a trip through Te Tatau Pounamu Wilderness Area when we'd exited via Waihohonu Springs and Tama Lakes, but we'd had our heads down in bad weather and hadn't noticed anything much, just hunched over and motored.

I discovered that Jock Graham's book *Ruapehu: Tribute to a mountain* mentioned Holl's Cairn, which was erected 'in the vicinity' of where he died,[10] and I got concrete answers from the Wanganui Tramping Club, which had been 'caretaking' the cairn and repainted its lettering in 2007. The club gave me rough directions to where it stood in the Mangaturuturu Valley.

After all that, I had gathered two crucial pieces of information: I wasn't just looking for Holl's Rock, I was also looking for his memorial cairn; and the Tongariro National Park Management Plan was wrong — the cairn wasn't on the true right of the Mangaturuturu.

My mate Toby had been instructing outdoors pursuits for the army down south and was briefly back in the North Island and keen for a few missions. I told him about Holl's Rock and he said, 'I'm in.' As he was travelling he didn't have much trad climbing gear with him, just basic kit: harness, rope, carabiners, some quickdraws and slings. I owned the same, mostly for alpine purposes. I asked my friend Jezza if we could borrow some of his trad gear, and I knew when he hesitated slightly that even though he said yes, he was a bit uncomfortable lending it out. I reneged, and Toby and I proceeded with our basic kit. (Later on when I told Toby I'd asked Jezza if we could borrow some trad gear, he was incredulous: 'That's like asking to borrow someone else's undies!')

We had a clear but windy day and got an early start walking out via Tama Lakes, where we both set about removing more than a few rocks from a large and pointless cairn that marred the landscape. (Cairns violate the 'leave no trace' principle of national parks, they can lead people astray as many trampers now build them for Instagram photos rather than for navigation, and shifting rocks around can cause erosion and destroy the homes and habitats of tiny critters.) We ascended the ridge above Lower Tama Lake and skirted south of Upper Tama Lake. There's a rough ground trail along here, and the bare ridgelines make travel easy. Then we dropped down to the Great Rift, an expanse I'd thought of as the 'Gates of Tama' before I knew of the old name for it, and from here we could see Holl's Rock winking at us lusciously.

We got up close and had lunch behind a huge boulder where we could shelter from the wind and put our harnesses on. Toby ran around the corner to scope it out from afar and concluded: 'Yeah, I reckon it goes.'

We were ignoring the long, vertical, highly aesthetic columns that would attract most rock climbers in favour of the sloping, shattered ledge: Holl's classic climb, which he used to test beginners.

We ascended a short approach, then I tucked my poles into my pack and eyed up the ledge. It looked fairly wide, like something you'd tramp cautiously in wilder backcountry — such as the ascent to Browning Pass or the climb to Waterfall Face — using your hands and arms as well as legs and feet, sort of 'four-wheel-drive tramping'.

'Okay, I'll lead, and we'll both be tied in, and just use natural rock features for protection,' Toby explained. Depending on what it was like around the corner, he said, he might use some climbing gear to secure us to the rock as he went.

'This is how Horace Holl would have done this climb, actually,' he called back as he wound the rope around various rock features. I waited, overconfident that it would be easy. After all, Holl had done it in just a tweed jacket and a handlebar moustache.

'On belay!' Toby called.

'Climbing!' I called back. I walked along the ledge, removing rope from behind sharp features, strong pieces of rock and smaller flakes that looked dodgy, but Toby had

ABOVE: The splintered rock of the western side of Pt 1562. Holl's Rock is on the far left.

BELOW: View down to the Great Rift and back to Upper Tama Lake from the summit of Pt 1562.

pre-tested them. You push on New Zealand rock, you don't pull, I reminded myself.

I could see the rope disappearing back around the corner as Toby took it in. I peered around and saw him, perched on solid terrain and prepared for another pitch. Then he disappeared around the next corner and took some time. I sat below the belay station holding the rope and peered over the vertical cliff below me. Retreating was still an option, I felt, and if we had more gear I'd be happy to abseil down directly off the bluff.

Toby took so long I began to wonder, and then to worry. I was about to call out when I heard him call, 'Just doing some gardening!' — he was pulling tiny tree roots and dirt out of crevices to 'clean' the route. He was putting in an extra sling around an anchor as a runner on the trickiest bit where it fell away entirely and I'd need to rely on my fancy footwork and hand holds to traverse across. He'd put the sling up and around a tall rock, with a snaplink carabiner down the bottom and the rope running through, and a couple of little rocks as chockstones for added safety on top. As a setup using minimal gear it was impressive. As I went across I had to cling to the rock with one hand (and the tips of two feet), remove the chockstones and the sling, unclip the rope, and get the gear back onto my harness one-handed so I had two hands free for this business of clinging to things as part of my new role in this peculiar fraternity.

I think Toby was internally chuckling with joy at all of this, in the same way Holl probably had.

I made it over. 'That was the crux,' Toby said, and I exhaled.

I looked around. We were surrounded by shattered rock. From here it was a direct climb up to the high point 1562 metres, just west of Tama peak. Easier, more direct, and just a case of grab at the rocks and go.

At the top we high-fived (as you do), snapped a few pics, breathed some more, coiled the rope and sorted our gear, which tends to get mixed up as you're moving.

We walked off the top of point 1562 metres along the ridge to the east of the Great Rift. We'd done Holl's classic climb, in about four pitches.

Next time I'll do it in a tweed jacket.

After any fatality in the wilderness, people begin to question the risk inherent in whatever activity was responsible for the person's demise, and after the Stanton search in 1931, adventurer Eric Burton wrote of Holl's superior ability to read the weather. 'Mr Holl knew the National Park and its mountains as few men are likely to know them,' Burton wrote.

He'd been in a climbing party led by Holl, and they were planning to go the next day. The weather looked perfect and promised well for the climb, but Holl tried to shut it down.

'I don't like the look of it for tomorrow,' Holl said.

'Why, it looks now as if it will be perfect,' Burton said.

Holl knew otherwise, and insisted the party leave for the ski club hut that afternoon, even though it was late, so that they could get an early start the next morning in case the weather changed for the worse during the day. The next morning

there was a little bit of cloud but otherwise it seemed fine to Burton. Still, Holl hesitated. It was only 6 a.m. so they decided to have a go, and turn back if need be. They ascended to the Whakapapa Glacier, above the clouds, and couldn't see anything below, just Ngāuruhoe peeking through with a sea of clouds beneath it. Then mist and cloud completely surrounded them, reducing visibility to just a few metres. Everything was white.

The wind began, a cold wind, and the wet mist soaked them through. Holl decided to continue to the top, get their bearings and return. However, in going up, they did exactly what the Stanton party had done — they veered to the left. Holl had a compass, and when the cloud parted briefly he was able to take a bearing, which saved the day and all was fine. But Burton realised Holl had known much earlier than he had that it wasn't going to be good.[11]

Holl had established several camps around the mountain, including one in the bush just below Tawhai Falls on the route up to Whakapapa, and another in the Mangaturuturu Valley. It was an easy walk to follow the Mangaturuturu River up from the viaduct where the highway now lies, just before Pokaka in the west. The river valley is reasonably wide, and the rocky riverbed offers uncomplicated travel. Just before the valley opens out into wide flats dotted with tussock, there's a 23-metre waterfall to navigate. Above that, several stands of beech trees near the river are ideal for sheltering from the elements, and the Mangaturuturu waterway splits, with its true left fork running pure and clear. The true right fork was sometimes referred to as the 'sulphur stream' for its occasional tendency to become dirty and smell of chemicals.

On Friday, 27 May 1927, a cold, wet and stormy day with heavy rain and snow from the outset, Holl set out with John Bartrum, a professor in geology at Auckland University College. Bartrum was known for his 'almost masochistic' attitude to physical danger in the outdoors while pursuing geology — he and his wife had spent their first six months as newlyweds in a tent in the Buller Gorge — coupled with extreme modesty, self-deprecation, permanently damaged ankles from his geological pursuits, and chronic arthritis.[12] They set out from Pokaka around midday and headed for Holl's camp near the Cascades about 7 miles above the railway. Making their way up the swollen Mangaturuturu River, they had to traverse the waterway at least 20 times before they reached the safety of camp.

Holl was leading a packhorse just ahead of Bartrum, and both were carrying 15-kilogram rucksacks. It was slow and difficult, and they had to steady themselves on each crossing by clutching at their horses' trappings. Around 4 p.m. they reached a major ford, a place where the Mangaturuturu was usually one and a half chains wide, but the water was now waist high. Rain and snow had converted it into a raging torrent. Large rocks, up to five feet in width, studded the flooded stream, and boulders were constantly on the move, pushed around by the force of the water.

The men were about 8 feet away from each other. Holl turned to Bartrum and acknowledged the risk they were taking. 'We're only about a quarter of an hour from camp,' he yelled over the loud noise of the roaring water.[13]

Holl was nearly at the opposite bank when his legs began to slip out from underneath him. His hands were numb from the intense cold and rain, making it difficult to hold onto the horse's bridle for long enough to allow Bartrum, who was separated from Holl by his own horse, to get to him and lend assistance. The current was too strong, and Holl was swept away in a flash. Bartrum could do nothing but watch Holl bobbing down the torrent like a cork. Later, he reflected that the rocks probably killed Holl rather than drowning.

'It was only a matter of seconds before the body was out of sight,' Bartrum said. 'The stream was wide at the point where we were crossing. The fall in the stream is excessive, particularly where the accident occurred,' he told the coronial inquiry.[14]

Bartrum tethered the horses to a nearby tree and ran down the river for just over a mile, but Holl was long gone. He conducted a thorough but fruitless search, and returned to his horse as the skies blackened with night and heavy rain. Worried for his companion, he spent the night in the open with just a canvas sleeping bag for protection. The next day he left and raised the alarm back at Pokaka.

'Owing to our positions and the suddenness of the occurrence together with the swiftness of the river I was quite unable to render Holl any assistance whatever,' Bartrum said. He was the less experienced of the two. 'Holl was the principal of the party. I was his guest. On my return to Pokaka on Saturday I searched the stream but could see no sign of the body, the stream was in high flood all Saturday.'[15]

A search party including local expert Joe Blyth was sent in, under trying conditions of driving snow, thunder and lightning. They found Holl's body in a creek about two miles below the scene of the accident on the Sunday morning, at 10.40 a.m. His body had been caught up in a snag in the river, and most of his clothes had been torn off by the river.[16]

Ohakune police constable James Annison told the coroner that the Mangaturuturu, when in flood, was one of the swiftest streams he knew of in the district, being a mountain torrent with an excessive fall. 'The body was badly knocked about through coming in contact with the rocks, and the skull was also badly crushed,' he said. 'The bed of the stream is full of boulders which are constantly on the move when the stream is in flood. My experience of the stream convinces me that any person swept away by the stream would have no chance of coming out of it alive.'[17]

'The scene . . . is in one of the most beautiful gorges in the National Park,' the *Wanganui Chronicle* had reported in an article about his death in June 1927.

> It is traversed for almost its full length by the Mangaturuturu Stream, which is regarded as perfectly safe in normal times, but which becomes very dangerous in the rainy season. Mr Holl found a site set in beautiful surroundings, about seven miles above the railway line. This spot, which became known as Holl's camp, he

THE RUAPEHU TRAGEDY.—Mr. Horace Arthur Holl, principal of the University Coaching College at Auckland, was drowned in attempting to ford the Mangaturuturu Stream on Friday. Mr. Holl was one of the most experienced amateur alpinists in the Dominion. On the south side of Ngauruhoe is a rock named after him. Left: A photograph of the unfortunate climber on Holl's Rock. On the right, another snapshot of Mr. Holl in alpine "kit."

ABOVE: Horace Holl's newspaper obituary. Bagnall Collection, Massey University Library

BELOW: Holl's Cairn, a memorial to the man, in the Mangaturuturu Valley.

> was in the habit of using as a half-way stop on his many ascents of the mountain. The route from it provided comparatively easy access to Pare-te-tai-tonga, the centre peak of 9025ft. Many waterfalls were to be found near the camp site, and wonderful panoramas were to be obtained in the vicinity.[18]

The Mangaturuturu Valley is a place of magic and delight. Most people only engage with it to see the Cascades, to tramp the Round the Mountain Track or to stay at Mangaturuturu Hut, and never venture any further off track. Up high the Mangaturuturu Glacier still exists, and in winter it's a rewarding ski down from the saddle that gives access to the Crater Lake, an area known as Te Pā-tatau-o-te-rangi (the Gates of Heaven), a place where Ngāti Rangi believe souls depart earth for the afterlife.

Further down, the waterways draining from the glacier are often a stunning glacial blue set against volcanic rock worn smooth by the pressure of passing ice. There are green meadows and terrifying cliff bands, pretty stands of beech forest and impossibly clear pools of perfect water to indulge in.

I camped out in the lower Mangaturuturu once with a friend, sheltered only by a lightweight tarp propped up with my tramping poles. We lit a fire, watched some Bush TV, and counted stars as they appeared. That trip we discovered a deep, curving swimming hole just above a waterfall in the main part of the river, where we availed ourselves on a sweltering day of its 11-degree water, alternating between cold swims and baking ourselves on hot rocks. I've returned many times to that swimming hole as a sort of pilgrimage. It's very close to where I suspect Holl came to grief that day in 1927. I later found out we'd camped pretty much where his old Mangaturuturu campsite was: half a mile above the falls below the Wanganui Tramping Club hut (Mangaturuturu Hut), on the river's true right bank.[19]

I found Holl's Cairn, finally, just off track in a position that makes it hard to spot unless you're specifically hunting it out. I saw what I thought was a pile of stones on top of a very large rock, and walked around to the other side to check. And there, in fresh white paint on a lichen-covered grey rock, was the simple text:

27.5.27
HORACE ARTHUR HOLL

It's said that Holl's Cairn is near the site where he was swept away, but I disagree. The cairn is higher up, in between two narrow tributaries to the Mangaturuturu, not near the main river where it widens out, and Holl's camp would have been on the flats near the river where several stands of beech forest offer good shelter — somewhere between where the Mangaturuturu Hut now stands and the 23-metre waterfall to the southwest.

Of all people, Holl knew the risk in crossing a flooded river. 'It was pure misadventure,' Bartrum told the coroner. 'Mr Holl had so often pitted his knowledge and strength against Nature, and succeeded, and I suppose it was inevitable that Nature should sometimes win.'[20]

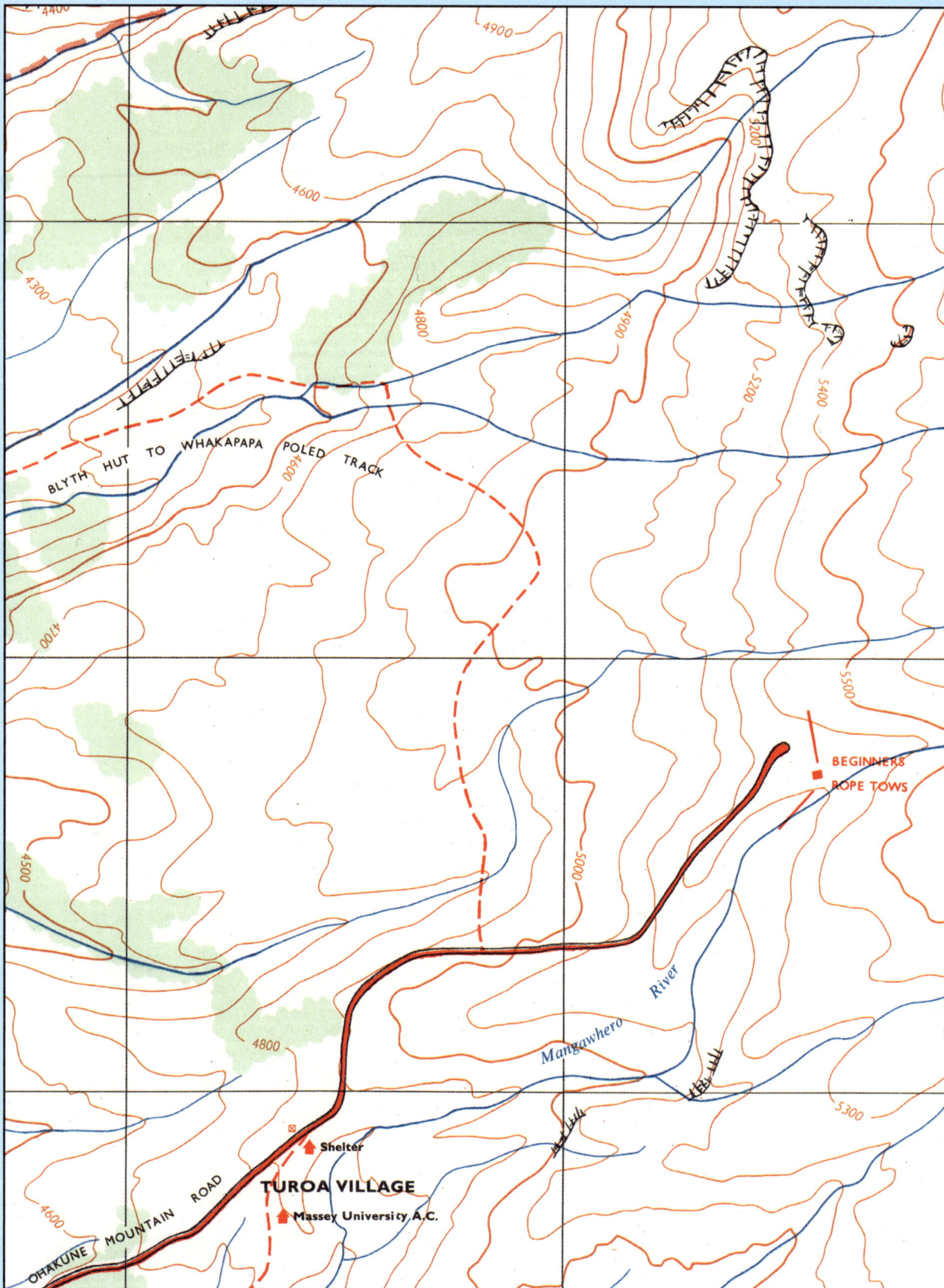

4400
4900
3200
4600
4300
4800
4900
5200
5400
BLYTH HUT TO WHAKAPAPA POLED TRACK
4600
4700
5500
BEGINNERS
ROPE TOWS
4500
5000
River
Mangawhero
4800
5300
Shelter
TUROA VILLAGE
Massey University A.C.
OHAKUNE MOUNTAIN ROAD
4600
To Ohakune
To Blyth Hut

Map showing the Tūroa ski field area and Mangawhero catchment, where fuel has been spilled. National Library of New Zealand, 38239634

CHAPTER 18

The mauri of the maunga

In 1979, a diesel spill from the newly constructed Tūroa ski field affected the pure and beautiful Mangawhero Stream. Since then, both Tūroa and Whakapapa have suffered fuel spills. I spent several summers finding swimming spots on the maunga and exploring the water-supply infrastructure. Meanwhile, we were being watched . . .

Hugh Girdlestone, that enthusiast of early exploration on Ruapehu, held a firm opinion about drinking cold water from the mountain: 'On no account should the cold ice-water be drunk, as it is very bad for the heated body,' he wrote in 1909. 'If one must drink, put some snow in a hollow in a rock exposed to the sun, and wait until it melts and gets the chill off it; but it is much better to do without it whilst climbing.'[1]

I beg to differ on many fronts — for example, cold water is the fastest way to cure heatstroke (the 'heated body'). I suppose science has come a long way since Girdlestone wrote that advice. But most of all I beg to differ simply because the cold, pure water on Ruapehu is one of its greatest delights.

DOC, on behalf of iwi, asks people not to touch the water in the national park. In its information section about the Tongariro Alpine Crossing, the department advises: 'All waterways including the lakes on Tongariro and his peaks Ngāuruhoe and Ruapehu are sacred to local iwi, Ngāti Hikairo ki Tongariro. Kaumātua Te Ngaehe Wanikau asks visitors to the area to respect the sanctity of the maunga tapu (sacred mountains) by not touching or entering any of the waterways including the alpine lakes.'[2] DOC also points out that high mineral concentrations are present in many of the national park's waterways, particularly Mangatepopo Stream, Emerald Lakes and Ketetahi Hot Springs (and if you go to Ketetahi, you're trespassing, too — it's not and has never been part of the park). 'For cultural and health reasons, swimming is not advised in many of the lakes, streams and rivers of the park.'[3]

This edict not to touch the waterways blew my mind a little bit. Sure, I hadn't been swimming in Emerald Lakes or trespassing in the dead of night to Ketetahi. But I had been swimming in jewel-coloured pools in unfrequented places around the mountain, delighting in the contrast of cold water in the heat of summer, sometimes drinking it while I swam in it, flouting Girdlestone's health advice with each dip and, in a sense, 'consuming' Ruapehu. I held an intense desire not just to visit the waters of the national park, but also to get into them, to become one with them. And I loved to drink them. Now, I wasn't sure what to think.

At the Ohakune Library I stumbled across a book about Ngāti Rangi perspectives on water. (Ohakune Library is one of the carrot patch's little-known gems — it's well funded but hardly anybody ever borrows books, so while in the main centres you might wait months and months for a new release, at Ohakune you simply walk in and the book you want is instantly available. Additionally, Aucklanders will be amazed to know there is parking right outside. Right outside!)

The book was called *Mouri Tū Mouri Ora: Water for wisdom and life*. Genesis Energy, a Crown-owned operation, diverts water from the Moawhango and Whanganui rivers, as well as tributaries of the Whangaehu, to operate the Tongariro Power Scheme. In 2003, Ngāti Rangi, Whanganui iwi and Tamahaki appealed the 35-year renewal of a concession to continue diverting the waters, arguing that the scheme disrupted the rivers' ability to follow their natural paths unbroken from the mountains to the sea. In fact, iwi had opposed this for more than 40 years. *Mouri Tū Mouri Ora* was a collection of perspectives from the court case, and they resonated with me, particularly the piece

ABOVE: Swimming in a remote, clear pool of water on the southern side of Ruapehu, fed by the Mangaehuehu Glacier, which can be seen in the background.

BELOW: One of the best swimming holes on the Mangawhero River, the Pearl aka Paradise Pool.

from Colin Richards (Pahake, Marangai Pā, Ngāti Rangi, Whanganui Iwi mai i Te Kāhui Maunga ki Tangaroa):

> I often heard our old people speak of the streams and springs that flow from Koro Ruapehu, as toto (blood). They were referring to the life essence that flows in our ancestral streams and rivers, from The Mountains to The Sea. And if we look into the depth of that, they were referring to the life-force within water that provides all living things with their life sustenance. Without it, there can be no life. It is very simple to look at water and say that's just another river. That is a very Westernised view of things . . . as tāngata tiaki, our responsibility is to nurture and care for that life-force, so it may sustain all living things.[4]

I wanted to touch the water, to get into the water and drink it, and that came with responsibility: to nurture and care for it.

'Of all the elements, water is the first because without it there can be no life sustenance of Papatuanuku,' Richards wrote. 'If we disturb that, then we have upset the balance, and if we upset the balance then there is retribution. Each living thing has a mouri, a life-force, and if we upset the life-force then we have caused an imbalance in the world.'[5]

I spent a couple of summers discovering pools of pure water around the mountain. My friend Jezza gave me some information to find one in the upper trickles of the Mangawhero, one that's a bit of a local secret. It's a round pool, emerald in colour, with a short waterfall that kids often use as a slide. Beech forest crowds one bank, while the other has clusters of smooth rock that heat up in the sun and are ideal for rewarming yourself. Initially I skinny-dipped there, until one day I nearly got caught and realised its secrecy was anything but watertight. I put a pin in on my topo map app to mark the spot and its coordinates and named it Paradise Pool. Another friend calls it the Pearl. When I found the Ohakune Hut site, I discovered the old marker poles for the track to the hut led right past Paradise Pool, the Pearl. It was close to the road, perhaps 10 minutes' walk, and I was amazed by its relative secrecy.

The Hairpin Spa was another favourite, a pool just off the hairpin bend on the Ohakune Mountain Road, with a view to Ruapehu and more hot rocks and beech forest. Jezza and I went exploring above Tūroa one day when he showed me a sort of infinity pool above a waterfall, and some very hidden swimming holes in the catchment above, all green-blue and crystal clear. I called the infinity pool the Top Tūroa Tub, and again, marked it on the topo map. Then I got to thinking that perhaps some of these swimming holes could be discerned from the satellite map. I did some 'finger tramping' on the map above Blyth Hut and spotted one I thought had potential. Jezza and I struck blue gold: another pure, clear, cold pool with a view to the mountain, and absolute privacy. I called that one the Secret Spa, for obvious reasons.

Another favourite was a glacial pool below Mangaturuturu Hut, which I'd found while exploring the area with Horace Holl in mind. That one: Holl's Heaven. Another was a deep, dark-blue pool just off the track near the Cascades, which we called 'FKK', short for 'Freikörperkultur', a German term for 'free body culture' — or, in other words, voracious and enthusiastic nudity. Jezza also introduced me to a secluded spot on the Mangawhero Stream, reached via a hidden track off the road, where the water was emerald green and clear. Because of the bush cover on both sides it was best visited at midday, so that one became the Lunchtime Spa. On the northern side of Ruapehu I found a stream dotted with stunning swimming holes right up to its headwaters, and spent a hot day wandering up and down and dipping into each of them without bothering to take my boots or clothes off.

Jezza and I both took a passing interest in the hype cult of Wim Hof, famous for his cold-water immersion routine, and these swimming spots came in handy. We found a convenient place for an after-work Wim Hof session, a pool just off the bottom of the Ohakune Mountain Road, hidden but easy to reach. It was tinged with moss on the opposite bank where the flow had cut into the ground, creating some water depth, and a small beach provided easy access. The forest overhung on both sides, creating a tunnel where the river flowed. I always brought my tramping cooker and we'd put the billy on before we got in so we had hot chocolates ready to go as soon as we got out.

One day we were shivering on the beach, hands wrapped around our keep cups for warmth, when two whio flew straight through the tunnel of bush, narrowly missing both our heads. Blue duck! So close to town. And so that one became known as Whio Beach.

Whio were common around the mountain streams before the evil stoat arrived and began knocking off the bird life. Another threat to whio is, erm, hydro schemes, because hydroelectric dams alter rivers and reduce the birds' available habitat. Handily, Genesis Energy runs a 'Whio Forever' programme. Make of that what you will. (In reality, the programme has been very successful, and predator control has resulted in significant increases in number and distribution.)

Whio are also found in the Manganuioteao River on the western slopes of Ruapehu. In 1988, in response to the Ministry of Energy and various hydroelectric development groups proposing schemes to dam or divert the Manganuioteao, an MP by the name of Helen Clark pushed through a National Water Conservation Order on the river.[6] The order preserved the river for its wild and scenic characteristics, to maintain a whio habitat, and for recreational fishing. And who knows how many whio might call the Manganuioteao home — the upper sections of the river are notoriously difficult to access.

Bill Mead noted the decline of 'blue mountain ducks' from around the 1940s: 'Three noxious animals began to spread into the Park — deer, opposums and stoats. Before they arrived there were no deer tracks through the subalpine scrub, which was difficult to walk through till we had cut tracks, and the undergrowth in the bush was thicker before deer and possums had thinned it. The animals also reduced the number of flowering plants in the open country. The stoats had a serious effect on some of the bird life. For example, before they arrived, blue mountain ducks were common along the mountain streams, but before long they were very rare.'[7]

As with heather, releasing deer into the park was once deemed a good idea. The

1897 annual report of the Department of Lands and Survey reads: 'The Wellington Acclimatisation Society has also supplied some red deer for the park, which were successfully turned out in April last. There are four of them, and latest accounts say they are doing well in their new home.'[8] By the next year, they were happily roaming: 'The four red deer turned out at the foot of the mountains have been constantly seen, but it is not known whether they have increased or not.'[9]

In 2013, a diesel spill from Tūroa ski field leached about 19,000 litres into streams high up on the mountain, and — among other things — contaminated Raetihi's town water supply, via the Makotuku River. Ruapehu Alpine Lifts (RAL), then-operator of Tūroa, pleaded guilty to unlawful discharge of a contaminant, failure to maintain the fuel storage system, failure to test an emergency plan every 12 months, and failure to notify WorkSafe. RAL ordered more diesel to replace the lost fuel even before notifying any of the relevant agencies.[10]

History does seem to repeat itself, perhaps nature's way of forcing us to learn the lessons we refuse to learn. On Sunday, 9 December 1979, a party of Scouts from Waiouru had been crossing the Mangawhero Stream several kilometres below Tūroa ski field when they detected the distinct smell of fuel. The day before, 17,000 litres of fuel oil — a mixture of diesel and kerosene — had been spilled while fuel was being transferred from a master tank.[11] The fuel had flowed down into the national park's rivers, including the Mangawhero, and into the water supply in Raetihi. It wasn't until the Tuesday that officials in Raetihi were notified, and the foreman visited the settling ponds to find an oily substance on the surface and turned off the supply.

Raetihi locals were forced to go without water, with some travelling to Ohakune to fill up, but they took a patient and practical approach. Raetihi mayor Peter Jones said: 'We have to accept these things with the industrialisation of the area. We would be more unhappy if Tūroa was not there.'[12] Jones also said he hoped some measures would be taken so that spills wouldn't happen in the future.

A dam of sorts was built near the Tūroa carpark to prevent the spill continuing into the Mangawhero and Makotuku streams. It was thought that most of the fuel had been washed away by heavy rain, but that traces would continue to flush down.[13] Fuel persisted in the water for up to five months, and although larger animals such as whio and trout were seemingly not killed by it, aquatic insects in the upper reaches were disturbed and killed during the two weeks after the spill. A researcher who monitored the water ecology after the spill concluded that a recovery time of at least six months wasn't uncommon.[14] However, some species took 8 to 12 months to recover to pre-spill status. (Happily, the research was supported by a Mobil Environmental Grant of $425. Make of that, also, what you will.)

There wasn't a lot of public information about the 1979 oil spill — in fact, I'd only become aware of it thanks to a one-line mention on the Wikipedia page for the Mangawhero River — but I found files stuffed with pages of letters, reports and information about it at Archives New Zealand.

A Tūroa report later identified that there had been a 'considerable delay' between the incident occurring and management being informed. The pump had been running for 20 hours and the overflow had happened at a rate of three gallons per minute, through a seal on a vertical rod indicator at the top of the tank. The cause, according to the report, was human error.[15]

Alex Harvey Industries (AHI), which developed Tūroa, had been warned of the risk earlier that year, well before the spill. In March, conservation field officer Bryan Williams wrote to the Conservator of Wildlife to express his concern that since the start of the development of the ski field there had been a number of diesel spillages, most of which had found their way into the Mangawhero River.[16] The most recent spillage, Williams wrote, had occurred while diesel was being pumped to a tank and an employee left a tap turned on, leaving diesel to flow onto the ground and into the Mangawhero River, with more than 100 litres lost. 'I have expressed concern to both AHI and park board rangers at the number of oil spillages that are occurring on the site and which end up in the Mangawhero River,' Williams wrote. 'AHI are given a warning by the park board whenever there is a spillage [but] no other action is taken to my knowledge.'[17]

This prompted an inspection in early April by the Inspector of Explosives, after which AHI was instructed to make several changes to its diesel storage and pipes, including an above-ground tank, by 'constructing a concrete bund around the tank with a concrete floor'. The bund was to be 'of sufficient size to contain the total quantity of fuel stored'.[18]

The year before, the main concern around Tūroa had been the possible impact of the new ski field on whio habitats. Assistant Conservator of Wildlife D. J. Stack wrote to Bryan Williams instructing him to keep a watching brief. 'As you are aware our involvement . . . should be played low key as the main areas of dispute are between the developers and the Tongariro Park Board,' Stack wrote. 'Recent publicity records possible downstream effects through siltation on Blue Duck habitat. This I am sure you are aware is somewhat of a red herring and in fact has very little substance. Would you please continue to maintain some surveillance over the development activities.'[19]

Tūroa also had a spill of an unknown quantity in 2007. Whakapapa ski field spilled 600 litres from an underground tank in 2000; this followed the loss of 200 litres during a transfer operation in 1994, and before that an unknown quantity from a workshop at Iwikau Village in 1993.[20]

We are damned to repeat the lessons we don't learn, I suppose.

I made a small personal project out of visiting bodies of water — streams, lakes, rivers, waterfalls — mostly in the national park, but also occasionally outside. Hugh Girdlestone had written of 'magnificent waterfalls' on the western slopes, which fall dramatically first 55 metres, then 28 metres, below a flat-top bluff named Te Kohatu. Reaching Te Kotahu, roughly halfway between Whakapapa and Tūroa, required some off-track navigation and enthusiasm for traversing rocky obstacles. Some bodies of

An early postcard of Rangataua Lakes, with Ruapehu in the background. Bagnall Collection, Massey University Library

water were more theoretical, or seasonal — a small tarn on the map below Holl's Rock turned out to be dry, and the lakelet in South Crater on Tongariro was often patchy, and just a line of hard ice in winter. I didn't visit them all — the sulphur lagoon in the large crater below Te Mari I deemed far too dangerous to go tootling around just for the sake of it.

Just south of Ohakune on the road to Raetihi is Ngā Roto-o-Rangataua Reserve, where a walking and biking track loops around a small, dark lake. Formerly known as Ohakune Lakes Scenic Reserve, the area's original name was restored as part of the Ngāti Rangi Claims Settlement of 2019.[21] There are in fact two lakes (both craters), Rangatauanui (the larger one) and Rangatauaiti (the smaller one). I found this curious, as Rangataua is a township well out of Ohakune, on the way to Waiouru.

The first time I went there for a walk, I got out of the car, looked around, and was instantly cloaked with an inexplicable sense of worry. It was raining slightly and in the middle of a weekday, so my car was the only one at the carpark. I hesitated long enough for the momentary pause to turn into something longer, and the slight unease — just some sort of feeling, the hairs on the back of my neck standing up — encouraged me to get back in the car and go for a walk elsewhere.

I returned one day determined to walk around the lake and prove to myself that all was fine (and it was), and I've walked it a few times with a friend and her dog, it being one of the few dog-friendly areas around town. But that slight hesitation and sense of unease stayed with me for some time.

I didn't think of it again until I was researching another topic entirely and came across some information about the lakes. The site is sacred for Ngāti Rangi, I read. An enemy war party from Ngāti Raukawa came to the area in the early 1800s. Most Ngāti Rangi fled, but some were caught and killed. Ngāti Raukawa then subjected their bodies to cannibalistic ritual and threw the remnants into the lakes. Those who fled or survived the attack moved to Ohakune, where the town is now located. The name 'Rangataua' means 'war party', and the word is also the name of a demi-god and famous warrior who lived in the clouds and used rain, hail, snow and lightning as his weapons. Ngāti Rangi would call upon Rangataua to fight for them.

The two lakes at the site are believed to be the lowest vents of the Ruapehu volcanic area, and are estimated to have formed 25,000 years ago. Ngāti Rangi consider them to be the bottom of the mountain.[22]

I commented to Ngāti Rangi rep Korty Wilson that there wasn't any signage there with info about the site, its history or any potential tapu status — in fact, the Visit Ruapehu website mentioned it was a good spot for a swim. Korty said that it was progress that you now can't drive around the lake — the map shows a paper road, and it used to be open access.

After that, knowing the history of the lakes, I felt placated, and instead of feeling concerned, I welcomed the feeling of somehow connecting with the spirits who lived there.

Jezza told me one day about a secret dam in the bush, close to town and thought to be part of the old water-supply network. I'd become curious about the water supply in Ohakune versus the water in Wellington, which I visited often for work. I seemed to be particularly headachy whenever I went to Wellington, but not so living in Ohakune, and the water tasted dramatically different. It's hard to find out exactly what they do to the water in Wellington, but in Ohakune it trickles off the Mangawhero, is put through a sand-filtration process, and the plant is chlorinated, but not enough to affect the taste or be noticeable.

Actually, there were multiple dams — Jezza showed me one with swimming potential in the lower reaches of the Mangawhero catchment, a short walk beyond the Mangawhero Campsite on the lower Ohakune Mountain Road. Remnants of the old logging operations in the area were dotted around, including an old Ford flatbed truck whose headlights jutted just out of the ground. The other dam was on the southern slopes of Raetihi hill (893 metres), a thickly forested area that was notoriously hard to access (or an exciting new opportunity, if you relish bush bashing).

We went to find the Mangawhero dam with another friend, Mac, as a lunchtime outing one rainy day, first walking up the old Bennett & Punch tramline through the lower Mangawhero bush. Work was due to begin the next week on Te Ara Mangawhero, a mountain-biking pathway from the top of the mountain road to the bottom. We wanted to walk the old tramline while it was still an historic footprint, rather than a work site.

Jezza exploring one of the dams in the lower Mangawhero catchment.

Mac knew mostly where to go, and we approached from a paper road until we had to leap over a locked gate. Then a gap appeared in the trees, a portal to an impossibly green dimension. A few paces in we found remnants of an old hut: corrugated iron, a rusty bed frame, some large pieces of metal and old booze bottles — one with the lid still attached and some milky liquid inside. I couldn't get the lid off to find out what it was so I took the bottle home and prised it open. It was very old Maltexo — malt extract — and I regretted opening it, for the smell that emerged was unholy.

I peered around the site, poking through the undergrowth to see what else was underneath. It occurred to me: was this yet another of Les and Merv Bergersen's huts, the men who had hid out to avoid conscription? I got a shiver. So much of the area was covered by bush litter from the constantly shedding canopy. Ponga trees had fallen over and were becoming soft and returning to soil. I recalled that the Bergersens had used several huts, and one had been near the old ranger's station, just down the road. That meant that this was quite possibly one of their hideouts.

The old path offered us a small stream crossing and some old waterworks infrastructure in the middle of the bush — large pipes and a giant tap going into a hole in the ground, but without a handle. The track was easy to follow and very well benched, currently being used as a biodiversity line and denoted by large pink triangle markers and pink tape tied to trees. At one point it led through a distinctive cutting, with walls high on both sides and green shoots popping out.

'This would be glowworm central at night,' I said.

Mac agreed. 'Amazing how benched it is, really wide in places.'

Jezza hugged a tree.

Eventually the old path spat us out onto the upper part of the Mangawhero Forest Walk, quite suddenly — a transition from thick bush with a line of possibility through it to a wide and obvious track proper. Standing on the Mangawhero track, it was difficult to tell that another track led down that way aside from the tell-tale pink tape, which I would've just ignored as being an indicator of a trapping line.

We followed the line back down to another track, the Rimu Loop. Jezza had told me the track to the dam departed from this loop and I'd gone to look by myself but couldn't spot the entrance. Jezza led the way, and after 20 seconds of pushing through a gappy spot in the bush we were on the old 'road' that led up to the dam — I guess way back, they must have had to get vehicles up there to work on the dam. We hopped over some sizeable windfall and wove through trees. Then a DOC sign warned us that the structure was closed and not to be used. We paused momentarily to pay our respects to the sign's concern for our safety, then ducked under some yellow tape designed to act as a barrier, and found ourselves standing on a flat section with a stream running through it — not deep at all.

'Er, where's the dam?' I asked.

'We're standing on it,' Jezza said.

Mac began to descend directly into the bush, hidden by fronds, next to where the stream went over a short waterfall. I looked over and saw he was using a ladder to get down. I went next, poked by branches, clinging to the metal ladder which felt clunky

but secure at the same time, avoiding the waterfall on my left. Mac gave me some beta: 'Put your right foot over this pipe and hang on to the tree.' I managed to execute a few dodgy moves and get off the ladder without ending up in the drink. Meanwhile Jezza descended and ducked behind the waterfall, then pointed out the sloped concrete structure we were standing underneath.

'Imagine everything on the other side of this was filled up with water, not with sand and dirt and so on. That was once the dam.'

Then I got it. The flat section with the stream above us had filled entirely with silt, branches, leaves and other natural matter.

'The first time I came up here I was thinking we'd be swimming in the dam,' Mac said.

A noise cut across the sound of our voices and the falling water.

'Shhhh,' Jezza said. 'What's that?'

'I heard it too,' Mac answered.

On our right close by we could hear an animal, breaking through sticks and branches, trampling leaves. Then: silence.

'It's gone,' Jezza said. 'Let's go.'

We decided to visit Rochfort Crater on the way back. Or one of the craters, anyway — there are actually three, and the upper one at the back is hidden by bush and requires a short bush crash. I hadn't seen it before and was amazed to discover it was in fact a shallow swamp covered in a thick mat of floating moss. It was dense and sturdy, but when we walked on it, we could feel the water underneath, although our feet didn't get wet. You could jiggle on the mat of moss and make it undulate.

We stood in a circle facing in, looking down at the moss, just contemplating.

'It's sort of like it's—' Jezza broke off. Our heads snapped up in unison.

I could see the whites of Jezza's eyes. Mac's face was frozen. Not fear, but disbelief.

It was the same animal as before, the noises that had been on our right-hand side while we were at the dam. Now it was on our left. Tracking us. Grunting, deep, throaty, and maybe not all that happy. Jezza made pig noises, three in a row. Low voiced, throaty. The animal responded in kind. All three of us were glued to the spot.

Jezza reached out a hand to me. 'Give me one of your poles,' he said in a low voice.

I handed him one walking pole and kept the other in case I needed to act in the interests of self-preservation. Mac was behind me. I was in the middle. I was either the meat in the sandwich, or I was protected on both sides by humans who'd be picked off first from the herd.

'I'll go left,' Jezza whispered. 'And you guys go right and back to the track.'

We'd be safe but Jezza would be the sacrificial lamb.

He did. We did. Jezza caught up to us, pole in hand, unbloodied.

'I reckon it was a wild boar.'

Just like in *Wild Pork and Watercress* when Uncle Hec and Ricky have to stab the pig while it's charging at them, and then they feast on it later, roasted over an open fire. This was real adventure!

'Happened to a guy I know,' Jezza said. 'He got chased by wild pigs, three of them, and he went missing. Eventually they found him on top of a water tank on someone's property, the pigs circling below. He couldn't get off.'

In *Mouri Tū Mouri Ora* Colin Richards said: 'As tāngata tiaki, our responsibility is to nurture and care for that life-force, so it may sustain all living things.'[23] I felt a particular responsibility to the Mangawhero River. It flowed past my house, and on a quiet night I appreciated listening to its subtle sounds as I lay back in my hot tub staring at the stars. Such calm and quiet seldom occurred in Ohakune, so it was noticeable when it did.

I continued to dip in the Mangawhero's upper reaches, where the pristine pools beckoned. I began to notice, though, how much rubbish the catchment held. Jezza and my local friend, DOC worker Lois, regularly put in efforts to clean it up. Lois told me that one summer, she and another DOC worker decided to make a project out of combing the entire length of the Mangawhero from top to bottom and they pulled out multiple large rubbish sacks full of trash. Jezza and I hauled out a few things, and I made my own project of cleaning up the waterways.

That summer followed a lean snow year when the ski field at Tūroa had barely operated, but the impact on the environment was still noticeable. We picked up old gloves, plastic ski-pass cards, drink bottles, food wrappers, ski poles — so much detritus from the lifts above.

One day I was standing on the water's edge, my buddy cleaning up from the other side. 'There's something at your foot,' he said. 'See that purple thing?'

I looked down to see the very purple face of Sir Apirana Ngata staring back at me from a $50 note partially embedded in the soft sand. Sometimes when you love the mountain, the mountain loves you back.

'Our old people didn't so much teach us by telling us, but we were taught by being taken with them and watching them,' Ida (Morna) Taute said on behalf of Ngāti Rangi at an Environment Court hearing in 2003. 'You could tell by the way they touched the water — it was like a caress. There was and still is a sacredness about our rivers and springs, and the relationship we have with them. It is the same for all our kin of the natural world.'[24]

Ruapehu maunga swathed in clouds. Te Heuheu (2732m) is on the far left, Paretetaitonga (2751m) is on the right.
Mike Heydon/ChopperWorx

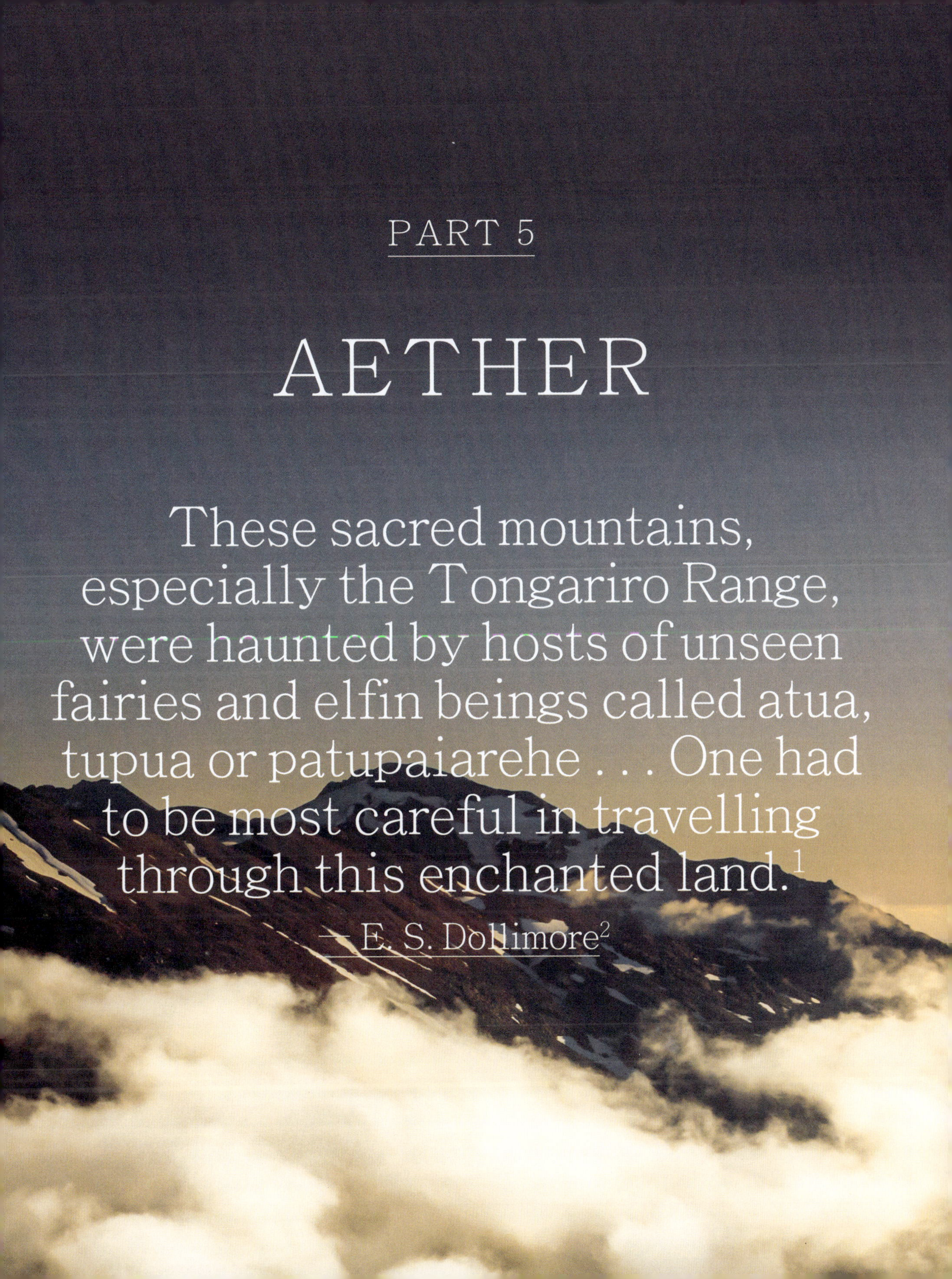

PART 5

AETHER

These sacred mountains, especially the Tongariro Range, were haunted by hosts of unseen fairies and elfin beings called atua, tupua or patupaiarehe . . . One had to be most careful in travelling through this enchanted land.[1]

— E. S. Dollimore[2]

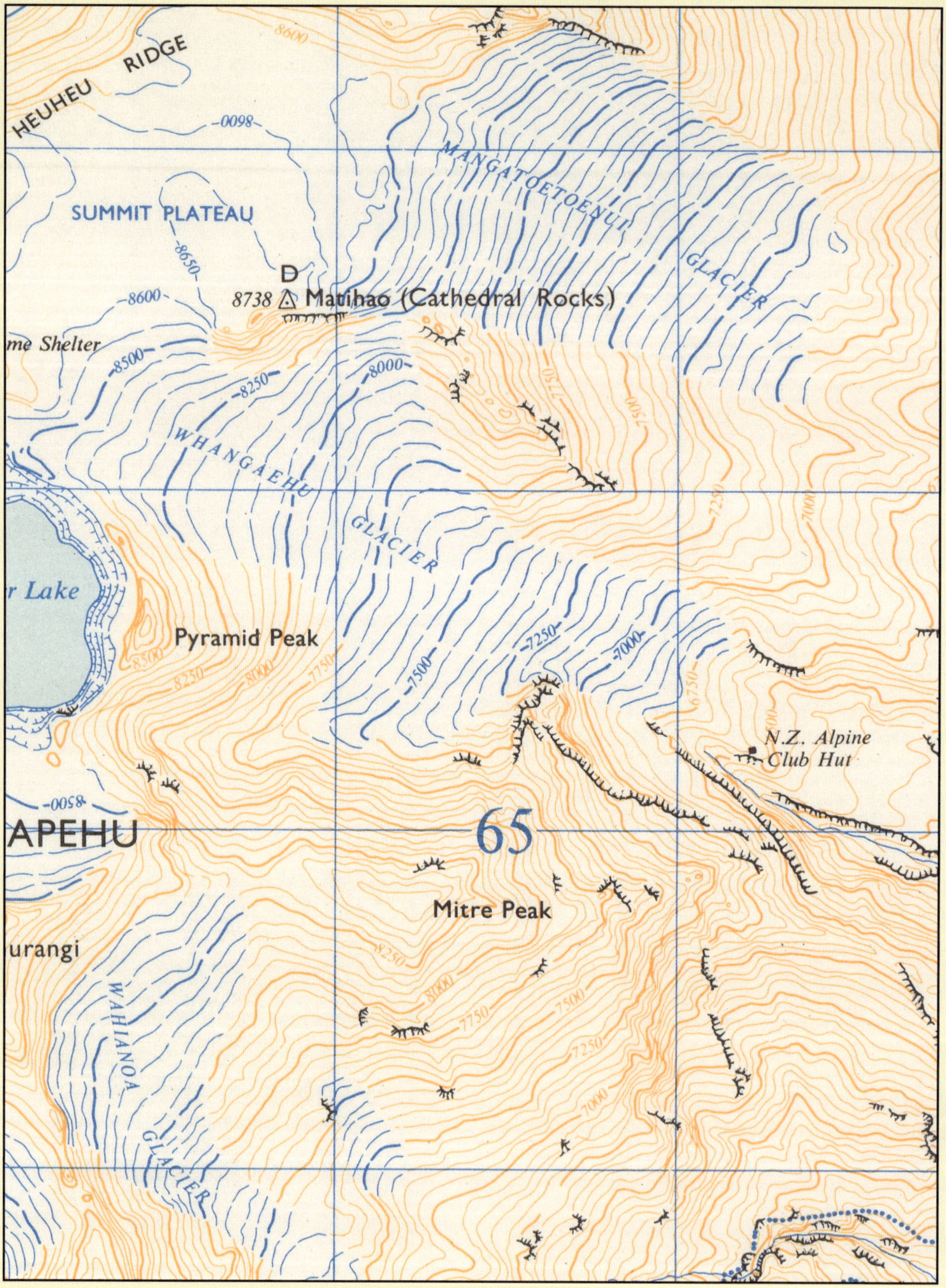

HEUHEU RIDGE
8600
SUMMIT PLATEAU
8650
MANGATOETOENUI
GLACIER
D
8738 Matihao (Cathedral Rocks)
8600
me Shelter
8500
8250
8000
7750
7500
WHANGAEHU
GLACIER
7250
7000
r Lake
Pyramid Peak
8500
8250
8000
7750
7500
7250
7000
6750
N.Z. Alpine
Club Hut
8500
APEHU
65
Mitre Peak
urangi
WAHIANOA
GLACIER
8250
8000
7750
7500
7250
7000

Map showing Mitre Peak, now known as Ringatoto, and the committing east ridge. National Library of New Zealand, 23363041

CHAPTER 19

Missing climbers on Mitre Peak

In June 1977, two climbers left Wellington for Rangipo Hut, from where they struck out to climb the east ridge of Ringatoto. A storm hit Ruapehu, and in spite of an extensive search operation the climbers weren't found. The following summer, a pilot spotted something in the snow on the Wahianoa Glacier. It was one of the climbers.

I heard whispers of skeletons found on the mountain, stories of people who'd gone out and never come home. I was told that in 1991 a group of mountain runners found a body huddled up in a nook near Waihohonu Hut, someone who had clearly sought shelter but had not survived. Another found on the slopes of Tongariro in the early 1980s was thought to be the outcome of self-harm. In 1983 a skeleton was found on Ruapehu; a glasses case with a name inside was nearby. These stories are all impossible to verify because the coroner's office doesn't yet have the capability to search for deaths by location, and you need a name to get the information. So the stories remain just that — stories.

But some cases are easier than others to verify — whispers that a Scout had gone missing in the Mangaturuturu Valley in the 1980s are indeed true. In 1985 an 11-year-old from Raetihi, John Brough, simply disappeared between Mangaturuturu Hut and Lake Surprise. He was walking in file as part of a group of six Scouts and two supervisors when he just stepped off the track and disappeared. Local rumours were that he might have been playing hide and seek. The search was extensive but hampered by dense cloud and rain, and Brough has never been found.[1]

I found mentions of Egon Lehner, who was 21 and had just immigrated to New Zealand the month before he went missing.[2] He was inexperienced in climbing but enthusiastically joined a party intending to ascend Ruapehu. Early on the morning of Saturday, 20 April 1957 the party left a hut lower down on the Whakapapa side, but by 7 a.m. Lehner was exhausted and decided to turn back. When the party got back to the hut and found that Lehner hadn't materialised, they immediately raised the alarm, and alpine clubs and ski clubs turned out to help. A blizzard had struck the mountain and searching was difficult. It was thought Lehner wouldn't survive if he was still on the exposed slopes, but if he'd managed to descend into the bush in the Whakapapaiti catchment he could still be alive — a situation similar to the Stanton episode of 1931. It wasn't looking hopeful, though — Lehner was lightly clad, had no experience in the outdoors, and had no food or supplies with him.

The search continued that week in atrocious weather. It cleared fine and warm on the Thursday, but by then hopes for Lehner's survival had diminished. The next day search parties found footprints, believed to be about a week old, on the eastern slopes — far away from where Lehner should have been. They also found a set of 'unusual footprints' at around 2100 metres leading from the Whakapapa Glacier down to the Amphitheatre, a bluffy, rocky area, then on to the end of the snowline and down into the bush at Erua. In several places the footprints changed abruptly to a slide then back to footprints. It is unlikely that Lehner had managed to ascend that far alone. By this point more than 700 people were scouring the mountain in patchy weather.[3] Searchers also found further footprints and a ski cap on the western slopes. By now they'd combed everywhere from east to west, from Whakapapa Glacier to Restful Rocks and even over to Tama Lakes on the lower northern slopes of Ruapehu, heading to the base of Ngāuruhoe.

The search was abandoned after more than a week. Lehner's body was finally found 13 years later, in April 1970, by a climber who was 2400 metres high on Te Heuheu ridge — a steep area unsuitable for an inexperienced person, higher than anticipated, and

This photo of Anthony Morrison appeared in the newspaper after he and Bill Olsen went missing. Bagnall Collection, Massey University Library

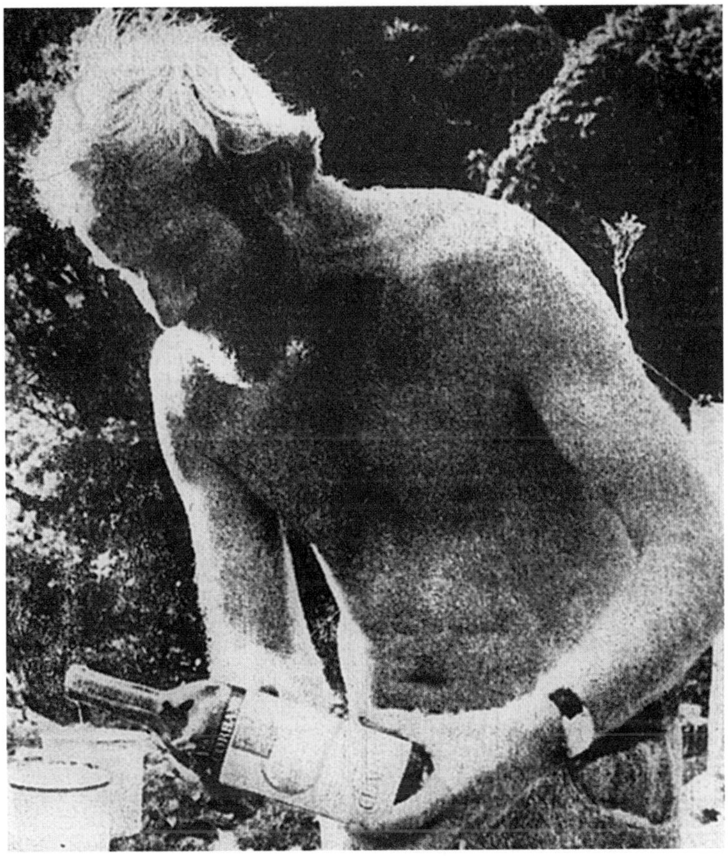

far away from the usual route to the top via Restful Rocks or the Whakapapa Glacier. A watch and camera were found near the remains. How and why he'd gone over and up there was a mystery.[4]

I heard also about some missing climbers who'd disappeared without a trace in the 1970s. Nobody seemed to know anything more than just 'missing climbers', 'some time during the 1970s', and that they'd never been found. But that was enough to go on. I went on the hunt, and found that some, but not all of it, was true.

On the Friday of Queen's Birthday weekend 1977, two climbers left Wellington bound for Ruapehu. Arthur William Olsen (known as Bill) was a psychologist with the Education Department. He was 42, married, and lived in Lyall Bay with his wife Violet. Antony Morrison (Tony) was a tutor at the Technical Correspondence Institute in Lower Hutt. He was 41, married, and lived in Petone. Both were members of the Tararua Tramping Club and the New Zealand Alpine Club, and thrived on adventure in the outdoors. A photo of Morrison appeared on the front page of the *Dominion* newspaper the week after they went missing. Taken while he was adventuring in the Tararuas that March, he's shirtless, pouring Corbans wine into an enamel mug with the twitch of a smile on his face. You can tell he's a large-format male — not fat, but strong and lean, with a bushy beard. A proper Ed Hillary-style climber.

Ringatoto Peak, formerly Mitre Peak, viewed in winter conditions from Tahurangi.

Olsen picked Morrison up in his blue Hillman station wagon around 4.30 p.m. on Friday, 3 June, after waving goodbye to Violet. He'd shown her maps of the area where they intended to climb. The two climbing partners wanted to tackle the east ridge of Mitre Peak (Ringatoto), 2591 metres, on the eastern side of Ruapehu. It's a long, sloping ridge, a 1000-metre climb from nearby Rangipo Hut, which starts off as a wide rocky area, then sharpens into a more defined ridge. There are obstacles to be turned, gendarmes, on the upper part of the ridge, which are usually sidled on the southern, or Wahianoa, side. It's also a fairly committing climb — once you're on the ridge, there's no easy way off. Except to fall.

Rangipo Hut sits just under 1600 metres' altitude on the eastern slopes of Ruapehu. It's known for stunning sunrises but also extreme exposure — there's really nothing around it to protect it except a small hump of a hill just behind. The army training area lies below it, quite near, and for the unaware, the booming noises of artillery can be disconcerting.

As to the meaning, 'rangi' means day, sky or heaven, and 'po' means night. Historian James Cowan wrote that the word Rangipo was a combination of the words for 'sky' and 'dark', or 'day' and 'night', 'meaning the place where the sky was darkened by a volcanic eruption' or 'the place where the sky is dark'.[5] It feels poetic.

Olsen and Morrison arrived at Rangipo Hut some time before Saturday night on the holiday weekend. Inside, arranging their gear and cooking dinner, they met climbers Brin Williman and Mark Prebble, who were leading a party with two other, less experienced people. Their group departed around 8 a.m. on Sunday and travelled up the Whangaehu River to Whangaehu Hut, the New Zealand Alpine Club hut perched on a knoll above the waterway, which had been their intended objective before bad weather the day before had prompted them to change their plans. Olsen and Morrison left for the east ridge to Mitre Peak. Prebble later recalled they seemed dressed adequately for their climb, and took packs with climbing equipment and food. The weather was broken cloud, alternating between dark sky when it clouded over then bright sunshine. Showers had been off and on before they left, but then the weather cleared, with moderate winds. Nothing to be too worried about.

Prebble said later in a statement: 'I would have been prepared to go out by myself and carry out the same climb and would have classed it as a dirty weather climb. I will say, however, that if the two persons were only carrying extra clothing and climbing equipment and had no bivvy equipment, they would have been in real trouble later in the day when the weather worsened. The winds came up throughout the day and conditions really deteriorated towards evening. The mountain is not extremely difficult, however with any deterioration in the weather this mountain can be as difficult as any other.'[6]

The east ridge climb Olsen and Morrison were attempting was not technical, but given the conditions, not comfortable. 'Ruapehu is not a difficult mountain and, with habitation virtually surrounding the mountain, all one would have to do is keep walking to come to signs of life,' Brin Williman said later.[7]

ABOVE: This photo shows the conditions Mark Prebble and Brin Williman battled on Ruapehu — a car engine filled with snow. Brin Williman collection

BELOW: Mark Prebble (right) and fellow climber Bill on the summit of Mitre Peak on a subsequent trip. Brin Williman collection

During the afternoon the winds increased and the tops became obscured by cloud. As Prebble and Williman ascended the snow gully towards Whangaehu Hut, they thought they could hear shouting. Prebble thought it was in the general area above them, around 150 metres below the top of Mitre Peak. The climbers discussed the shouting they could hear as they battled their way in the increasingly bad weather, and concluded that it was probably just a sign of difficult conditions for communication for the party on the ridge, not aimed at them. At any rate, there was little they could do, given they couldn't see the people who were yelling out. 'I gained the impression that it could have been someone who was "hullowing" us from some position on the mountain,' Williman said later. It didn't seem to be important at the time; it only became so in retrospect.

The climbers in Prebble and Williman's group were beginning to worry about the deteriorating weather conditions so they pressed on to the shelter of Whangaehu Hut. They could occasionally make out Mitre Peak through the blowing cloud across the valley. Even after they'd arrived at the hut, the wind that night was sufficiently strong and concerning that when one of the women in their party, who wasn't an experienced mountaineer, went out to the toilet they roped her up to mitigate any risk of her being blown off the bluff.

By 3 p.m. on the Sunday, a full-on blizzard gripped Ruapehu and its surrounds. Motorists on the Desert Road became trapped, and dozens of cars were stuck in snowdrifts. Many drivers had minor accidents after running off the road and into banks. Winds reached 160 kilometres per hour and cars at the Whakapapa ski field carpark were buried. Visibility on the Desert Road was down to three metres. The army came in to help, pulling out 30 or 40 cars — some of which had housed the occupants for the night.

The blizzard raged until late Monday morning,[8] when Prebble, Williman and their party headed out again. The winds had shifted to the south, so they were again walking into a headwind of blowing snow. They were relieved to get their car going and head home to Wellington.

Olsen and Morrison didn't return as scheduled on the Monday, and early on the morning of Tuesday, 7 June, Violet Olsen called the police.

Constable Jim Gosman, stationed at National Park, and Norris Galbraith, senior sergeant at Taihape, sprang into action. Initially they weren't worried; with so much snow falling in the severe conditions, they knew the Tukino Mountain Road would be blocked by large snowdrifts, and many people were stranded in huts at Tukino ski field. There were no specific fears for Olsen and Morrison — they were just assumed to be part of the wider community of folk on Ruapehu who needed to wait patiently for the snow to clear and access to resume. But by Wednesday afternoon, all stranded parties had been accounted for except the two men, and the weather and snow had cleared enough to begin searches.

Police checked the Tukino huts. Olsen's station wagon was found on the Tukino Mountain Road, at the intersection with the Ruapehu Round the Mountain Track to

Rangipo Hut. Gosman checked Rangipo Hut, where he found the men's packs, sleeping bags, clothing and food. He found an entry by Olsen and Morrison in the hut intentions book, from 5 June: 'Arrived in snow. Heading towards Mitre and, depending on snow conditions, to return tonight.'

A full search was mounted on Thursday, 9 June, and helicopters were used to search the entire area with emphasis on Mitre Peak. Around midday they found footprints in the snow on the ridge leading to the peak, clearly visible from the air. The footprints disappeared approximately 300 metres below the summit, where the ridge begins to properly sharpen and a ring of bluffs appears on the northern side.

The next day, police called in expert mountaineers led by Graeme Dingle to conduct a ground search of the area where footprints had been seen. This party found more footprints made by two people to a height of 2370 metres, about 210 metres below the peak — an area consistent with Williman's reports of hearing 'hullowing' at them from above.

Gosman later reported: 'At this point the tracks became confused, indicating that the climbers had been attempting to find shelter or seek some escape route off the ridge. There were signs of descent tracks to about 7700 feet [2350 metres] and some isolated marks at this point, but there was no conclusive sign of descent below that point. This area was about 800 yards [730 metres] in a direct line from Whangaehu Hut and it was very possible that the climbers were attempting to reach this hut. The descent on all sides of the ridge is steep and bluffy.'[9]

Dingle's party thought that the men were attempting to descend on the north side of the ridge to try to escape the gale-force winds that began on Sunday afternoon.

The search and rescue continued with helicopter flights, and police brought in a dog to search the snow basins below the ridge — the first time a dog had been used in a national park for search and rescue purposes. The dog showed some interest in a pile of avalanche debris and the party dug into it but found no trace of the men.

They decided there was no hope of finding the men alive. Jim Gosman concluded: 'It was apparent that they had met with some mishap on the Mitre Ridge at about 1pm on the previous Sunday when the blizzard had struck.'[10]

Dingle and his mountaineers offered a couple of theories. Firstly, that the men fell or were blown from the ridge, in which case their bodies would be either on the north or the south side of the ridge at around 1800 metres. Secondly, that they decided to shelter and died of exposure, and their bodies would be covered with snow drifts from the blizzard. Lastly, they were attempting to descend to Whangaehu Hut to get shelter and were avalanched, and their remains were in the debris found at the bottom of the northern slopes. They concluded that it was unlikely the men had been killed outright, but rather that they would have died of exposure.

The search was called off, after a total of 560 human hours and 17 hours of helicopter time.[11] No other tracks or sign had been discovered, and as the entire mountain was coated in snow, there was little chance of finding their bodies until the thaw came later in the year.

Tongariro National Park Board Chief Ranger Kerry Mawhinney concluded in a statement to the media: 'There is no hope at all of them still being alive.'[12]

As the snow melted in late 1977 and into summer 1978, the searches continued, albeit sporadically. Then, in January 1978, Jim Gosman received notification that something had been seen from the air, lying in the snow below the peak on the southern side of Mitre Ridge, descending into the Wahianoa Glacier. Teams were helicoptered up and found the body of a man lying face up in the snow in an area about 300 metres below the ridge, and below the area where they'd found footprints on the ridge during the search in June. Police, along with Graeme Dingle, returned the next day to retrieve the body.

It was Bill Olsen. A rope was attached to his body, and the other end disappeared into deep snow. The searchers theorised that Tony Morrison was attached to that end, and they spent hours digging into the snow to free the rope, but found nothing. Dingle thought there was a strong possibility that the men had been roped together, and that Morrison had undone the rope when Olsen slipped over the ridge so he would be free to go for assistance or to look for shelter.[13]

'There has been no trace of the body of Morrison to date,' police told the coroner. 'There is every possibility that it has fallen into one of the many deep crevasses in the area or is buried beneath avalanche debris.'[14]

I contacted Graeme Dingle, now Sir Graeme, whose long list of achievements and high profile made it much easier to track him down, and asked for his recollections. Dingle had been climbing on Bomb Arête, a rock climb just a short walk up the Mangatepopo Valley, on the Sunday when the Queen's Birthday storm started, and its ferocity immediately concerned him.

'I thought, Jesus, I hope people aren't on the tops, because this is a real screamer,' he told me. 'Then I heard that the two guys were missing.'

When the storm cleared, Dingle's friend, helicopter pilot Otto Gram, came to get him. They flew over Ringatoto, where Dingle could make out marks on the snow.

'On the ridge just below the summit were two sets of marks, like ice-axe marks, one on each side of the ridge. I told Jim Gosman that I thought one had been blown off the ridge, and the other had jumped onto the other side.'

Later, when summer came, Gram and other pilots had been keeping a lookout whenever they flew over the area. When something was spotted on the snow, Gram fetched Dingle and they helicoptered up to check it out. 'And sure enough, there was the body — of Olsen — and a rope coming off it.'

Dingle pulled on the rope but couldn't get it out of the snow. They dug and dug. Then he tied it onto the chopper and got Gram to apply pressure on it. Nothing gave.

'I walked up to the rope and gave it a jerk with one hand. It went zizzing through the snow and stopped. I did it again, and it popped out with nothing on the end, almost as if, as weight had come on the rope, the knot had come undone or it was never actually tied on.'

Dingle asked Gram to take him to the foot of the face where he'd seen the ice-axe marks the winter before, during the search. He probed a field of avalanche debris with no success. He remembers asking Jim Gosman to send a police dog in, and the animal being very interested in the debris: 'He kept returning to one place and peeing on it. I kept probing and probing and couldn't find anything.'

Dingle recalled loading Bill Olsen's body onto the skid of the chopper, but then they came across someone who had injured their leg, so they loaded him onto the helicopter too, and it made it too heavy to take off. 'I got out and pushed the chopper down the hill until it had enough momentum on it to get going, then I jumped on the skid.'

Some time later, Dingle gave a talk, as he often did. A woman approached him and asked: 'Do you think you could tell me where my father is?' She was referring to Tony Morrison. 'I told her, he's almost certainly down in the Whangaehu as there was quite a big lahar a few months afterwards, and I think that whole area was taken out.'

I asked Dingle whether he thought it was possible, then, that Bill Olsen had fallen off the ridge onto the Wahianoa side (on the south), and Tony Morrison onto the Whangaehu side (on the north), then Morrison had untied himself and gone for help, and perished? 'It's possible Morrison took off and died in the storm. But had he done that, he probably would have been found.'[15]

Tony Morrison's body is unlikely ever to be discovered, I think, and when I suggested that to Graeme Dingle, he agreed. The terrain on both sides of the ridge to Mitre Peak is bluffy and precipitous, and seldom visited in summer conditions — partly because the rock crumbles easily and partly because access is so difficult. Bill Olsen's body was found in the Wahianoa catchment, on the southern side, where the terrain is impossibly steep. Continuous rockfall, as well as avalanches in winter, mean that any remains are probably thoroughly covered.

I got in touch with Mark Prebble and Brin Williman and asked for their recollections of events, my strange enquiries sliding into their lives and pulling up memories long buried. Incredibly, Williman had kept brief notes of all his trips, and together with their collective memories and the coroner's report on Bill Olsen's death they pieced together a thorough account. They'd had further adventures in the same area.

Undeterred by their experiences of the howling blizzard on Ruapehu's eastern slopes, Prebble and Williman returned for another trip seven weeks later with a third climber, Bill Foster. The trio spent Friday night at a hut near Tukino ski field, then went up to Whangaehu Hut on the Saturday, climbing a rocky outcrop known as the Watchtower in the afternoon and returning to the hut for the night. On the Sunday they climbed Tahurangi by the crater face and dropped off the Mitre Peak ridge into the Whangaehu valley. As they were sidling on the true left to get back to Whangaehu Hut the snow slope avalanched, carrying all three 100 metres down into the valley. The crack went for 500 metres across the slope and the headwall was some 30 centimetres deep.

As Prebble felt the debris slow and stop, he made a galvanic spasm to avoid being frozen hard into the snow, which sets hard as soon as it comes to rest, thanks to the dissipation of the energy from the avalanche's movement. That meant he was able to extricate himself quickly from his partial burial and went to dig Foster out. Williman was further down the slope, more thoroughly buried, but not completely.

'I was tumbled down the mountain within the snow not knowing what was up or what was down,' Williman recalled. 'Fortuitously I finished up about 85 per cent buried, on my back with my knees clear of the snow and my head almost out and forearms free, about the degree of burial that I would have if swimming on my back.'

He controlled his panic and managed to clear the snow off his face and breathe deeply, but he couldn't get himself free. When Prebble and Foster arrived about five minutes later, Foster inadvertently kicked snow into his gasping mouth.

'Panic all over again,' Williman said.

It took about half an hour for the pair to dig him out.

'The snow had compacted like concrete, particularly around the pack on my back, and after a while we realised if we undid the pack straps that would make extrication a lot easier,' Williman recalled.

Foster had sprained his ankle and was mentally shaken up from the slide. The party got back to the hut at Tukino that evening but not all the way out and home as they'd originally intended, so a ranger came looking for them, prompted by Williman's wife reporting that they hadn't made it back to Wellington. Foster was later sledged on a stretcher out to a four-wheel-drive vehicle driven in by the ranger.

'Looking back I now think how lucky I was, but at the time did not get too upset by it all,' Williman told me. 'My trip notes on the avalanche laconically state "Returned (from Tahurangi) via Mitre and was involved in a wind slab avalanche just above the hut". Nothing more.'

Prebble agreed. 'You and I got on with it. I suppose we just thought it was one of those things.'

The snow science of avalanches wasn't so well known in those days, and transceivers weren't in existence as companion rescue equipment, and nor were locator beacons. Indeed, Williman recalled: 'I remember a rumour at the time that avalanches seldom occurred on Ruapehu.'[16]

I also tracked down the coroner's report for Bill Olsen. It was sealed for privacy reasons for 50 years, so I applied to access it. To my surprise, my request was approved. At time of writing, the report was due to be sealed for another five years. I also tried to find Bill Olsen and Tony Morrison's families, to no avail.

A pathologist had done a postmortem examination of Olsen's body shortly after it was found. He found Olsen had fractured his left leg just above the ankle and cracked his ribs. The report concluded that Olsen had died that Sunday from exposure, unable to move or help himself because of his injuries.[17]

Through Archives New Zealand I also found Bill Olsen's will. It was short; mostly, he left various sums of money to family members. But there was a tiny line there, in small typewriter print: 'The sum of $100 and the ice axe owned by me at the date of this, my will, to my friend, Tony Morrison.'[18]

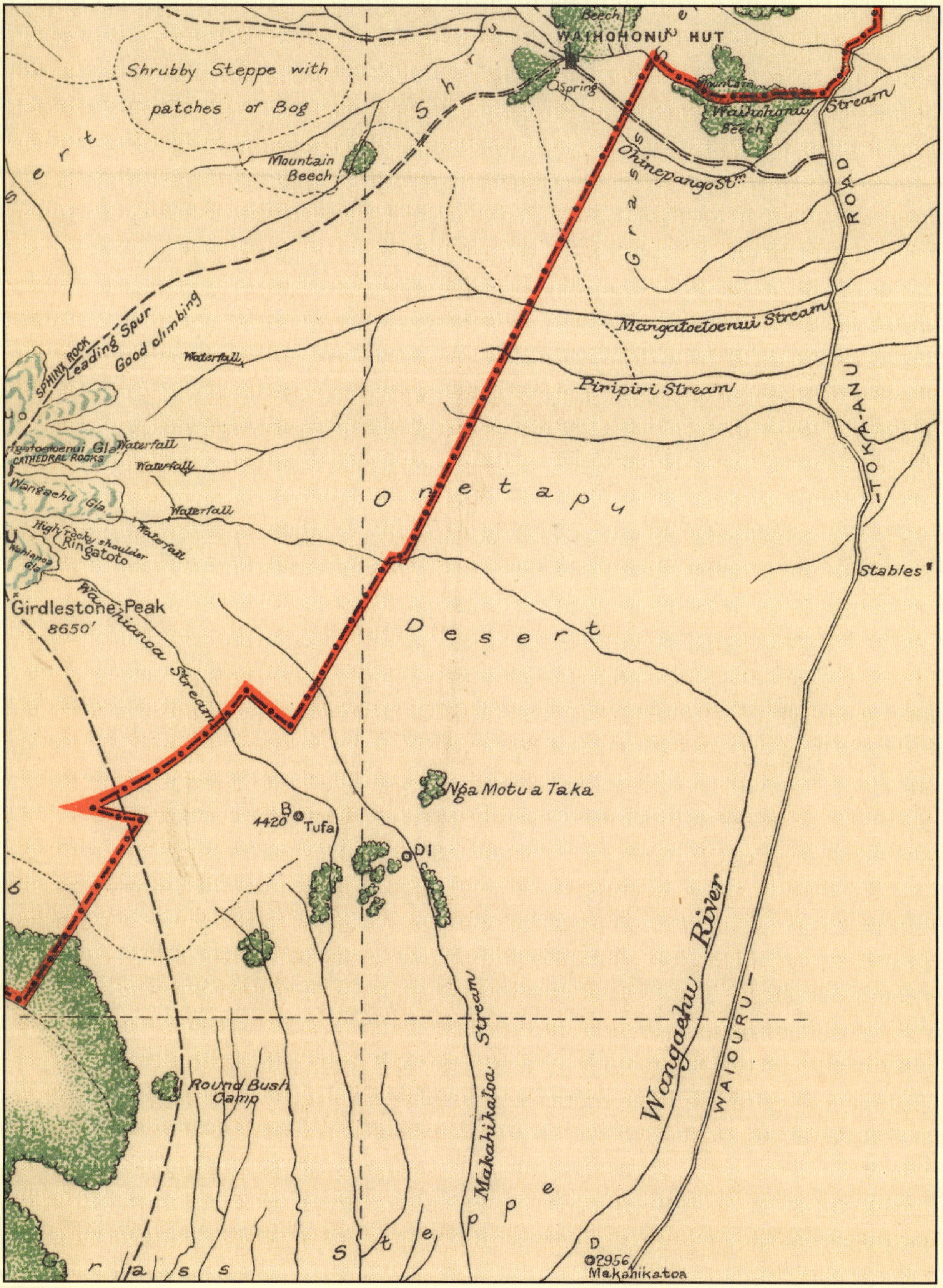

WAIHOHONU HUT
Beech
Spring
Shrubby Steppe with patches of Bog
Mountain Beech
Waihohonu Beech
Stream
Ohinepango St.
ROAD
TOKAANU
WAIOURU
Mangatoetoenui Stream
Piripiri Stream
SPHINX ROCK
Leading Spur
Good climbing
Waterfall
CATHEDRAL ROCKS
Wangaehu Gla
High rocky shoulder
Ringatoto
Girdlestone Peak
8650′
Wahianoa Stream
Onetapu
Desert
Stables
Nga Motu a Taka
B
4420
Tufa
DI
Makahikatoa Stream
Wangaehu River
Round Bush Camp
Grass Steppe
D
2956
Makahikatoa

Map showing Te Onetapu, the Sacred Sands, formerly known as the Rangipo Desert, 1959. National Library of New Zealand, 30876251

CHAPTER 20

Te Onetapu — the Sacred Sands

Ghost Bush, known as Ngā Motu a Taka, is a stunning oasis on the eastern side of the mountain, in the alpine desert William Colenso described as 'a fit place for Macbeth's witches'. Army legend has it that an entire battalion of soldiers went into this small patch of bush in Te Onetapu — the Rangipo Desert — and were never seen again.

A friend who knew I was researching Tongariro National Park asked if I'd heard about Ghost Bush. I hadn't, but I wasn't surprised — no matter how much research I did, no matter how well I thought I knew Tongariro and Ruapehu, new material always seemed to be popping up.

'It's an area within the military zone on the eastern side, near Rangipo,' she said. 'An entire battalion of army men went in there and never came out. Supposedly about a hundred of them died — or disappeared.'

Her husband worked for the army and had mentioned it as a common urban legend in the Waiouru and Rangipo area. But to me it seemed deeply unlikely that so many people could go missing in the bush and remain unnoticed by recorded history.

'I'm sure there's a lot of GST added to the story,' she said.

I put in an information request with the New Zealand Defence Force, and noticed that they were very careful not to respond directly to my (admittedly sometimes rather ridiculous) questions. Instead, they referred me to a representative for Ngā Waihua o Paerangi, the iwi authority for Ngāti Rangi, for whom the area is a site of significance. I then discovered that the proper name for Ghost Bush is Ngā Motu a Taka, the bushes of Taka, a rangatira who lived in about 1700. Taka was travelling through the area and stopped in the Rangipo Desert to collect food with his large following of people. A raging storm blew through and the entire party perished.[1]

Once I knew the name — Ngā Motu a Taka — I found more threads online. Ngāti Rangi's Statutory Acknowledgements document says the area is 'often referred to by Army personnel as "Ghost Bush"', and mentions that these bushes were a source of food and sometimes shelter.[2] 'During the summer months the area is spectacular,' the document enthuses, although it's more or less impossible to visit unless you're part of Ngāti Rangi or you have access via the army (I tried, and failed).

I found a website that gave a different reason for the name Ghost Bush but told a similar story of Taka, which made me think that the figure of a hundred deaths was perhaps accurate, just not related to the army:

> The treeless Muri-motu plains could be quickly traversed in fine weather, but provided no shelter if a southerly storm brought snow. One of the patches of mountain beech in Zone One, just below Rangipo Hut, is said to be haunted by the ghost of an 1880s sheep stealer frozen to death in a snow storm, and so it is called Ghost Bush. But he was not the only one to be trapped there by snow. Those patches of trees were close to the walking track between Waihohonu and Karioi, across Rangipo desert, and have long been known as Ngā Motu a Taka. Taka, the then chief of the Ngatihau, went from the Whanganui river valley to settle at Murimotu, but his party were trapped by a snow storm while catching birds at Rangipo. A hundred and four of them died, and the bones of those people are on the road to Rangipo to this day.[3]

So, the tale of people perishing at Ghost Bush had some sort of a grain of truth to it.

Later in the DOC archives I found an old Tongariro National Park handbook that listed Ngā Motu a Taka, or as it called the area, NGAMOTUATAKA. The book described

Stunted growth in the frost-covered Te Onetapu, under the watchful eye of Ruapehu. Mark Watson

'several large clumps of native timber on the plateau east of Ruapehu and between the mountain and the Whangaehu River after the latter makes its bend southwards'. One of the three main patches of bush is known as Round Bush, which appears on early maps, and another is Ghost Bush. The handbook has a slightly different version of Taka's story:

> According to legend a sad fate befell one Taka and his companions in one of these motu ('islands' of bush). They were a bird-hunting party — men, women and children — who camped while seeking mutton birds that bred in the rocky heights, and weka, tui and kaka that were to be found on the plains and in the forests. A great storm came on the party and they perished of cold in the poor shelter of the motu. Their dogs, however, did not perish. They lived on the flesh of their late owners and when searchers came to the place there was nothing left but closely picked bones. The dogs multiplied and the Tongariro-Ruapehu country came to have packs of wild dogs.[4]

Ngā Motu a Taka was often mentioned in conjunction with the name Te Onetapu, which I'd seen on the map plastered across the eastern plains of the Rangipo Desert, often overlapping the Defence Force zone. Te Onetapu translates beautifully to 'the Sacred Sands', and was so named after the death of the ancestor Taiteariki near the summit of what is now the Desert Road. Taiteariki was killed by slings and stones as an act of vengeance, and had his brains knocked out. A small volcanic cone at point 1082 just west of the Desert Road is known as Te Roro o Taiteariki — literally, the brain matter of Taiteariki.

Taiteariki's killing made the area sacred to Ngāti Rangi, and Te Roro o Taiteariki is a wāhi tapu — a site of immense cultural significance. In fact, Te Onetapu, Te Roro o Taiteariki, and nearby Nukuhau (a rocky ridge that divides the pure waters of the Mangatoetoenui from the sulphuric waters of the Whangaehu River) are ancient sites and landmarks used to describe iwi boundaries. Under the 2019 settlement between Ngāti Rangi and the Crown the name of the Rangipo Desert was changed back to its original, Te Onetapu, an act that will forever commemorate the spilling of Taiteariki's blood, a story that is told in the settlement deed.

After Taiteariki was killed, his body was prepared for 'ritual interment' at Ngā Rimutāmaka, an area at around 1000 metres altitude on the lower slopes of Ruapehu below Girdlestone Peak, in what is now the Karioi Forest. Later, his body was transported to the summit areas of Ruapehu and buried at Te Pā-tatau-o-te-rangi,[5] an area near the Crater Lake, as was considered befitting of the reigning nobility of the time.[6]

High-born Ngāti Rangi ancestors were interred in summit areas on Ruapehu up until the 1920s. A sacred whare wānanga known as Te Rangiwanangananga was established on the mountain's slopes, and Ngā Rimutāmaka near Round Bush was the renowned spot where rites of passage for deceased nobility would take place before they were taken higher on Ruapehu via Te Ara-ki-Paretetaitonga. The whare wānanga only became inactive in 1966 because of colonial intrusion. Ngāti Rangi's settlement document describes the practice: 'This ritual practice of interment on the mountain summit is generic with tikanga practices of external iwi and highlights the connection of the elite nobility to their respective sacred maunga.'[7]

I had long been staring at Ngā Rimutāmaka on the topo map, just on the fringes of the pine forests of Karioi, but again, it was a site I'd probably never be able to visit.

Ghost Bush and Te Onetapu appear on some of the oldest maps of Tongariro National Park, but as I tend to focus on huts and tracks, I'd never noticed their existence. Te Onetapu seems to be inextricable from Ghost Bush, both in history and in place, sharing the plateau of sand and snow, suffering sandstorms and blizzards, its pumice badlands punctuated by stunted shrubs. Tussock and other cushion plants dot the landscape, and water-flows erode the gravel to expose pumice from Taupō's AD232 eruption in alluring lines you can trace with your fingers. Te Onetapu, the area known as the Rangipo Desert until the name reverted to the original, is a desert but not a desert — it receives two metres of rainfall annually in the north and a metre in the south. That level of moisture is enough to support a forest, but no forest can tolerate the huge lahars that have swept across much of the area in the past 1500 years. Except Ghost Bush. Lahars seem to have gone around it, just not touched it. Now, the altitude, frosts and wind affect the growth of vegetation in the area, and the resulting vegetation mosaic is testament to the lahar history and extent, and other harsh environmental factors.

Te Onetapu was noticed, by name, by Europeans early on. Historian James Cowan wrote: 'At the heart of Rangipo, the desert region, is Onetapu, the sacred or enchanted sands. It is a black, shivering land.' He refers to travelling the 'Waiouru–Tokaanu Road' (the Desert Road) as 'traversing a sterile waste'.[8] European explorers seemed to hold a binary view of the land they encountered — either it was fecund and ripe for farming and planting, or it was sterile and therefore terrifying or somehow haunted. Te Onetapu fits the latter, but to conceptualise it as 'pointless' is to, er, miss the point.

Botanist and adventurer William Colenso wrote of an eerie experience he had while travelling from Ahuriri, Napier, to Lake Taupō, crossing Te Onetapu en route, in 1847. Colenso is a tricky person to introduce. He's known as the godfather of the printing industry in New Zealand, but he was also a pious and rather tiresome religious adherent, who sought to convert Māori with a brand of zeal that many found abrasive. With equal zeal he explored and botanised, and so he pops up like a meerkat across many aspects of New Zealand's history. He was known to be inflexible, overbearing and devoid of a sense of humour. Colenso married Elizabeth Fairburn in a sort of convenience arrangement. They had a child together, but he then cheated on her with the housemaid. He was suspended as a deacon and the wheels fell off the shopping trolley of his life. His shortcomings are perhaps best encapsulated in his biography in *Te Ara — the Encyclopedia of New Zealand*, which records that his 'highly developed sense of sin' meant that many people 'took quiet pleasure in his misfortunes'.[9] So, he was accomplished and a high achiever, but also thoroughly insufferable.

Anyway, in 1847 Colenso crossed Te Onetapu, describing it as 'a most desolate weird-looking spot', 'a fit place for Macbeth's witches! or Faustus' Brocken scene!'[10] The desert was about 2 miles wide where he crossed it, and the burnt logs scattered and embedded in the sand had been polished by sandstorms. A southerly storm came through but the party had no shelter — similar to the experience of Taka at Ghost Bush — and they searched in vain for cover. The guide lost his way, unable to see any landmarks in the storm. After about four hours they found water and stopped in a deep gully that had recently been scoured by fire. Unable to find level ground to pitch their tent, they had to dig into the ground with axes and passed a miserable night. The next day was bitterly cold, and the southerly gale and heavy rain continued. The guide refused to retrace their steps and go back over Te Onetapu: 'Our guide flatly refused, and my natives joined him; he saying, that high desert sand was now covered with snow, and that from the falling snow and sleet he could not tell the course — which, perhaps, was really the case.'[11]

The guide told the story of Taka and his people, who perished in a storm: 'From him we had the story of 70 men having been once lost at one time in attempting to cross that place in snowy weather.' Colenso noticed the others discussing how he had been the reason for the bad weather, due to uprooting some dacrydium shrubs, eating some gaultheria berries while crossing Te Onetapu, and failing to observe 'certain superstitious ceremonies'. He wrote of his observation that these fears of the fierce powers of Te Onetapu were well founded:

> The old Maoris have many peculiar stories and superstitious fears [about Te Onetapu], some of which, I have no doubt, are agglutinated around a nucleus of reality . . . some of my natives [insisted] that the sounds they heard among the fitful ravings of the blast among the trees, were not merely those of the trees creaking and of the denizens of that forests — parrots, owls, and wood-hens (Ocydromus australis) — but of the justly irate patupaiarehe (wood nymphs or fairies), or of the ghosts of the dead! . . . I shudder now, while writing this, in thinking of that wretched time, though more than 46 years have since passed.[12]

Nearly a century after Colenso's journey, Lands and Survey Research Officer Edward Dollimore compiled a 'handbook' of Tongariro National Park, in which he wrote of the spirit world. The sacred mountains of Tongariro were 'haunted by hosts of unseen fairies and elfin beings' called atua, tupua or patupaiarehe, he said, and these spirit guardians of the highlands were said to take human form but few Māori ever beheld them. Regardless, the fairies and elfins constantly watched the Māori people, notably surveilling them for any transgressions:

> Violators of the tapu who incurred the anger of these mysterious beings were sometimes seized suddenly and borne off to unknown enchanted regions; sometimes they were kept under fairy spells for indefinite periods. The victims of such spells saw the tupua and their mountain villages, houses and dwelling-caves; saw and talked with the spirit inhabitants. Travellers who passed around the bases of the mountains heard the ghostly voices shouting, speaking or singing though no creature was visible. Ill luck befell every person who committed some

> hara — an offence against the tapu of the peaks — even an unwitting crime. The mildest punishment might be to have a sudden storm descend upon one (no light affliction in this region), or, perhaps, the spirits might whisk the offender away and return him demented and incoherent to his people after many days.

Dollimore noted that people had to be careful when travelling through the Sacred Sands. It was a hara, a transgression, to cook food in Te Onetapu, or to kill or snare birds that could be wairua (spiritual).[13]

I was delighted to discover that springs existed in Te Onetapu, but again I knew I'd probably never get to see them. They were noted in an article in the *Wanganui Chronicle* in 1886, along with other hot springs: 'One of these [springs], Onetapu, on the eastern slope, is near the source of the Wangaehu, and is the means of defiling that river with sulphate of iron and alumina. Another hot spring is on the western slope, and is visible from near the head of the Whanganui River.'[14]

For Ngāti Rangi, the natural resources of Te Onetapu are not just water sources but also a sort of portal for spirits. The statutory acknowledgements document from the iwi's 2019 settlement reads: 'Of special importance are the springs that bubble up from the vast artesian aquifer, known as Te Wai Hohonu — he moana ki raro whenua. Spiritual guardians are present, known and communicated with by members of the iwi.' There is also a nod to the Onetapu springs, which are equally spiritual: 'The Tomowai are an important spring source located on Te Onetapu. The springs fall into the Whangaehu River.' The springs were used in 'tohi' rites, a ceremony performed over a child in flowing water while asking the atua (god or spirit) to endow the child with certain desired mental and physical qualities. 'The Tomowai has been described as being a "portal" for both the spiritual and the physical.'[15]

For a while there, all I wanted in life was to go into Ghost Bush. A couple of my adventure buddies who also worked for the Defence Force, Toby and Hayden, tried to get access for us to no avail — evidently the area is a popular haunt for four-wheel-drive enthusiasts. Hayden did take me four-wheel driving in the opposite direction, through the army training area directly east of Waiouru, and I got a sense for how the land was used by the Defence Force. We stopped at a hut for morning tea, boiling the billy in frigid air that hung in front of our faces as we breathed. A military map on the wall showed the mountains of the central plateau in much more detail than I'd seen on regular topo maps, which simply showed an expansive area sectioned off with the warning:

> ARMY TRAINING AREA
> INTERMITTENT LIVE FIRING
> UNAUTHORISED ENTRY PROHIBITED

The regular topo map was bare, other than two places where it sang: TE ONETAPU. But this one showed all the goodies. And just below Rangipo Hut, if you walked downhill and in a southeasterly direction, there it was: Ghost Bush. Four-wheel-drive tracks were marked on the map, criss-crossing all over zone 1, as it's known. I later checked the satellite images in Google Earth. Ghost Bush itself looked healthy and green, while the desert landscapes around it were marred by four-wheel-drive tracks and, in places further down, what looked like small craters from live-firing practice. That jarred with me, such blatant scarring of the landscape in a sacred and spiritual area.

I found some DSIR papers from the late 1970s, which contained descriptions of the Defence land, acknowledging the destruction of the landscape: 'Parts of this area are scarred by shell craters and there may be some unexploded shells present. Clearly much more information is needed about this land before its merits for inclusion in the Park can be assessed.'

Evidently, in the 1970s the DSIR's Botany Division was making recommendations for more land to be included in Tongariro National Park. I'd noticed a governmental desire to keep adding to the park over time, not always successfully. The DSIR papers described 'Te Onetapu sand dune', as if the Sacred Sands consisted of just one dune:

> The small alpine sand dune located immediately south of the Tukino road and immediately west of State Highway 1 is a type of landform and community not known to occur elsewhere. The Board's attention was drawn to its unique character in a report made some years ago (Atkinson 1964) where it was described as an 'area of exceptional biological interest'. It has not become part of the Park . . . The area would require a thorough inspection to determine whether its present state warrants its inclusion.[16]

The 2019 settlement between Ngāti Rangi and the Crown also admits the damage to the sacred site: 'The Crown acknowledges that sites sacred to Ngāti Rangi have been damaged or destroyed on defence land around Waiouru, particularly on Te Onetapu, and further acknowledges that this has had an ongoing, detrimental impact on Ngāti Rangi's physical and spiritual relationship with the land.'[17] You can sort of hear the Crown shrugging its shoulders. The 'agreement in principle' document expanded on this:

> The activities of the New Zealand Defence Force on and near wāhi tapu on Te Onetapu continue to be offensive to Ngāti Rangi. Ngāti Rangi recognise the role of the New Zealand Defence Force to protect New Zealand and the critical importance of the New Zealand Defence Force training area at Waiouru to the activities of the New Zealand Defence Force. The New Zealand Defence Force's continued use of the training area at Waiouru is considered by Ngāti Rangi to be Ngāti Rangi's sacrifice for and on behalf of the nation.[18]

The agreement states that Ngāti Rangi's sacrifice for the nation will be recognised, and that the New Zealand Defence Force will establish a relationship of 'meaningful dialogue' and ensure access for iwi to sites of cultural significance. It may blow your mind that any sort of access and 'meaningful dialogue' wasn't already in place before.

So I couldn't access Ghost Bush but I could do the next best thing: camp in Te Onetapu outside of the military zone. I knew I'd need to keep out of the way of the Whangaehu River as a lahar risk, but I fancied the idea of camping between the Whangaehu and Waikato catchments, as the Upper Waikato Stream ran down the eastern side of Ruapehu. I drove in on a clear, cloudless day, parked the car on the Tukino Mountain Road and peeled off in a southerly direction, tramping over humps and fans of sand and past charred, stunted timber — the remains of ancient forests destroyed by hot pumice showers raining down and the pyroclastic flow from the AD232 Taupō eruption — noting the same effect Colenso had described, of the wooden remnants being polished smooth by sand.

I picked a camping spot as close to the army training area as I dared, on a gravel plateau backed by a small clump of obliging shrubs — my very own version of a ghostly bush, perhaps — and so close to the words TE ONETAPU on the map that I was deeply satisfied. Importantly, I had, firstly, access to the pure water source of the Upper Waikato Stream for drinking, and secondly, a comprehensive view to Ruapehu for the sunrise show I hoped Koro would put on.

I was still a way off from Ghost Bush itself, but I felt I was thoroughly in the middle of Te Onetapu and its sacred sands, feeling and seeing a little slice of what Colenso might have felt and seen on his travels.

Adhering to the rule not to cook anything, not wanting to call down any unexpected southerly storms or the spiritual wrath of the patupaiarehe upon myself, I opted for a cold dinner, then set about pitching my tent. I'd just got a replacement tent under warranty and had only hastily assembled it in my living room to see what it was like. The old one had been multipitch — meaning I could pitch it with the fly and the inner or just the fly — so I'd left the inner of the new one at home and opted to sleep under just the fly that night. But, disaster: the manufacturer had changed the setup and this new tent couldn't be pitched with just the fly. I was in the middle of the desert with a tent that was largely useless. However, I was also far too stubborn to give up and walk back out, so I simply wrapped myself up in it, the world's first waterproof alpine burrito, and lay back to watch the stars.

I was disappointed to wake up and discover that I had fallen asleep and absolutely nothing exciting had happened; any ghosts from nearby bushes had resisted taking an interest in my existence. The only thing of note was that a frost overnight had frozen my outgoing breath all over the top of my sleeping bag, and I was sort of caked in ice, yet still quite warm inside. I waited until the sun peeked over the horizon properly — sunrise show in full panorama, with pink light hitting the peaks — and was then coaxed out of my burrito setup by the increasing warmness, going from frosty toes to a baking core within the space of minutes.

Like the ghost lady who had visited the Haunted Whare over on the Whakapapa side of Ruapehu, these spirits seemed equally reluctant to materialise — for me, at least.

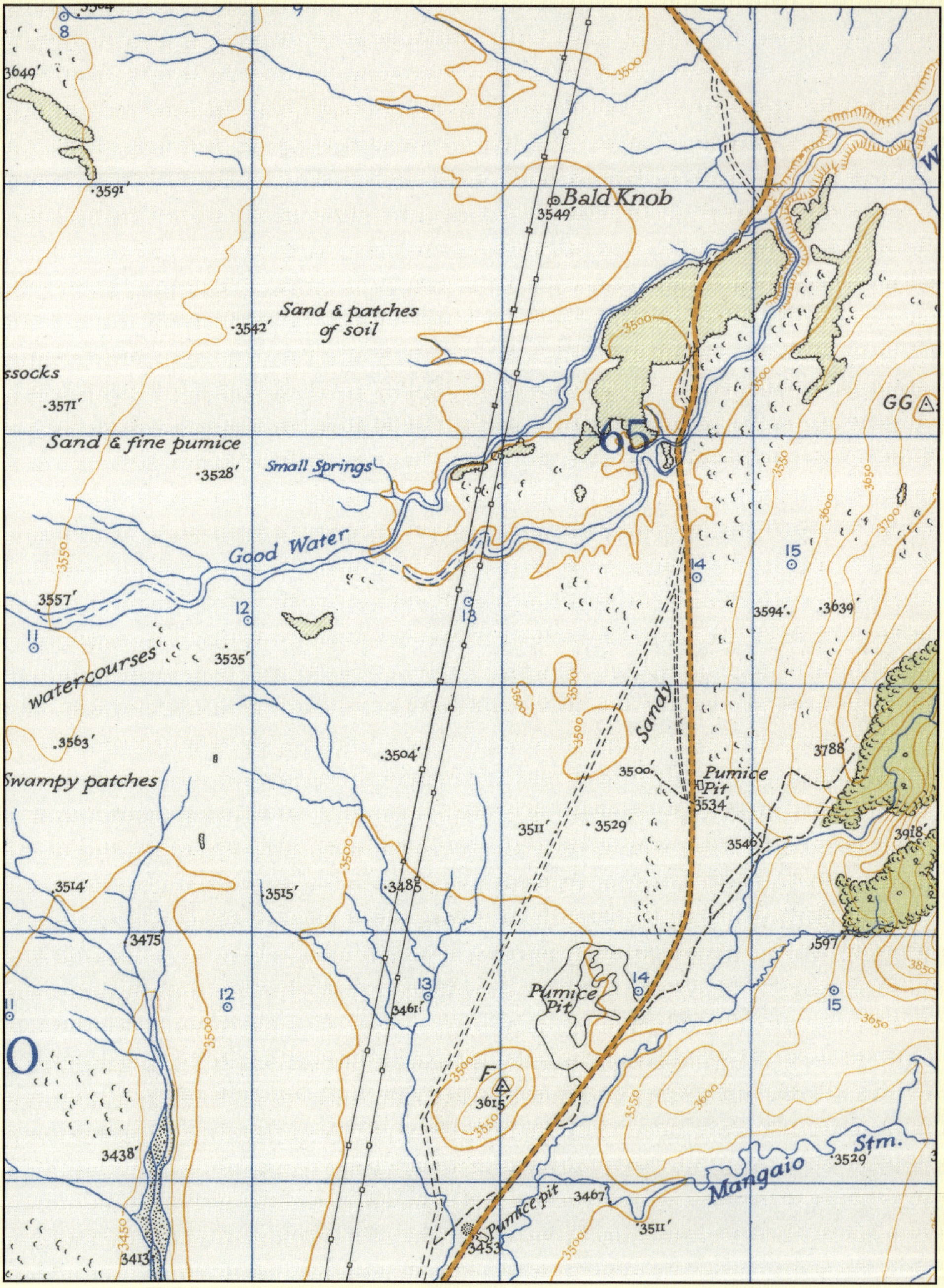
Bald Knob
3549′
Sand & patches
of soil
3542′
3591′
3649′
ssocks
3571′
Sand & fine pumice
3528′
Small Springs
Good Water
3557′
watercourses
3535′
3563′
Swampy patches
3504′
Sandy
Pumice
Pit
3534′
3500
3511′
3529′
3546′
3788′
3918′
3594′
3639′
GG
65
3514′
3515′
3488
3475
3461
Pumice
Pit
F
3615′
Mangaio
Stm.
3529′
3467
Pumice pit
3453
3511′
3438′
3413′
3500
3550
3600
3650
3700
3850
3450

Map showing the Desert Road area of the national park, where Goatman roams. National Library of New Zealand, 30876251

CHAPTER 21

Searching for Goatman

Goatman, aka Hoofman, is reputed to live on the Desert Road, where he hitchhikes and crusades in the name of safety. He's hairy, smelly and doesn't say much. One dark Rangipo night, I hoped to encounter him.

While searching for information on Ghost Bush, I stumbled across Goatman, a creature also known as Hoofman. Such half-human, half-goat creatures are common in mythology around the world, although more recently claimed to be the product of US government DNA experiments gone wrong in the 1950s.

Our Ruapehu Goatman (I felt a sense of ownership, although I'd not met him yet) lives on the Desert Road at the foot of the mountain but is known to cruise down to Taihape and up to Tūrangi and even as far as Taumarunui on the regular. He's also rumoured to live under the banana bridge in the Paraparas, between Raetihi and Whanganui, as well as at the Hatupatu rock on the road between Taupō and Tokoroa, and occasionally on the western side of 'Feature Foxtrot' on the Desert Road, postcode 3382. So he's done quite well in the property game. (Probably votes ACT.) Goatman hitches a ride, doesn't say much, then dissipates from the vehicle rather than properly exiting, leaving dirty hoofprints in the footwell on the passenger side. Which, frankly, is actually terrible etiquette.

His modus operandi, according to one online expert, is as follows: 'You stop and give him a lift, but just a short way up the road he asks to get out. Sometimes he just disappears from the car, having safely gotten you past the stretch of road you were about to have an accident on. Just seeing him on a dangerous piece of road has avoided you from an accident about to happen, most probably right where he stood.'

He's around 7–8 feet tall, smells putrid, is covered in thick, matted fur, and can be rather vicious. Sometimes he's naked, sometimes he's clothed, but he's consistently hairy and very wild. Incredibly, he's reported to be successful with the ladies. (I'm told there's a woman in Ruatāhuna who claims she was snatched away by him for several weeks.)

Goatman is in fact a twin. One of the goats is goaty in the upper half, human in the lower half; the other one, human on top and goaty down below. One brings good, but the other inflicts misfortune and even death, because he's impatient. Illustrations of Goatman do indeed show him to be prodigiously hairy, and he's usually represented as a goat upper half, with two large curved horns protruding from his head, paired with an extremely athletic bottom half.

The other version (with the goat bottom half) is not commonly represented visually but I would imagine that this the version most people would pick up, partly because his twin's horns would be glaringly obvious from a distance, and drivers would be reluctant to give him a lift on account of the risk of him banging his horns on the paintwork while trying to get into the passenger seat. He's described as 'a massive bugger', and to be fair he needs a few rounds of Invisalign and 40 to 45 minutes alone with a sharp razor and a hot towel.

One commenter on a Facebook post about Goatman summed up what you might now be thinking: 'So after reading this you're telling me that some people have stopped to pick up a hitch-hiker seven feet tall with a goat head and then once underway he just disappears . . . where you get your weed from bro?' I just think it sounds like an entertaining Friday night.

Stories abound from Waiouru Military Camp, but Goatman is most commonly

Looking over Te Onetapu and Ngāuruhoe from Tukino ski field at dawn.

spotted further up the Desert Road, either leaping into the bush as cars approach or thumbing a lift. Many people won't drive the Desert Road at night, lest Goatman be looking to order an unofficial Uber.

Another commenter dismissed the idea entirely: 'The only thing I saw in the Waiouru Training Area while freezing my arse off were my questionable career choices.'

In all seriousness, Goatman is thought to be a kaitiaki, just making sure everyone is safe, and protecting the natural resources. Alternatively, he's considered to be an ancestor who has come to warn of impending bad news or traumatic events to come. I became intensely interested in the idea of encountering him.[1]

I'd certainly driven the Desert Road alone and in the dark, and I'd done a fair amount of driving between Goatman's regular known haunts of Taumarunui, Tūrangi and Taihape also alone and in the dark, without ever seeing him. But that was before I knew about the disappearance of an entire battalion of soldiers and the existence of the Goatman (it seemed too coincidental that the two were in the same area, and surely they were related). But in the same way that once you start thinking about buying a certain make of car, you then see it everywhere, I began to see potential Goatmen in my travels. I saw shapes, things moving on the side of the road, too swiftly to make out. It could've been a large bunny, or it could've been a goaty movement.

One morning in the pitch black I was driving from Ohakune to National Park to guide a group on the Tongariro Alpine Crossing, navigating frosty road and black ice, when I came around a corner to see a person waving at me. I'd just been through Erua and noticed the temperature had creepily and suddenly plummeted from -1 degrees to -5. I was right near the derelict buildings of the Waikune Prison, abandoned more than 30 years ago. This was the western side of Ruapehu, well away from Goatman's usual haunt, but the Desert Road was closed due to black ice, so perhaps he was taking a diversion up to Taumarunui?

I drove past two sets of headlights and a human waving furiously. I couldn't make out any goat-like features although things were a blur. One of the cars flashed its lights at me.

What if they needed help?

I'd just done outdoor first-aid training and the thought of someone having a medical event on the side of the road while I drove merrily past was untenable. I carefully executed a U-turn in the frost and went back around the corner.

One of the pairs of headlights had disappeared and the other car sat on the side of the road. Two young boys, perhaps around 13 years old, came up to my window.

'You got any petrol?' one asked. I had none.

'Can you give us money for petrol?' I didn't carry cash. They were too young to drive, surely. I sized them up: too short to reach the pedals.

Was Goatman in the car?

'Where are your parents?'

It turned out Dad was in the car, completely off his cookies, and petrol was the least of their problems. There was no phone reception and, selfishly, I was concerned I was going to be late. I gave them snacks and a bottle of water, and told them to wait until daylight, when help would come.

I called it in to police, but didn't mention Goatman, lest the fuzz question my sanity.

I was still thinking about Goatman that evening as I drove up the Tukino Mountain Road after a stunning day on the Tongariro Alpine Crossing. I was meeting a climbing buddy for some technical mountaineering skills practice. My Subaru was too low to get past the 2WD carpark, so I asked for a pickup, and one of the ski patrollers, Pete, came down in his ute to collect me.

On the way in, I drove past someone in a small car, a Ford Fiesta. In the almost-dark of the imposing Rangipo night, I noted he had a large afro-like head of hair, and a lean, muscular body. Was it Goatman? So much hair was ideal for hiding two giant horns, I rationalised, but on the other hand, was Goatman really going to fit into a Ford Fiesta? He'd appreciate the fuel economy with all the miles he racked up going from Taumarunui down to the Paraparas, but surely he'd find a hatchback rather constricting. Not to mention the potential for paintwork scratches. Marks would be a tell-tale sign, I thought, but it was too dark to make out any damage.

I got out of my car and into the pitch black. Someone else was there, and he got out of a dark-coloured ute. I assumed it to be Pete.

'Hi Pete!' I sang out. 'How you going?'

It was either Pete or someone who was going to pretend to be Pete for the sake of abducting me. Still, it was Friday night and I was up for an adventure. I locked my car and got into his ute.

'There's someone else down here who wants a pickup,' Pete said. He did a three-point turn and headed back down the road.

'Have you ever heard of Goatman?' I asked him. (It's one of my top strategies: be so weird that they'll regret abducting you.)

I began to garble about Goatman, aka Hoofman, and the logistics of him choosing a Ford Fiesta as his daily ride, and how paint scratches would be a dead giveaway. Pete looked at me sideways, gave an occasional nervous, token 'haha', and focused on the road. I took the hint and stopped babbling.

God, it was dark.

Soon a Ford Fiesta came into view. There are two small fords on the road where a stream intersects it. Pseudo-Goatman hadn't even made it past the first waterway, and I concluded that any Goatman worth his salt would surely know how to manoeuvre around such basic obstacles on his home turf. It couldn't be him.

We pulled up and the afro guy got into the ute with his gear. I couldn't make out any damage on the driver's door from any horns. But that weekend, I still couldn't help staring at him occasionally, just thinking, what if?

I haven't encountered Goatman yet. But I keep an eye out for him, on the Desert Road at night, peering into the inky blackness in case he's waiting on the side of the road for a pickup. One day . . .

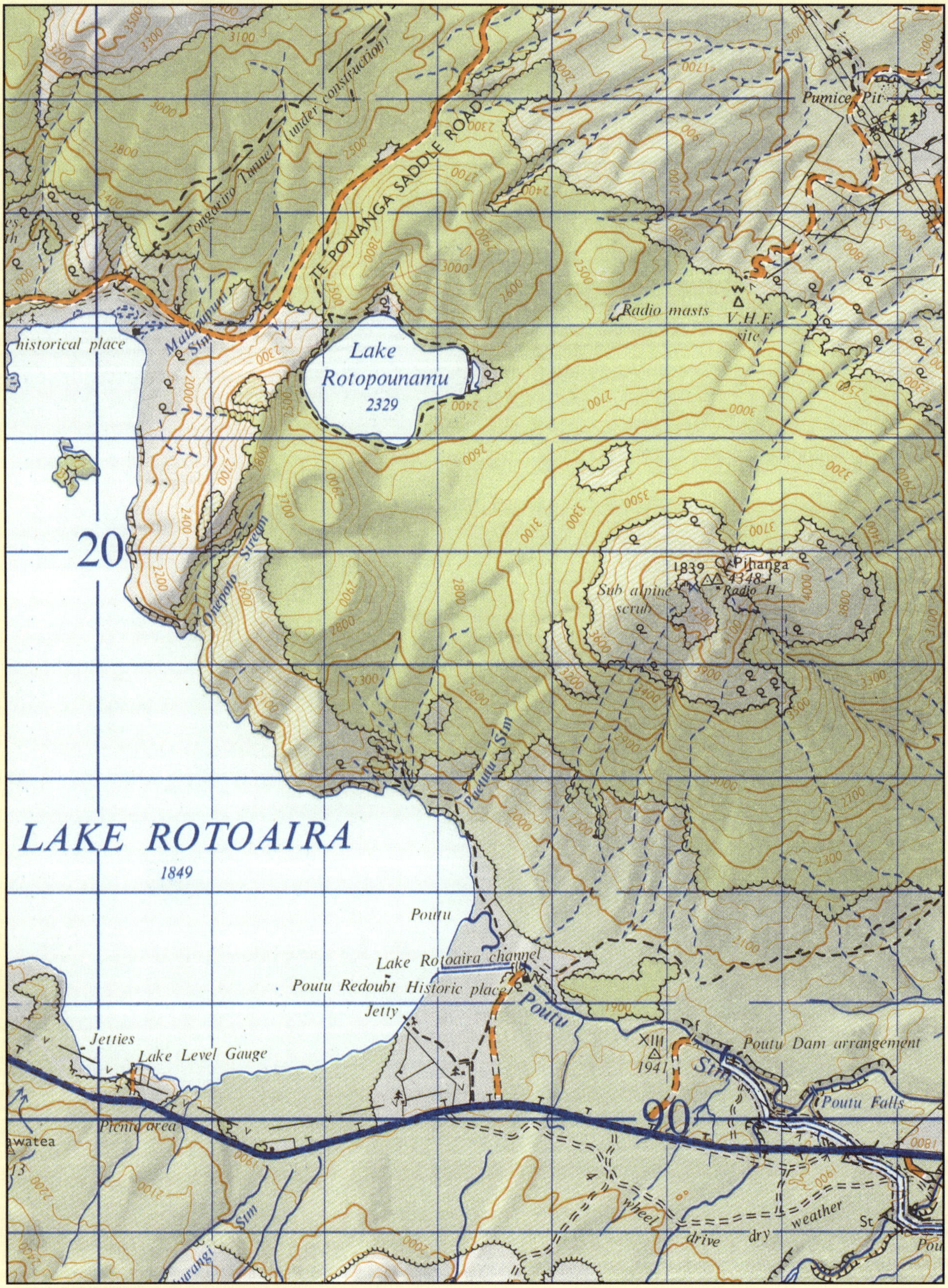
LAKE ROTOAIRA
1849
Lake Rotopounamu
2329
TE PONANGA SADDLE ROAD
Tongariro Tunnel (under construction)
Pumice Pit
Radio masts
V.H.F. site
Pihanga
4348
1839
Radio H
Sub alpine scrub
historical place
Mangamawhitiwhiti Stm
Onepoto Stream
Pukehunahuna Stm
Poutu
Lake Rotoaira channel
Poutu Redoubt Historic place
Jetty
Jetties
Lake Level Gauge
Picnic area
Poutu Dam arrangement
Poutu Stm
Poutu Falls
1941
wheel drive dry weather
20
90

Map showing Lake Rotopounamu, Lake Rotoaira and Onepoto Stream, where the gurgler probably drains. National Library of New Zealand, 23362321

CHAPTER 22

The water vortex of Rotopounamu

I'd walked around Lake Rotopounamu many times without knowing it was one of earth's four elemental chakras, with great healing power. The lake has seven feeder streams but no visible overland outlet — just a 'gurgler', a sort of drain hole, near its edge. Rotopounamu is considered the vortex of the water element, so you must be careful to always walk it in an anticlockwise direction — the same direction the water goes down its 'gurgler'.

Lake Rotopounamu and the central plateau volcanoes behind. Mike Heydon/ChopperWorx Taupō

I drove the guiding company's van up the Bruce Road past the Chateau to pick up a client from his on-mountain accommodation. I had basic information: the client, Max, had booked a private guide (me) for the day, so it was just the two of us doing the Tongariro Alpine Crossing; he was 75 but rated himself quite fit, and he was from Switzerland, where he'd hiked and climbed in the Alps. As I got out of the van, a man from the accommodation approached me.

'Max is on his way,' he said, rushing to get the words out. 'Look, I just need to let you know — he needs watching closely. He's got dementia. He went walkabout last night in the dark and we had to go looking for him.'

I thanked him for the heads-up as Max came out to meet me. He was lean and muscular, his frame speaking clear statements of years spent in mountainous terrain. But fitness was one thing — managing a client with dementia in an exposed alpine environment was another.

The weather was forecast to close in and the wind was already picking up. I communicated the client information back to base and my directive in return was that it wasn't safe to take him over Red Crater on the Crossing, but rather up to the 6-kilometre mark at South Crater at most, and then do another short walk, close to a road end. Max and I walked to Soda Springs and turned back from there as dark and angry skies approached from the south. His fitness wasn't an issue — in fact he would have been one of the fitter clients had we been in the usual big group with a ratio of one guide to 10 clients.

To fill in the rest of the day we headed to the Lake Rotopounamu track just beneath Mount Pihanga, where a 5-kilometre loop track undulates around a small lake. I'd only ever walked around it in bad weather as a 'Plan C' option when the ski fields were closed or the weather made tramping a bad idea, and usually as a token activity en route to the mineral hot pools at Tokaanu. It was never a first choice.

As we set off on the track, I realised that although we had chatted a lot already, I hadn't yet been able to figure out what Max had done as a job throughout his life. It appeared he wasn't independently wealthy as he'd saved for this trip and was being managed from afar by his sisters. I asked a few questions, determined to find out.

'I was an artist,' he said. 'I studied art history at college.' We stopped to peer through the trees at the lake's edge. 'Well,' he self-corrected. 'I didn't study it formally. I studied other things, but what I was *really* interested in was art history, so I sat in on all the lectures for four years and did all the assignments for myself.'

We moved off to stare up at some tōtara, rimu and mataī trees. Lake Rotopounamu sits in a catchment that is entirely indigenous podocarp forest. It's rare, because it's close to being in pristine and original condition.

'So I got into painting, oil painting. And for 10 years I focused very intensely on getting the colours *just* right. Just mixing colours to get *exactly* the right colours.'

I waited for a conclusion, perhaps a successful career as an artist.

'Then I stopped that. I abandoned art entirely, after I lost my sense of smell from all the turpentine.'

I interrupted him to point out some bush lawyer, tātarāmoa, across the track and hooked it back with my pole.

'After that, I got really into cinema. I got very focused on film, and I watched thirty thousand films over nine years.'

We walked past some hūpiro, otherwise known as stinkwood — or, if you're particularly affected by the smell, shit shrub.

'But then I realised Hollywood was really going downhill, you know? So I stopped that entirely. And then I got really into world events, and I just read and studied everything I could about the world, and politics, and Donald Trump and how it all works on a global scale.'

I realised that whatever Max had done for a day job was irrelevant; it simply supported whatever his interest of the day was. And here was a life lesson: to go, relentlessly, after the things that fascinate you.

So far I hadn't seen many signs of his supposed dementia, although on a couple of occasions he stopped on the track to look at the forest or scenery, and was prone to walking back in the direction we'd just come, albeit briefly, before he realised and self-corrected. He was from the other hemisphere, after all.

'I could walk all day, you know, Hazel,' he said. 'Yesterday I did the Taranaki Falls walk, and up and down the Whakapapanui track, and up the Silica Rapids track. Then I thought I had time before dinner, so I went out again in the dark just for another look. I forgot my torch, that was silly. They came looking for me, you know? They were really worried. But I just didn't want to stop walking.'

Was it dementia, and had he gone walkabout, or was he simply enjoying the world in a way we don't expect of a 75-year-old man? He thought he was out for a nice night-time walk, while the accommodation manager deemed him to be in trouble and in need of rescue. The truth was probably somewhere in the middle. Still, I was glad I'd been warned, so I could watch him closely to make sure he didn't wander off the track in search of just the right colours, or an interesting bird, or something. It's all perspectives, I suppose.

That day I came to appreciate several new things, thanks to Max. Firstly, the idea that life can be endlessly fascinating if you simply decide that it is. And secondly, that Lake Rotopounamu was a worthy spot in its own right, valuable for its forest, birds and history, not just as a sheltered walk as a last resort in bad weather.

Lake Rotopounamu is also valued for its spiritual properties. It is considered to be the planet's elemental water vortex, one of four vortexes that govern earth's four elements; the others are Table Mountain in South Africa (earth), the Great Pyramid of Giza (air), and Haleakala Crater, Hawai'i (fire). These elemental vortexes are spinning energy portals where rituals done in a circle can open and heal the earth, the participants and other human beings. The four 'spinner wheels' generate the energy of the four elements, and they are nature's 'secret code', reminding us that we all come from the same source, and that if we lose our way, we will remember and 'spiral back'.

So, Lake Rotopounamu is the 'spinner wheel' associated with the element of water. The lake is fed by seven streams but has no visible outlet other than a drain hole or 'gurgler', which drains in an anticlockwise direction, so if you walk the track for spiritual or healing purposes you should walk it in an anticlockwise direction also.

I am not making this up, but at this point you might be asking what sort of factual basis these ideas are grounded in, and the answer is: well, not much. The idea of the four vortexes was created by self-appointed 'Earth chakra expert' Robert Coon in 1967. Enthusiasts believe these vortexes give off a healing energy. Exactly how one is supposed to harness this energy seems to vary — for example, praying to the goddess, throwing items in as a gift back to the unseen world, meditating while facing the lake, or uploading a selfie to Instagram.

Now this is where it gets really weird, if it wasn't weird enough for you already. Some people believe that there are 12 'dragon lines' in the world (sort of like ancient power lines), and they meet in the centre of something called the 'Holy Grail Net' at Lake Rotopounamu. The lake is therefore home to a powerful water dragon; if there is mist on the lake, the dragon is awake. Further, the lake is green, which is the colour of the heart chakra; some believe that the heart chakra 'vibrates' the lake to green. You can go to the lake to 'recharge' your 'internal power grid'. Just don't get too close to the dragon, lest he be looking for a snack.

This is all very similar to the holy rock on Mount Wakefield in the heart of Aoraki Mount Cook National Park. In 1960, Mount Wakefield was 'charged' by 'The Master Jesus' with 'majestic spiritual powers that can never be depleted'. The Aetherius Society believes that the Cosmic Avatar Jesus (who is possibly different to the garden-variety Jesus) sent energies via yoga master George King into the mountain on Christmas Eve 1960, and the mountain now waits quietly for people to go to the rock and send its energies out to the world.[1] Again, I am not making any of this up. (Embarrassingly for King, he lost his way coming down from the summit and spent the night out.)

Robert Coon's earth chakra ideology states that for each of these vortexes there is an 'auspicious time', about once every six months, when these locations are in their most powerful phases and can advance the planet's purpose. For Lake Rotopounamu this is the Pisces full moon, which happens around August or September, and the Pisces new moon, which happens around February or March. You can harness the healing power during this time and your Instagram following will double virtually overnight.

Coon has a mathematical equation for this: 'In the water vortex, the quality is love. Multiply the speed of light by itself, and you arrive at the velocity of love.'[2]

I couldn't believe this was all right here in my backyard! I had the potential to heal the world, make it a better place, and arrive at the velocity of love, all from Lake Rotopounamu. But seriously, I wondered about sacred and mystical sites. There was something about Ruapehu and Tongariro that seemed to draw people in, and incite them to describe it as 'magic'.

After all that woolly business I went in search of some cold hard facts about Rotopounamu. I'd always assumed it to be outside of Tongariro National Park, but in fact it had been included as a sort of extension after the Pihanga Scenic Reserve was created in 1965, encompassing 12,700 acres (around 5000 hectares) of land.[3] In 1968 the Park Board created the loop track around the lake in partnership with the Justice Department, and today the reserve is looked after by DOC.[4] The lake, which covers an area of about one square kilometre, was formed by a landslide about 10,000 years ago. In places it's almost 9 metres deep, although most of it is actually fairly shallow. The National Institute of Water and Atmospheric Research (NIWA) has identified the body of water as a priority freshwater site for conservation management because it's rare to find a lake in New Zealand in such original condition.[5]

The lake is fed by up to seven streams and has no visible overground outlet. Ernst Dieffenbach explored the area in 1841 and couldn't find an outlet (bearing in mind that just getting to the lake in those days was an epic achievement).

> I gained with difficulty the precipitous and rocky basaltic shore of the Rotu-Ponamu [sic], which is surrounded by almost impenetrable underwood. This little lake lies in a perfect funnel, formed by the surrounding mountains, which rise on one side to a crest of considerable height. It is about a mile and a half in circumference, and apparently of great depth, and has no visible outlet.[6]

One outlet was discovered in 1994 by Turangi Field Centre staff and is commonly referred to as the 'gurgler', as you can hear it gurgling when the lake level is low. Field Centre manager Dave Lumley described it as a small drain hole in the lake's bed.

'The gurgler was in relatively silent mode when I rediscovered it, so I had to use all my panther like stalking skills to track it down,' Lumley wrote in the *Tongariro* journal.[7]

He gave directions: it was 10 minutes' walk along the track heading southwest from the southern end of Long Beach, a pristine white sandy beach with clear water at the eastern side of the lake. Keen gurgler spotters should stroll along in that direction, and look for a large kahikatea tree that's fallen into the lake, a little way past a wooden seat. The gurgler was located approximately 20 metres southwest along the lakeshore from the fallen tree, Lumley wrote, and if it was a windless day, you would be able to hear it gurgling. He noted it was approximately 1.5 metres from the track and about a metre into the lake from the current lake edge, and the water was about 30 centimetres deep.

'The gurgler is unremarkable in itself, just a small whirlpool disappearing into a small crevice in the lake bed. However, as I discovered when I put my arm down into the crevice, quite a volume of water (as indicated by the powerful suction which threatened to drag me down into the bowels of the earth) disappears down the gurgler.'

Lumley thought it was unlikely that the gurgler would completely drain the lake, as it was only a metre from the lake shore and in shallow water. But he noted that the lake level had dropped significantly in the past month, after being higher than he had seen in the nine years he'd been there.

'The gurgler is an interesting feature on a great local walk and I suspect that many visitors will discover it when walking past when the lake is still. However, on most days the lapping of waves onto the shore will disguise its telltale sound and they will stroll past completely oblivious to the presence of this new phenomenon only a few metres away.'[8]

I'd been told someone had tipped dye into the lake to see where it might run out, but it had never emerged. I felt this could be a bit of a fairy story, given that the most likely place it drains to is Lake Rotoaira, which has a huge surface area and any dye would be quite diluted by the time it emerged. My enquiries about the dye went unanswered by various departments and institutions.

Ngāti Hikairo ki Tongariro representative Bubs Smith told me that for Ngāti Hikairo ki Tongariro, the drainpipe for Rotopounamu is via Onepoto Stream, southwest of the lake on the northern edges of nearby Rotoaira. 'Local observation over time has shown that when the Tokaanu pools are high and generally colder, the lake at Rotopounamu is a bit lower, and the reverse is true, too,' Bubs told me. 'It affects the northern side of Rotopounamu more than the southern side.'

I came across a chap in the tramping world who'd been to the gurgler with a group of spiritualists in tow.

'I used to do a bit of guiding around the mountain while I was living in Taupō,' he told me. 'My boss called me one day and said he had a group of people staying at the Hilton for a conference, and they really wanted to walk around Lake Rotopounamu. I said, sure.'

His boss told him it was extremely important that he take them around anticlockwise.

'I thought, okay. I mean, toss a coin as far as I'm concerned.'

And, his boss told him, before you meet them, google the word 'chakra'.

'Turns out, they were all chakra fanatics, from overseas, and that's what the conference was about. I have to say they were the most charming people. All aged about fifty to seventy, mostly women, I took them around anticlockwise and they grinned from ear to ear all the way, even hugging a few trees.'

They never saw the gurgler, which he said was rather 'nondescript' and tricky to locate.

'It's some 20-odd metres from the track through reasonably thick bush to the lake edge, where it's a metre or so into the lake.'

He's of the view that the gurgler might not always be active, and that it comes and goes at various times.

I had walked past the gurgler so many times on rainy, windy days and never known. Moreover, I had walked around the lake so many times without even thinking about the fact that there was no obvious outlet. I hadn't known I was circling a spiritual vortex that might have assisted in my own healing. It frequently occurs to me that I still know very little about the landscape where I live.

It struck me: How do we know there is only one gurgler? What if there's another? What if there are several gurglers, only they are in locations that make them tricky to

spot? We don't know how thoroughly Dieffenbach examined the area, and scientists seemed to be more focused on fish species and water quality than anything else.

I decided I couldn't rule out the existence of further gurglers, and this led to one conclusion: I'd need to go in search. The lake was relatively shallow, and quite clear around the shore, at least. If I tramped in with a wetsuit and snorkelling gear, I could explore underwater around the lake's edges and look for other outlets.

I roped in three unsuspecting victims to join me on this folly by convincing them it would be fun. One, Maria, refused to get into the water, so she was appointed safety officer and would stay on the shore. David and Pete committed to getting into the lake with me on the basis that we'd be in line for King's Birthday honours on account of making a groundbreaking scientific discovery.

When Pete and I arrived at the carpark we discovered David had assumed we'd wear our wetsuits for the walk in. Meanwhile Pete and I had our gear packed into backpacks and our boots on. David declined to borrow a spare pack, stuck with his plan, and changed into his diving wetsuit on the side of the busy road while we all watched. He slipped on a pair of Crocs to protect his feet. Maria occasionally shook her head and

Pete, the author and David ready to snorkel Lake Rotopounamu in search of undiscovered gurglers.
Maria Niva

sighed. I realised it looked quite shady, three clothed people standing around watching a man take his pants off in a roadside carpark.

'You can be in charge of the cooker,' I said to Maria. I'd packed a cooker to boil water for hot drinks afterwards. It was May, and the air temperature was around 5 degrees, with a layer of fog slowly burning off. She shook her head. 'You want no part of this, don't you?' I said, and she laughed. Maria was once a victim of one of my bright ideas when I took her on a tramp that largely consisted of walking up a river. 'There's a couple of river crossings,' I had told her, meaning 'a lot'. We did 42 crossings that day — it was July, too, and our feet froze — and Maria is now, somewhat understandably, and very sensibly, reluctant to sign up for my trips.

A car pulled up and three women got out in tramping gear. They surveyed David, who by now had most of his lower body into the wetsuit.

'What are you guys doing?' one asked.

'Body recovery,' I called out. They stopped and looked serious.

'Not really,' I said. 'We're going to snorkel in the lake.' And I told them all about the gurgler, the spiritual healing vortex, the spinner wheel and the possible dragon resident and the need to walk the lake anticlockwise under a Pisces full moon. I think I left out the bit about George King supercharging the Jesus rock, but at the time I deemed it would've been overkill.

Jan, Sally and Tobi were from the west coast above Wellington and hadn't bargained on meeting some local crazies. Later, when we were decked out in wetsuits and into the freezing lake, hooting at the stabbing cold, they turned up to watch. Our efforts were largely pointless — the visibility was around a metre so identifying anything other than our hands and fins was impossible, and the lake's bottom was covered in bright green weed and silt. I grabbed handfuls of it and took photos. I'd read the lake had the invasive weed *Juncus bulbosus*, the same plant that had plagued the Emerald Lakes on the Tongariro Alpine Crossing for some years until DOC managed to eradicate it.

I cooked up more ideas that day about wheeling tanks into Rotopounamu and scuba diving the lake, maybe in summer when the visibility might be clearer and the temperatures less brutal. Turns out NIWA had already done that, several times — in 2019, 2014, 1990 and some time in the 1980s, to survey submerged vegetation. At one point they used a boat to get around to five different sites and a wheelbarrow to get tanks and gear in.

That trip, we entirely failed to find any further gurglers, and the only discovery of the day worthy of King's Birthday honours was David's dulcet Scottish tones as he pronounced the word 'gurgler'. (David also claims to have 'supercharged' a 'Jesus tree' at 5 Minute Beach while the rest of us were busy getting changed.) You might find us there, next summer, surveying the water's edges, or perhaps under a Pisces full moon, heading out for a healing walk in the moonlight. Anticlockwise, of course.

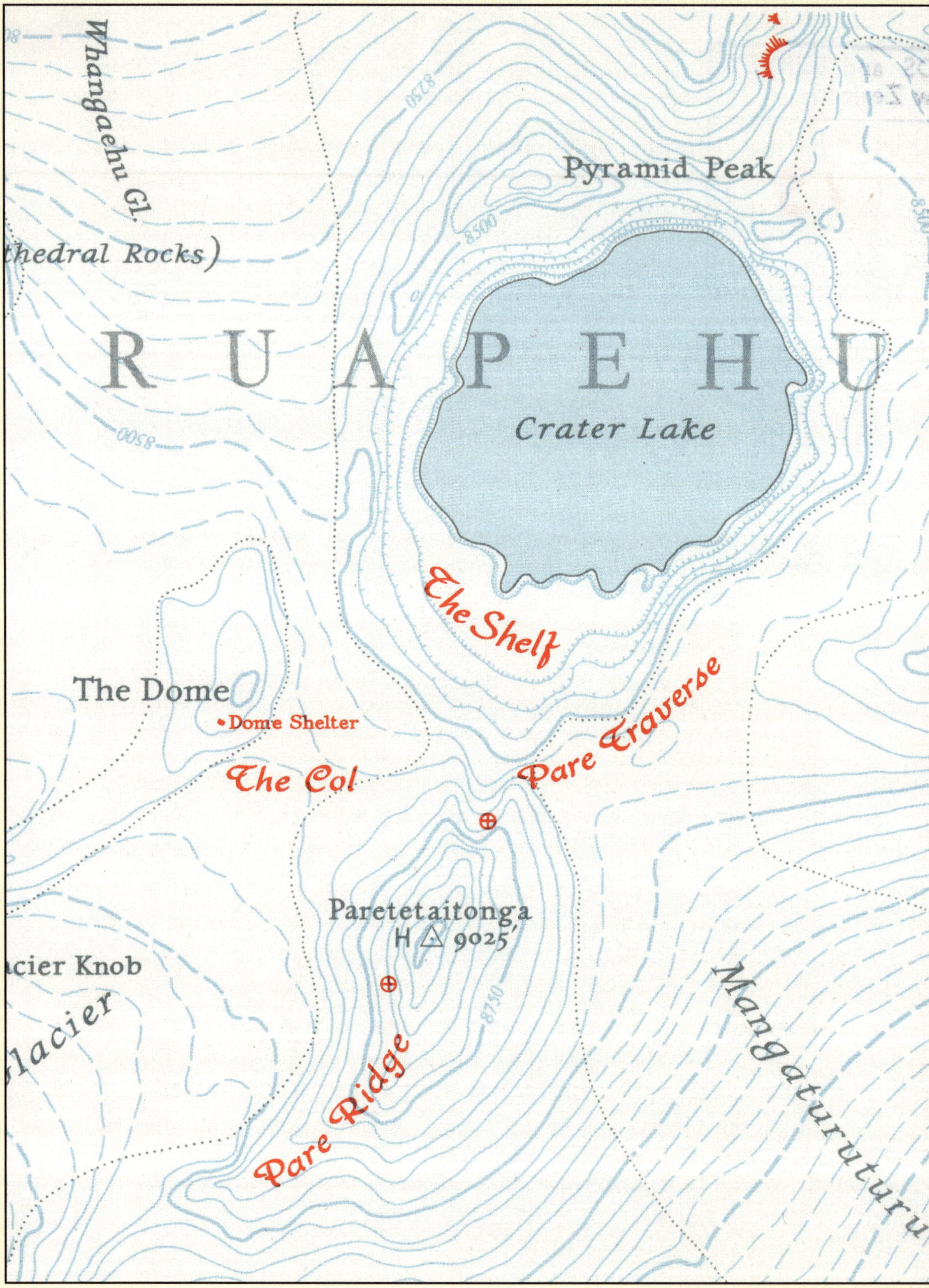
Whangaehu Gl.
thedral Rocks)
Pyramid Peak
8250
8500
RUAPEHU
Crater Lake
The Shelf
The Dome
Dome Shelter
The Col
Pare Traverse
Paretetaitonga
H △ 9025′
acier Knob
lacier
8750
Pare Ridge
Mangaturuturu

CHAPTER 23

Skull on a summit

In 2002 trampers near Dome peak on Ruapehu found a small, weathered skull, partially encased in glacier ice. Could it be the lost climber of 1977? Or had someone come to grief by falling into one of Ruapehu's crevasses, and had perished there, unable to get out?

The Summit Plateau area looking to Matihao/Cathedral Rocks in summer.

I heard whispers of a skull that was found high on Ruapehu. One person said it was at the Notch, the V-shaped terrain feature that offers easy access between the steep slopes on approach and the Summit Plateau, where glacier ice used to flow through. Another person told me it was found inside a crevasse on the upper Whangaehu Glacier. Yet another told me it was very close to Crater Lake itself. Nobody knew any dates, nothing showed up in online searches, and aside from rumours, there was little to go on. But I was captivated by the whispers. Could this be Anthony Morrison, the climber who went missing while on Ringatoto in 1977, and who somehow had gone higher in the storm rather than lower? Egon Lehner, too, had been found somewhere thoroughly unexpected.

Eventually I found a story in an issue of the *Ruapehu Press* that was more than 20 years old.[1] It was 2002, at a time when tiny local stories stayed tiny and local rather than being picked up and thrown at the main page of Stuff, which explained how it had flown under the research radar and was still unknown today.

On Saturday, 16 February 2002, a group of trampers ascended Ruapehu for a day walk. Arriving at Dome, where Dome Shelter then stood, they found a skull, partially encased in old snow and ice, and close to the structure. They left the skull on a rock, took photos of it and informed DOC staff at Whakapapa on their return.

The next day, police, DOC staff and iwi representatives from Ngāti Tūwharetoa and Ngāti Rangi flew to the site, following protocol for any incidents involving human remains in the national park. The skull was respectfully uplifted and sent to the Institute of Environmental Science & Research (ESR) in Porirua for a detailed forensic examination. At first glance, it was fairly worn and appeared to have a hole in the side, near the top of the head. It only had four teeth left and was fairly small.

The skull was quite old, and police were clear they weren't treating the find as suspicious. DOC and police representatives said that as far as they knew, skulls were rarely found on Ruapehu. Senior sergeant Steve Mastrovich made it clear: 'There are no missing people outstanding from that area.' So, not Tony Morrison; he had gone missing from further down on the eastern side of the mountain, away from Dome, and I knew it was unlikely to be him, if the skull was old and small.

The newspaper article concluded: 'Whether the region was an urupa or burial ground is not known but the *Ruapehu Press* understands it was a custom of Ngāti Rangi, the iwi most closely associated with Mt Ruapehu, to re-inter the bones of high-born ancestors high on the mountain and possibly in the crater itself.'[2]

I put in an Official Information Act request to police for whatever notes they had from the find, and another to ESR for the forensics report. Police had nothing — they simply responded that the information didn't exist. I checked with local police sources and they confirmed it was like searching for a grain of white rice on a glacier. I held my breath when I opened the ESR response, anticipating a long report on the details of the skull. But it simply read: 'A pathologist examined the skull in my presence. In his opinion the skull was probably pre-European Māori. As it was small and light he believed that it was probably that of a female or young adult. The damage to the skull appeared to have been the result of weathering rather than a traumatic event.'[3]

So what happened to it, I wondered? Where does the skull reside today? Ngāti Rangi representative Korty Wilson told me it was taken back up to the Crater Lake, placed in a kete and left there in a crevasse, as is appropriate for the iwi.

'What if someone stumbled upon it again?' I asked. I had visions of it coming out again thanks to the shifting ice.

'Sometimes you're meant to come across something,' Korty said, and raised her eyebrows. 'Sometimes you're not.' And I thought, in that moment, of the ashes at the site of the *Kaka*.

South Island backcountry history has stories of people going into crevasses and popping out lower down years later, often broken up into body parts rather than as whole skeletons. I'd found one story in which part of a man was found on one side of a pass, and part of him on the other side, and other stories where cameras had popped out and the film had been developed and the climbers were identified thanks to the photos being published on social media. North Island crevasses didn't have that same sort of history. It's likely Ruapehu's crevasses just aren't big enough and grunty enough, or that we don't have the same sort of summer climbing traffic that's seen in the Southern Alps. Crevasses had historically been a thing, though. I found a photo of the Mangaehuehu Glacier from 1934 that showed a distinctive ice fall during winter, a maze of crevasses open although the snowfall had offered extensive cover, and another from the Whakapapa Glacier with decent cracks.

I asked Harry Keys about it.

'There used to be slots on most of the glaciers when they were bigger, many decades ago,' Harry told me. 'Some of the glaciers still have active slots — such as the Tūwharetoa and Crater Basin glaciers, and like those on the Mangatoetoenui, could be hazardous when covered by thin drifts of snow.'

Harry sent me an old photo of the summit plateau and Crater Lake area, age unknown, in summer conditions — Te Heuheu peak and Cathedral Rocks are devoid of snow cover, as is the distinctive ridge leading from Te Heuheu down to Tukino, and the ridge from Tukino Peak sloping west. The whole Summit Plateau area is distinctly crevassed and the cracks run down the Mangatoetoenui Glacier and Whangaehu Glacier. What's astounding to me, though, is that Dome was still surrounded by snow and ice. Harry confirmed that Dome indeed used to be totally covered, year-round. It's essentially a nunatak, a rock that protrudes through a glacier.

The summit plateau also looks far more full than it does now, even in winter — ice used to spill over in several places, including through the Notch. Today, even with major midwinter snow cover, there's a ridge that separates the Summit Plateau, creating two depressions, a northern crater and a southern crater. This picture shows just one huge, bulging ice field. In fact, the ice seems to spill over between point 2642 and the ridge to Tukino Peak — an area that has several contour lines' worth of prominence. The vast differences blow my mind.

But what's absolutely clear to me, looking at this photo, is that the owner of the skull must have fallen (or been placed) into a crevasse. The glaciers are ablating, and in the same way that they move and shift and re-produce unlucky folk from decades

ABOVE: Climbers survey the crevassed terrain of the Mangaehuehu Glacier. Surveying cadet Walter Dunnage nearly came to grief in a deep crevasse on the Mangaehuehu. Auckland Libraries Heritage Collections

BELOW: Crater Lake and the Summit Plateau in the 1920s or 1930s, showing many crevasses compared to present day. Auckland Libraries Heritage Collections

past in the South Island, on the North Island's rooftop they are revealing long-hidden secrets. Maybe one day they will reveal others.

I conducted a thorough hunt for stories of people who'd come to grief in Ruapehu's crevasses and came up empty-handed, except for one, a story of a near miss. In January 1886, when James Park, C. Dalin and Walter Dunnage ascended Ruapehu, the first patch of snow they encountered was at around 1600 metres, the same height as the ski field carparks now (it is an incredible concept, now, that snow once extended that far down in summer, and the permanent snowfields extended just below 2000 metres).[4] Each member of the party wore heavy hobnailed boots and carried an alpenstock, and without this climbing gear and the sun's rays softening the snow and ice, they would otherwise not have been able to ascend. They intended to climb the Mangaehuehu Glacier but found it too icy, and couldn't dig their alpenstocks in or make safe steps. They went straight up Girdlestone — then simply referred to as 'the south-east peak' — aiming for the saddle between Girdlestone and Tahurangi, which they found tricky due to the crevassed nature of the glacier.[5] Park wrote: 'A sharp lookout had to be kept for the numerous crevasses and fissures which, in places, cut the ice into an intricate network, more especially where the snow-fields were moderately flat.'

They crossed over onto the Wahianoa Glacier.[6] It was late in the day and the refreeze had begun. Snow that had been dripping was now freezing again, not into a cohesive block but into loose pieces. They moved fast but lightly, making for 'a high boss of volcanic agglomerate' where they thought the snow would be sticking to the ice better. They were within reach of the rocks when Dunnage slipped and began to slide.

'His destruction seemed inevitable,' Park wrote, 'for he was rapidly approaching an immense crevasse that traversed the whole field, and had particularly attracted our attention a short time before. It was the dangerous description of a crevasse well known to alpine tourists, which has one side higher than the other.' Park estimated a difference of about 20 feet (6 metres).

'Both sides were corniced, and from its concave roof and sides hung innumerable long blue icicles and sharp projections of ice. Its depth appeared to be many hundreds of feet, extending probably to the bottom of the valley.' Dunnage was in a right pickle.

> To this crevasse Dunnage was rapidly sliding, and there seemed but small chance of his recovering himself. He was sliding with his back to the snow, and his weight started the dry snow, which accelerated his speed; but he had fortunately stuck to his alpenstock, which, getting in front of him, ploughed into the ice, so that eventually he was able to swing himself clear of the sliding snow; but none too soon, for with a few feet more he would have dashed into the icy chasm below.

Dunnage had slid about 200 feet (60 metres), in what is arguably Ruapehu's first recorded episode of successful self-arresting.

Harry told me he didn't know of any history of fatal accidents by crevasse fall in the national park. 'I don't know of anyone disappearing into a crevasse on Ruapehu, but I suspect some people's legs have broken, though — especially earlier, say, prior to the 1960s . . . but then, I haven't heard of any serious accidents, either. It's possible to climb or walk in the crevasses if you are confident the floor is stable and safe, but not a lot of people have the knowledge and experience to be able to assess that.'

I added another objective to my Ruapehu trip list: one day I'd go up in the height of summer and monkey around in the crevasses. I was particularly interested in the cracks on the Mangaehuehu Glacier, which I could see from Ohakune, and the top of the Mangatoetoenui. I'd take Harry with me for safety assessments, I decided, and to further the Mallowpuff Test on the southern slopes. My Ruapehu wishlist was expanding even as I ticked things off.

Some time later in a kōrero with Bubs Smith from Ngāti Hikairo ki Tongariro I brought up the skull. He'd been notified when it was found. 'When that happened I talked to a number of kaumātua and let them know it was with police and ESR for checking and forensics,' he told me. 'When they came back to me and said it was pre-European, female, maybe 18–20 years old, I thought of an old waiata my mother had told me about. It speaks of a young girl who was betrothed to someone in Ngāti Rangi, which was something that was done to keep the ties strong between iwi. She didn't want to leave her homeland and went up the mountain never to be seen again.'

This meant that none of our European climbers were the first to get to the top of Ruapehu, I said, and Bubs agreed, pointing out that Ngāti Rangi interred chiefs in the crater, so they had a history of ascents. Although mountaineering was a European construct and dominated by older men, the first ascent of Ruapehu — incredibly — probably belonged to a young Māori woman.

'Chances are,' Bubs said, 'these are her remains.'

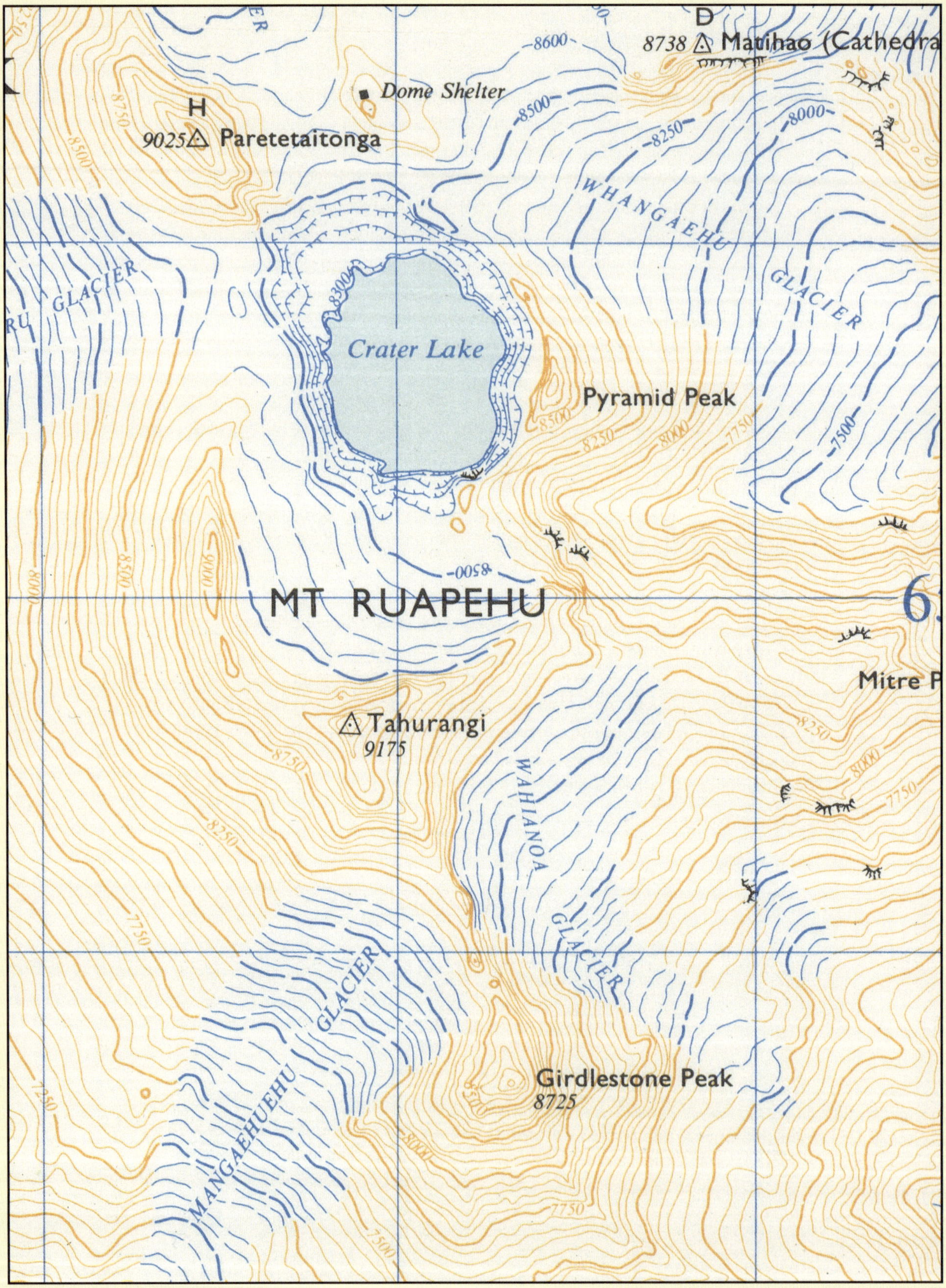

D
8738 Matihao (Cathedra
Dome Shelter
H
9025 Paretetaitonga
8600
8500
8250
8000
WHANGAEHU GLACIER
RU GLACIER
8300
Crater Lake
Pyramid Peak
8500
8250
8000
7750
7500
9000
8500
8000
8500
MT RUAPEHU
6
Mitre P
Tahurangi
9175
8750
8250
WAHIANOA GLACIER
8250
8000
7750
7750
MANGAEHUEHU GLACIER
Girdlestone Peak
8725
8500
8000
7250
7750
7500

Map showing Tahurangi, Ruapehu's highest peak at 2797 metres. National Library of New Zealand, 23363041

CHAPTER 24

Peak obsession

Could we engage in a way of mountaineering that didn't involve summits? A way of spending time on a mountain and really knowing its history, culture and context rather than always angling for a peak or a route? And after all this time, and all these trips, did I really know Ruapehu any better?

Contemplating the Ruapehu massif from Hauhungatahi. Mandy Rothe Photography

I began my exploration of Ruapehu with the summit that is the most distinctive to me, Girdlestone Peak (Peretini, 2658 metres), a sharp peak that captures the eye when viewing the mountain from the southern side. It's perhaps fitting to end my Ruapehu journey with the highest peak in Tongariro National Park, in fact the highest in the North Island, Tahurangi (2797 metres).

This habit of angling for summits is, I realise, very much a European preoccupation. I read up on the history of mountaineering in New Zealand, which seemed to be focused tightly on the idea of 'topping out'. 'Mountaineers differ from trampers, tourists and other visitors to the mountains: they want to get to the top,' wrote John Wilson in *Te Ara — the Encyclopedia of New Zealand*. 'They do it for adventure, for a sense of physical wellbeing and for fun.'[1] In this conceptualisation of mountaineering, getting to the top is an essential part of the pastime, and without it, it's not mountaineering at all.

This idea of 'mountaineering as summits' means doing hard stuff. 'Real' mountaineers are revered for their first ascents, for dreaming up exploits others haven't achieved. I was in an alpine club lodge one day chatting to a man who had a reasonable mountaineering history himself, and I happened to mention Alastair McDowell. A passionate mountaineer, runner and cyclist, Alastair had recently linked up all the peaks over 3000 metres in the Southern Alps in a groundbreaking project called 'Enchainment'.

'Oh yes,' the man said. 'Well, Alastair is a *mountaineer*.'

He spoke with verbal italics, the emphasis serving to indicate that Alastair was a 'proper' mountaineer (and he is; you really don't get much more 'mountaineer' in New Zealand right now than Alastair). This man also had mountaineering exploits on his adventure résumé, but he didn't consider himself a *mountaineer*, the sort that deserved italics.

I didn't consider myself a mountaineer, italics or no italics, either, simply because I hadn't done a lot of properly hard ascents (Ruapehu, Tongariro and Ngāuruhoe are considered very 'easy' mountains in the climbing world). But I wondered, was there a model of mountaineering where I could identify as such, without really being that bothered about getting to the top? A model where I could engage with the mountain on its icy flanks, in its streams and rivers, in rock crevices and in fields of hairy alpine buttercups, rather than straining to stand on a tippy-top peak? There certainly used to be. Early climbers around Ruapehu and Tongariro largely went for the botany or for some other sort of scientific fieldwork (Ludwig Krenek tracking the size of the glaciers, or Robin Oliver and James Witten-Hannah dangling into the crater), for tourism and for general exploration and enjoyment.

Mountaineering historian Graham Langton suggested making a distinction between 'mountaineers' (as a term that can include trampers as well as climbers) and 'mountain climbers' (those who tend to aim for summits or routes), while the more general term 'climber' can include rock climbers, wall climbers, ice climbers and so on. 'Early climbers on Ruapehu did aim for the summits,' Langton told me. 'Others rambled around looking at glaciers, botany and so on, without aiming for the summits.'

Someone once asked George Mallory why he wanted to climb Mount Everest and he famously replied: 'Because it's there.' And maybe that's how I felt about Ruapehu, a bit — it was just *there*, looking at me, enchanting me, calling me in.

On descending from Everest, Ed Hillary announced to expedition member George Lowe: 'Well George, we've knocked the bastard off.' It's a phrase that positions a mountain as something that needs to be conquered, or overcome, although Hillary later wrote, 'It is not the mountain we conquer, but ourselves.' (Sir Ed also said 'my solar plexus was tight with fear', and I identify hard with that.) Conquering is about victory, and sometimes about ownership, and I never feel any different for summiting peaks; I don't *feel* like I've conquered them, or that I now 'own' them. You expect you will; you stand on the summit waiting for a sensation of some sort to overcome you, to be somehow changed as a person. For me, that feeling never comes.

Perhaps there's a model of mountaineering where we could lay down our weapons and get up close to the mountains, and simply see what they have to teach us. There's infinity outwards and upwards, but also infinity inwards, if you look down at the tiny alpine plants, the pebbles in a stream, the striations left behind on volcanic rock as glacial ice recedes. The mountain can talk to you, if you slow your roll and take the time to listen.

'Most climbers who do any sort of thinking about their recreation realise that they learn more about themselves in climbing than anything else,' Graham Langton told me.

I read Nic Low's book *Uprising*, which chronicles his journey to understand how Ngāi Tahu had travelled across the divide, in a bid to connect the land to some sort of spirituality, to think about it differently. One of his quotes sat with me for a long time:

> I mounted an expedition to not climb Aoraki/Mount Cook, to set out up the Linda Glacier route and to find out just how far I would go to pay my respects, to not think about it in terms of conquering the mountain or standing on top of his head, because Ngāi Tahu asks that climbers do not stand on the very top of Aoraki . . . I just wanted to go to his shoulder to speak aloud some of our old traditions, to mihi (pay tribute) to him from right up close.[2]

Yeah, maybe we *could* think about mountains as more than peaks and summits. I set out on my own journey to fully know my old friend Ruapehu. I wanted to walk joyfully in the streams that ran down his flanks, and to touch the shimmering diamonds of ice on his arms in winter. I wanted to tramp off track in places others didn't go, to explore the wilderness areas and walk alongside huge deer footprints unseen by other humans. If Ruapehu was a person, I think I'd want to hug him, and sit by the fire with him as he told the stories of old.

In 1918 mountaineer Hugh Strutfield wrote an essay titled 'Mountaineering as a Religion' for the British *Alpine Journal*. It's a piece that was before its time, and stands in sharp contrast to New Zealand mountaineers such as Samuel Turner, who was overly proud of his physical prowess, skipping ability and summit achievements. Strutfield wrote: 'The true mountaineer is not a mere gymnast, but a man who worships the mountains . . . he demands closer contact with the objects of his passion; but this passion is never otherwise than devout and reverential in its quality. To us the great ranges and the glaciers lying at their feet are sacred things.'[3]

I wasn't a gymnast of any kind, but I loved going to the church of the outdoors to worship Ruapehu on any day of the week.

My friend Toby, who was a captain in the army, told me a yarn about something he called the Rock of Excellence. While he was living at the army camp at Waiouru he ascended Tahurangi and uplifted a rock about the size of a compressed sleeping bag. This he painted gold and named the Rock of Excellence. Toby was leading several groups of soldiers and he wanted to create a competition between the groups, so he would award the Rock of Excellence to one of the teams for various attributes or feats. There was a catch: the rock had to be protected, and if another group managed to uplift it, the rock was theirs.

Indeed, an opposing team did, and a confrontation ensued. Instead of stealthily snatching the rock back, a guy from the first team showed up at the door of the barracks, demanded it back, and performed what Toby described as a 'jumping headbutt' on another soldier.

Sufficient drama had been caused by the Rock of Excellence for Toby to begin questioning whether the rock had some sort of bad spirit. After all, he'd taken it from the summit of Tahurangi on a sacred mountain.

'I took it back up,' Toby told me. 'And left it up there. There was still some snow around on the very top, left over from winter, so I left it just down from the summit. But I felt that I had taken it away from its rightful place, and it needed to go back. What I'd done wasn't right.'

I, too, had taken a rock — a much smaller one — and later returned it, and I told Toby about this. In summer I frequented the Lunchtime Spa, one of my favourite swimming holes. Accessed via a hidden track off the lower Ohakune Mountain Road, the Lunchtime Spa was fringed with overhanging greenery and its swimming hole curved slightly, with rock worn smooth from centuries of water flowing down it. The water itself was a curious shade of green compared to other Mangawhero swimming spots, which tended towards a bluer hue.

One day I adopted a tiny, smooth rock from the Lunchtime Spa. I named him Dwayne (the Rock) and took him home. I'm not really sure why I did it — it was sort of unthinking at the time. But I couldn't shake a strange feeling every time I looked at Dwayne, and I kept thinking about the fact that I'd removed him from his home, and how would I like to be removed from mine? I wouldn't.

I took Dwayne back for a swim, and put him into the swimming hole at the deepest point, where I'd found him. He was a distinctive light colour and stood out among the other dark rocks.

When I visited the next day, Dwayne was gone.

The first ascent of Ruapehu is very much a Pākehā preoccupation, and its history is peppered with men of European descent who sometimes disregarded the wishes of tangata whenua in their pursuit of climbing glory. George Beetham and Joseph Maxwell are widely accepted as being the first ascensionists of Ruapehu, but historically there has been some confusion because of the number of different summit peaks on the massif.

Sir George Grey, who was Governor of New Zealand from 1845 to 1853 and was a major influence in colonisation, partially ascended the northern peak Te Heuheu (not the highest peak), against the wishes of tangata whenua, in the late 1840s. Grey climbed some distance up the mountain, and claimed to have reached the summit icefield in 1853.

In 1877, John and Thomas Allison from Whanganui ascended Te Heuheu. Then in 1879 politician and alpinist George Beetham and civil engineer Joseph Maxwell 'discovered' the Crater Lake after doing a 'complete' ascent of Ruapehu from the southern side. It was Beetham's second attempt.

In 1881, brothers Arthur and Herbert Russell, along with husband and wife team Ethel and William Birch, successfully ascended Te Heuheu and Tahurangi. Ethel Birch is thought to be the first woman to ascend Ruapehu.

Along with obsessing over summit peaks and first ascents, European climbers also enjoyed engaging in the pastime of leaving objects on mountain tops for others to later find or ferret out, in what seems to be a very early version of geocaching, or perhaps littering. Maxwell and Beetham deposited two sixpences on their summit climb 'for the benefit of future mountaineers', and a record of their visit tucked away in a matchbox.[4]

In 1886 James Park, C. Dalin and Walter Dunnage summited Girdlestone Peak (then called Little Matterhorn) and Tahurangi (which Park called Ruapehu Peak). On the Tahurangi summit, they made sure to leave their mark. Park wrote:

> There was nothing to be gained by a prolonged stay on the summit and, without delay, we prepared for the descent. A stout beech sapling, which we had carried to the top, was driven securely into the frozen snow and to it we tied a ball of black calico. Our names and the date of ascent were placed in a sealed bottle and carefully stowed in a cairn of stones on a rock ledge, about 20 yards to the north of the summit and about 15 feet lower.[5]

Hugh Girdlestone once led a party to the summit of Little Matterhorn, where he discovered a flask of whisky, left there 14 years previously by another climber. Its presence on the summit had become something of a local rumour, and so Girdlestone referred to the peak colloquially as Whisky Peak. After so many years exposed to the elements, the felt covering the flask had rotted away and the whisky inside had turned black due to corrosion. Rumour had it that a sovereign had been left with the flask, but no coin was found. They also found the skeletons of six horses on the side of the mountain, which had presumably taken shelter among some rocks but perished from the cold.[6] (That wasn't the first time Girdlestone had found a horse in the alpine environment — at Easter 1910 he found a dead horse in the summit crater of Ngāuruhoe.)

In 1890, an unnamed writer published a five-part series about Ruapehu in the *Hawke's Bay Herald* titled 'Up Ruapehu, and how to get there'. The writer had found a cairn of stones erected on Ngāuruhoe by an earlier climber, Kerry Nicholls, as well as a matchbox recording that a party of boys from Wanganui Collegiate School had previously reached that point.[7] In the matchbox was a Jubilee shilling, a lead whistle and a paper containing the date of ascent, and the names of those who ascended, with some 'poetry':

> In box five gentlemen from Wanganui College
> (Read signatures for your more certain knowledge)
> Ascended here Jan. 18th 1900
> And Kerry Nicholls' cairn and safety sought
> With Mr Len McLauchlan as their guide
> And now this document conjointly hide
> To appease the wrath of mountain deities
> They gave a Jubilee bob and here it is.[8]

BELOW: A dead horse found in the crater area on Ngāuruhoe. Bagnall Collection, Massey University Library

FOLLOWING PAGES: Ruapehu's summit area as seen from Tahurangi col in early summer.

In 1882, Aucklander W. M. Leys Collie published an account of his travels in the *New Zealand Herald*. He knew of a mahogany camera that had been left inside the crater of Ngāuruhoe all winter and he was curious to find out if it was still in one piece. He discovered it to be completely wrecked: 'I came upon it completely spoiled, not from the weather, but the nearest sulphur fumes had blown round a rock to that direction, corroded all the metal work, wrecked the wood, and stained, irremediably, even the ground glass.' Inexplicably, a bag of biscuits had also been left there, and they were (unsurprisingly) found to be soft and bitter from the sulphur. Leys Collie then left a note with the camera with details of his ascents and visits to the crater, and thought it strange that other climbers hadn't come across this and other items — such as, he said, meat tins — when they summited only two years later.[9]

I hoped, as I researched these things, that our insistence on leaving things on sacred summit peaks to mark our existence had become a thing of the past. The more I researched, and the more I walked and thought, the happier I was with the idea that Girdlestone was now undisturbed by a plaque on his head.

A friend told me of her first trip to summit Tahurangi. She had miscarried a baby girl some time earlier, and the grief was ongoing. She stood on the summit with a friend, and suddenly felt something gripping her internally. A white cloud enveloped her, swirled around and departed swiftly. Her companion claimed to have seen no cloud and to have felt nothing. She later wondered if the soul of her baby girl had departed the earth in that moment, going through a portal from Tahurangi as the highest peak in the North Island.

The portal, known as Te Pā-tatau-o-te-rangi (the doorway to the heavens) is actually on an area west of the Crater Lake, in a col or saddle between Paretetaitonga and Te Ataahua, looking out west to Taranaki and down into the Mangaturuturu Glacier. The first time I stood on this area, after climbing up the Whakapapa Glacier and preparing to ski down to Tūroa, I felt as if I was on the edge of the earth itself, reaching out across the green land below, peering out above the clouds. Indeed, it felt like a portal to another dimension.

Writer Melanie Nelson described this in an article for the Federated Mountain Clubs magazine *Backcountry*, in which she interviewed Ngāti Rangi representative Che Wilson: 'Che Wilson described that when people in the greater Whanganui confederation pass away, they don't go to Cape Reinga in the north, but to the peaks of

Mount Ruapehu, and from there to Te Pā-tatau-o-te-rangi, the launchpad or doorway to the heavens,' Nelson wrote. 'They believe there is a vortex, Te Punga-o-ngā-rangi, above Ruapehu which takes them to the heavens where they become a star.'[10]

From earth to stardust, in the vortex of sacred fire.

Did I now really know Ruapehu, after years of researching the mountain, of wandering over his slopes, watching his sunrises and sunsets, and touching his volcanic earth? I felt as though I did, in a way, but there was still so much to discover; Ruapehu was more than summit peaks, but ridges and valleys and streams and bushes and rocks and springs and endless cracks in the space–time continuum containing deep, dark, sacred knowledge. On clear days, I couldn't look away. I felt it was home, found it hard to leave, and always took a sharp breath in when I saw Ruapehu on my way back from a trip away, rounding the corner to suddenly see Koro, faithfully waiting for me to come back to him.

I took solace in the knowledge that George Beetham, fellow lover of Ruapehu, had found it hard to leave, too. He wrote in 1926: 'Now, before returning from the wilds to civilization, I once more gazed on the snow-capped and ice-bound tops of the hoary-headed old mountain and bade it au revoir — not good-bye.'[11]

Tongariro and Ngāuruhoe seen from Ruapehu at sunrise. Mandy Rothe Photography

Notes

Glossary

Select bibliography

Acknowledgements

About the author

Index

Notes

A note on the text

1 Roderick Gray, *Tongariro: The sacred mountain of the Maori* (Digby, Long & Company, 1890), 4.

Introduction

1 George Beetham, *The First Ascent of Mount Ruapehu, New Zealand, and a holiday jaunt to Mounts Ruapehu, Tongariro, and Ngauruhoe* (Harrison and Sons, 1926), 19.
2 Ibid.

Part 1. Earth

1 Susan Graham, *Susan in Springtime* (A.H. & A.W. Reed, 1960), 146.

Chapter 1. The smashed summit stone

1 Dave Bamford, Facebook post, 10 April 2021.
2 Meetings: Girdlestone Memorial. H. E. Anderson, W. Perry, conveners, *New Zealand Times*, 17 January 1921, 3.
3 'Girdlestone Memorial: Tablet in Tongariro Park', *Dominion*, 20 January 1921, 8.
4 'Tongariro National Park: Girdlestone Peak', *Manawatu Times*, 16 April 1921, 7.
5 Republished in 'A Mountain Memorial: Little Matterhorn now Girdlestone Peak', *Dominion*, 16 April 1921, 7.
6 Ibid.
7 Ibid.
8 'Gentian', 'A Memorial in the Mountains: The late H.E. Girdlestone', *Otago Witness*, 16 May 1922, 54.
9 'On Girdlestone Peak: Memorial stone unveiled', *Evening Post*, 18 March 1922, 6.
10 'Gentian', 'A Memorial in the Mountains', 30–31.
11 James Park, 'The Ascent of Ruapehu', *Otago Witness*, 30 May 1922, 54.
12 Gavin McLean, 'Park, James', *Dictionary of New Zealand Biography*, first published 1996, updated November 2010. *Te Ara — the Encyclopedia of New Zealand.* https://teara.govt.nz/en/biographies/3p8/park-james
13 T. Arthur Johnston, 'Tongariro National Park: Girdlestone Peak', *Otago Daily Times*, 28 April 1921, 8.
14 Walter Dunnage, *Appendix to the Journals of the House of Representatives*, 1894 Session I, 70. https://paperspast.natlib.govt.nz/parliamentary/appendix-to-the-journals-of-the-house-of-representatives/1894/I/652
15 'Girdlestone Peak: Climbed in thunderstorm', *Gisborne Times*, 4 January 1927, 5.
16 Roger Mann, 'Slab Avalanche on Ruapehu', *New Zealand Alpine Journal* (1976): 74–75.
17 Ian Young, 'On Girdlestone', *New Zealand Alpine Journal*, 1991, 207–209.
18 Department of Conservation, *Tongariro National Park Management Plan Te Kaupapa Whakahaere mo Te Papa Rēhia o Tongariro 2006–2016*, https://www.doc.govt.nz/documents/about-doc/role/policies-and-plans/national-park-management-plans/tongariro-national-park/tongariro-national-park-management-plan.pdf. This is the current management plan for the park.
19 Tongariro National Park Act 1922, No. 31, Section 15. http://nzlii.org/nz/legis/hist_act/tnpa192213gv1922n31321.pdf
20 'The Sparrow Hawk as a Fighter', *Press*, 7 November 1899, 5.
21 Amanda Gillies, 'Mt Ruapehu Tragedy: Family disappointed they can't fix son's misspelt name on memorial plaque', *Newshub*, 12 August 2022. https://www.newshub.co.nz/home/new-zealand/2022/08/mt-ruapehu-tragedy-family-disappointed-they-can-t-fix-son-s-misspelt-name-on-memorial-plaque.html
22 Melanie Nelson, 'In the Shadow of Ruapehu: A kōrero with Ngāti Rangi leader Che Wilson', *Backcountry* (June 2018): 24–29.
23 'Girdlestone Peak: Memorial slab intact', *Evening Post*, 25 March 1924, 7.

Chapter 2. Secret huts on the southern slopes

1 'Lying Approved: Objector's views. Further cases heard', *Auckland Star*, 3 August 1945, 6.
2 *Tongariro: The Journal of Tongariro National Park*, No. 41, Winter 1991.
3 New Zealand Defence Force (NZDF) Personnel Archives and Medals. File of Leslie John Bergersen. New Zealand Police memorandum, 22 February 1943.
4 NZDF Personnel Archives and Medals. File of Mervyn Stanley Bergersen. New Zealand Military Forces Attestation for Service, 3 June 1941.

5 NZDF file, Mervyn Stanley Bergersen. Correspondence from military major to Wanganui area headquarters, 23 April 1942.
6 'Proceedings Against Defaulters', *Ashburton Guardian*, 10 November 1915, 3.
7 Karoline Tuckey, 'History of Shannon War Camps Uncovered', *Manawatu Standard*, 4 July 2016. https://www.stuff.co.nz/manawatu-standard/news/81697932/history-of-shannon-war-camps-uncovered
8 Ashley Cunningham, 'Memories of the Ohakune Track' (unpublished booklet, 1988).

Chapter 3. Lost on Ruapehu — the Stanton search

1 'Sports in the Snow', *Dominion*, 26 August 1931, 10.
2 'Salt Memorial Hut on Mount Ruapehu Opening This Week', *Hawera Star*, 25 August 1931, 9.
3 'Young Woman's Death', *Star* (Christchurch), 28 August 1931, 1.
4 'Ascent of Ruapehu: A difficult climb', *New Zealand Herald*, 29 August 1931, 10.
5 'J. M. B.', 'For Warwick Stanton: A reminiscence and an appreciation', *Craccum*, Auckland University College, Vol. V, No. 10, 17 September 1931: 3.
6 Susan Graham, *Susan in Springtime* (A.H. & A.W. Reed, 1960), 85–86.
7 'Lost on Ruapehu', *Nelson Evening Mail*, 1 September 1931, 5.
8 Graham, *Susan in Springtime*, 92–93. Paraphrased by the author here.
9 Ibid., 94.
10 'Successful Search', *New Zealand Herald*, 31 August 1931, 10.
11 Graham, *Susan in Springtime*, 97.
12 Ibid., 98.
13 Ibid., 101.
14 Ibid., 105.
15 'Directing Mind', *Auckland Star*, 2 September 1931, 9.
16 Graham, *Susan in Springtime*, 107.
17 '"Hopelessly Astray": Rescued students' stories', *Auckland Star*, 2 September 1931, 9.
18 Graham, *Susan in Springtime*, 87–123.
19 Ibid.
20 Ibid.
21 'Lost on Ruapehu', *Wanganui Chronicle*, 9 September 1931, 8.
22 Graham, *Susan in Springtime*, 117.
23 'Continuous Work', *Auckland Star*, 2 September 1931, 9.
24 'Stanton Still Missing', *Dominion*, 5 September 1931, 9.
25 Ibid.
26 'Search Trebled', *Evening Post*, 3 September 1931, 14.
27 'Inquest on Warwick Stanton', *Horowhenua Chronicle*, 1 October 1931, 3.
28 'Memorial on Ruapehu', *Hawera Star*, 6 September 1933, 9.
29 Today known as Federated Mountain Clubs.
30 'Safeguarding Climbers', *New Zealand Herald*, 3 September 1931, 10.
31 'Still Missing', *Nelson Evening Mail*, 3 September 1931, 7.
32 'Ruapehu Episode', *Northern Advocate*, 3 September 1931, 6.
33 Ibid.
34 'Ruapehu Tragedy', *Waikato Times*, 25 May 1932, 10.
35 'Lost Climber', *Timaru Herald*, 8 September 1931, 9.
36 Letter from Mr Graham Bell to A. Laird, coroner, Taumarunui, 6 October 1931. Sourced from Tongariro National Park Board — Chateau — Blyth Hut Track. Archives New Zealand (Auckland). Ref: R24156983. 1931–1980. Box 268.
37 Jock Graham, *Ruapehu: Tribute to a mountain* (A.H. & A.W. Reed, 1963), 51.
38 W. Robertson and Hon. E. A. Ransom, Department of Lands and Survey. *Public Domains and National Parks of New Zealand (annual report on)*, 1932, 5.
39 'Ruapehu Line Poled', *New Zealand Herald*, 22 March 1932. Sourced from Tongariro National Park Board — Chateau — Blyth Hut Track. Archives New Zealand (Auckland). Ref: R24156983. 1931–1980. Box 268.
40 Letter, T. A. Blyth to W. Robertson, chairman, Tongariro National Park Board, 14 June 1933. Sourced from Tongariro National Park Board — Chateau — Blyth Hut Track. Archives New Zealand (Auckland). Ref: R24156983. 1931–1980. Box 268.
41 'Rescued Climbers at the Chateau: Bridal group', *New Zealand Herald*, 5 September 1931, 8.
42 Graham, *Susan in Springtime*, 13.
43 Alan Graham, 'Biography of John Campbell "Jock" Graham; Biography of Maude Fitzgerald Susan Graham', November 2010. Supplied by Alan Graham, personal communication, 26 July 2023.
44 Graham, *Susan in Springtime*, 146.
45 'J. M. B.', 'For Warwick Stanton'.

Chapter 4. Mangaiti, the hidden hut

1 William Mead, *Memories of a Mountain and a River* (Wanganui Newspapers, 1979), 30.
2 Information in this passage is taken from material held by Archives New Zealand, including History of Mangaiti Hut from 'Ski clubs and lodges — Tongariro Tramping Club (Mangaiti Hut)', R23532699, 1969–1983. The file contains correspondence between Tongariro Tramping Club and the Tongariro National Park Board, and a Department of Lands and Survey memo about the hut from the chief ranger, dated 13 April 1983.
3 Mead, *Memories of a Mountain and a River*, 29–30.
4 Matt Davis, Department of Conservation, statement, 2 May 2024.

Chapter 5. The Dudley rescue

1 Anne Dudley, *Weekend Tramps in the Kaimai Ranges* (Self-published, 2009).
2 Roger Bates, 'Climbing Couple Overdue on Mount Ruapehu', in *Land Search and Rescue in New Zealand 1934–2020* (The Copy Press, 2020), 174–79.
3 '"We'd Have Died" Without Training as Venturers', *Auckland Star*, 18 July 1972, 1.
4 'Mounting Fear for Couple', *Auckland Star*, 13 July 1972, 1.
5 Bryan Dudley, personal communication, 13 July 2023.
6 'Lost Climbers Were Trying Warmth Test', *Auckland Star*, 14 July 1972, 1.
7 'Ruapehu Rescue', *Auckland Star*, 17 July 1972, 1; 30.
8 Bates, 'Climbing Couple Overdue on Mount Ruapehu'.
9 Advertisements column, *Press*, 10 July 1971, 2.
10 'Flights Over Crater Cut', *Press*, 19 May 1971, 1.
11 Ibid.
12 'Team with Doctor Near Holed-up Six', *Auckland Star*, 17 July 1972, 1.
13 Bates, 'Climbing Couple Overdue on Mount Ruapehu', 174–179.
14 Fraser Clark is sometimes referred to as Geoffrey Ian Clark.
15 'Rescuers Reported "in bad shape" After Burial in Snow', *Auckland Star*, 18 July 1972, 1.
16 'Couple Describe Mountain Ordeal', *Press*, 19 July 1972, 3; 'Voice in Snow: Of song, prayer and saviours', *Auckland Star*, 18 July 1972, 1.
17 'Men Rescued from Snow', *Press*, 19 July 1972, 1.
18 Ibid.; 'Rescuers Reported "in bad shape"'.
19 Mark Prebble, personal communication, 1 July 2023.
20 Bates, 'Climbing Couple Overdue on Mount Ruapehu'.
21 John Mazey, Chief Ranger, Tongariro National Park & Field Controller, Search & Rescue Operation. Mr & Mrs Brian & Ann Dudley [sic]. Supplied via personal communication, Mark Prebble, 6 January 2024.
22 Mark Prebble, personal communication, 1 July 2023.
23 Also known on later maps as Dome Equipment Shed; the name was changed to discourage people from staying there. It has also been referred to as Dome Hut.
24 Jock Graham, *Ruapehu: Tribute to a mountain* (A. H. & A. W. Reed, 1963).
25 'Climber Sleeping After Ordeal', *Press*, 31 December 1965, 1.
26 Monika Coles, 'Return to Dome Shelter', *Wilderness*, November 2017. https://www.wildernessmag.co.nz/return-dome-shelter/
27 Frances Ferguson, 'Ruapehu's Historic Shelter to be Removed', *Stuff*, 15 February 2018. https://www.stuff.co.nz/environment/101408329/ruapehus-historic-shelter-to-be-removed
28 'Climbers Lucky to Survive Blizzard', *Press*, 3 September 1971, p. 3.
29 John Mazey, Chief Ranger, Tongariro National Park & Field Controller, Search & Rescue Operation. Mr & Mrs Brian & Ann Dudley [*sic*]. Supplied via personal communication, Mark Prebble, 6 January 2024.
30 Mark Prebble, personal communication, 1 July 2023.

Chapter 6. Hauhungatahi's secret stone

1 Carl Walrond, 'Hunt for the Wilder Places', *New Zealand Geographic*. https://www.nzgeo.com/stories/hunt-for-the-wilder-places/
2 Department of Conservation, *Tongariro National Park Management Plan Te Kaupapa Whakahaere mo Te Papa Rēhia o Tongariro 2006–2016*, 118.
3 Shaun Barnett, 'The D'oh! of Wilderness', in Mich Abbott and Richard Reeve (eds), *Wild Heart: The possibility of wilderness in Aotearoa New Zealand* (Otago University Press, 2011), 21, 33.
4 In Department of Lands (Annual Report), 1909, 45. https://paperspast.natlib.govt.nz/parliamentary/AJHR1909-II.2.2.2.1/4
5 In Robert McNab, *Tongariro National Park (Report of the Board of the)*, 1908. 6. https://paperspast.natlib.govt.nz/parliamentary/AJHR1908-I.2.2.2.13

6 Ibid.
7 Letter, John Cullen to Minister of Justice, Wellington, 'Planting heather on Tongariro National Park and Upper Waimarino Plains', 18 May 1914. Bagnall Collection, Massey University Library.
8 Ibid.
9 'Tucking into Tongariro Heather', Manaaki Whenua Landcare Research. https://www.landcareresearch.co.nz/news/tucking-into-tongariro-heather/. Information also from Graham Bagnall, 'Heather at Tongariro: A study in developing conservation policy', draft text (date unknown). Bagnall Collection, Massey University Library.
10 Greta Stevenson, 'The Three Forest Belts of Hauhungatahi', *Forest and Bird* 197, (1 August 1975), 7–10.

Part 2. Air

1 Ernst Dieffenbach, *Travels in New Zealand* (John Murray, 1843), 363.

Chapter 7. The wreck of the *Kaka*

1 Statement to police. Beth Weedon Gilberd. Undated. Transport Accident Investigation Commission archives.
2 Statement to police. Robert Henry Schofield. Undated. Transport Accident Investigation Commission archives.
3 Statements to police. Barry George McFarlane; Edward Clive Ross; Jack Henry Johns. 18 November, 1948. Transport Accident Investigation Commission archives.
4 'Thirteenth Body Found Under Wing of Wrecked Airliner', *Gisborne Herald*, 2 November 1948, 6.
5 Ibid.
6 'Parts of Airliner *Kaka* Being Taken by Souvenir Hunters', *Wanganui Chronicle*, 19 February 1949, 3.
7 Ibid.
8 'Callous Thieves and Vandals', *Gisborne Herald*, 2 April 1949, 4.
9 'The Air Disaster', *Wanganui Chronicle*, 2 November 1948, 4.
10 Letter, R. G. Phyn to Minister of Civil Aviation, 16 December 1948. Transport Accident Investigation Commission archives.
11 'Boy Finds Diary of *Kaka* Victim', *Northern Advocate*, 31 December 1948, 2.
12 Information about Rod Winchcombe and Ray Christensen's trip to find the wreck comes from: Laurel Stowell, 'Memories of Air Crash Relived by Tramper', *Wanganui Chronicle*, 14 March 2015. https://www.nzherald.co.nz/whanganui-chronicle/news/memories-of-air-crash-relived-by-tramper/XOBPUUPUIFHXCPWTW2YYGACL44/. Rod Winchcombe also appears in *Descent from Disaster*, Season 2, Episode 6, 24 June 2015. Director: Ross Peebles. Ngā Taonga (Wellington), TZP462242: https://ngataonga.org.nz/collections/catalogue/catalogue-item?record_id=624049
13 Otaihape Hut Book, supplied by club member Judith Hamblyn. Personal communication, 20 July 2023.
14 Statement of Constable A. S. Ward, undated. Transport Accident Investigation Commission archives.
15 Ibid.
16 'Lockheeds Christened: Ceremony at Milson', *New Zealand Herald*, 19 October 1938, 17.
17 'Two New Lockheeds Christened: Function at Milson', *Manawatu Times*, 19 October 1938, 6.
18 'Fast Flying *Kaka* Established Record', *Auckland Star*, 22 November 1938, 12.
19 'Air Liner Skidded at Rongotai: No passengers injured', *Wanganui Chronicle*, 19 March 1946, 7.
20 Honourable Sir Harold Featherston Johnston, K. C., *Report of Commission to Inquire into and Report on Treatment of Press Representatives: Kaka Aircraft Disaster. Appendix to the Journals of the House of Representatives*, 1949, Session I, H-37A.
21 Matthew Scott, 'Officials Quietly Handle Ruapehu Skiing Death', *Newsroom*, 2 July 2022. https://www.newsroom.co.nz/officials-quietly-handle-ruapehu-skiing-death
22 'Weather Factors Associated with Flight of ZK-AGK', 23 October 1948. Transport Accident Investigation Commission archives.
23 'Mail Found', *Evening Post*, 3 November 1948. Page unknown. Transport Accident Investigation Commission archives.
24 'Ruapehu Plane Crash Focus of TV Show', *Ruapehu Bulletin*, date unknown.
25 'The Mountain Has Spoken', *New Zealand Geographic* 28 (Oct–Dec 1995). https://www.nzgeo.com/stories/the-mountain-has-spoken/
26 Details on temperature and radius from 'Report on Ruapehu (New Zealand) — September 1995', *Bulletin of the Global Volcanism Network*, Vol. 20, No. 9 (September 1995). https://volcano.si.edu/showreport.cfm?doi=10.5479/si.GVP.BGVN199509-241100

Chapter 8. A plane wreck hidden for decades

1 'Organisation of Rescue', *Press*, 17 December 1951, 6.
2 'Loss of Plane on Ruapehu', *Press*, 24 January 1952, 5.
3 'Like a Nightmare', *Star*, 3 September 1931, 5.
4 Ibid.
5 Williams, 1984, cited in Harry Keys, '1988 Survey of the Glaciers on Mt Ruapehu, Tongariro National Park', Science and Research Internal Report No 24 (July 1988): 11.
6 Brian Leach, 'But for 50 Feet . . .', *NZ Aviation News*, March 2010. Supplied by editor John King, personal communication, 19 January 2022.
7 Air Force Museum of New Zealand: Recovery of crashed Consul aircraft: NZ1902. Letter, Flight Lieutenant Angelo to Chief Conservation Office, Ohakune, 22 September 1988. Department of Conservation archives.
8 Crashed military aircraft of historical interest. Guidance to recovery groups. Ministry of Defence. Date unknown, included with: Air Force Museum of New Zealand, Recovery of crashed Consul aircraft: NZ1902.
9 Air Force Museum of New Zealand: NZ1902 crash site. Letter, Flight Lieutenant R.M. Angelo to Rob McCallum, Department of Conservation, Ohakune, 4 May 1989. Department of Conservation archives.

Chapter 9. A fireball above Te Heuheu peak

1 'Six Die: Ruapehu Crash', *New Zealand Herald*, 22 November 1961, 1. Richard Waugh collection. Includes: 'Guide Has Theory of "Killer" Peak'.
2 'Stretcher Party Battles Ice and Wind', Rotorua, New Zealand, 22 November 1961. Newspaper clipping, publication unknown; Richard Waugh collection.
3 Ibid.
4 Ibid.
5 Eye witnesses' accounts, *Press*, 22 Novemeber 1961, 16.
6 Title unknown, *Otago Daily Times*, 22 November 1961, 1. Richard Waugh collection.
7 Spellings of the men's names vary in the records; Reiser is sometimes spelt Rieser, and Imboden sometimes Ingboden.
8 Publication unknown, Tauranga, 22 November 1961. Richard Waugh collection.
9 Ibid.
10 'Air Crash Victims' Bodies Brought Down from Ruapehu', *Press*, 23 November 1961, 16.
11 Ibid.
12 Ibid.
13 '44-Year Fight to Clear Pilot's Name', *Bay of Plenty Times*, 16 August 2003, 3. Richard Waugh collection.
14 'Before Crash, Plane Had Been Checked'. Publication unknown. Richard Waugh collection.
15 Jock Graham, *Ruapehu: Tribute to a mountain* (A. H. & A. W. Reed, 1963), 49.
16 Cited in Richard Waugh, 'Air Crash Injustice', *NZ Aviation News*, 19 September 2011. Richard Waugh collection.
17 'Ruapehu Crash Caused by Fatigue, Turbulence,' *Press*, 25 November 1961, 10.
18 Cited in Richard Waugh, 'Air Crash Injustice'.
19 'Ruapehu Crash: Investigations by D.S.I.R.', *Press*, 7 December 1961, 13.
20 S. J. Swift, Principal Fatigue Engineer, Civil Aviation Authority, Australia, 'The Aero Commander Chronicle', paper presented at ICAF 95, Melbourne, Australia, May 1995.
21 Richard Waugh, 'Air Crash Injustice'. One propeller went missing after being recovered from the crash site for the purposes of investigation and has never been found.
22 Barbara Morris, personal communication, 18 November 2023.

Chapter 10. A test flight turns to tragedy

1 'Ruapehu Crash Kills Five', *Press*, 11 December 1982, 1.
2 Project Tongariro, 'Our Story'. https://www.tongariro.org.nz/our-story

Part 3. Fire

1 James Cowan, 'The Haunted Whare: A tale of the Tongariro country', *Otago Daily Times*, 30 July 1927, 2.

Chapter 11. The legend of the Haunted Whare

1 James Cowan, `The Haunted Whare: A tale of the Tongariro country', *Otago Daily Times*, 30 July 1927, 2.
2 James Cowan, *The Tongariro National Park of New Zealand: Its topography, geology, alpine and volcanic features, history and Maori folk-lore* (Tongariro National Park Board, 1927), 132–33.
3 Roderick Gray, *Tongariro: The sacred mountain of the Maori* (Digby, Long & Co, 1890), v–vi.
4 Cowan, 'The Haunted Whare', 2.

5 Ibid.
6 Ibid.
7 '"Wind" Romps into Hut', *Wanganui Chronicle*, 11 January 1936, 12.
8 Jack A. Tunnicliffe, 'The Haunted Whare: A true ghost story', *Auckland Star*, 22 August 1934, 16.
9 Cowan, 'The Haunted Whare' *Otago Daily Times*, 2.
10 Warden J. Cullen in W. Robertson and Hon. Frank Langstone, *Department of Lands and Survey. Public Domains and National Parks of New Zealand (Annual Report On)*, 1938, 8.
11 W. Robertson and Hon. Frank Langstone, *Department of Lands and Survey. Public Domains and National Parks of New Zealand (Annual Report on)*, 1936, 6.
12 Tongariro National Park — buildings — Haunted Whare. Archives New Zealand, R24156858.
13 Wendy Hunter Williams, *Out of Mind Out of Sight: The story of Porirua Hospital* (Porirua Hospital, 1987), cited in Karen Williams, 'More Haunted Whare Stories', *Tongariro* (2000): 20.
14 Williams, 'More Haunted Whare Stories', 20.
15 W. Robertson and Hon. Frank Langstone, *Department of Lands and Survey*, 1936, 6.
16 Tongariro National Park — buildings — Haunted Whare, ranger report, 1952, 1. Archives New Zealand, R24156858.
17 C. G. S. Ellis, 'Plan of Tongariro National Park: Showing localities and details of lots mentioned in general specifications' (Lands and Survey Department, 1926). https://ndhadeliver.natlib.govt.nz/delivery/DeliveryManagerServlet?dps_pid=IE366876
18 Tongariro National Park — buildings — Haunted Whare, Archives New Zealand, R24156858.
19 R. W. T., *Roll Back the Years*, Vol. 2, No. 38 (Aug–Sept 1983): 470–71.
20 Christine Williams, 'Tales from the Chateau', *Tongariro: The annual*, Department of Conservation, Vol. 7 (November 1998), 65–68. Richard Waugh collection.

Chapter 12. Te Wai ā-moe Crater Lake

1 'A Close View: Ruapehu eruption', *Nelson Evening Mail*, 14 July 1945, 3.
2 'Trapped on Cliff: Schoolboy's ordeal', *Patea Mail*, 18 August 1937, 3.
3 'Tragedy Avoided: Father of injured man expresses thanks', *Wanganui Chronicle*, 9 July 1945, 4.
4 Ibid.
5 James W. Alexandre, 'The Ruapehu Crater Lake: A little-known thermal phenomenon in the Tongariro National Park, New Zealand', *The Journal of the Royal Astronomical Society of Canada*, Vol. XXV, No. 10 (December 1931).
6 Likely to be Niels Sylow and Karl Sylow based on electoral roll data, but not known for sure.
7 'Crater Lake Swum', *Evening Post*, 9 January 1932, 12.
8 W. Robertson and Hon. E. A. Ransom, *Department of Lands and Survey. Public Domains and National Parks of New Zealand (Annual Report on)*, 1932, 5. https://paperspast.natlib.govt.nz/parliamentary/AJHR1932-I-II.2.2.2.11
9 N. E. Odell, 'Mount Ruapehu, New Zealand', *Alpine Journal* (UK), Vol LX, No. 290 (May 1955), 108–112.
10 George Beetham, *The First Ascent of Mount Ruapehu, New Zealand, and a holiday jaunt to Mounts Ruapehu, Tongariro, and Ngauruhoe* (Harrison and Sons, 1926).
11 Ibid.
12 'Telegraphic News', *New Zealand Mail*, 22 March 1879, 9.
13 Ibid.
14 James Park, Geological Survey Department, 'Narrative of an Ascent of Ruapehu' in *Transactions and Proceedings of the Royal Society of New Zealand*, Volume 19, 1886, Unnumbered Page. Read before the Wellington Philosophical Society, 24 February 1886. https://nzetc.victoria.ac.nz/tm/scholarly/name-208917.html
15 'Ascent of Mount Ruapehu: Crater Lake Frozen, *New Zealand Times*, 31 January 1913, 7; 'Unusual Happening: Crater Lake Frozen', *Manawatu Standard*, 31 August 1926, 3.
16 'Monday, May 27, 1889', *Otago Daily Times*, 27 May 1889, 2.
17 The Reverend Richard Taylor, in his book *Te Ika a Maui* (Wertheim and Macintosh, 1955), describes an avalanche of ice and mud, but this seems to have been accepted as a flood rather than a lahar.
18 Beetham, *The First Ascent of Mount Ruapehu.*
19 Alexandre, 'The Ruapehu Crater Lake', 449.
20 Tongariro and Ruapehu. In a state of eruption. *Opunake Times*, 19 March 1895, 3.
21 Alexandre, 'The Ruapehu Crater Lake', 449.
22 Benedict Friedländer, communicated by T .F. Cheeseman, 'Some Notes on the Volcanoes of the Taupo District', *Transactions and Proceedings of the Royal Society of New Zealand*, Vol. 31 (1898): 508.
23 L. Cockayne, 'Report on a Botanical Survey of the Tongariro National Park', Department of Lands, 1908, 9. https://paperspast.natlib.govt.nz/parliamentary/AJHR1908-I.2.2.2.16
24 Alexandre, 'The Ruapehu Crater Lake', 449.

25 'Mountain Discovery', *Poverty Bay Herald*, 19 March 1937, 12.
26 'Tangiwai Inquiry: Evidence by former chief guide at Chateau', *Press*, 5 March 1954, 10.
27 Ibid.,
28 A. J. D., 'Fumes and Mist in a Crater', *Weekly News*, 16 April 1958 (handwritten date unclear). Bagnall Collection, Massey University Library.
29 Ibid.
30 Jock Graham, *Ruapehu: Tribute to a mountain* (A. H. & A. W. Reed, 1963), 40, 14.
31 Ibid.; Further information in: 'Snow Vehicle on Ruapehu: Transport of skiers', *Press*, 1 September 1961, 20; 'Vehicle Climbs Mt. Ruapehu', *Press*, 22 August 1961, 11.
32 'Ringatoto Pk', Climb NZ. https://climbnz.org.nz/nz/ni/tongariro/mt-ruapehu/ringatoto-pk

Chapter 13. Sly groggers and a booze ban

1 'Faulty Packing: Carrot growers fined', *New Zealand Herald*, 3 October 1936, 18.
2 'Oly Ohakune: A libel on the King Country', *NZ Truth*, 23 November 1907, 4.
3 Megan Cook, 'Māori Smoking, Alcohol and Drugs — Tūpeka, Waipiro Me te Tarukino', *Te Ara — the Encyclopedia of New Zealand*. http://www.TeAra.govt.nz/en/maori-smoking-alcohol-and-drugs-tupeka-waipiro-me-te-tarukino; more information at: https://teara.govt.nz/en/interactive/39869/fighting-to-stay-dry
4 'The Sly Grogger: At work in the King Country', *Waipa Post*, 20 June 1922, 2.
5 'Trade Topics', *New Zealand Illustrated Sporting & Dramatic Review*, 6 September 1900, 18; 'House of Representatives', *Daily Telegraph*, 31 August 1900, 2.
6 'National Prohibition: Results of the polling', *Evening Star*, 11 December 1914, 8.
7 'Life Along the Railway', *Auckland Star*, 4 May 1907, 9.
8 'Police Raid in Ohakune: Liquor seized', *Opunake Times*, 17 December 1909, 2.
9 'The Sly-Grog Seller: Sales to a constable', *Auckland Star*, 20 January 1910, 5.
10 'Continuance Well in Lead', *Evening Post*, 15 November 1928, 13.
11 Untitled, *Waipa Post*, 8 June 1929, 4.
12 Untitled, *Manawatu Times*, 22 April 1908, 4.
13 I have to admit there's no proof he actually said this; I made this bit up. But he probably said something along these lines.
14 'Sly Grog at Ohakune', *Wanganui Chronicle*, 4 October 1907, 7.
15 Michael Kelly, *Ohakune Old Coach Road Conservation Plan* executive summary, Department of Conservation, November 2005, 3.
16 Jim Eagles, 'Ohakune: Historic trail frozen in time', *New Zealand Herald*, 9 February 2010. https://www.nzherald.co.nz/travel/ohakune-historic-trail-frozen-in-time/M3XLMVHGBPR74FRKVFNJLJRJJQ/
17 William Mead, *Memories of a Mountain and a River* (Wanganui Newspapers, 1979), 46–47.
18 'Spelling of Ohakune Correct Without Macron, Ngāti Rangi Chair Says', *Whanganui Chronicle*, 7 August 2019. https://www.nzherald.co.nz/whanganui-chronicle/news/spelling-of-ohakune-correct-without-macron-ngati-rangi-chair-says/WGVU73CHGVCL56TCJODVICGRHA/
19 'There and Back: Along the Main Trunk Line', *Evening Post*, 9 November 1908, 7.
20 'Main Trunk Line', *Waihi Daily Telegraph*, 7 November 1908, 2.

Chapter 14. Joe Blyth's Ohakune Hut

1 John R. Lythgoe, 'The History of Recreation and Development at Turoa, Mt Ruapehu' (PhD thesis, Lincoln College, 1985), appendix III, 94.
2 New Zealand Armed Forces Statement of Service. Thomas Arthur Blyth. Lieutenant, NZ Army. Supplied 13 June 1980 to Graham Bagnall. Bagnall Collection, Massey UniversityLibrary.
3 Lythgoe, 'The History of Recreation and Development at Turoa', appendix III.
4 Ibid., Fig. 45.
5 Ibid., 97.
6 F. A. Charlton, 'A Mountain and a School', in Lythgoe, 'The History of Recreation and Development at Turoa', appendix III, 94. It's possible this quote is by J. A. Blyth — source material unclear.
7 Ashley Cunningham, *Memories of the Ohakune Track* (unpublished booklet, 1988).
8 Ohakune Hut history from Lythgoe, 'The History of Recreation and Development at Turoa, Mt Ruapehu'.
9 Correspondence, Tongariro National Park Board, 17 April 1940. Tongariro National Park Board — Blyth Hut on Ohakune side of Mount Ruapehu. Archives New Zealand, TNP78. R24156945.
10 Cited in Lythgoe, 'The History of Recreation and Development at Turoa, Mt Ruapehu'; see also Letter, R. B. Watson, Secretary, Tongariro National Park Board, to R. Hall, Taihape Venturer Scouts, 30 August 1972.
11 Correspondence between R. A. Whale, Hon. Secretary, Waimarino Deerstalkers Association, and

Chief Ranger John Mazey, May and June, 1970. Tongariro National Park Board — Blyth Hut on Ohakune side of Mount Ruapehu. Archives New Zealand, TNP78. R24156945.

12 Letter, John Mazey to Secretary, Tongariro National Park Board, 9 October 1974. Tongariro National Park Board — Blyth Hut on Ohakune side of Mount Ruapehu. Archives New Zealand, TNP78. R24156945.

13 Blyth Hut replacement, 6 August 1973. Tongariro National Park Board — Blyth Hut on Ohakune side of Mount Ruapehu. Archives New Zealand, TNP78. R24156945.

14 Blyth Hut, 5 April 1974. Tongariro National Park Board — Blyth Hut on Ohakune side of Mount Ruapehu. Archives New Zealand, TNP78. R24156945.

15 Extract from the board meeting held over the period 29 November–1 December 1974. Tongariro National Park Board — Blyth Hut on Ohakune side of Mount Ruapehu. Archives New Zealand, TNP78. R24156945.

16 Karen Hawke Grimwade, *The Ohakune Mountain Road: Yard by yard* (Ruapehu District Council, 2010), 10.

17 Lythgoe, 'The History of Recreation and Development at Turoa, Mt Ruapehu'.

18 Transcribed by Graham Bagnall, Bagnall Collection, Massey University Library.

19 Elsewhere the date of Blyth's death is cited as 6 February 1939; however I take the date on his tombstone to be correct.

20 'Ohakune Pioneer's Memory Fresh After Twenty Year Period'. Date and publication unknown, Bagnall Collection, Massey University Library.

Chapter 15. Skiing Ngāuruhoe

1 Note that some material says the Killy filming occurred in 1974. However, newspapers of the time record it as 1968. See: 'French Ski Star to Visit New Zealand', *Press*, 28 August 1968, 19; 'Films, Wisecracks and Changes . . .', *Press*, 19 August 1982, 31.

2 'Ngauruhoe Erupts', *Press*, 20 August 1968, 1.

3 Carla Hay, Review: 'Ski Bum: The Warren Miller Story', starring Warren Miller, 28 February 2021. https://culturemixonline.com/tag/gary-nate/

4 Quotes and information from Warren Miller, 'Outskiing a Volcano', 26 November 2010. https://skitheworld.com/2010/11/outskiing-a-volcano; Warren Miller, 'Dumb Is as Dumb Does', *Ski* (January 2006): 144; Warren Miller, 'Warren's World: Travels with Jean-Claude', *Ski* (31 January 2018), 144. https://www.skimag.com/ski-resort-life/travels-with-jean-claude/

5 Paul Green, personal communication, 4 July 2023.

6 Laura Williamson, '*Flare — A Ski Trip*: A NZ Ski Film by Sam Neill'. https://1964.co.nz/flare/. See also *Flare: A Ski Trip*, Archives New Zealand. https://www.youtube.com/watch?v=q2qeHP1Pz1w and https://www.ngataonga.org.nz/search-use-collection/search/F7514/

7 'Films, Wisecracks and Changes . . .', *Press*, 19 August 1982, 31.

8 J. C. Bidwill, *Rambles in New Zealand* (W. S. Orr, 1841).

9 Ernst Dieffenbach, *Travels in New Zealand* (John Murray, 1843), 346–47. Among iwi the whole range is sometimes referred to as Tongariro, and sometimes Ngāuruhoe is referred to as Tongariro.

10 Ferdinand Hochstetter, *New Zealand: Its physical geography, geology and natural history, with special reference to . . . the provinces of Auckland and Nelson* (J.G. Cotta, 1867), 363.

11 Cited by Dr Ferdinand Hochstetter, 'Lecture on the geology of the province of Auckland', Delivered to the Members of the Auckland Mechanics' Institute, 24 June 1859, *Auckland Provincial Gazette*, 3 August 1859, 1.

12 Miri Schroeter, 'Trampers Told Not to Climb Tongariro Crossing's Mount Doom', *Stuff*, 16 October 2017. https://www.stuff.co.nz/manawatu-standard/news/97909833/trampers-told-not-to-climb-tongariro-crossings-mount-doom

13 National Parks Act 1980, Section 4.

Part 4. Water

1 H. Hill, F. G. S., 'Ruapehu: Retrospect and prospect', *New Zealand Alpine Journal*, Vol. II, No. 8 (October 1895): 82.

Chapter 16. Disappearing ice

1 Ludwig Krenek, 'The Mountains of Central Lahul', *The Himalayan Journal*, No. 13 (1946). https://www.himalayanclub.org/hj/13/5/the-mountains-of-central-lahul/

2 Steve Krenek, 'Why I Am a New Zealander, Not an Austrian', personal communication, 8 August 2023.

3 Source material on Krenek and Kolb: Ludwig Krenek. 'Lahul Expedition 1939', *Alpine Journal* (UK), Vol. LII (May 1940): 135; 'Shorter Notices', *The Geographical Journal*, Vol. 126, No. 1 (March 1960): 106; Jonathan Westaway, 'Lithanamnesis: Isolation, memory and longing in mountaineering narratives by POWs in World War Two', *Literary Geographies*, Vol. 6, No. 2 (2002): 235–38; Fritz

Kolb, *Himalaya Venture* (Lutterworth Press,1 959); Jeffrey S. Kargel, Gregory J. Leonard, Michael P. Bishop, Andreas Kääb and Bruce H. Raup (eds), *Global Land Ice Measurements from Space* (Praxis Publishing, 2014).
4 Ludwig Krenek, 'Changes in the Glaciers of Mt Ruapehu in 1955', *New Zealand Journal of Geology and Geophysics*, Vol. 2, No. 4 (1959): 643–53.
5 Ibid.
6 Cited in Noel Odell, 'Mount Ruapehu, New Zealand: Observations on its Crater Lake and Glaciers', *Journal of Glaciology*, Vol. 18, No. 2 (1955): 601–05.
7 Ibid.
8 Mike paid me to write that.
9 'The Waikato River', *New Zealand Herald*, 6 March 1928, 11.
10 'Ruapehu's Mystery: Crater lake now cold', *Evening Post*, 19 May 1926, 14.
11 This section was originally published as a story in *Wilderness*: Hazel Phillips, 'Finding Lake Madness', *Wilderness* (March 2019). https://www.wildernessmag.co.nz/finding-lake-madness/
12 Sue Miles (text) and Geoff Moon (photographs), *The River: The story of the Waikato* (Pearson Education, 1984).
13 'Scaling Everest', *Thames Star*, 1 September 1925, 6.
14 'Voices from the Past', Lost on Everest. https://www.pbs.org/wgbh/nova/everest/lost/mystery/voices.html#hillary
15 'No More Climbing', *Ashburton Guardian*, 7 July 1924, 5.
16 Bernard Gunn, 'Noel Ewart Odell, 1890–1987', *New Zealand Alpine Club Journal* (1987): 133–34.
17 Noel Odell, 'Mount Ruapehu, New Zealand', 601–605.
18 '"Lazy Attitude" in N.Z.', *Press*, 10 May 1952, 2.
19 Benedict Friedländer, 'Some Notes on the Volcanoes of the Taupo District, Communicated by T. F. Cheeseman', *Transactions and Proceedings of the Royal Society of New Zealand*, Vol. 31 (1898): 506.
20 A. J. Heine, 'Mount Ruapehu Ice and Snow Photo Survey', *New Zealand Journal of Geology and Geophysics*, Vol. 6, No. 2 (1963): 261–67.
21 'Caught in Avalanche: Skier Relates Escape', *Press*, 20 August 1957, 14.
22 Ibid.
23 Harry Keys, '1988 Survey of the Glaciers on Mt Ruapehu, Tongariro National Park: A baseline for detecting effects of climate change', *Science and Research Internal Report* No. 24 (July 1988). Unpublished.
24 'Glaciers on Ruapehu Volcano', Glaciers online, SwissEdu. https://www.swisseduc.ch/glaciers/new_zealand/ruapehu/index-en.html
25 Harry Keys, 'The Mallowpuff Project', *Tongariro* (2006): 26.
26 N. E. Odell, 'Mount Ruapehu, New Zealand', *Alpine Journal (UK)*, (1955): 108–12.

Chapter 17. Holl's Rock

1 'South East Buttress', Climb NZ. https://climbnz.org.nz/nz/ni/tongariro/mt-ruapehu/girdlestone-pk/south-east-buttress
2 'Unique Experience on Mountain', *Dominion*, 4 January 1927, 8.
3 J. W. Alexandre, 'The Ruapehu Crater Lake', *Journal of the Royal Astronomical Society of Canada*, Vol. 25 (1931): 433.
4 'Intrepid Alpinist', *New Zealand Herald*, 30 May 1927, 8.
5 William Mead, *Memories of a Mountain and a River* (Wanganui Newspapers, 1979), 17.
6 Richard Thomson, *Tongariro: A Climbing Guide to Tongariro National Park: Summer and winter alpine routes, ski-mountaineering and rock climbing* (New Zealand Alpine Club, 2006).
7 Graham Langton, 'Horace Holl: Mountaineer and Tongariro pioneer', *NZ Alpine Journal* (1999): 112–14.
8 Will of Horace Arthur Holl – Auckland – Schoolmaster, 15 December 1920. Archives New Zealand, R9380936.
9 Thomson, *Tongariro*, 134–35.
10 Jock Graham, *Ruapehu: Tribute to a mountain* (A. H. & A. W. Reed, 1963), 50.
11 Eric H. Burton, 'Is Ruapehu Dangerous?', *Auckland Star*, 4 September 1931, 6.
12 Alan Mason, 'Bartrum, John Arthur', *Dictionary of New Zealand Biography*, first published in 1998. *Te Ara — the Encyclopedia of New Zealand*. https://teara.govt.nz/en/biographies/4b10/bartrum-john-arthur
13 'Story of Death on Mt. Ruapehu', *Star*, 1 June 1927, 4.
14 Coroner's inquest report for Holl, Horace Arthur, 1927. Case files, Archives New Zealand, R23841449.
15 Ibid.
16 Other source material: 'Well-Known Climber Swept Off Feet and Drowned on Slopes of Ruapehu',

Star, 30 May 1927, 9; 'Popular Rambler Swept to Death', *Sun*, 30 May 1927, 1; 'Accidentally Drowned', *Sun*, 31 May 1927, 13.

17 Coroner's inquest report for Holl, Horace Arthur, 1927. Case files, Archives New Zealand, R23841449.

18 'Amid the Snows', *Wanganui Chronicle*, 6 June 1927, 3.

19 John R. Lythgoe, 'The History of Recreation and Development at Turoa, Mt Ruapehu' (PhD thesis, Lincoln College, 1985), Fig. 42.

20 'Story of Death on Mt. Ruapehu'.

Chapter 18. The mauri of the maunga

1 H. E. Girdlestone, *Department of Lands (Annual Report on)*, 'Appendix IV. The mountains of the Tongariro National Park', 25 May 1909, 42.

2 'Tongariro Alpine Crossing: History and culture', Department of Conservation. https://www.doc.govt.nz/parks-and-recreation/places-to-go/central-north-island/places/tongariro-national-park/things-to-do/tracks/tongariro-alpine-crossing/

3 'Walks in and around Tongariro National Park', Department of Conservation, November 2022, 6. https://www.doc.govt.nz/globalassets/documents/parks-and-recreation/tracks-and-walks/tongariro-taupo/tongariro-national-park-walks.pdf

4 Colin Richards, Pahake, Marangai Pā, Ngāti Rangi, Whanganui Iwi mai i Te Kāhui Maunga ki Tangaroa, in Āneta Hinemihi Rāwiri (ed.), *Mouri Tū Mouri Ora: Water for wisdom and life. Ngāti Rangi, the Tongariro Power Scheme, and the Resource Management Act 1991: Reconciling indigenous spiritual wellbeing, corporate profit, and the national interest.* (Te Atawhai o te Ao, Independent Maori Institute for Environment and Health, 2009), 15.

5 Ibid.

6 'Move to Save Blue Duck', *Press*, 25 March 1988, 14.

7 William Mead, *Memories of a Mountain and a River* (Wanganui Newspapers, 1979), 23–24.

8 S. Percy Smith, *Department of Lands and Survey (Annual Report on)*, 31 March 1897, vii.

9 S. Percy Smith, *Department of Lands and Survey (Annual Report on)*, 31 March 1898, 9.

10 Liz Brooker and Tony Wall, 'The Ruapehu Skifield Spill: A community's anger', *Stuff*, 24 May 2015. https://www.stuff.co.nz/national/68729679/the-ruapehu-skifield-spill-a-communitys-anger

11 Media reported 15,000 litres however a study later done cited 17,000 litres. Frances B. Michaelis, 'Effect of Turoa Oil Spill on Aquatic Insects in the Mangawhero River System', *New Zealand Entomologist*, Vol. 7, No. 4 (1983).

12 'Big Oil Spill Raetihi, Water Shut Off', *Ruapehu Guardian*, 19 December 1979, 1; 'Raetihi Water Cut by Diesel Spill', publication unknown, 13 December 1979, Bagnall Collection, Massey University Library.

13 Ibid.

14 Michaelis, 'Effect of Turoa Oil Spill on Aquatic Insects in the Mangawhero River System'.

15 A. D. R. Wright, Company Manager, Turoa Skifields, *Turoa Report on Oil Spill*, 1979, 6.

16 Williams' forename is spelled variously Brian and Bryan in documents accessed at Archives New Zealand.

17 Communication to wildlife conservator, Rotorua, from Bryan Williams, field officer, 27 March 1979, Archives New Zealand.

18 Inspection on 5 April 1979, further communication, 11 April 1979. Communication to Mr D. Johns, technical manager, Turoa Ski Fields, from R. Jackson, inspector of explosives for district superintendent, 11 April 1979, Archives New Zealand.

19 Communication to wildlife conservator, Rotorua, from Bryan Williams, field officer, 27 March 1979, Archives New Zealand.

20 Brooker and Wall, 'The Ruapehu Skifield Spill'.

21 Ngāti Rangi Claims Settlement Act 2019, Section 59. https://www.legislation.govt.nz/act/public/2019/0040/latest/LMS48219.html

22 Ngāti Rangi Deed of Statutory Acknowledgement, 13–14.

23 Richards, in *Mouri Tū Mouri Ora*, 15.

24 Quoted in *Mouri Tū Mouti Ora*, 7.

Part 5. Aether

1 The full quote reads: Violators of the tapu who incurred the anger of these mysterious beings were sometimes seized suddenly and borne off to unknown enchanted regions; sometimes they were kept under fairy spells for indefinite periods.

2 E. S. Dollimore F. R. G. S. (ed), *Folk Lore of the Mountains: Handbook of the Tongariro National Park* (The National Parks Authority, 1953). Lands and Survey Department, Department of Conservation archives, ref A1197318.

Chapter 19. Missing climbers on Mitre Peak

1 'Search for Missing Boy to Resume This Morning', *Press*, 3 December 1985, 8.
2 The name is spelled in various ways, such as Lehrner, Lerner, Leaner. The most common on record is Lehner.
3 'Search for Climber', *Press*, 23 April 1957, 10.
4 Information on the Lehner search also taken from 'Youth Lost on Ruapehu', *Press*, 22 April 1957, 10; 'Ruapehu Search Revived', *Press*, 29 April 1957, 8; 'Ruapehu Search Abandoned', *Press*, 30 April 1957, 14.
5 James Cowan, *The Tongariro National Park, New Zealand: Its topography, geology, alpine and volcanic features, history and Maori folk-lore* (Tongariro National Park Board, 1927).
6 Coroner's Report, Arthur William Olsen, 18 September 1978. Official Information Act request, June 2023.
7 Ibid.
8 'Snow Traps Motorists', *Dominion*, 7 June 1977, 1.
9 Coroner's Report, Arthur William Olsen.
10 Ibid.
11 'Ruapehu Search Called Off', *Press*, 11 June 1977, 1.
12 'Searchers Abandon Hope', *Dominion*, 11 June 1977, 1.
13 From the coroner's report, which is typed but with amendments in handwriting. Original typed text says: 'At some stage the rope had either broken or been deliberately untied by Morrison . . .', and the words 'had either broken or' have been crossed out with the initials of Gosman, and the word 'loosened' has been substituted for 'untied'.
14 Ibid.
15 Interview with Graeme Dingle, 13 July 2023.
16 Personal communication, Brin Williman and Mark Prebble, 5 July 2023.
17 Coroner's Report, Arthur William Olsen.
18 Will of Olsen Arthur William, 1978. Archives New Zealand, R23084380. https://collections.archives.govt.nz/web/arena/search#/entity/aims-archive/R23084380/olsen-arthur-william?q=olsen+arthur+william&source=aims-archive

Chapter 20. Te Onetapu — the Sacred Sands

1 Review of James Cowan's book *The Tongariro National Park, New Zealand*, in 'Book of the Week: Ruapehu's story', *Taranaki Daily News*, 5 September 1931, 17.
2 Ngāti Rangi Statutory Acknowledgements. https://www.horizons.govt.nz/HRC/media/Media/Iwi%20and%20Hapu/Ngati-Rangi-Statutory-Acknowledgements.pdf
3 *Ancient History of the Maori*, Vol VIII, 1855. https://www.folksong.org.nz/waiouru_history/7_polynesia/index.html
4 E. S. Dollimore F. R. G. S. (ed), *Folk Llore of the Mountains: Handbook of the Tongariro National Park* (The National Parks Authority, 1953). Lands and Survey Department. Department of Conservation archives, ref A1197318.
5 Sometimes written as Te Pātatau o te Rangi.
6 Ngāti Rangi and the Crown, 'Agreement in Principle to Settle Historical Claims', 15 March 2017, 15. https://assets.prod.ngatirangi.com/2017_0315_ngati_rangi_draft_aip_printed_3a59c9c009_35a9d11393.pdf
7 Ibid.
8 James Cowan, *The Tongariro National Park, New Zealand: Its topography, geology, alpine, volcanic features, history and Maori folk-lore*, (Tongariro National Park Board, 1927), 77–78.
9 David Mackay, 'Colenso, William', *Dictionary of New Zealand Biography*, first published in 1990. Te Ara — The Encyclopedia of New Zealand. https://teara.govt.nz/en/biographies/1c23/colenso-william.
10 William Colenso F. L. S., 'Memorandum of a journey into the interior, in which succeeded in crossing the Ruahine mountain range, with notes on the peculiar local botany of that region, etc.' Read before the Hawke's Bay Philosophical Institute, 14 October 1878, 40–42. https://nzetc.victoria.ac.nz/tm/scholarly/tei-Stout65-t14-body-d2.html
11 Ibid.
12 Ibid.
13 Dollimore, *Folk Lore of the Mountains*.
14 George Allen, 'Ruapehu's Activity, Wanganui, July 20, 1886', *Wanganui Chronicle*, 21 July 1886, 3.
15 Ngāti Rangi Statutory Acknowledgements, Horizons Regional Council, undated, 19.
16 I. A. E. Atkinson, 'Recommendations for Additions to Tongariro National Park', Department of Scientific and Industrial Research (DSIR), 18 July 1979, 8. Department of Conservation archives, ref A1226898; I. A. E. Atkinson, 'Unique scientific areas of Tongariro National Park', unpublished DSIR report, 1964.
17 Ngāti Rangi Claims Settlement Act 2019, Section 9(25).
18 Ngāti Rangi and the Crown, 'Agreement in principle to settle historical claims', 15 March 2017, 25.

Chapter 21. Searching for Goatman

1 Goatman information from 'The Goatman', Mark Wallbank, Paranormal New Zealand. https://hauntedauckland.com/site/goatman/ and Facebook page 'Feels like home bro', 29 July 2018. https://www.facebook.com/feelslikehomebro/posts/1625412717588203/

Chapter 22. The water vortex of Rotopounamu

1 'Mt Wakefield — Holy Mountain', The Aetherius Society. https://www.aetherius.org.nz/about/holy-mountains/mt-wakefield/
2 Robert Coon, 'Earth Chakras'. https://www.earthchakras.org/page-3/
3 'Scenic Reserve Near Turangi', *Press*, 3 December 1965, 3.
4 'Trips by Branches to Ruapehu Lodge', *Forest and Bird* (1 May 1968): 18; 'Rotoiti Lodge Opened in Nelson Lakes National Park', *Forest and Bird* (1 May 1968): 9; *Tongariro National Park Management Plan Te Kaupapa Whakahaere mo Te Papa Rēhia o Tongariro 2006–2016* (Department of Conservation, October 2006), 67.
5 Ian Kusabs and Dave Rowe, 'Taonga and Mahinga Kai of the Te Arawa Lakes: A review of current knowledge — Koaro', National Institute of Water and Atmospheric Research report, July 2007. https://niwa.co.nz/sites/niwa.co.nz/files/te_arawa_species_report_koaro_0.pdf
6 Ernst Dieffenbach, *Travels in New Zealand* (John Murray, 1843), 360.
7 Dave Lumley, manager, Turangi Field Centre, Tongariro (1994): 7, reproduced in 'The Rotopounamu Gurgler', *Tongariro: The annual*, 41.
8 Ibid.

Chapter 23. Skull on a summit

1 Geoffrey Darling, 'Rare Skull Find on Mt Ruapehu', *Ruapehu Press*, 21 February 2002.
2 Ibid.
3 Forensics Report, Institute of Environmental Science & Research Limited (ESR). Author anonymous — redacted for privacy reasons. ESR reference WSC02472, Ruapehu Skull 020218/8636. 28 March 2002. Official Information Act request.
4 Park's account is found in: James Park, Geological Survey Department, 'Narrative of an Ascent of Ruapehu'. Read before the Wellington Philosophical Society, 24 February 1886. *Transactions and Proceedings of the Royal Society of New Zealand*, Vol. 19 (May 1887). https://nzetc.victoria.ac.nz/tm/scholarly/name-208917.html.
5 Park calls the highest peak Paretetaitonga, not Tahurangi, but here I have adopted the naming as it currently stands to avoid confusion.
6 This is my assumption; Park writes that they took the 'north-east approach' to the mountain, which would indicate they were attempting to ascend via the Wahianoa Glacier.

Chapter 24. Peak obsession

1 John Wilson, 'Mountaineering', *Te Ara — the Encyclopedia of New Zealand*. http://www.TeAra.govt.nz/en/mountaineering/print
2 Nic Low, 'Following historic routes through the Southern Alps', *Nine to Noon*, RNZ, 25 June 2021. https://www.rnz.co.nz/national/programmes/ninetonoon/audio/2018801289/nic-low-following-historic-routes-through-the-southern-alps
3 Hugh Strutfield, 'Mountaineering as a Religion', *Alpine Journal* 32 (1918): 241–47.
4 H. Hill, F. G. S., in 'Ruapehu: Retrospect and prospect', *New Zealand Alpine Journal*, Vol. II, No. 8 (October 1895): 8–14.
5 James Park, Geological Survey Department, 'Narrative of an Ascent of Ruapehu', Read before the Wellington Philosophical Society, 24 February 1886. *Transactions and Proceedings of the Royal Society of New Zealand*. Vol. 19 (May 1887). https://nzetc.victoria.ac.nz/tm/scholarly/name-208917.html. Also in James Park, *The Life and Times of James Park* (Geoscience Society of New Zealand, 2017). https://gsnz.org.nz/assets/Uploads/Shop/Products/MP144_James_Park/MP144_2017_Life_and_times_James_Park.pdf
6 *Nelson Evening Mail*, 3 April 1903, 1.
7 The school was renamed Whanganui Collegiate School in 2019.
8 'Up Ruapehu and How to Get There', *Hawke's Bay Herald*, 1890.
9 'Ngauruhoe: Narrative of excursions to the great volcano', *New Zealand Herald*, 18 February 1882, 6.
10 Melanie Nelson, 'In the Shadow of Ruapehu: A kōrero with Ngāti Rangi leader Che Wilson', *Backcountry* (June 2018): 24–27. https://melanienelson.co.nz/wp-content/uploads/sites/201/2021/09/In-the-shadow-of-Ruapehu-1.pdf.
11 George Beetham, *The First Ascent of Mount Ruapehu, New Zealand, and a holiday jaunt to Mounts Ruapehu, Tongariro, and Ngauruhoe* (Harrison and Sons, 1926), 19.

Glossary

alpenstock	A long walking stick with a metal spike at the bottom, used before ice axes.
arête	A narrow ridge of rock that separates two valleys.
belay	Using a rope in case of a fall.
beta	Information about a climb or route.
buff	A neck scarf, used to stop heat escaping, or as a beanie or headband.
choss	Crumbling rock, often found in New Zealand mountains.
col	A saddle between two peaks or higher points.
downwasting	Thinning of a glacier due to melting of ice. A glacier retreats horizontally but downwastes vertically.
gendarme	A rock pinnacle or outcrop on a ridge that prevents easy access.
gunnysack	A sack made from rough fibre, also known as a hessian sack or a burlap sack.
lahar	Volcanic material and water, usually released in an eruption, which flows from the eruption zone and typically down a valley. On Ruapehu, a lahar comes from the Crater Lake.
névé	The upper part of a glacier, usually consisting of hardened snow rather than glacial ice.
permolat	Material used to make venetian blinds, which used to be used as track markers in New Zealand.
quickdraws, slings	Technical climbing gear.
skinning	Ascending on snow using skins, which are placed on the bottom of skis for grip and traction.
spot height	A height marked on a topographical map but not named.
tephra	Volcanic material produced in an eruption.
true right/left	On the right/left side of a watercourse when looking downstream.

Select bibliography

Bamford, Dave. *The Boys from Waipu*. Self-published, 2020.

Beetham, George. *The First Ascent of Mount Ruapehu, New Zealand, and a holiday jaunt to Mounts Ruapehu, Tongariro, and Ngauruhoe*. Harrison and Sons, 1926.

Cowan, James. *The Tongariro National Park of New Zealand*. Tongariro National Park Board, 1927.

Debreceny, Peter (ed.). *The Restless Land: The story of Tongariro National Park*. Department of Lands and Survey, 1981.

Harris, Ralph. *Recollections of Ruapehu: Tongariro National Park in the 1950s*. Self-published, 2011. ISBN: 978-0-473-19844-2.

George, Merrilyn. *Ohakune: Opening to a new world*. Kapai Enterprises, 1990.

Graham, Alan. *Ruapehu: 100 years of skiing*. Balasoglou Books, 2013.

Graham, Jock. *Ruapehu: Tribute to a mountain*. Reed, 1963.

Graham, Susan. *Susan in Springtime*. Reed, 1960.

Gray, Roderick. *Tongariro: The sacred mountain of the Maori*. Digby, Long & Company, 1890.

Lythgoe, John R. *The History of Recreation and Development at Turoa, Mt Ruapehu*. Lincoln College, 1985.

Mazey, John. 'Sheep Farming Tongariro District 1855–1918'. Unpublished dissertation, Lincoln University College, Canterbury, undated.

Mead, William. *Memories of a Mountain and a River*. Wanganui Newspapers, 1979.

Williams, Karen. *Volcanoes of the South Wind: A volcanic guide to Tongariro National Park*. Random House, 2013.

Williams, Karen and Dave Bamford. *Skiing on the Volcano: Historical images of skiing on Mount Ruapehu*. Ruapehu Alpine Lifts & Tourism Resource Consultants, 1987.

The author in the South Crater with Ngāuruhoe behind. Mike Heydon

Acknowledgements

Thanks to Massey University Press publisher, Nicola Legat, for seeing the merit in *Fire & Ice*, and to the MUP team for bringing it to life. Thanks to Anna Bowbyes, editor Susan Brierley, project editor Anna Jackson-Scott, proofreader Tracey Lowndes and indexer Diane Lowther. Thanks to Lisa Moes (@ lovethyland) for her beautiful, vintage-inspired cover illustration and Megan van Staden for the design.

I am indebted to the early readers of the manuscript for their time, thoughtful feedback and attention to detail: Dave Bamford, Paul Hersey, Harry Keys and Penelope Whitson. Thanks also to Dave and Harry for lending me valuable research material, books and documents.

Many others also read through sections of the text, gave feedback and checked it for accuracy: Eleanor Arnst, Lois Cooper, Graeme Dingle, Bryan and Anne Dudley, Jane Dudley, Alan Graham, Paul Green, Bruce Jeffries, Graham Langton, Barbara Morris, Mark Prebble, Conrad Smith and Brin Williman.

I am grateful for research help from Judith Hamblyn (Otaihape Ski Club), Austin Hutcheon (Taupo Tramping Club), John King (*NZ Aviation News*), Pauline Knuckey (Massey University Library), Hugh McKeesick (Taupo Tramping Club), Kaye Rabarts, Dave Scoullar (Wanganui Tramping Club), Ron Thomas, Dave Wilton and Pete Zimmer. Particular thanks to aviation historian Richard Waugh for trusting me with his archives and reading over draft material.

Thanks to Jeff Bergersen and Susan Pulman for their help researching the lives of their relatives — Jeff's father Merv Bergersen and Susan's grandfather Les Bergersen, and to Steve and Gita Krenek for research help and photos of their incredible dad Ludwig Krenek.

Several departments and organisations were instrumental in providing information and research help: Archives New Zealand, the Department of Conservation (Will Brocklesby), National Library of New Zealand, New Zealand Police (Sonia Bauerfeind) and the Transport Accident Investigation Commission.

Thanks to Mike Heydon for his striking images of Ruapehu, Tongariro and Ngāuruhoe, and to Carl Thurston at ChopperWorx Taupō for giving us permission to use them. Thanks also to Conrad Smith/Alpine Jesus for his stunning image of the Whakapapanui Stream, and Peter Laurenson/The Occasional Climber for his striking image of Whangaehu Hut.

Ngā mihi nui to the iwi of Tongariro National Park for their kōrero: Korty Wilson from Ngāti Rangi, Bubs Smith from Ngāti Tūwharetoa and Aiden Gilbert from Uenuku.

This book mentions many people who lost their lives in Tongariro National Park. I trust that any surviving family and whānau of the deceased will know that I have considered the lives and stories of their loved ones with the utmost respect and regard.

This book was supported by grants from Tūpiki Trust, New Zealand Alpine Club's DOW Hall fund and Ruapehu District Council. I was awarded a 2024 residency at the Michael King Writers Centre in Devonport, Auckland, and the time and space was instrumental in finishing the final draft for submission. I am grateful to these organisations for their support.

Thanks to everyone who contributed to the crowdfunding campaign to cover production costs for the book: Megan Arden, Lisa Arthur, Naomi Arnold, Chris Auld, Brian Bannister, Stew and Rob Barclay, Amy Barnes, Luke Benefield, Mr Biscuits Whitson-Smith, Garth Boggiss, Matt Britton, Philip and Helen Browne, Jacqui C, Scott Campbell, Andrew Carleton-Brown, Tim Carpenter, Patrick Caudle, Fleur Chalk, Cheese McCheese, Jane Cherrington, Rhoda Chignall, Slasher and Percy Chirnside, Stuart Clark, Diana Clement, Marie Clotworthy, William Cohen, Amanda Collins, Ian Collins, Louise Conville, Lucy Conway, Owen Cotton, Dion Cruse, Mal Dawson, Dennis de Monchy, Orla Drylie, David Eaton, Michelle Ebbett, Simon Edmonds, Rob Eller, Terry Fenn, Cara Fergusson, Sue Foley, David Forsyth, Catherine Gafa, Annabelle Gibb, Janina Gillies, Dori Gillming, Fiona Gilmour, Esther Goh, Pablo Gomes Ludermir, Joanna Greig, Saarah Gul, David H, Alistair Hall, Judith Hamblyn, Lisa Hart, Sally Heppenstall, Marie Hessey, Greg Holland, Travis Holman, Leigh Hopkinson, Margaret Huggins, Harriet Jackson, Peter James, Alpine Jesus, Mitchell Job, Aly Learmonth, James Littlejohn, Little Red Hen, John Lyttle, Mac Madsen, Malcolm Team Xtreme, Rachel Mariu, Ben McKay, Lachlan McKenzie, Kerri McMaster, Jo Merson, Richard Neeson, Jan Nisbet, Sharon Noyce, Elliott O'Brien, Suzanne Oliver, Marie Parsloe, Stephen Prendergast, Jacob Pynenburg, Jacki Ramson, Tim Robertson, Kelda Robinson, Mandy Rothe, Sue Rowe, Conor Rutherford, Kiri Saul, Anais Schanzel, Deborah Shaw, Vonney Silvester, Kerry Sinclair, Bill Smugs, Papa Smurf, Julie Spiers, Amy Stonestreet, Grace Stratton, Dean Stringer, Aaron Tasker, Will Them, Emma Therese, Neroli Thomson, Jess Thompson, Rob Thompson, Shell Tomlin, Jesse Turner, Sarah Vaz, Mel Weddell, Whakapapa Mount Ruapehu, Janette Williams, Rissa Williams, Murray Wilson, Virginia Winstone, Ray Wong, Glen Young and Claudia Zimmer, and Anonymous, who donated repeatedly. Without you, it wouldn't have happened.

An extensive hug to my friends and family for tolerating my obsession with Ruapehu and Tongariro over the past few years and patiently allowing themselves to be either the target of a monologue about what I'd just discovered, or a victim of a trip in the wilderness, many of which were wild goose chases: Conrad Smith, David Forsyth and Maria Niva (just a couple of river crossings!), Emma Gregg, 'Henry', Howie Nicholson, Ken Mercer, Lois Cooper, Jeremy Hamer, Mac Madsen, Mandy Rothe, Mike Heydon, Papa Smurf, Pete Hart, Preston Hatcher and Toby. Credit to Garth Boggiss for taking the time to vacuum-pack Mallowpuffs and plunge them to 40 metres in Lake Taupō in the name of science. Thanks to Hayden Ricketts, Dion and Brian Cruse, and Arron and Victoria for housing me while on various research trips.

Last but never least, to my Alpine Potato, for listening to me rabbit on and enthusiastically embracing my ideas for silly adventures. P. S. — that's us on the cover.

About the author

Hazel Phillips is a Ruapehu-based writer and outdoors enthusiast. She has published three previous books, including *Solo: Backcountry adventuring in Aotearoa New Zealand* (Massey University Press, 2022), a New Zealand nonfiction bestseller. Hazel holds a Master of Creative Writing with first-class honours, with a creative thesis that explored fundamentalism and rigid thinking. She is usually found somewhere near a mountain or a lake, and she is passionate about bringing the history of our wilderness spaces to life through storytelling and contemporary narratives. In her spare time she enjoys multi-day tramping, skiing, ski touring, mountaineering, mountain biking and scuba diving. Her writing pursuits have so far caused her to wear out eight keys on her laptop keyboard.

Index

Page numbers in **bold** refer to images.

M

N

O

P

R

S

T

U

V

W

Y

MASSEY UNIVERSITY PRESS

First published in 2025 by Massey University Press
Private Bag 102904, North Shore Mail Centre
Auckland 0745, New Zealand
www.masseypress.ac.nz

Design by Megan van Staden
Cover artwork by Lisa Nicole Moes, International Rescue
Map on page 5 by Lisa Nicole Moes, International Rescue

A catalogue record for this book is available from
the National Library of New Zealand

Printed and bound in China by 1010 Printing Asia Limited
ISBN: 978-1-99-101684-3
eISBN: 978-1-991309-14-3